DIVE

THE ULTIMATE GUIDE

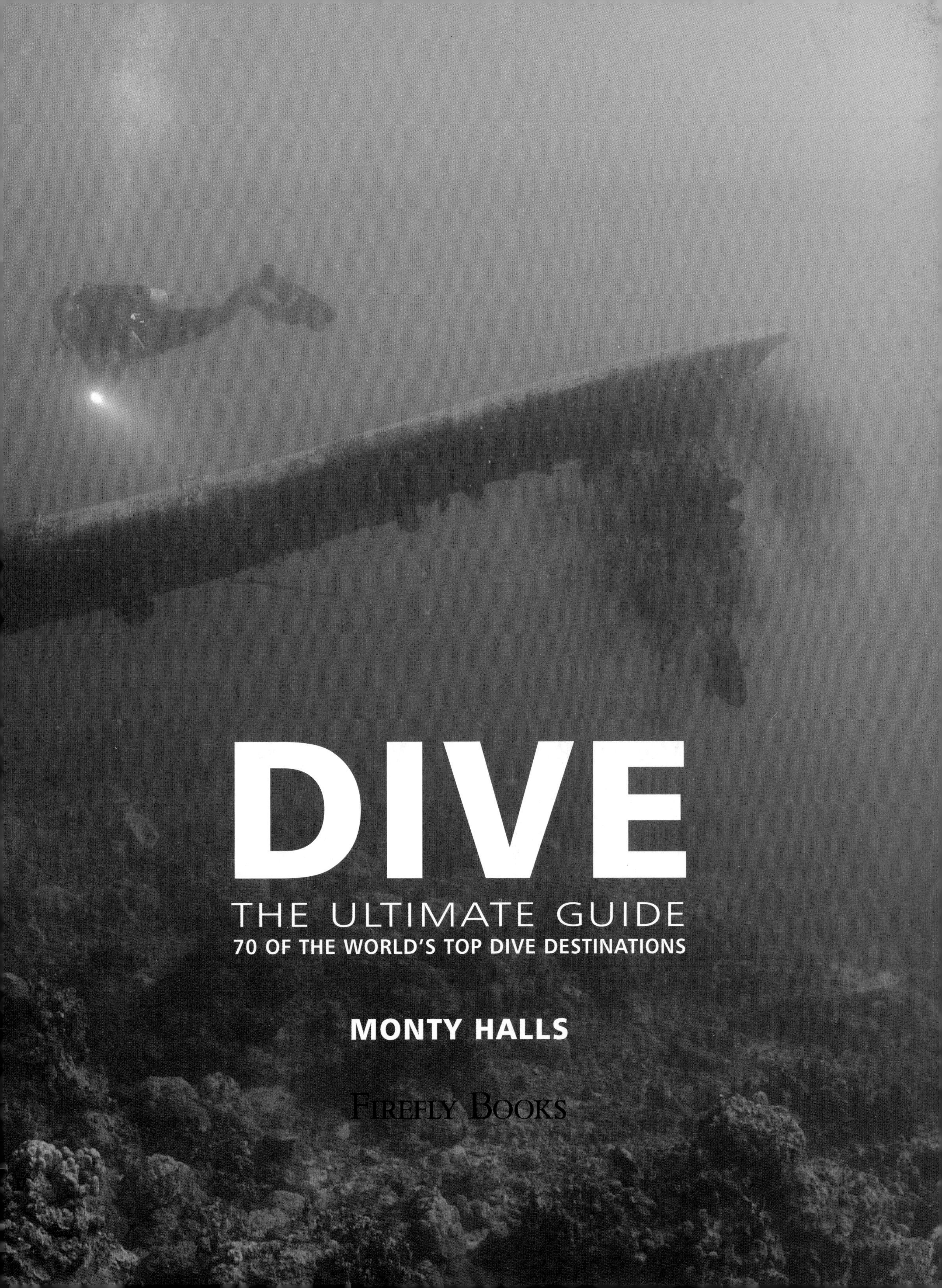

DIVE
THE ULTIMATE GUIDE
70 OF THE WORLD'S TOP DIVE DESTINATIONS

MONTY HALLS

FIREFLY BOOKS

A FIREFLY BOOK

Published by Firefly Books Ltd. 2008

First printing

Publisher Cataloging-in-Publication Data (U.S.)

Halls, Monty.
    Dive : the ultimate guide : 70 of the world's top dive locations / Monty Halls.
Rev. ed.
Originally published as: Dive : the ultimate guide to 60 of the world's top dive locations, 2004.
[352] p. : col. photos., maps ; cm.
Includes index.
ISBN-13: 978-1-55407-402-0 (pbk.)
ISBN-10: 1-55407-402-9 (pbk.)
Summary: Guide to the best locations for scuba diving around the world.
1. Scuba diving – Guidebooks. I. Title.
797.2/3 dc22   GV838.672.H35 2008

Library and Archives Canada Cataloguing in Publication

Halls, Monty
    Dive : the ultimate guide : 70 of the world's top dive locations / Monty Halls. – Rev. ed.
Includes index.
ISBN-13: 978-1-55407-402-0
ISBN-10: 1-55407-402-9
    1. Scuba diving – Guidebooks. I. Title.
GV838.672.H34 2008   797.2'3   C2008-900446-9

Published in the United States by
Firefly Books (U.S.) Inc.
P.O. Box 1338, Ellicott Station
Buffalo, New York 14205

Published in Canada by
Firefly Books Ltd.
66 Leek Crescent
Richmond Hill, Ontario L4B 1H1

Planned and produced by
Ultimate Sports Publications Limited.
8 Grange Road
Barnes
London SW13 9RE
United Kingdom
www.artofdiving.com

For Ultimate Sports
Publisher David Holyoak
Project Managers Gillian McDonald and Jonathan Hayden.

Contributors: Tony Baskeyfield, Jane Burnett, Rebecca Corbally, Mark Evans, Jason Heller, Arun Madisetti, Lesley Maw, Gillian McDonald, Jane Morgan, Gavin Parsons and JP Trenque.

Cover design by Marcus Nichols

Printed in India by Ajanta Offset.

Thank you:
The publishers and the author would like to thank all of the photographers and divers who have so generously contributed towards this book. Thanks also to the advertisers for their valued support.

Acknowledgments:
A list of photographers whose work appears in the book can be found on page 349.

All requests for permission should be addressed in writing to David Holyoak, Managing Director, Ultimate Sports Publications Limited, and a copy to Firefly Books Ltd.

Database right Ultimate Sports Publications Limited.
Reprographics by: PDQ Digital Media Solutions Ltd., Bungay, U.K.

Cover image: Dr. Alex Mustard
Page 2–3: Jake seaplane, Palau (Dan Burton)
Page 5: Tube sponge, Indonesia (Tony White)
Back cover: Lionfish, Cuttlefish, Blue Star and Coral, Wakatobi (Jason Heller); Whaleshark, Seychelles (Tony Baskeyfield); Turtle, Sipadan Island (Jane Morgan)

This book is dedicated to the memory of
Major Jason Ward, Royal Marines.
He loved the sea.

"Come, my friends.
'T is not too late to seek a newer world.
Push off, and sitting well in order smite
The sounding furrows; for my purpose holds
To sail beyond the sunset, and the baths
Of all the western stars, until I die."
from Ulysses – Alfred, Lord Tennyson

CONTENTS

LINDE WERDELIN

LINDE WERDELIN produce the only true sports watches on the market. These elegant timepieces allow for the digital functionality, available in the LINDE WERDELIN Sea Instrument, to attach on top when required, for the ultimate diving experience.

It is simply the most advanced and easy to use dive computer in the world.

The LINDE WERDELIN Sea Instrument, pushing the boundaries of the modern day dive computer, blends groundbreaking technology, precision and craftsmanship with the very best in Danish design and software. Cased in lightweight aluminium, it is an ultra-light style piece for divers of all abilities, whether worn on its own or attached on top of the beautiful and architectural LINDE WERDELIN Biformeter watches.

Boasting the most advanced technology available in any dive computer, the Sea Instruments' sophisticated colour screens are protected by scratch resistant sapphire crystal, second only to diamond in hardness. Automatically switching on when entering the water, it provides superior legibility while responding to the environment and conditions underwater bestowing a first class display even in the most awkward of light situations.

In addition, the LINDE WERDELIN Sea Instrument guides divers by tracking the critical pieces of information needed on any dive.

Features include:
> Digital and graphical displays
> Alarm systems
> Dive depths and times
> Decompression stops
> Temperature
> Maximum depth
> Surface interval times
> Logbook functionality
> Computer upload and download
  software

Be guided by and re-experience the best dives around the globe with the LINDE WERDELIN Sea Instrument.

LINDE WERDELIN; redefining sports watches and dive instruments.

Test it for 5 days, to buy or for more information please contact LINDE WERDELIN:

e: info@lindewerdelin.com
w: lindewerdelin.com
t: +44 (0) 207 727 6577

lindewerdelin.com

INTRODUCTION

WELCOME TO DIVE—THE ULTIMATE GUIDE TO SEVENTY OF THE WORLD'S TOP DIVE LOCATIONS.

This book was born out of necessity, based on my experience of organizing trips for diving groups to various locations around the world. It came to me that I was re-inventing the wheel every time I began the laborious business of planning the logistics and administration for these trips. Worryingly, the most difficult information to acquire often concerned the safety aspects of the diving—details such as where to find the nearest recompression chamber or hospital? Who is the governing body for diving in that area? Which airlines are "diver friendly"?

Therefore, from its inception, the purpose of this guide has been not only to provide diver-friendly descriptions of the selected dive sites—the standard information of any dive guide—but also to list the key support facilities—dive centers, dive organizations, recompression chambers, hospitals and conservation societies—at each location so no one need ever be in doubt as to where to go for immediate aid or information. And, of course, DIVE includes addresses, telephone numbers, email, and websites for these facilities, as well basic information on first aid in case of emergency.

Also included for each location is essential information about visibility, water temperature (winter and summer), useful travel information about getting there, visa requirements, and currency. There is information on the geography, marine life and the dive area in general as well as detailed reports on selected dive sites. Each of the dive sites reported on is graded according to experience and located on a diver-friendly map for the area. We also record the existence and location of some of the other dive sites in the area. Last, but not least, you will find information on other activities and not-to-be-missed places of interest for rest-days and for non-divers.

This book has been a labor of love. Not just for me, but for everyone else involved especially the team at Ultimate Sports and the hundreds of divers and specialists throughout the world who also thought the time was right for a one-stop reference guide for today's globe-trotting diver. They have helped me to list some of the greatest dive spots on Earth, most of them run by operators who care passionately for their own piece of the blue planet, often policing their reefs and dives with missionary zeal.

There are also a good sprinkling of obscure sites known to and loved by locals but often hidden in the small print of some other dive guides—and for these I thank the many divers who have shared their secrets with us. In addition, some of the most talented underwater photographers I have had the pleasure of working with in more than two decades of diving have helped bring the book to life with their spectacular images. The result is a unique glimpse of what each site can offer, an irresistible draw for the diving aficionado.

By no means is this guide the final word on the subject of world diving. It is very much a "live" work, waiting for feedback, updates, and the steady flow of information required to keep pace with the discovery of new sites and the ever-changing face of diving. Listing any selection of top dive locations is always a touchy business, so please feel free to translate your righteous indignation into advice and feedback—your contribution is invaluable and will help to extend and improve future editions of this guide in years to come.

We are the first generation to have explored beneath the surface of the sea on a regular basis. Divers have a unique insight into the steady decline of key marine species and habitats in the delicate coastal fringes they frequent in ever greater numbers. The dive operators in this book have all shown a responsible approach to their dive sites and the spectacular species therein—it is incumbent on us all to do the same.

I hope this book gives you the chance to make your own explorations a little easier and more successful. Safe diving!

Monty Halls

Monty Halls

◀ JELLYFISH LAKE, PALAU

THE OCEAN

OCEAN DATA

MAXIMUM DEPTH

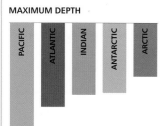

	feet	meters
PACIFIC	35,830	10,924
ATLANTIC	28,230	8,605
INDIAN	24,440	7,450
ANTARCTIC	23,740	7,235
ARCTIC	18,400	5,608
AVERAGE	26,128	7,964

AREA

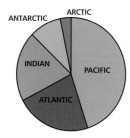

	million sq miles	million sq km
PACIFIC	64.0	166.0
ATLANTIC	31.7	82.0
INDIAN	28.4	73.6
ANTARCTIC	13.5	35.0
ARCTIC	4.7	12.2
AVERAGE	28.5	73.8

VOLUME

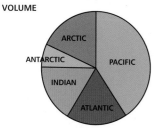

	million cubic miles	million cubic km
PACIFIC	173.6	723.7
ATLANTIC	77.2	321.9
INDIAN	70.1	292.1
ANTARCTIC	28.1	177.3
ARCTIC	77.2	321.9
AVERAGE	85.3	355.4

SOME 71% OF THE EARTH IS COVERED BY WATER, AND EVEN IF ALL LAND MASSES WERE REMOVED, THE WATER IN THE OCEANS WOULD STILL COMPLETELY COVER THE EARTH IN A LAYER 1.5 MILES (2.5 KM) DEEP.

The oceans of the world have an average depth of 2.3 miles (3.8 km) and contain 426 million cu miles (1.8 billion cu km) of water. Life on Earth began in the ocean and exists in every part of it. There are more living creatures in the ocean than on land, adapted for survival in a medium that is 830 times denser than air, can conduct sound four times faster, is able to bend light and absorb the colors of the spectrum, and requires 3,200 times more heat to raise its temperature by one degree than the same volume of air. The density of seawater enables the largest animal on Earth, the blue whale, to live eternally suspended in a medium that itself seethes with microscopic life.

WATER

Pure water is a simple molecule of oxygen and hydrogen, with the formula H_2O. Both hydrogen atoms are at the same end of the water molecule. They carry a positive charge and are attracted to the negative oxygen atom of other water molecules. This attraction, known as cohesion, is a crucial factor in supporting life. Cohesion gives viscosity, viscosity gives physical support, and physical support creates a cradle for life as well as a medium in which living organisms can reproduce and migrate over massive distances. The cohesive nature of water also means it has the strongest surface tension of any common liquid, creating a canopy that supports its own ecosystem.

THE WATER MOLECULE

The attraction between the negative oxygen and positive hydrogen atoms of separate water molecules is what creates its remarkable cohesive qualities.

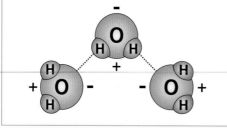

SEAWATER

Most of the world's water is in the sea. Since water has the capacity to dissolve more substances than any other liquid, seawater contains a variety of dissolved gases and solids (salts.) Chemical processes such as the weathering and erosion of rock or direct input from underwater hydrothermal vents add salt to the sea. Every 1,000 g of seawater contains on average 35 g of salt, although the salt content may be as high as 40 g in some places (for example in the Red Sea) and as low as zero in others (for example, close to large rivers.)

The remarkable physical and chemical properties of seawater have a direct bearing on the development of particular ecosystems, influenced by local conditions such as the temperature and clarity of the water, and whether it contains the key nutrients upon which life depends. A strong determining factor of a particular system's capacity to support life is the amount of oxygen it contains. Oxygen is produced by photosynthesizing plants in the water or is absorbed from the surface. As the temperature of water increases, its capacity to hold oxygen decreases. The shallow, crystal-clear tepid waters of a tropical reef are actually low in oxygen content, but where deep, very cold currents well up to the surface, the water is oxygen-rich. Thus thriving ecosystems often develop where deep water currents clash with the continental shelf.

Water also has a great capacity to store heat. The vast repository of the oceans is in effect the thermostat of the planet. Water heats up and cools down 3,200 times more slowly than the land does, and gigantic ocean currents, acting like conveyor belts, distribute heat around the world, keeping temperatures within a range that allows life to exist. Without water the planet Earth would be a barren lifeless lump of rock, subjected to daily extremes of boiling heat and icy cold.

OCEAN CURRENTS

As a look at a map of the world shows, Britain is at the same latitude as Newfoundland and Labrador. Yet winter temperatures in Britain are considerably higher.

This is because the Canadian seaboard is cooled by the Labrador Current, flowing south from subpolar waters, and the British Isles lie in the path of the North Atlantic Drift, the ocean current that diverts warm water carried from the Caribbean by the Gulf Stream east across the North Atlantic. This is a classic example of how ocean currents regulate temperature as they sweep past like great rivers, their surface waters losing or gaining only a single degree of heat a day.

MARINE ECOSYSTEMS

Local ecosystems are shaped by the conveyor belt of currents, whether it is the cold, nutrient-rich waters of the Benguela Current striking the southwest coast of Africa to create super-abundant fishing grounds off Namibia, or the warm South Equatorial Current producing ideal conditions for the largest natural structure on Earth, the Great Barrier Reef. Thus, although the oceans are broadly divided into polar, tropical, and temperate zones, there is an immense variety of marine life within them. Most recreational diving explores the ecosystems of temperate seas, tropical seas, and the open ocean, though the polar regions are also opening up.

TEMPERATE SEAS

The temperate zone is the part of the Earth between the polar regions and tropics, and its richest marine ecosystems are found in cold, nutrient- and oxygen-rich waters where phytoplankton, the microscopic photosynthesizing plants that are basis of the marine food chain, abound. Typical coastal shelf communities are great kelp forests and rocky reefs covered in a matrix of seaweed and fixed animals, with larger predators overhead, drawn to their rich food sources. The range of local conditions in temperate waters is greater than that of any other ocean system, and a community of migratory species moves from area to area to make the most of these changes throughout the year.

TROPICAL SEAS

Tropical seas, particularly around the fringes of landmasses, give an impression of immense species richness, reflected in the bewildering array of fish and coral species that inhabit coral reefs and coastal mangrove swamps. But tropical seas, being warm, are poor in oxygen. That an ecosystem survives here at all is notable. Much of the tropical abundance is down to reef-building hard corals, which grow in saline warm seas at between 18°C and 30°C (64°F and 86°F), and to an extraordinary plant/animal relationship.

The coral polyp is a single animal that has evolved to live in colonies. Microscopic algae called zooxanthellae shelter within the skeleton of the polyp and live off the carbon dioxide and nutrients it excretes. The polyp in return benefits from the oxygen and sugars given off by the plant. This wonderful symbiotic relationship has resulted in one of the most efficient recycling systems on Earth, with oxygen and energy being constantly re-used within a reef. It is this that makes the coral reef such a productive ecosystem, an oasis for animals at every level of the food chain. But corals are fragile: they die if the water becomes too warm or cloudy, as the zooxanthellae need plenty of sunlight to photosynthesize. They are therefore highly vulnerable to pollution and to global warming.

THE OPEN OCEAN

The oceans stretch across 142 million sq miles (369 million sq km) of the Earth's surface. The Pacific Ocean alone, some 10,500 miles (17,000 km) wide, contains almost 50 percent of all the world's water. The average max depth of the oceans is 26,128 feet (7,964 m), and through this apparently three-dimensional desert drifts and swims a great array of organisms. Species that live in the open ocean are called pelagic.

The distribution of life in the open ocean varies between day and night, with migrations taking place through the water column that extends from the ocean bottom—the benthic zone—up through the twilight zone between 3,280 and 650 feet (1,000 and 200 m) to the surface layers, the top few hundred feet. In the day, 75 percent of open ocean species remain in the twilight zone, but at night this drops to only 45 percent as great numbers of animals move up from the darkness to feed in the richer surface layers. This vertical migration is the greatest daily movement of animals anywhere on Earth.

The open ocean is the realm of the great cruising predators and stately plankton eaters. More and more divers want to encounter large pelagics such as sharks, whales, great swordfish and shoals of nomadic tuna, animals supremely well designed for their opportunistic life in the open ocean, and several dive operators now specialize in organizing ocean-going expeditions.

POLAR REGIONS

Although still a highly specialized area of diving, recreational expeditions to the polar regions have increased in the last decade. With air temperatures as low as −70°C (−94°F) and water temperatures around 0°C (32°F), the polar waters are rich in oxygen and nutrients from the shallow continental shelves that abound in the Arctic, and from the upwelling of cold water around the Antarctic Convergence, where warm and cool currents mix. Life forms are specialized and hardy, with only 120 species of fish having the adaptations to live in the Antarctic year-round. But the rewards of diving through great cathedrals of ice are addictive, the visibility spectacular, and the marine life unique.

PACIFIC OCEAN

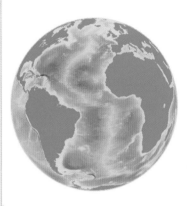

ATLANTIC OCEAN

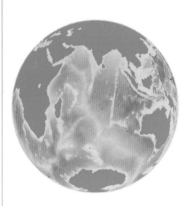

INDIAN OCEAN

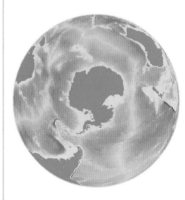

ANTARCTIC OCEAN

diver: doug allan, award winning underwater photographer
project: BBC series, Planet Earth
location: tonga, south pacific ocean
exposure protection: fourth element thermocline neutrally buoyant wetsuit system

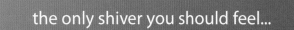

the only shiver you should feel...

...is that of anticipation

fourth element

THE WORLD OF DIVING

WE DEFY THE LAWS OF PHYSICS EVERY TIME WE DIVE. THE ABILITY TO EXPLORE BENEATH THE WAVES IS A TRIUMPH OF HUMAN PERSISTENCE AND INGENUITY.

The quest to move freely for long periods underwater was finally achieved with the development of the aqualung in the mid 20th century. Since then the boundaries have extended year after year, as the development of increasingly technical equipment and complex mixtures of gas allows divers to push ever deeper into unexplored territory in the oceans. And yet humans are still no nearer to overcoming the laws of physics than were the first divers to venture beneath the waves using pioneer scuba sets.

THE AIR WE BREATHE

Humans evolved to breathe the gases of the atmosphere on the surface; they do not have the physiological luxury of the adaptations shown by marine mammals to cope with those same gases when they are breathed under greater pressure at depth. Nitrogen and oxygen, the principal components of air, become narcotic or toxic when breathed under pressure and are absorbed at higher rates. Both these factors place severe limits on the use of scuba to explore the oceans.

The human form has air spaces within the body that must adapt to the pressure of depth. Certain spaces are rigid (e.g. the sinuses and middle ear) and must have air introduced to them by the diver through natural mechanisms and trained techniques. Others, such as the lungs, are collapsible, and they must be maintained at normal volume by introducing greater volumes of air than at the surface. The extra volume of air required for one complete breath at depth means that the diver is exposed to greater amounts of the constituent gases in air. This can cause narcosis in the case of nitrogen and extreme toxic reactions in the case of oxygen.

Decompression Sickness is a consequence of the increased absorption into the bloodstream of nitrogen breathed under pressure. As the diver surfaces and the pressure decreases, the nitrogen comes out of solution into the diver's bloodstream. Barotraumas result from the rapid expansion of gases within a body space as pressure is decreased quickly, for example in a rapid, uncontrolled ascent. To prevent this happening, divers must limit their time at depth and should surface in a controlled and graduated manner to allow the gases to be removed from the blood naturally by means of gas exchange between the blood and the lungs.

The immutable laws of physics and the limitations of human physiology inevitably set boundaries on how far divers can explore the deep oceans. Although the depth limit for diving on air (that is, without complex gas mixes) is usually accepted as being 270 feet (80 m), recreational divers are normally limited to the shallow zone—that is, the first 150 feet (45 m) of the surface waters. The deepest dive ever undertaken using air was in the region of 490 feet (150 m), a figure that represents a mere half of one percent of the average height of the water column throughout the world's oceans.

THE DEVELOPMENT OF SCUBA DIVING

The first open-circuit demand scuba set was developed by two Frenchmen, Benoit Rouquayrol and Auguste Denayrouze, as early as 1865. But it was deeply inefficient owing to the inability of the cylinders of that period to maintain the required amount of pressure, and to the lack of a reliable regulator.

The earliest piece of equipment to allow true independent movement underwater was the closed-circuit rebreather invented by Henry A. Fleuss in 1879, a system that differed only slightly from the rebreathers of today. Then, in 1908, the Scottish physiologist John Scott Haldane, one of the great pioneers of diving, undertook a remarkable study into the physical limits of scuba diving. Using himself as a guinea pig, Haldane developed the forerunner of modern dive tables and essentially established the limits to which humans can descend in the sea, paralyzing himself in one buttock in the process (amongst other novel injuries.)

The real milestone in recreational scuba diving came in 1943, when a French naval officer and diver, Jacques Cousteau, developed the first open-circuit regulator with Emile Gagnan. At the same time John Scott Haldane's son, biologist J.B.S. Haldane, carried on his father's studies of underwater safety, refining the diving decompression tables yet further. Up until then, diving had been largely confined to the military arena. Now the stage was set for recreational diving to sweep the world.

THE FOUR LAWS

Four laws relating to the behavior of gases under pressure apply to the human body when diving to any depth.

BOYLE'S LAW

The pressure of a given quantity of gas at constant temperature is inversely proportional to its volume.

CHARLES'S LAW

The volume of a given quantity of gas, kept at constant pressure, is directly proportional to its absolute temperature.

DALTON'S LAW

The total pressure exerted by a mixture of gases is equal to the sum of the pressures of each of the different gases making up the mixture.

HENRY'S LAW

The amount of gas dissolved into a liquid at a given temperature is directly proportional to the pressure of that gas.

▶ **WHALE SHARK**
Man's curiosity and inventiveness have allowed our generation to become the first to explore the oceans *en masse*. The rewards speak for themselves.

No one did more to spread the message of diving in the 1950s and 1960s than underwater filmmakers Hans and Lotte Haas, and Jacques Cousteau himself, who used the new medium of television to popularize exploration of the oceans and marine biology through series such as *The Silent World*. Organizations such as the British Sub Aqua Club (B.S.A.C.) sprung from military diving practices in 1953, and began to train civilians to enjoy recreational diving. In 1966 the Professional Association of Diving Instructors (P.A.D.I.) was formed. It now operates throughout the world and has introduced more people to the sport of diving than any other organization. Diving continues to grow at a phenomenal rate around the world. In 2003, more than an estimated 1.5 million diving certifications were issued, a number that looks set to increase year by year.

DIFFERENT FORMS OF DIVING

Much as we pride ourselves on our complex equipment and our ongoing journey ever deeper into the water column, the recreational sector is just one face of diving. Diving can be an occupation, a means of getting to the work place, of taking photographs or making films, of gathering scientific data and observations, or an end in itself. Since its inception in 1943, scuba diving has evolved and branched into a multi-faceted sport covering a whole range of disciplines.

PROFESSIONAL DIVING

Recreational Instruction

With scuba diving still growing at an immense rate, there are continued opportunities for making a living in recreational instruction. However, the entry of instructor-qualified individuals into the diving market over the last decade has diluted the market somewhat. The largest international organization, P.A.D.I., trained 100,000 new instructors in the decade from 1990 to 2000, a workforce that few industries could absorb without experiencing a glut of qualified personnel. Diving instruction is not the utopian existence imagined by many, as it is invariably poorly paid for unremittingly hard work. Nonetheless, for many divers it is the only opportunity to combine work and play effectively.

Commercial Diving

A wide range of activities and qualifications come under the blanket heading of commercial diving, from the scuba-trained scientific diver through to the offshore diver, a specialist in mixed-gas saturation, who works underneath an oil platform. For all of them, the fundamental principle is the same—diving is merely a means of traveling to the work place—and all commercial divers are certain to be qualified to carry out some kind of specialist tasks once they get there.

All aspects of commercial diving, including training and operation, are generally regulated by government agencies responsible for overseeing safety standards at work, reflecting the demanding conditions most divers encounter in their day-to-day work. Commercial regulations also apply to working within the media industry (for example as an underwater cameraman or safety diver on a film set.)

Military and Police Diving

An area of diving with a long and fine pedigree, the first records of which date back to 332 B.C. when Alexander the Great used divers to clear the harbor at Tyre. Once again, this is specialized work in which the diving is merely the means of allowing a specialist to perform a role underwater, whether this involves carrying out searches, recovery, or operations of war.

RECREATIONAL DIVING

Standard Scuba

Today recreational diving has never been more accessible. Training organizations have grown into great multinational corporations, with the largest (P.A.D.I.) now training 55 percent of the world's divers from 4,300 recognized dive centers in 175 countries.

Recreational diving covers a whole range of activities but is, by definition, diving purely for pleasure. It can effectively be described as diving on air only, as opposed to using complex gas mixtures, although the emergence of technical diving over the last decade has seen nitrox diving (that is, artificial mixtures of nitrogen and oxygen) becoming a standard feature of the recreational diving scene.

Technical Diving

Although various gas mixtures for diving had been explored since 1924, the true birth of technical diving took place in 1987 when the U.S. Navy began testing helium as a deep diving gas. After Dr. Bill Stone, in an extraordinary series of dives, descended to depths of 320 feet (97 m) in a cave system in Florida, the ensuring explosion in technical diving that followed was initially driven by specialists in cave exploration. But swiftly spread to the rest of the diving community, who have widely adopted mixed-gas techniques in the last decade.

Ice Diving

Although ice diving remains a specialized sphere of diving, with correct training and applied safety techniques, it can also be pursued by recreational divers. Borrowing techniques developed by scientific divers working for research groups such as the British Antarctic Survey, divers can safely access some of the rich ecosystems beneath ice shelves, and indeed dive beneath favored

HISTORY TIMELINE

1535: The first true diving bell is developed by Guglielmo de Loreno.

1788: Further refinements to the diving bell, including replenishment of air from the surface.

1823: Charles Deane develops a diving helmet that is simply weighted on to the shoulders without an attached suit.

1837: Augustus Siebe develops a suit that acts as a sealed unit with the helmet.

1839: Combination of hard helmet and sealed suit, with air supplied from the surface, is adopted by British military divers.

1878: Dr. Paul Bert publishes *Barometric Pressure*, a study of oxygen toxicity, hypoxia, and decompression sickness.

1878: Henry Fleuss invents the first self-contained dive apparatus using the forerunner of modern rebreather technology.

1908: J.B.S. Haldane publishes his work on decompression sickness.

1911: The first commercially available oxygen rebreather is developed by Draeger in Germany.

1912: The U.S. Navy develops tables based on the work of Haldane and his associates.

1933: Louis Ce Corlieu develops and patents the first fins.

1937: First successful dive conducted using helium/oxygen mix.

1939: Hans Hass makes the first underwater film, *Stalking Underwater*, for spearfishermen and photographers.

1941: Italian military divers use closed-circuit rebreathers in wartime.

1942: Jacques Yves Cousteau meets engineer Emile Gagnan.

1943: Jacques Yves Cousteau and Emile Gagnan invent the aqualung.

1943: Enriched air nitrox first proposed as a diving gas to reduce decompression problems.

1951: Conrad Limbaugh develops the first civilian scuba training course.

1953: Cousteau publishes The Silent World.

1954: Dr. Hugh Bradner develops and introduces the neoprene wet suit.

1954: The Y.M.C.A. develops the first nationally available scuba training program in the United States.

1957: Fredrick Dumas develops the buoyancy compensation device (B.C.D.).

1959: Confederation Mondiale des Activités Subaquatiques (C.M.A.S.) is established.

1960: The National Association of Underwater Instructors (N.A.U.I.) is established.

1966: Ralph Erickson and John Cronin form the Professional Association of Diving Instructors (P.A.D.I.) in the United States.

1967: Tom Mount establishes the National Association of Cave Divers

1983: The ORCA Edge dive computer becomes commercially available.

1986: The International Association of Nitrox Divers (I.A.N.D.) is founded by Dick Rutkowski to provide nitrox training to sport divers.

1987: Wakulla Springs Project test dives the first fully redundant rebreather, the Cis-Lunar Mk-1.

1993: Dive Rite Manufacturing launches the Bridge, the first variable-mix computer.

1994: Technical Diving International (T.D.I.) is formed.

freshwater recreational sites in the winter months. Effective communication, specialized equipment, surface support, and experience are all essential for exploring the cathedrals of ice in the more remote areas of the world, but the rewards are rich indeed.

Cave Diving

Another area that requires specialized training, cave diving has been described as the most dangerous sport on Earth. It has developed hand-in-hand with technical diving to meet the never-ending desire of divers to push still further and deeper into unexplored cave systems, where there is no free access to the surface. This makes it absolutely essential to have the right training, equipment and personnel, and various specialized training organizations have formed to meet these demands.

DIVING EQUIPMENT

Diving equipment is constantly evolving and improving, in line with developments in the creation of new materials and ever-increasing knowledge of the science of scuba diving. Early divers required considerable physical strength and resilience to cope with their primitive equipment, but the advances of the last 50 years now make it possible for anyone who is in reasonable physical condition to take up diving. Diving equipment will not stand still as technology continues to throw up new improvements, and the divers of the next century will almost certainly appear as alien to us today as the frogmen of the 1940s.

Exposure Suits

No single piece of equipment has had a more significant impact on the comfort of divers than the exposure suit. Water conducts heat away from the body 20 times faster than air, and the evolution of modern materials such as Lycra and crushed neoprene has had a huge impact on the sport. Wet suits, the most common form of thermal protection, are made from closed cell neoprene, and vary in thickness from 0.1 inches (2.5 mm) to 0.4 inches (10 mm). Dry suits, developed by the commercial diving industry (although the zips were developed by N.A.S.A.), prevent any water getting inside the suit. These suits are made of strong vulcanized rubber, neoprene, or crushed neoprene, and require various levels of thermal protection beneath.

Masks

Now manufactured to be low volume, with silicone replacing rubber as the material of choice, modern diving masks provide excellent all-round vision and are strong enough to last a lifetime. Features of the last few decades include the introduction of clear silicone prescription lenses, and feathered skirt edges. These have the benefit of creating a complete seal where the mask meets the face.

Snorkels

Modern snorkels have wide bores and dual vent systems, so that the snorkeler can breathe and expel water easily. They have adjustable offset mouthpieces to avoid fatigue, and hug the contours of the diver's head. Once again, the materials of these snorkels have evolved considerably. Hard plastics are used for the tube and flexible silicone for the mouthpiece.

Fins

Fins today use complex composite construction techniques, with the foot pocket made of plastic and rubber, and the blade made of compounds called thermoplastics. The clips on such fins are a quick-release swivel type, and most fins have vents and channels developed over decades of research to allow maximum output from a single fin kick. Fin designers tend to replicate features seen in nature, a particularly successful example being twin-bladed Force Fins.

Regulators

The most significant development to have affected regulators since Cousteau's 1943 model has been the creation of balanced systems, allowing greater ease of breathing at depth. Modern regulators are small and lightweight, and frequently have manual controls to allow the diver to regulate airflow. Many are made of molded composite materials, adding durability and decreasing weight.

Buoyancy Compensators

The need to control buoyancy whilst changing depth is a problem fish and divers face alike. The modern diver's version of a swim bladder is the Buoyancy Compensation Device (B.C.D.), a jacket-style support for equipment and cylinder, as well as a crucial buoyancy aid both on the surface and underwater. B.C.D.s today may have in-built air sources, integrated weight systems, and even incorporate gauges and regulators.

Diving Computers

Perhaps one of the most significant developments in modern diving, the dive computer was introduced to the recreational sphere in 1983, and is now widely considered to be a crucial accessory. Computers monitor the depth and time of repeated dives, building a profile for the diver and warning of impending decompression problems. They may also be air-integrated, incorporating the diver's breathing rate into their calculations, and have the capacity to download their data to conventional computer systems.

PROTECT THE AQUATIC ENVIRONMENT

DIVERS AND SNORKELERS ARE OBVIOUS AMBASSADORS FOR THE UNDERWATER ENVIRONMENT. 10 WAYS YOU CAN HELP:

1. Dive carefully in fragile aquatic environments.

Although, at first, they may look like rocks or plants, many aquatic organisms are fragile creatures that can be damaged or harmed by the bump of a tank, knee or camera, a swipe of a fin or even the touch of a hand. It is also important to know that some aquatic organisms, such as corals, are extremely slow growing. By breaking off even a small piece, you may be destroying decades of growth. By being careful, you can prevent devastating and long-lasting damage to magnificent dive sites.

2. Streamline yourself.

Much damage to the environment is done unknowingly. Keep your gauges and alternate air source secured so they don't drag over the reef or bottom. By controlling your buoyancy and taking care not to touch coral or other fragile organisms with your body, diving equipment or camera, you will have done your part in preventing injury to aquatic life.

3. Continue your education.

If you haven't dived in a while, your skills (particularly buoyancy control) may need sharpening. Before heading to the reefs, seek bottom time with a certified assistant or instructor in a pool or other environment that won't be damaged by a few bumps and scrapes. Better yet, take a diving continuing education course such as P.A.D.I. Scuba Review, the P.A.D.I. Adventures in Diving programme, or a P.A.D.I. Speciality Diver course. AWARE continuing education diving courses provide you with the skills practice and practical application of environmentally sound diving techniques.

4. Consider your impact on aquatic life.

Very few forms of aquatic life pose a threat to us. In fact, some creatures even seem friendly and curious about our presence. As we become bolder and more curious ourselves, we may even feel compelled to touch, handle, feed and even hitch rides on certain aquatic life. However, our actions may cause stress to the animal, interrupt feeding and mating behaviour, introduce food items that are not healthy for the species or even provoke aggressive behaviour in normally non-aggressive species. Interact responsibly with the aquatic environment.

5. Understand and respect underwater life.

Through adaptation to an aquatic environment, underwater life often differs greatly in appearance from life we are used to seeing on land. Many creatures only appear to look like plants or inanimate objects. Using them as 'toys' or food for other animals can leave a trail of destruction that can disrupt a local ecosystem and rob other divers of the pleasure of observing or photographing these creatures. Consider taking part in a Project AWARE programme to become more familiar with the importance of, and the interdependent nature of, worldwide aquatic ecosystems. Dive sites that are heavily visited can be depleted of their resources in a short time. Collecting specimens, coral and shells in these areas can strip their fascination and beauty. If you want to return from your dives with trophies to show friends and family you may want to consider underwater photography instead.

6. Be an ECO-Tourist.

Protected areas, such as parks, reserves and sanctuaries are one of the best tools for conserving the aquatic environment. Support the creation of protected areas, follow all local laws, and learn to appreciate that all aquatic habitats (such as grass beds, mangroves and rubble zones) are important and interesting environments. Do not confine your diving only to sites highlighted in brochures and articles. When planning a diving trip, choose ECO-Tour Operators involved with ECO-resorts and ECO-operators. Make informed decisions when selecting a destination and support the Project AWARE Go ECO environmental campaign.

7. Respect the underwater cultural heritage.

Divers and snorkelers have the privilege to access dive sites that are part or our cultural heritage or maritime history. You should help preserve these sites for future generations by obeying local laws, diving responsibly and treating wrecks with respect. Wrecks can serve as important habitats for fish and other aquatic life.

8. Report environmental disturbances or destruction.

Divers and snorkelers are in a unique position to monitor the health of local waterways, lakes and coastal areas. If you observe an unusual depletion of aquatic life, a rash of injuries to aquatic animals, or notice strange substances or objects in the water, report them to your local authority or similar organisation.

9. Be a role model.

As a diver or snorkeller, you realise that when someone throws a plastic wrapper or other debris overboard, it is not out of sight, out of mind. You see the results of such neglect. Set a good example in your own interactions with the environment, and other divers and non-divers will follow suit.

10. Get Involved.

There are plenty of opportunities to show your support of a clean aquatic environment, including local beach clean-ups, surveys and attending public hearings on matters that impact local coastal areas and water resources. Divers' skills in particular are always needed and appreciated by many environmental organisations.

FOR MORE DETAILS VISIT: www.projectaware.org

To take great underwater images with your compact digital camera, you need INON.

INON is the accessory range for your camera that makes professional results possible, fun and easy. All without breaking the bank.

Interactive Website for INON Underwater Photographers
INON Advisory Panel helps ensure you get the right advice to make the most from your INON underwater photography equipment. Leading panel experts include Martin Edge, Mark Webster and Maria Munn.

The Best Dealers
Carefully selected dealers who really understand compact digital underwater photography techniques and equipment. All specially product trained to make sure you always get the Inon underwater camera equipment that's right for you.

Matchless Back Up
The best back up is available through your local INON dealer. Generous guarantees that go far beyond our legal obligations. With INON, it probably won't go wrong. But if it does, as a minimum, we'll swap it and extend your warranty.

UFL165 Fisheye Lens
Massive field of view lets you take sweeping reef vistas and evocative shipwrecks and capture even large subjects in poor visibility. Focuses right down to the lens itself for stunning creative perspective shots.

UCL165 Close Up Lens
Brilliantly sharp two element close up lens lets you zoom in for revealing detail in the tiniest subject like pygmy seahorses, nudibranchs and cup corals.

L105 Wide Angle
npact wide-angle lens
's great for largesubjects
divers, sharks and rays.
y to light with just one
be.

Inon D-2000 Strobe.
High powered, wide angle,
compact and lightweight, this
is the ideal strobe. TTL
exposure for fuss free perfect
exposures automatically. Full
manual override for creative
control. Built in modelling light.

www.inonuk.com

CARIBBEAN SEA

The Caribbean Sea, on the western side of the Atlantic Ocean, occupies a basin of 1 million sq miles (2.6 million sq km), bounded on the north and east by the island chains of the Greater and Lesser Antilles, on the south by South America, and on the west by Central America. It connects with the Gulf of Mexico in the northwest through the Yucatán Channel, and its undersea topography is characterized by a series of basins and ridges, with the greatest depths being found in the Cayman and Venezuelan Basins. The deepest point of all is Bartlett Deep, at just over 3 miles (5 km.)

The waters of the Caribbean tend to be warm because the sills on its eastern edge prevent the circulation of cold water from the Atlantic. There are only two key points where significant amounts of water enter the Caribbean: the Anegada Passage between the Virgin Islands and the Lesser Antilles, and the Windward Passage between Cuba and Haiti. The tides tend to be higher on the western edges of the Caribbean due to the prevailing wind essentially driving the water mass westwards, where it rises into the Central American landmass. Because the incoming winds invariably deposit rain on the windward, or eastern side, of the high volcanic islands of the Caribbean, the areas to the lee of hills and mountains are normally extremely barren.

A recent scientific study recorded a total of 949 fish species in the Caribbean Sea, a figure that falls markedly short of the diversity of marine species found in the Pacific. What immediately strikes visiting divers is the paucity of coral species. Only 70 different kinds are known to exist in the Caribbean, and of these a mere 10 species provide 90 percent of the coral cover. More noteworthy are the Caribbean's spectacular sponges. Some of the larger barrel and tube sponges are the most impressive specimens to be seen in any of the world's oceans.

Its proximity to the United States means that the Caribbean has been attracting large numbers of divers to its shores for a good number of years, and a well-organized diving infrastructure exists throughout much of the region. The Caymans, the Virgin Islands, and Mexico in particular have long been popular destinations, offering a range of dives from shallow reefs to thrilling drifts, but there are also a number of places where diving is just getting going, one of the most exciting being the burgeoning dive industry in Cuba. To the north, the Bahamas have gained quite a reputation within the global diving community for delivering big animal encounters, particularly with dolphins and sharks.

◄ SAN JUAN WRECK
As well as the colorful corals and marine life, the Caribbean also offers some great wreck diving.

Dan Burton

FLORIDA KEYS

STRETCHING AWAY FROM THE SOUTHEAST TIP OF NORTH AMERICA INTO THE GULF OF MEXICO, THE FLORIDA KEYS PROVIDE THE ONLY OPPORTUNITY TO DIVE CORAL REEFS IN THE UNITED STATES. RICH IN MARINE LIFE, WARM, AND RELATIVELY BENIGN, THEY ARE THE PERFECT INTRODUCTION TO THE WORLD OF DIVING.

The colorful past of the Florida Keys is reflected in the names of the individual groups of islands that make up the chain, redolent as they are of Native American, Spanish, and Colonial history. Today the Florida Keys have a well-developed dive industry that operates within a network of marine parks and sanctuaries. They offer professional access to reasonably pristine reefs, particularly as the diver moves west toward the less crowded parts of the Keys.

GEOGRAPHY

The Florida Keys consist of 200 limestone and coral islands stretching in an elegant bow for 120 miles (193 km) away from the southeastern tip of Florida into the Gulf of Mexico. Thirty-four of the main islands are connected by a network of 42 bridges, creating the 120-mile (193-km) Highway Number 1, surely one of the most dramatic highways to be found in the United States.

From east to west the Keys are loosely divided into five regions—Key Largo, Tavernier/Islamorada, Marathon, Lower Keys, and Key West. Navigating through the Keys is relatively easy as long as you pay attention to the mile markers indicating progress along the long ribbon of bridges and highway.

The shores of the islands, particularly to the west, are mainly mangrove and shallow lagoon. The main reef, running parallel to the Keys, is found approximately 5 miles (8 km) offshore.

MARINE LIFE

The entire chain of the Florida Keys is protected under the mantle of the Florida Keys National Marine Sanctuary, and contains the oldest Marine Park in the United States—the John Pennekamp Coral Reef State Park, established in 1960. The protected parts of the Florida Keys are subdivided into 18 smaller zones. They cover a huge area and extend for 3 miles (5 km) beyond the outer reef. This legislation is essential, as there is evidence of over-fishing in certain areas of the reef, and diver traffic can be very heavy at the more popular sites, placing the fragile corals and their attendant species under severe pressure.

The inner regions of the Keys are a vital nursery for various coral species, with mixed mangrove swamps and seagrass beds providing ideal cover for juvenile fish, as well as grazing for the Florida manatee. Farther out on the main reef, washed by the waters of the Gulf Stream, there is rich biodiversity. Several species of angel fish, snappers, grunts, large groupers, hawksbill turtles, lone great barracuda, some magnificent green morays, eagle rays, and nurse sharks move in and around the coral reefs, which are characterized by stark elkhorn and staghorn coral structures and large barrel and tube sponges.

THE DIVES

The vast majority of diving in the Florida Keys is boat diving. Typical of the inshore regions are shallow lagoons and flats covered in seagrass, giving way to the occasional patch reef until the true reef begins some 5 miles (8 km) offshore. This reef takes many forms, but is essentially a spur and groove formation running down to depths of 70 to 80 feet (21 to 24 m).

The Keys offer something for every level of diver, from shallow dives on the isolated inshore reefs for the beginner to more challenging wreck and reef dives on the outer reef. Even on the main reef, depths rarely

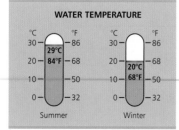

WATER TEMPERATURE

°C	°F	°C	°F
30 —	— 86	30 —	— 86
29°C			
20 — **84°F** — 68		20 — **20°C** — 68	
		68°F	
10 —	— 50	10 —	— 50
0 —	— 32	0 —	— 32
Summer		Winter	

FLORIDA
(United States)

✈ ●Miami

Key Biscayne

Sands Key

Elliott Key ●**Long Reef**

Old Rhodes Keys

●**The Wall**

●**Turtle Rocks**

Key Largo

●**Carysfort Reef**

●**Grecian Rocks**

Key Largo● ●**Christ of the Deep**

Tavernier Key

Tavernier● ●**Molasses Reef**

Plantation● ✚ 🕐

Upper Matecumbe Key *Windley Key*

●**Davis Reef**

Lower Matecumbe Key

●**Eagle**

Layton●

Long Key

Marathon●

Key Vaca

●**Samantha's Reef**

●**Sombrero Reef**

Marquesas Key

Big Pine Key

Saddlebunch Key ●**Looe Key**

Key West● *Boca Chica Key* ●**Adolphus Busch Sr.**

Key West

Joe's Tug● ●**Sand Key Reef**

0   30 km

0   20 mi

▼ NURSE SHARK

Although the Keys lack the diversity of shark species found in other areas of the Caribbean, there are nonetheless extremely healthy populations of nurse sharks in the region.

John Bantin

John Bantin

► **ANGELFISH**
A pair of gray angelfish warily eye the approaching photographer.

►► **JOE'S TUG WRECK**
The Florida Keys has numerous wrecks to explore including Joe's Tug.

 DIVE CENTERS

OCEAN DIVERS
Marina Del Mar Resort, 522 Caribbean drive, Key Largo, FL, U.S.A.
Phone: +1-800-451-1113
E-mail: info@oceandivers.com
Web: www.oceandivers.com

ABYSS PRO DIVE CENTER
13175 Overseas Highway,
Marathon, FL, U.S.A.
Also at the Holiday Inn Marina, MM 54
Phone: +1-800-457-0134
E-mail: info@abyssdive.com
Web: www.abyssdive.com

 DIVING ORGANIZATIONS

The U.S. Coast Guard is responsible for the safety of dive vessels.
Phone: +1-800-368-5647
E-mail: uscginfoline@gcrm.com

 RECOMPRESSION

Mariners Hospital
50 Highpoint Road, Tavernier,
FL 33070, U.S.A.
Phone: +1-305-852-4418

 HOSPITAL

Mariners Hospital
50 Highpoint Road, Tavernier,
FL 33070, U.S.A.
Phone: +1-305-852-4418

 CONSERVATION SOCIETY

The Marine Sanctuaries in Florida are administered by the National Oceanic and Atmospheric Administration. For more information go to:
Web: www.floridakeys.noaa.gov

OTHER DIVE SITES

Long Reef
The Wall
Turtle Rocks
Carysfort Reef
Grecian Rocks
Davis Reef
Eagle
Samantha's Reef
Sombrero Reef
Looe Key
Adolphus Busch Sr.
Sand Key Reef
Joe's Tug

exceed 70 feet (21 m) and the water remains warm pretty much throughout the year—although on the deeper dives in winter water temperatures can drop down to 20°C (68°F), so a wetsuit is certainly required for these. Currents are a factor on the outer reef, a measure of the presence of the Gulf Stream sweeping past these reefs, as well as the tidal range and upwellings from deeper water to the southeast.

The diving infrastructure on the Keys is highly professional and well organized. All boat operators have to pass a stringent set of requirements established by the U.S. Coast Guard. Medical facilities, good communications, excellent accommodation, and hyperbaric facilities are all part of the set up. Some deeper wrecks are a draw for the technical diver, and nitrox and technical diving equipment are readily available.

MOLASSES REEF

• **60 feet (18 m)** • **beginner**

Possibly the most popular dive in the Keys, Molasses Reef is easily accessed from Key Largo and represents a classic spur and groove reef that typifies diving in this region. The site lies at the southern region of the Marine Park, and has a slightly wider range of coral species than other areas in the park.

The main section of the reef is a sloping coral bank cut with deep canyons and ridges that create numerous overhangs and crags—a varied topography providing numerous holes and sanctuaries for green morays, crayfish, and shoals of silversides. This is a particularly good reef for observing shoals of the larger fish species on the reef, with horse-eye jacks and Bermuda chub present in dense aggregations. The reef itself is divided into a number of smaller sites whose names such as Coral Cave, Eagle Ray Alley, Hole in the Wall, and Spanish Anchor—the latter the site of a splendid large anchor—speak for themselves.

THE CHRIST OF THE DEEP STATUE

• **25 feet (8 m)** • **beginner**

This famous statue reaching up from the seabed is actually the third cast made of the same sculpture. The first is off Genoa in Italy, the second is in the harbor at St. George's in Grenada (to commemorate the hospitality of the Grenadian people after the sinking of the *Bianca C*), and the third was placed here in 1966.

The statue is 9 feet (2.7 m) high, and stands in 25 feet (8 m) of water surrounded by reef at a site called Key Largo Dry Rocks. Directly opposite the statue is a huge brain coral, while built-up bommies and reefs surround it on all sides.

The reef is an ideal location for less experienced divers, being well-sheltered and shallow. The marine life here is particularly accustomed to the presence of divers, especially as fish feeding has taken place here in the past. Keep a watchful eye for lots of emboldened barracuda on the lookout for hand-outs, as well as Bermuda chub and stingrays on the sandy patches. There are a number of cleaning stations dotted around the immediate area of the statue, and these can provide fascinating glimpses of local fish life, particularly if the diver is patient and is prepared to keep watch at one station for a sustained period.

ADDITIONAL DIVES

It is also well worth attempting a dive on the wreck of the *Adolphus Busch Sr.*, a 210-foot (64-m) long former island freighter that was purchased by the local dive community and sunk perfectly upright and intact in just over 100 feet (30 m) of water on December 5, 1998. This is a deeper dive, and currents can be a factor, but the reports from this site are enthusiastic to say the least. The Keys also has a number of other notable wreck dives for the dedicated wreck diver.

OTHER ACTIVITIES

Close to Miami is the Everglades National Park, which is well worth a visit when journeying to, or from, the Florida Keys. The park covers a massive 1.5 million acres (600,000 ha), and its network of wetlands and grassy plains provides safe havens for alligators, snakes, otters, and an array of bird life including cranes, blue herons, and ospreys.

As ever with this style of park in the United States, there are excellent facilities on hand for visitors. Several visitors' centers are dotted throughout the park, and the more adventurous should not pass up the opportunity to canoe through some of the Everglades' deserted backwaters. A large lodge in the park—Flamingo Lodge—provides accommodation for those planning a longer stay.

☎ **TELEPHONE NUMBERS**

Recompression chamber	+1-305-852-4418
Hospital	+1-305-852-4418
U.S. Coast Guard	+1-800-368-5647

💻 **WEBSITES & E-MAIL**

State of Florida travel planner	www.visitflorida.com
Florida Keys information	www.fla-keys.com
Dive information	www.flkeysdivesites.com

Dan Burton

LITTLE BAHAMA BANK

  VISIBILITY
Regularly 100 feet (30 m) plus

 MUST SEE
Spotted dolphins

DOWNSIDE
Frequently rough
Not guaranteed to see dolphins
Remote site
Expensive diving

 GETTING THERE
Little Bahama Bank: fly direct from Miami into Freeport, or liveaboard direct from the east coast of Florida.
Walker's Cay: direct access by seaplane from Fort Lauderdale, or from Freeport on Bahamas Air.

 VISA
Visas are not required by U.S. and Commonwealth citizens (for up to 8 months), E.U. citizens (for up to 3 months), and certain South American countries (for up to 14 days). Assured onward/return passage is required in all cases. Passports should be valid for at least 6 months.

 MONEY
Currency is the Bahamian dollar. U.S. dollars are readily accepted throughout the country. Most operators take all major credit cards.

DIVERS ARE DRAWN TO THE CRYSTAL WATERS OF THE BAHAMAS WITH TWO MAIN TARGETS IN MIND—TO ENJOY THE THRILL OF SHARKS FEEDING AND TO SWIM WITH WILD DOLPHINS.

The islands of the Bahama chain contain approximately 5 percent of the world's total number of coral reefs. They offer some truly wonderful diving in waters with crystal-clear visibility above a white sand bottom. But it is the near certainty of shark and dolphin encounters that makes the Bahamas an irresistible destination for the itinerant diver looking for life on the wild side.

There are few places on Earth where divers are guaranteed sightings of large numbers of either sharks or dolphins. Yet within the Bahamas are two absolute gems of dive sites that offer the chance to swim with both of these magnificent creatures in their ocean environment. Divers flock to Walker's Cay for the chance to watch sharks feeding, and to Little Bahama Bank for the matchless experience of encountering wild dolphins. Thanks to well-managed programs put in place by local dive operators, the populations of both species are carefully maintained and very special relationships have developed between man and animal.

▼ DOLPHIN ENCOUNTER
The dolphin encounters in the Bahamas draw divers from all over the world.

Dan Burton

WATER TEMPERATURE

°C	°F		°C	°F
30	86		30	86
28°C				
20 — **82°F**	68		20 — **24°C**	68
			75°F	
10	50		10	50
0	32		0	32
Summer			Winter	

Walker's Cay
Shark Rodeo

Stangers Cay

Great Sale Cay

White Sand Ridge
Mangrove Cay

Little Abaco
Cornishtown

Little Bahama Bank

The Sugar Wreck
End

Great Guana Cay

Grand Bahama

Hope Town
Marsh Harbor

Freeport
Shark Junction

Elbow Cay

BAHAMAS

Great Abaco

Moore's Island

0		40 km

0		30 mi

Gorda Cay

GEOGRAPHY

The Bahama chain consists of 700 islands and 2,000 smaller sand cays extending for 750 miles (1,207 km) southeast of Florida and north of Cuba. Only 30 of the islands are inhabited. They are low-lying, the highest point being the distinctly unimpressive Mount Alvernia at 197 feet (60 m), and are surrounded by deep oceanic trenches. The northernmost island is Grand Bahama; the capital, Nassau, is on New Providence Island. The combination of the ocean trenches and the warm waters of the Gulf Stream, which run up from the Gulf of Mexico between the island chain and the eastern seaboard of the United States, has the effect of creating an oasis of clear water around the islands.

Little Bahama Bank lies between Grand Bahama and Abaco Island. Its northern end is approximately 70 miles (112 km) east of the Florida coast. The Bank consists of white sand, seagrass beds, and patch reefs in 10 to 50 feet (3 to 15 m) of water, the outer edge of which is lined with cays, rocks, reefs, and wrecks. Towards the edge, water depth starts to increase to 200 feet (60 m) before dropping off precipitously to a maximum depth of over 6,500 feet (2,000 m) in some places.

Little Bahama Bank can be accessed directly from Florida or from many departure points within the Bahamas themselves. A number of specialized dive operators organize liveaboard trips of several days' duration to the Bank in search of the dolphins.

Walker's Cay is a 100-acre (40-ha) island at the western end of the chain of cays north of Grand Bahama. It can be reached from the Florida coast, about 100 miles (161 km) to the west, and Grand Bahama, 40 miles (64 km) to the south. A reef encircles the island, and while this contains interesting gullies, drop-offs, and some pleasant reef dives, the main attraction is unquestionably the world-famous Shark Rodeo.

MARINE LIFE

Although lacking the grandeur of reef walls and canyons found in the Caribbean Sea proper to the south of Cuba, Little Bahama Bank is exciting in terms of the large pelagic animals that patrol the warm shallow waters of the area. The reefs themselves are low relief and rarely rise more than a few feet above the seafloor. However, there are some spectacular sponges and sea fans amongst these reefs, particularly around the wrecks that dot the Bank. Angelfish, grunts, and snappers are present on virtually every dive, as well as ubiquitous patrolling barracuda. Some of the barracuda in the area grow very large indeed, and compete for food with Nassau groupers and many different species of sharks, including intimidating bull and tiger sharks—two of the classic shark encounters in diving—as well as the occasional great hammerhead shark. At certain sites on Little Bahama Bank you are virtually guaranteed an encounter with several large sharks. There are also some real bruisers of loggerhead turtles present, particularly

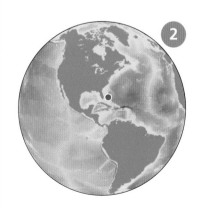

DIVE CENTERS

DOLPHIN DREAM TEAM
P.O. Box 530714, Lake Park,
FL 33403-8911, U.S.A.
65-ft liveaboard *Dream Too* departing from
Lake Park in Florida. Owner Scott Smith is an
experienced skipper working the Banks.
Phone: +1-888-277-8181
E-mail: info@dolphindreamteam.com
Web: www.dolphindreamteam.com

BRENDAL'S DIVE CENTER INT'L, LTD
Green Turtle Cay, Abaco, Bahamas
Phone: +1-242-365-4411
E-mail: brendal@brendal.com
Web: www.brendal.com

NEAL WATSON'S UNDERSEA
ADVENTURES
P.O. Box 21766, Ft. Lauderdale, FL
33335-1766, U.S.A.
Phone: +1-954-462-3400
E-mail: info@NealWatson.com
Web: www.nealwatson.com

 DIVING ORGANIZATIONS

The water sports industry in the Bahamas is
not carefully regulated, and visitors should ask
about an operator's insurance coverage and
insist on sufficient training before using their
equipment.
The website of the Bahamas Diving
Association provides a comprehensive guide to
diving the Bahamas, accommodation, and
alternative shore-based activities.
Web: www.bahamasdiving.com.

 RECOMPRESSION

Jackson Memorial Hospital, Miami, FL, U.S.A.
Phone: +1-305-585-3483
Contact: Dr Luis Matos

Mariners Hospital, Tavernier, FL, U.S.A.
Phone: +1-305-852-4418
Contact: Dr J. W. Loewenherz

 HOSPITAL

Medical care is generally good in Nassau and
Freeport, but is limited in other areas. Persons
with serious or life-threatening conditions are
normally airlifted to hospitals in the United
States for treatment.

Rand Memorial Hospital, Freeport
Phone: +1-242-352-6735

Princess Margaret Hospital, Nassau
Phone: +1-242-322-2861

 CONSERVATION SOCIETY

Bahamas Reef Environmental Education
Foundation (B.R.E.E.F.),
P.O. Box N-7776, Nassau,
New Providence, The Bahamas
Phone: +1-242-327-9000
Web: www.breef.org
E-mail: breef@coralwave.com

around the wrecks. These seem to have very little fear of divers, so you may be fortunate enough to experience some tremendous encounters. But dolphins are the obvious attraction of the site, especially spotted dolphins, although bottlenose dolphins are also present in considerable numbers.

The reef life at Walker's Cay is considerably more diverse in nature. There are some particularly rich hard coral reefs at this site—one particular brain coral measures a thumping 9 feet (3 m) in diameter. Such abundant reef systems support healthy populations of larger species such as groupers and barracuda, as well as an eclectic mix of angelfish, triggerfish, and butterfly fish. In addition, there is every likelihood of encountering larger animals such as spotted eagle rays and loggerhead turtles. The site's famous shark populations include large numbers of blacktip reef sharks, and unique gatherings of bull sharks, Caribbean reef sharks, and nurse sharks. Hammerheads, lemon sharks, and tigers are also occasionally sighted.

THE DIVES

The diving on the Little Bahama Bank is generally very shallow—in the 15 to 40 feet (4 to 12 m) range. Visibility can be decreased markedly in stormy weather; this is, after all, a gigantic shallow sand bank. However, the conditions here are very benign once under the surface, with warm clear Caribbean water over flat reefs. Diving to the south can be more demanding, with the more remote islands rapidly gaining a reputation.

DOLPHIN ENCOUNTER

• Snorkeling • beginner

Dolphins are encountered all over Little Bahama Bank, although there do seem to be certain areas where they are more prolific. White Sand Ridge, 35 miles (56 km) north of the port of West End, seems to have particular success with dolphin encounters. However, operators report regularly swimming with dolphins as far north as Walker's Cay.

Reputable operators all have their own favorite sites, as well as their own techniques and rules for swimming with the dolphins once they have been found. You will lessen your chances of a close encounter if you chase the dolphins (you never seem to catch them anyway!), and you should avoid attempting to touch them. Scuba diving with the dolphins is not permitted, and indeed seems a positive discouragement to them to interact.

The standard technique is to cruise the Bank, wait for the dolphins to approach the boat, an indication that they are willing to interact, and then still the engines. Mid afternoon to early evening seems to be the most fruitful time for encounters. But even when the dolphins have been apparently giving positive signals, it is not unusual for them to lose interest rapidly and move away from the immediate area soon after the snorkelers have entered the water. This can make dolphin encounters extremely frustrating. Nonetheless it is

▼ NASSAU GROUPER
The Nassau groupers on the Banks are large, curious, and very confident.

John Bantin

Linda Pitkin

worth persisting, as a sustained encounter can be tremendously rewarding, and to be in the water with the dolphins for a number of hours as they play around you is simply unforgettable.

Many of the operators use scooters to keep pace with the dolphins and have developed close relationships with individual animals. Animal behaviorists believe that dolphins not only communicate with each other with clicking sounds, but use body language as well, so feel free to try your own brand of communication with these intelligent animals —they certainly seem to enjoy the divers' efforts!

THE SUGAR WRECK

• 20 feet (5 m) • beginner

This shallow wreck was a classic three-masted schooner sunk at the beginning of the last century, and is so named for the cargo of molasses she was carrying from

Havana, Cuba, to the northeastern United States. She sits in shallow water and is well broken up, with only a few spars and a fallen main mast standing proud of the seabed. Nonetheless the wreckage is a beacon for marine life in the surrounding desert of the sand flats, and is a gloriously relaxing dive.

What superstructure remains is heavily encrusted with sea fans, corals, sea whips, and sponges. Cruising above this growth are large schools of snappers and grunts, while goatfish forage in the sand beneath. Morays and sleeping nurse sharks may be seen in the darker nooks and crannies of the wreckage. French angelfish are particularly abundant, while stingrays are frequently sighted in the flats between the wreckage. Such an abundance of life inevitably attracts predators, and the large shoals of barracuda cruising low overhead are particularly impressive. As night falls reef and bull sharks may move in to explore the area of the wreck.

▲ **GREAT BARRACUDA**

Some very large barracuda can be seen cruising above the reefs of Little Bahama Bank.

OTHER DIVE SITE

Shark Junction

THE BULL PIT

• 25 feet (8 m) • intermediate

This is a classic shark dive, and the site has been regularly visited by a number of operators over the last ten years. As a result, the resident shark populations now associate the noise of boat engines with the distribution of food. They will move in to the area as soon as a dive boat arrives on the scene, whether it is chumming or not. This, of course, allows those opposed to feeding fish to enjoy a guilt-free dive, although there is no getting away from the fact that the sharks' behavior is caused by many years of human activity at the site.

The Bull Pit consists of a series of low reefs and bommies that create a labyrinth of channels and gullies. The best approach is to settle in one of these gullies and await the arrival of the sharks. They are of course aware of the presence of divers, and will move in very close to inspect your bubbles and investigate you for handouts. Although the site has a reputation for being a very safe dive, inexperienced divers can find it very alarming to find themselves in close proximity to such large, potentially aggressive animals as bull sharks, so it is highly recommended that novices and those unfamiliar with diving with sharks dive under close supervision.

SHARK RODEO

• 35 feet (11 m) • intermediate

The famous shark rodeo takes place on a flat patch of sand about the size of a football pitch in the waters around Walker's Cay. The dive boats frequently circle the site first, gunning their engines to draw in the sharks. On entering the water, the divers settle on the seafloor in sight of a "chumsicle"—a large frozen mass of fish contained in a porous cylinder. The advantage of the chumsicle feeding system is that it avoids having fish pieces floating within range of the watching divers—it can be mildly disconcerting, to say the least, to have a large chunk of fish land in your lap in the midst of a group of excited sharks. The sharks—often more than 100 of them, belonging to several different species—home in on the chumsicle and the show begins. Divers are instructed to stay extremely still, but this does not stop the sharks approaching to within inches of them, and there have even been reports of sharks swimming between the legs of kneeling divers on the seabed.

OTHER ACTIVITIES

A word of warning! If you are not a diver, Walker's Cay may hold little to occupy you beyond a bar, a small beach, a couple of swimming pools, and some world-class fishing if your interests lie in that direction. A transient population of sailors makes use of the large yachting marina that contributes a significant slice of income to the island's economy. But there is absolutely nothing in the way of scenery or nightlife, and the attractions of the island lie strictly beneath the surface of the sea.

Little Bahama Bank offers more in the way of alternative activities. It lies close to Grand Bahama, a classic tourist center visited by cruiseships, and boasts all the facilities you would expect of a popular vacation spot. The main town of Freetown has a population of 25,000, with excellent shopping and lively nightlife. The interior of the island possesses fine nature reserves, including the Lucayan National Park and the Parrot Jungle. Golfers take note—some of the best courses in the Bahamas are found on Grand Bahama.

☎ TELEPHONE NUMBERS

Recompression chamber	+1-305-585-3483
Hospital	+1-242-352-6735
Ministry of Tourism	+1-242-302-2000
Emergency services	911
Air Ambulance	+1-242-377-1606

🖥 WEBSITES & E-MAIL

Bahamas Diving Association	www.bahamasdiving.com
Bahamas Tourist Board	www.bahamas.com

◄◄ SHARK RODEO
Sharks are drawn to the shark rodeo by a "chumsicle", a kind of fishy popsicle.

▼ SQUIRRELFISH
A squirrelfish raises its spiny dorsal fin in a classic defensive response to the presence of a diver.

Monty Halls

TURKS & CAICOS
ISLANDS

 VISIBILITY
100+ feet (30 m) off deep walls

MUST SEES
Northwest Point
Grand Turk walls

 DOWNSIDE
Boat trips to remote sites easily disrupted by sea conditions

 GETTING THERE
Travelers from the U.S. have the best access to the Turks and Caicos Islands, with direct flights on several airlines fom Miami, Fort Lauderdale, and New York to Providenciales. For Canadians, there are charter flights between Toronto and Providenciales. European visitors have to connect with flights in Miami, Fort Lauderdale or New York. A departure tax of U.S.$23 is payable on all international flights.

 VISA
U.S. and Canadian visitors may enter without a passport, if they have an original birth certificate (or a notarized copy) and photo I.D. (e.g. driver's license). Visitors from other countries do require passports, but no visas are necessary.

 MONEY
U.S. dollar and all major credit cards.

WATER TEMPERATURE

°C	°F	°C	°F
30 — 30°C	— 86	30 —	— 86
20 — 86°F	— 68	20 — 27°C 81°F	— 68
10 —	— 50	10 —	— 50
0 —	— 32	0 —	— 32
Summer		Winter	

▶ **CORAL PINNACLES**
The Turks and Caicos Islands have some dramatic scenery both under and above the water.

DIVERS ARE DRAWN TO THE QUINTESSENTIAL SLEEPY CARIBBEAN ISLANDS OF THE TURKS AND CAICOS BY THE VARIETY OF DIVES AVAILABLE—FROM THE SHALLOW SEAGRASS BEDS TO PRECIPITOUS WALLS, FROM CAVES AND BLUE HOLES TO DRIFT AND WRECK DIVES.

The Turks and Caicos Islands, perched on the southeastern end of the Bahamas island chain, offer a range of diving reflected in the distinct characters of the two main island clusters. Shallow slopes and crystal visibility predominate to the west, whereas barreling currents and deep walls are the order of the day to the east. However, the islands remained something of a well-kept secret to divers until the opening of the international airport on Providenciales.

GEOGRAPHY

The two groups of 40 islands that make up the Turks and Caicos have a total land area of only 166 sq miles (429 sq km) which is spread over a mere 193 sq miles

Linda Pitkin

Whitby

North
Caicos

Bottle Creek

Football Field

Eagle Ray Pass

Conch Bar

Shark Hotel

Northwest Point

Eagle's Nest

The Amphitheater

The Crack

Grace Bay

The Pinnacles

Blue Hills

The Cathedral

The Hole in
The Wall

Turtle Cove

Five Cays

Land of the Giants

Highway to Heaven

Providenciales

Elephant Ear Canyon

Dolphin Dip

Driveway

Whiteface

Middle
Caicos

Lorimers

East
Caicos

CAICOS ISLANDS

TURKS & CAICOS ISLANDS
(British Overseas Territory)

0 — 10 km

0 — 20 mi

South
Caicos

Cockburn Harbour

Six Hill Cays

Long Cay

Turks Island Passage

Grand Turk

Cockburn Town

The Tunnels

TURKS
ISLANDS

Cotton Cay

East Cay

Fish Cays

Balfour Town

Salt Cay

Ambergris Cays

Bush Cay

Big Sand Cay

(500 sq km) of ocean. Low-lying, arid, and lacking in vegetation, the islands are formed of coral limestone fringed by dense mangroves, and are extensions of the submarine sandbank of the West Atlantic. The Caicos Islands sit on the northern edge of the bank, while the Turks Islands are located on another, much smaller bank to the east, separated from the Caicos by the 1.2-mile (2-km) deep Turks Island Passage.

Only 8 of the islands are inhabited. The population of the Turks and Caicos (a British Overseas Territory) is around 19,000, mostly concentrated in the capital of Cockburn Town on Grand Turk, although the island of Providenciales (popularly known as Provo) has grown in importance since the building of the international airport there.

MARINE LIFE

Under the National Parks Ordinance, passed in 1988, there are 33 protected regions and parks within the Turks and Caicos Islands. Moreover, the islands' government was the first in the Caribbean to pass legislation banning spearfishing. Mooring buoys abound, and the islands have an active program of "reef balling"—the sinking of artificial structures to create the foundations for new reefs. The islands' marine life is thus in healthy shape and provides a representative cross-section of Caribbean reef organisms.

The islands are particularly notable for the presence of many larger pelagic animals, including a tame dolphin "Jo-Jo" who has been interacting with divers for 18 years. It is quite possible to encounter mantas off the west wall at Grand Turk, and an unforgettable event, for those fortunate enough to witness it, is the migration of humpback whales through the Turks Island Passage between December and April each year.

While Caribbean Reef sharks are by far the most common shark species sighted around the islands, bull sharks and tigers are also occasionally seen. Southern stingrays are present in some numbers at key locations around the islands, and loggerhead, green, and hawksbill turtles nest on many of the cays.

THE DIVES

The two island groups that make up the Turks and Caicos Islands have distinct personalities, and the diving at each location reflects their different nature. The Caicos Islands sit on a vast sandbank, creating perfect conditions for learner divers or casual visitors (although the presence of drop-offs and deeper reefs to the west means that there are also options for the more experienced diver). The Turks Islands to the east are more dramatic in pure diving terms, for a short boat-ride from the shore puts the diver over walls plunging into the Turks Island Passage, a massive ocean trench 1.2 miles (2 km) deep.

This trench performs several important functions. It serves as an undersea highway for large pelagics such as humpbacks, and it also acts as a giant thermostat providing stable water temperatures. For divers, the trench presents classic wall-diving opportunities, although the currents are worthy of respect, particularly to the north and south of Grand Turk.

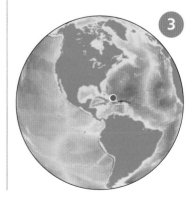

3

DIVE CENTERS

On Grand Turk:

BLUE WATER DIVERS
P.O. Box 124, Grand Turk,
Turks & Caicos Islands
Phone: +1-649-946-2432
E-mail: info@grandturkscuba.com
Web: www.grandturkscuba.com

SEA EYE DIVING
P.O. Box 67, Grand Turk, Turks & Caicos Islands
U.S. toll free: +1-800-786-0669
Phone: +1-649-946-1407
E-mail: ci@tciway.tc or cari@tciway.tc
Web: www.seaeyediving.com

On Providenciales:

BIG BLUE
P.O. Box 159, Providenciales,
Turks & Caicos Islands
Phone: +1-649-946-5034
E-mail: enquiries@bigblueunlimited.com
Web: www.bigblue.tc

DIVE PROVO
P.O. Box 413, Providenciales,
Turks & Caicos Islands
Phone: +1-649-946-5029
E-mail: diving@diveprovo.com
Web: www.diveprovo.com

Liveaboards:

TURKS & CAICOS AGGRESSOR II
Turtle Cove Marina, Providenciales,
Turks & Caicos Islands
AGGRESSOR FLEET LIMITED
P.O. Box 1470, Morgan City,
L.A. 70381-1470, U.S.A.
Phone: +1-985-385-2628
E-mail: turkscaicos@aggressor.com
Web: www.TurksandCaicosAggressor.com

 DIVING ORGANIZATIONS

None. Contact Turks & Caicos Islands Tourist
Board for recommended operators.

🕐 **RECOMPRESSION**

Providenciales has a multi-lock 60-inch
recompression chamber, run by hyperbaric
experts, and located at Miramar Resort, Turtle
Cove, Providenciales, Turks & Caicos Is.

➕ **HOSPITAL**

Associated Medical Practices
Leeward Hwy., Glass Shack, Providenciales,
Turks & Caicos Islands
Phone: +1-649-946-4242

Grand Turk Hospital
Hospital Rd., Grand Turk, Turks & Caicos Is.
Phone: +1-649-946-2333

 CONSERVATION SOCIETY

Turks & Caicos National Trust
P.O. Box 540, Providenciales,
Turks & Caicos Islands
Phone: +1-649-941-5710
E-mail: tc.nattrust@tciway.tc

In character with many other linear island sites (the islands are arranged in a rough curve following the edge of the bank), the breaks between the smaller islands attract congregations of large pelagics, and are known as reliable areas for dramatic encounters with dolphins, sharks, and mantas.

▼ BARREL SPONGE

Barrel sponges are some of the largest structures found on Caribbean reefs.

GRACE BAY

- **10 to 100 feet (3 to 30 m)**
- **beginner to intermediate**

A huge bay protected by a 14-mile (22-km) barrier reef, Grace Bay is an ideal site for new arrivals in the islands who wish to brush up their skills before moving onto more challenging sites, and for learner divers.

There are numerous sites dotted around the bay, most of them a short boat ride away from the north

John Bantin

John Bantin

shore. The most popular site in the bay is the Pinnacles, a classic spur and groove reef interspersed with deep gullies, cuts, and canyons. Gorgonians and sponges make the most of the shallow reef formations, while in the recesses and folds of the reef lurk some big morays, crayfish, and scorpionfish. The great asset of this particular site is the variation at any depth, with reefs that extend almost to the surface and yet offer more experienced divers the chance of deeper mini walls.

The Cathedral is a large sand patch leading to a steep-sided gully that drops to nearly 100 feet (30 m). If you follow the exit of the gully round the wall to the north you come across a smaller cave that sometimes contains large groupers. Watch out for garden eels on the sand patches at the early stages of this dive.

NORTHWEST POINT

• 45 to 130 feet (14 to 40 m) • advanced

Northwest Point is essentially a 3-mile (5-km) strip of steep wall, dropping from 45 feet (14 m) to over 5,000 feet (1,524 m)! This a classic wall dive, with beautiful coral and gorgonian growth clinging to vertical walls cut with canyons and steep gullies, while off in the blue lurk schooling fish, rays, and cruising sharks.

The cuts and ridges in the wall provide a number of excellent dive sites, including Eagle's Nest, centered around several deep cuts in the wall.

The Crack is perhaps one of the best-loved sites along the Northwest Point. The dive begins on a large sand patch in 40 feet (12 m) of water close to the lip of the wall. As you approach the wall, take time to investigate the jumbled matrix of plate corals at the lip, which provide hiding places for small morays, octopuses, and scorpionfish.

The diver has two options at this point—head out directly over the wall, or descend through the deep cut in the reef wall. This cut continues all the way down to an exit leading to a ledge that extends 30 feet (9 m) out from the face. Close to this exit point is the Crack itself, running the entire height of the wall and flanked by plate corals, sea whips, sponges, and gorgonians. Don't get too fascinated by the goings-on in the Crack, as much of the action in this dive takes place out in the blue and it is always worth glancing away from the wall every now and then.

Shark Hotel is a dive for the slightly more experienced diver. As you head north from the mooring buoy a small gully appears that leads to an impressive cavern. This frequently contains resting white tip reef sharks and turtles. Exiting this cavern through a beautiful arch, the diver emerges on to a large platform at 130 feet (40 m), before ascending diagonally back up the wall.

▲ OCTOPUS
It is always worth paying close attention to the reef, whether deep or shallow, else you might miss a sight such as this octopus sliding out of a small hole.

DIVER'S TIP

From late December through April, the entire Atlantic herd of 2,500 humpback whales passes through the channel on their annual migration to the Mouchoir Bank, just 20 to 30 miles (32 to 48 km) to the southeast. During this period divers can listen to an underwater concert of the whales' songs.

John Bantin

▲ SEAGRASS
Seagrass beds provide a crucial habitat for both large and small species.

Eagle rays and the odd cruising reef shark may be seen in the blue as the diver ascends.

THE TUNNELS

• 30 to 120 feet (9 to 36 m) • intermediate

This is a classic Grand Turk site, with a steep wall plunging to abyssal depths within a stone's throw of the shoreline.

The site is located at the southern end of Grand Turk, and gets its name from the two tunnels that burrow into the wall. The dive begins on the lip of the wall over white sand, before the divers move to the top of the wall and a large coral head containing the entrance to the first tunnel. Take a moment to explore this area, as stingrays, garden eels, and parrotfish are all common on the lip of the wall here.

The main tunnel emerges from the reef wall at 60 feet (18 m), where the divers exit to follow a large crack. Turning south, the second, smaller, tunnel comes into view. Fish life is profuse in this region—barracuda, jacks, jewfish, eagle rays, and tuna out in the blue, and shoals of snappers and grunts nearer to hand. This is also a renowned spot for encountering feeding mantas

during the summer. Try to remember to take a look back up the reef, as you will be rewarded with a stunning view of overhanging gorgonians and plate coral silhouetted against the reef crest. Continuing north on the dive, you dip slightly deeper before slowly ascending toward the lip of the wall.

THE AMPHITHEATER

• 30 to 120 feet (9 to 36 m) • intermediate

This site owes its name to the shape of the reef wall framing a large sand patch—the stage for the show that takes place in the blue water of the drop-off. The sand chutes that lead to the Amphitheater are home to southern stingrays as well as large patches of garden eels. Follow a gap in the coral from the Amphitheater down to the exit at around 80 feet (24 m) and you will find yourself suspended above a drop-off more than a mile deep! Off in the blue in the winter it is possible to hear the singing of passing humpbacks, and the unpredictability of this site is one of its great attractions. Turtles, eagle rays, mantas, reef sharks, large schools of barracuda, and Atlantic spadefish—even the locals don't know what will appear in the deep waters of the channel. On ascending the reef wall at the end of this dive watch out for schools of Bermuda chub and beautifully colored queen triggerfish.

WEST CAICOS

• Various depths and experience levels

This uninhabited island offers some of the most adventurous diving in the Turks and Caicos, and is about a 60-minute boat-ride away from Providenciales. The names of the dive sites are tremendously evocative—Land of the Giants, Highway to Heaven, Dolphin Dip—and all refer to the passage of large pelagics in the nutrient-rich channel to the north and the stark drop-offs to the west. At dives such as the Driveway there are vast numbers of barrel sponges, and at Elephant Ear Canyon there is an elephant's ear sponge that measures 11 feet (3 m) in diameter and is thought to be the largest in the whole archipelago.

OTHER ACTIVITIES

Tourism is well-developed on the Turks and Caicos Islands, and there is a wide range of accommodation and vacation package deals to suit most budgets from the medium through to the very pricey indeed. Essential stops for the nature lover include Little Water Cay, which is a haven for rock iguanas and forms part of the Alexandra Nature Reserve. There are guided tours along specially constructed boardwalks through the heart of the reserve. For the birdwatcher, Flamingo Pond on North Caicos is a must, where huge flocks of flamingoes can be observed from hides along the road. For the more adventurous, the Middle Caicos Conch Bar Caves is the largest cave system in the Caribbean, and is well worth a visit.

Cockburn Town is a typical sleepy Caribbean town, with some beautiful beaches nearby. Do take some time to wander along the seafront in the capital to admire historic buildings and the famous Colombus Monument —marking the spot where Colombus is supposed to have landed in 1492. The Philatelic Bureau's stamps are famed throughout the stamp-collecting world, and the Turks and Caicos National Museum displays artefacts from ancient and modern island history.

☎ TELEPHONE NUMBERS

Recompression chamber	+1-649-946-4240
Hospital	+1-649-946-2333
Turks & Caicos Islands Tourist Board	+1-649-946-4970

🖥 WEBSITES & E-MAIL

Turks & Caicos Islands Tourist Board	www.turksandcaicos.tc
Travel guide	worldtravelguide.net/country/286/country_ guide/caribbean/turks-and-caicos.islands

▼ **GRUNTS**
A school of blue-striped grunts keep close together in a defensive formation.

John Bantin

ISLA DE LA JUVENTUD

CUBA'S ISLA DE LA JUVENTUD, THE ISLE OF YOUTH, HAS A PIRATICAL PAST AND A RAPIDLY DEVELOPING FUTURE AS ONE OF THE BEST DIVE SITES IN THE CARIBBEAN. WITH GENTLE REEF TOPS LEADING TO PRECIPITOUS DROP-OFFS THAT POSITIVELY SWARM WITH MARINE LIFE, ITS REPUTATION IS WELL DESERVED.

 VISIBILITY

100 feet (30 m). Not good in Sept and Oct due to storms.

 MUST SEE

Tarpon

 DOWNSIDE

Unpredictable tourist facilities

 GETTING THERE

Direct flights are available to Havana from most major international hubs, from where you transfer to Nueva Gerona. Limited flights operate from Miami.

 VISA

Virtually all visitors require a Cuban visa or Tourist Card for a stay of one month, available from travel agencies, tour operators, or a Cuban consulate. U.S. citizens are still officially forbidden to travel to Cuba without a special license; travel restrictions are relaxing, however.

$ MONEY

Currency is the Cuban peso. U.S. dollars are highly desirable. Transactions using U.S. credit cards may be stopped as illegal, but non-U.S. Visa and MasterCard are fine.

Isla de la Juventud is by far the largest of the hundreds of islands that make up the Canarreos Archipelago lying in the Gulf of Batabanó off the southwestern coast of Cuba. The island was discovered by Christopher Columbus on his second voyage to the Caribbean in 1494. He named it La Evangelista, and since then it has enjoyed a succession of colorful names reflecting its checkered past as the haunt of pirates and brigands, including the Isle of Parrots, the Isle of Treasure, the Isle of Exiles (when it was being used by the Spanish as a penal colony for political prisoners), and the Isle of Pines. It acquired its most recent name, meaning the Isle of Youth, in 1978.

GEOGRAPHY

Isla de la Juventud, some 60 miles (97 km) from the coast of Cuba, was colonized by the Spanish governors of Cuba at the beginning of the 19th century and today forms part of the province of Havana. Of Cuba's many islands, it is second only in size to the mainland, and covers some 849 sq miles (2,200 sq km). It is mostly flat, with a large interior swamp, the Ciénaga de Lanier. The island is the least populated region of Cuba. Most people live on the north coast in and around the capital, Nueva Gerona. The island welcomes tourists and has undeniably some of the best diving in the whole of Cuba, most of it centered on the Pirate Coast of the

WATER TEMPERATURE

°C	°F		°C	°F
30	86		30	86
29°C				
20	68		20	68
84°F			**24°C**	
10	50		10	**75°F** 50
0	32		0	32
Summer			Winter	

Linda Pitkin

▶ **GOLDENTAIL MORAY**

While it may not yet have gained the reputation of some other Caribbean dive sites, Isla de la Juventud has a lot to offer.

island's southwestern peninsula, particularly within the area of the Marine National Park at Punta Francés.

MARINE LIFE

Marine biologists estimate that there are approximately 1,000 fish species in the waters around Cuba. But while the reefs in the region are particularly impressive—three of them exceed the entire Florida Keys in length—they do not have the reputation for attracting the large pelagics associated with other great diving locations around the world. However, as most of the diving on the Isla de la Juventud has the advantage of taking place in a nature reserve, the reefs here are of superb quality. Moreover, the walls are contorted and pitted with numerous caverns and overhangs—the perfect environment for divers to come face to face with larger reef residents.

One of the most famous of these fish is the tarpon. These magnificent predators, which resemble huge bars of silver, frequent caves and gullies when not out hunting. They appear to be hugely confident and will allow divers to inspect them at close quarters if approached correctly—a spectacular sight. Also present in the reefs are large marbled groupers. These fish are used to being fed and will follow a diver throughout a dive looking for hand-outs, so be prepared for some persistent attention on these dives.

Numerous sponges and large gorgonians characterize the reefs, with classic Caribbean reef species such as snapper and barracuda present in considerable numbers. Stingrays are almost invariably to be found in many of the sandy gullies and reef tops.

John Bantin

▲ FRENCH ANGLEFISH
The French anglefish is inquistive and confident, making it an ideal subject for photography.

Nueva Gerona

Cayo el Navio

Cayo Triángulo

Cayo Guayabo

Cayos Balandras

La Fe

Cayo San Juan

ISLA DE LA JUVENTUD
(Cuba)

Cabo Francés

Shark Valley

The Queen's Garden

Trail of the Deep

Magic Kingdom

Siguanea

Tunnel of Love

Point Pedernalés

Black Coral Wall

0   20 km

0   14 mi

Cayo Matías

Punta del Este

Caleta Grande

4

▶ **TARPON**
Large schools of tarpon can be found swimming the waters around Isla de la Juventud.

 DIVE CENTERS
HOTEL EL COLONY
Carretera de la Siguanea, KM41, El Colony,
Isla de la Juventud, Cuba
Phone: +53-619-8282
E-mail: info@wowcuba.com
Web:www.wowcuba.com/cuba2.html

 DIVING ORGANIZATIONS
None

 RECOMPRESSION
Nueva Gerona Recompression Chamber
Ospedale General Docente Heroes del Baire
Ave. 39, Nueva Gerona, Isla de la Juventud
Phone: +53-462-3012
Physician in charge: Dr. José Luis Manso

 HOSPITAL
Ospedale General Docente Heroes del Baire
Ave. 39 Nueva Gerona, Isla de la Juventud
Phone: +53-462-3012

 CONSERVATION SOCIETY
National Headquarters
257 Park Avenue South, New York, NY 10010
Phone: +1-212-505-2100
E-mail: members@environmentaldefense.org

OTHER DIVE SITES

Shark Valley
The Queen's Garden

THE DIVES

The diving on the Isla de la Juventud is largely based around the activities of the largest and longest established operation on the island—the El Colony International Dive Center within the Punta Francés Marine National Park. This well-organized operation has access to at least 50 buoyed sites within a narrow band of the island's western coast.

Numerous spur and groove formations, caves, caverns, and large gullies characterize the reef tops on this part of the western coast, leading in turn to stepped drop-offs that plunge into the Caribbean Sea to depths in excess of 3,250 feet (1,000 m). The dive sites here are noted for excellent visibility and benign currents, and the reefs are classically Caribbean.

CABO FRANCÉS REEF

• **60 to 120 feet (18 to 36 m)** • **beginner**

The reef at Cabo Francés is essentially a step leading to the abyssal wall on the western edge of the island, which extends for a considerable length. Typically for a Cuban reef, the reef top is a mass of arches and overhangs, providing perfect hideaways for lurking tarpons and hungry groupers.

One of the characteristics of many Caribbean reefs is the presence of large sponges. The Cabo Francés reef and wall is no exception. The tube sponges here really are magnificent, like huge organ pipes rising from the reef top. Snaking elephant ear sponges seem to writhe over the reef top in great folds and curves. Just off the lip of the wall there are some splendid gorgonians. Note how they stretch themselves right out into the waters off the reef in order to maximize their exposure to passing currents.

Look out for the Tunnel of Love, a deep cut in the wall festooned with sponges and encrusting organisms on either side. These conceal many a Nassau grouper or schools of snappers. French angelfish patrol the edges

Linda Pitkin

shallow dives, approachable reef fish, and gentle currents. It is a reputation well deserved, and makes Punta Francés an ideal location for divers to visit in the early stages of their diving careers.

OTHER ACTIVITIES

The way of life on the Isla de la Juventud is slow and leisurely. There are certain aspects to it that some visitors may find difficult to handle—everyone wants tipping, transport is hideously unreliable, and the tourist infrastructure somewhat unpredictable. Accept these limitations, however, and you will find the island a fascinating and colorful destination.

A number of attractions on Isla de la Juventud are well worth visiting if you want time off from diving, including Native American cave paintings at Punta del Este. The walls of the cave, which has been described as the Sistine Chapel of aboriginal art, are covered with more than 200 paintings. Bibbijagua beach on the northeastern side of the island is notable for its unusual black sand. Only a short drive away is the Presidio Model, the prison where Cuban President Fidel Castro was jailed between 1953 and 1955 and where he drew up his plans for the Cuban Revolution of 1959. It is now a museum.

☎ **TELEPHONE NUMBERS**

Recompression chamber	+53-061-2-3012
Hospital	+53-061-2-3012

🖳 **WEBSITES & E-MAIL**

Cuban Tourist Board	www.cubatravel.cu
Cuban Travel and Culture	www.havanajournal.com
Cuban information	www.cuba.com
Cuban Government	www.cubagob.cu

DIVER'S TIP

At night, and if you're feeling particularly brave, shine a torch on a passing fish while close to a tarpon. The resultant strike from the tarpon happens in the blink of an eye.

▼ CRAYFISH
Crayfish spend much of the daylight hours holed up in the reef, only emerging at night to forage further afield.

of the reef wall, and schools of surgeonfish and grunts are a permanent feature. You may also see patrolling barracuda in the blue water off the main wall.

CABO FRANCÉS TO POINT PEDERNALÉS

• 30 to 130 feet (9 to 40 m) • **beginner to advanced**

This region, incorporating the Marine National Park of Punta Francés, has been divided into a number of separate dive sites, their names highly evocative of the dives themselves—Trail of the Deep, Magic Kingdom, Black Coral Wall, and the promisingly named The Site of All! Nearly all of these sites are characterized by a reef shelf pitted with gullies and caverns, some as deep as 240 feet (73 m), that leads eventually to the deeper water or wall of the shelf at the western end of the island. Don't miss the opportunity to look out into the blue water for passing green turtles, eagle rays, and the occasional gray reef shark. All of these dive sites have the reputation of being particularly benign, with great visibility,

John Bantin

JARDINES DE LA REINA

words by Jane Morgan

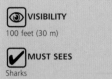

VISIBILITY
100 feet (30 m)

MUST SEES
Sharks
Tarpon

DOWNSIDE
Long transfer from Havana

GETTING THERE
Direct flights are available to Havana from most major international hubs, from where you transfer to Nueva Gerona. Limited flights operate from Miami.

VISA
Virtually all visitors require a Cuban visa or Tourist Card for a stay of one month, available from travel agencies, tour operators, or a Cuban consulate. U.S. citizens are still officially forbidden to travel to Cuba without a special license; travel restrictions are relaxing, however.

MONEY
Currency is the Cuban peso (CUC). U.S. dollars, credit cards and travelers' cheques are not accepted in Cuba. ATMs can also be a little unreliable. The best option is to take cash and change it to pesos at the airport.

CUBA'S JARDINES DE LA REINA (GARDENS OF THE QUEEN) HAS BEEN DUBBED THE "GALAPAGOS OF THE CARIBBEAN". A PROTECTED MARINE PARK COVERING 2,400 SQUARE MILES (6,200 SQ KM), IT BOASTS A CHAIN OF 250 VIRGIN CORAL ISLANDS, TOGETHER WITH REEFS TEEMING WITH LIFE AND AN UNUSUALLY PLENTIFUL SHARK POPULATION. ITS REPUTATION IS WELL DESERVED.

Jardines de la Reina is an archipelago in the south of Cuba, off the coast of Ciego de Avila, Camaguey, and Las Tunas provinces. The islands were discovered by Christopher Columbus on his second voyage to the Caribbean in 1494, and named "Gardens of the Queen" in honor of her Highness Isabella, Queen of Castile. This spectacular region of cays and mangroves was once inhabited by fishermen and a favourite fishing spot for Fidel Castro. The area has now been declared a protected marine reserve and makes up part of the third longest barrier reef in the world, with the only permanent inhabitants being a park police officer and dive center staff. Marine park status bans any commercial fishing and the collection of shells and turtles, which has resulted in a superb ecosystem.

GEOGRAPHY

Jardines de la Reina is Cuba's second largest archipelago (smaller only than Jardines del Rey). It lies 60 miles (96 km) off the southwest coast of the mainland and 80 miles (130 km) north of Cayman Brac in the Caribbean Sea. Stretching for over 75 miles (120 km) and in some places 20 miles (32 km) wide this is the largest marine park in the Caribbean. The archipelago is a saltwater wilderness consisting of hundreds of little cayos surrounded by rich mangroves and endless flats. Access to the area is a three- to four-hour boat transfer from the small fishing town of Jucaro, which in turn is a six-hour road transfer from Havana. The only inhabitants to be found on the tiny islets are birds such as heron, pelicans and egret and small mammals and reptiles including the iguana and the jutia, which is the largest endemic land mammal of Cuba and can grow to around 24 inches (60 cm) in length. Fly fishermen, who come to fish the plentiful stocks of tarpon and bonefish, have historically frequented the region far more than divers. Thanks to the lack of commercial fishing, the whole area is extremely rich in fish stocks and sharks.

The climate in Cuba is tropical and moderated by trade winds, and there are two main seasons. During the dry season (November–April), the average temperature is 72°F (22°C), although cold wet snaps can come from North America in December and January. The rainy season (May–October) has an average temperature of 77°F (25°C) and the days are hot and humid. Hurricane season is July–October and is more likely to affect the south of the country.

The best time for diving is November–April, with the latter part of this period being the warmest. December-February normally has the best visibility and November is the prime time for whale sharks in the Jardines de la Reina. During May and June, there tend to be more tarpon around, while the September full moon sees the coral spawning.

MARINE LIFE

The reefs are in pristine condition swathed with beautiful gorgonian fan corals and sea plumes interspersed with stunning colored vase, barrel and pipe sponges. Look closely for the usual Caribbean suspects snuggled inside the sponges—a menagerie of shrimps, decorator crabs and the charismatic arrow crab. Flamingo tongues cling on to the gorgonians and tiny blennies peek out from their rocky homes. Ask your guide to show you a jawfish: you won't just get one, but hundreds of them hovering above the sand as far as the eye can see. Marine biologists estimate that well over 900 species of fish live in these rich waters. There are numerous mangroves that provide a perfect nursery environment for the smaller fish that in turn populate the teeming reefs.

Groupers are common, and you'll often see the huge goliath grouper along with big tarpon and barracudas. With so little fishing, the residents seem less skittish and you can get really close to them. Large stingrays are also common here, and on some dive sites they can be found lying on the sandy bottom, particularly between rocky gullies.

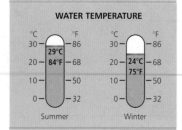

WATER TEMPERATURE

	Summer		Winter
°C	°F	°C	°F
30	86	30	86
29°C			
20	**84°F** 68	20	**24°C** 68
			75°F
10	50	10	50
0	32	0	32

Peruano •

CUBA

El Farallon •

*Jardines de
la Reina*
El Galeón •

Ancilitas • • Plus Reef

0   5 km

0   5 mi

Black Coral One • •

Las Cruces •

But in this region the star attractions are definitely the sharks, of which there is a very healthy population. The dive guides say this is due to the area's marine park status and claim they've seen a 100 percent increase in sharks, jacks and tarpon in the 10 years since it was established. Fish carcasses are used to bait the water and sometimes to feed the sharks, and it's normal to see dozens of silky sharks around the dive boat. Other frequent visitors are the larger Caribbean reef sharks that greet divers as they enter the water and escort them to the dive sites. During the months of October and November a popular visitor is the beautiful whale shark on its migration route through the reserve. Great hammerheads can also be seen occasionally, as can nurse and lemon sharks.

THE DIVES

The only dive center within the reserve is Avalon, who have exclusive rights to all activities in the area and offer diving from a choice of three liveaboards: La Reina, Caballones and Halcon. There is also the option of staying on the Tortuga, a floating hotel, and diving daily from a day boat. A permit is required to enter the marine park and the profit is used to finance the maintenance and preservation of the area. This also enables a team of dedicated marine biologists to work alongside the dive guides on a tagging project to track shark birth rates in the reserve. Eighty dive sites have been mapped and are scattered across the entire marine park, but there are still many more waiting to be discovered. With only 300 divers per year permitted into the park, the dive sites are uncrowded and undamaged. The shallow reefs are pristine and smothered with beautiful fan corals interspersed with brightly colored sponges providing plenty of homes for the prolific amount of critters. The topography is impressive with plenty of swimthroughs, gullies, overhangs, small caves and dramatic walls that plunge into the depths.

EL FARALLON

• **15 to 100 feet (5 to 30 m)** • **intermediate**

Stunning swimthroughs along with small caves and gullies ensure that this site stands out from the rest. At the far end of a swimthrough at 100 feet (30 m), large schools of jacks, tarpon and barracuda race around the

pinnacles and coral bommies. The reefs are all carpeted with gorgonians and soft corals. In the gullies you'll see black coral, whip corals and colorful sponges. Large groupers looking for an easy meal follow the divers throughout the dive. However, the safety stop is the highlight with an abundance of silky sharks waiting in the shallows around the dive boat. It's normal to see up to 20 or 30 sharks on this dive and they are very used to divers allowing you to get very close to them.

BLACK CORAL ONE

• **45 to 130 feet (14 to 40 m)** • **intermediate**

Caribbean reef sharks turn up here as soon as the boat arrives, indicating years of regular feeding. The sharks are perfectly comfortable with divers in the water and

5

▼ **SILKY SHARK**
Smooth-skinned silky sharks feed mainly on inshore and pelagic bony fish.

Jane Morgan

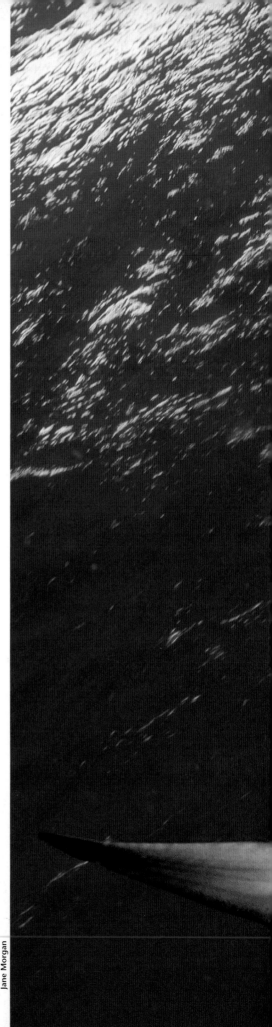

Jane Morgan

 DIVE CENTERS

HOTEL EL COLONY
Carretera de la Siguanea, KM41, El Colony,
Isla de la Juventud, Cuba
Phone: +53-619-8282
E-mail: info@wowcuba.com
Web: www.wowcuba.com/cuba2.html

 RECOMPRESSION

Nueva Gerona Recompression Chamber
Ospedale General Docente Heroes del Baire
Ave. 39, Nueva Gerona, Isla de la Juventud
Phone: +53-462-3012
Physician in charge: Dr. José Luis Manso

HOSPITAL

Ospedale General Docente Heroes del Baire
Ave. 39, Nueva Gerona, Isla de la Juventud
Phone: +53-462-3012

CONSERVATION SOCIETY

National Headquarters
257 Park Avenue South, New York, NY 10010
Phone: +1-212-505-2100
E-mail: members@environmentaldefense.org

▶ **UP CLOSE AND PERSONAL**

Silky sharks are very used to divers, so you
can get close to them as 20 or more
gather around the dive boat on your
safety stop.

even escort you through the blue water to the reef top.
A large hole is etched out of the reef, its walls covered
in corals and sponges. At one end there is a small
accessible cave and if you spend any time inside, the air
bubbles will permeate through the reef top making
trails up to the surface. This reef hosts an incredible
amount of life, including large fan corals covered in
flamingo tongues. There is also a large, hard coral
pinnacle standing proud from the reef and surrounded
by a mixture of angelfish and butterflyfish.

ANCILITAS

• **27 to 45 feet (8 to 14 m)** • **beginner**

This is a beautiful shallow reef, particularly good for
night diving and suitable for all levels of experience. At
night large gorgonian fan corals struggle to support
giant basket stars that cling onto their branches feeding
in the nutrient-rich waters. Brittlestars, arrow crabs and
flamingo tongues can also be seen jostling for space.
Plenty of sleepy fish including filefish, trunkfish and
groupers can be found hiding among the corals. Under
the ledges moray eels can be found with their
entourage of cleaner shrimps, and the overhangs are
also a good place for spotting spiny lobsters.

PLUS REEF

• **33 to 66 feet (10 to 20 m)** • **intermediate**

The spectacular reef top is covered with a vast array of
gorgonians, soft corals and sponges. Huge and plentiful
barrel sponges provide homes in their furrows for arrow
crabs and banded coral shrimps. A vast variety of fish
can be found here, with angelfish, butterflyfish,
goatfish and triggerfish all making an appearance.
Barracudas hang off the reef being cleaned and tarpon
gather together in the gullies. Keep a regular lookout
into the blue as there is always the chance of a pelagic
encounter.

OTHER ACTIVITIES

After a day's diving, the Avalon dive staff will take
you by skiff for trips though the mangroves where you
can spot a number of different birds, including heron.
Trips are also offered to some of the tiny coral islands
where fruit is taken to feed the local jutias and iguanas.
Off the beaches you can see many crustaceans and at
the surface you can often spot crocodiles. Most of the
dive guides are also experienced fly-fishing guides. Trips
are made by skiff into the shallow water flats where
anglers can fish for bonefish and tarpon. Although
Avalon dive center is based in the middle of a complete
wilderness, incredibly there is wi-fi Internet access—so
if you need something else to do you can always surf
the Web.

CAYMAN
ISLANDS

VISIBILITY

Low water run-off means consistently excellent visibility. In the range of 100 feet (30 m) plus year round.

MUST SEE

Stingray City

DOWNSIDE

Crowded

Expensive

GETTING THERE

Most travelers arrive in the Cayman Islands from the United States, with services to George Town from Miami and other cities. Travelers from Europe have to connect in the U.S. There's a departure tax of U.S.$13.

VISA

U.S. and Canadian citizens don't need visas, only proof of citizenship. Citizens of the E.U., the Commonwealth, Israel and Japan need passports but not visas.

MONEY

Currency is the Cayman Island dollar. U.S. dollars and traveler's checks are accepted throughout the islands. Major credit cards are accepted by all the larger tourist facilities.

WATER TEMPERATURE

°C	°F	°C	°F
30 —	— 86	30 —	— 86
29°C			
20 —	— 68	20 — **27°C**	— 68
84°F		**80°F**	
10 —	— 50	10 —	— 50
0 —	— 32	0 —	— 32
Summer		Winter	

STEEP WALLS, CRYSTAL VISIBILITY, AND THE BEST 10-FOOT (3 M) DIVE ON EARTH IS A HEADY COMBINATION THAT DRAWS DIVERS FROM AROUND THE WORLD TO THREE LOW-LYING, RUGGED, AND RELATIVELY BARREN ISLANDS BATHED IN THE WARM WATERS OF THE CARIBBEAN—THE CAYMAN ISLANDS.

Christopher Columbus discovered the Cayman Islands in 1503. Had he had the opportunity to venture beneath the waves, he would have noted a startling contrast to the harsh terrain above. Rising from an undersea mountain range, the islands have all the characteristics that are associated with a classic dive location—steep walls creating currents and rich upwellings, clear water, sheltered bays, and broad fringing reefs. The islands still have areas that represent particularly healthy examples of Caribbean reef systems, and although diving has had a heavy impact on some parts of the reefs, other areas are remote enough to harbor real gems of wild wall diving. The Cayman Islands have something for everyone.

GEOGRAPHY

The three islands that make up the Cayman Islands group (a British Crown Colony) lie approximately 150 miles (240 km) south of Cuba and 180 miles (290 km) northwest of Jamaica. Most of the islands' population of more than 33,000 live on Grand Cayman, the largest and most southwesterly of the group, particularly in George Town, the capital. Grand Cayman is an extended oval-shaped island with a total area of 77 sq miles (200 sq km.) A lagoon dominates its eastern end, and like all three islands, it is low-lying, reaching a maximum height of only 60 feet (18 m.) Its bowl-like shape, combined with its lack of high cliffs, is highly significant because rainwater leaches through the porous limestone rocks of the interior rather than running off through rivers and streams onto the reefs and walls of the immediate coastline. This lack of run-off means that the surrounding waters have exceptional visibility.

Little Cayman and Cayman Brac share the same low profile. The two islands lie parallel to one another

northeast of Grand Cayman, with Little Cayman rising only 46 feet (14 m) above sea level. Consisting of rugged rocks and brackish pools, it is the least hospitable of the islands. Cayman Brac is rather more developed, with a resident population of more than 1,000, although the island still retains very much of a classic Caribbean feel to it.

The undersea topography of the Caymans is broadly summarized as flat fringing reefs extending several hundred feet out from the coast, leading to craggy reef tops at approximately 50 to 70 feet (15 to 21 m), leading in turn to precipitous reef walls. Two distinct undersea shelves surround the islands, thought to be a legacy of sea level rise in the distant past.

MARINE LIFE

The topography of the islands lends itself to a variety of reef formations, from gently shelving fringing reefs to precipitous walls. The reefs themselves are broadly characterized by the presence of large tube and barrel sponges—a common feature of Caribbean diving but particularly abundant here—mixed in with beautiful gorgonian fans. The stingrays of North Sound on Grand Cayman are one of the great wildlife encounters of diving anywhere in the world, and the gatherings of manta rays at sites such as Bloody Bay Wall off Little Cayman are beginning to achieve similar fame. The reefs also offer huge schools of snappers, eagle rays, some impressive Nassau groupers, and large great barracuda, as well as healthy populations of gray reef sharks in certain locations. Hammerhead sharks may also occasionally be encountered off some of the more remote walls.

The Cayman Islands are well managed in terms of marine conservation, with a three-tier protection system covering 18 separate marine parks. Although

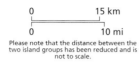

Cayman Brac

Greenhouse Reef

Bloody Bay Wall   Jackson Pointe   M.V. Captain Keith Tibbetts

CAYMAN ISLANDS
(British Overseas Territory)

Little Cayman

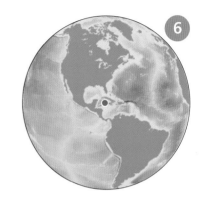

6

```
0                15 km
├────┼────┼────┼────┤
0                10 mi
```

Please note that the distance between the
two island groups has been reduced and is
not to scale.

Ghost Mountain   Eagle Ray Pass   Grand
                                    Cayman

West Bay   Stingray City

            Coral Gardens

✚ 🕐 ✈   ●East End
   George Town

Smith's Cove

STINGRAY ENCOUNTER
Stingray City may feel slightly
contrived, but it is nonetheless a
thrilling encounter.

John Bantin

DIVE CENTERS

BOB SOTO'S REEF DIVERS
P.O. 11800 A.P.O., Grand Cayman,
Cayman Islands
Phone: +1-345-949-2022
E-mail: info@bobsotosreefdivers.com
Web: www.bobsotosreefdivers.com

DON FOSTER'S DIVE
P.O. Box 31486, Seven Mile Beach,
Grand Cayman, Cayman Islands
Phone: +1-345-945-5132
E-mail: dfd@kandw.ky
Web: www.donfosters.com

BLUE WATER DIVERS LTD
P.O. Box 35 LC, Blossom Village,
Little Cayman, Cayman Islands
Phone: +1-345-948-0095

PETER HUGHES DIVE & PHOTO
P.O. Box 238 S.T.B, Divi Tiara Beach Resort,
Cayman Brac, Cayman Islands
Phone: +1-345-948-1553

DIVING ORGANIZATIONS

The Cayman Islands Watersports Operators
Association operates a code of practice and
provides direct links to approved operators in
the islands.

P.O. Box 31495, Seven Mile Beach,
Grand Cayman, Cayman Islands
Phone: +1-345-949-8522
Email: info@cayman.org
Web: www.cayman.org

RECOMPRESSION

George Town Hospital
Hospital Road, George Town, Grand Cayman,
Cayman Islands
Phone: +1-345-949-8600

HOSPITAL

George Town Hospital
Hospital Road, George Town, Grand Cayman,
Cayman Islands
Phone: +1-345-949-8600

CONSERVATION SOCIETY

To find out more about conservation in the
Cayman Islands contact the Cayman Islands
Watersports Operators Association at the
address above.

some areas such as Seven Mile Beach have undoubtedly suffered from intensive diving, there remain a number of relatively pristine and unspoiled Caribbean reefs that are accessible by the diver who is prepared to take the time and invest the money in longer boat trips beyond the better-established sites.

THE DIVES

Diving in the Cayman Islands is generally well run by an established and professional dive industry that has grown up to cater for the needs of the North American market in particular. Overseeing dive operations is the Cayman Islands Watersports Operators Association, a body that has done its best to establish a set of diving protocols and etiquette in order to control what is undoubtedly a crowded industry on the islands, achieving its aim with a fair degree of success.

It is no idle boast that there is always a site to dive in the Cayman Islands, almost regardless of the weather conditions. A sheltered bay or reef is nearly always a short boat ride away—although in hurricane season late in the year even these sites may be off limits.

The great variety of reef systems means that there really is a dive for every level of experience around the islands, all the way from gently sloping reefs interspersed with patches of sand through to steep walls over deep trenches. Most of the classic dives are done by boat, although it is also quite realistic to dive from shore if gentler exploration of the fringing reefs is the order of the day.

The dive operations around the islands are concentrated on the western coast of Grand Cayman in the heavily developed region of Seven Mile Beach a little way north of the capital, George Town. Nonetheless, the north wall, which plunges to an impressive 1.2-mile (2-km) depth, offers more challenging and less crowded diving opportunities, and is only a boat-ride away. There are also a limited number of operators based on the northern side of the island itself. Cayman Brac and Little Cayman offer broadly similar dives but without the pressure of diver numbers associated with the larger island.

STINGRAY CITY

- 15 feet (4 m) • beginner

Located on the western side of the sheltered mouth of the North Sound, Stingray City is an amazing phenomenon. The local guides have been feeding southern

Cayman Islands Tourist Board

▶ **SEA ANEMONE**
Anemones, like this one, have millions of harpoon-like stinging cells that are activated when touched.

Linda Pitkin

stingrays at the site for more than a decade, and over 200 of these magnificent animals may congregate at the feeding stations at any one time. The stingrays gather the moment they hear a boat engine, and are hand fed with individual tit-bits by the guides.

The fish are remarkably trusting and docile, even for animals that have actively chosen to interact with humans, and will sweep above, under, and around the divers in the group. As with all wild animals, their space should be respected. It is not unknown for divers to grab them for photographs or even attempt to ride them. Such activities can be extremely stressful for the animals and can damage their health by removing their protective covering. It is also potentially highly danger-ous for the diver in question, poetic justice perhaps!

Stingray City is one of two sites on Grand Cayman where it is possible to swim with the stingrays. The other, the Sandbar, is also located in the sheltered mouth of the North Sound, to the east rather than the west. It offers a similar experience to Stingray City, but is possibly slightly less crowded.

BLOODY BAY WALL

• 130 feet (40 m) • beginner to advanced

Situated on the northwest coast of Little Cayman, this site is widely regarded as the finest dive in the island group. The wall is split into a variety of smaller sites, although in broad terms the wall comes to within 20 feet (6 m) of the surface at some points, before drop-ping via a series of shelves to true abyssal depths. Thus it offers a range of possibilities for all levels of diver, although two absolute musts are the Chimney, a narrow passage through the coral down to 90 feet

(27 m), and the congregations of mantas on the reef shelf in the summer months. Other attractions of this tremendous wall are large numbers of turtles, gray reef and nurse sharks, sweepers, and barracuda. Visibility is consistently good here.

OTHER ACTIVITIES

Deep-sea fishing is the other great activity of the Cayman Islands; ask your private operator if you want to arrange a trip. Though no license is required, regulations require that you keep only what fish you can consume (some restaurants will cook your catch for you.) Tarpon and bonefish are fished for sport only, and must be released.

The islands offer outstanding birding, with nearly 200 native species. Cayman Brac has a parrot reserve and colonies of boobies and yellow-bellied sapsuckers. Little Cayman is home to the Booby Pond Nature Reserve, where red-footed boobies, herons, and egrets are common sights. Meagre Bay Pond, on the southern coast of Grand Cayman, features grebes, plovers, shovelers and snowy egrets.

The nightlife is concentrated in George Town. There are a few hotels and restaurants on Cayman Brac.

☎ **TELEPHONE NUMBERS**

Recompression chamber	+1-345-949-8600
Hospital	+1-345-949-8600
Department of Tourism	+1-345-949-0623

🖥 **WEBSITES & E-MAIL**

Department of Tourism	www.cayman.org
Travel site	www.caymanislands.ky

OTHER DIVE SITES

Ghost Mountain
Eagle Ray Pass
Coral Gardens
Smith's Cove
Jackson Pointe
M.V. Captain Keith Tibbetts

COZUMEL &
THE YUCATÁN

THE SPECTACULAR WALL DIVES OF COZUMEL ISLAND, THE WRECK DIVES AROUND CANCÚN, AND THE CAVE DIVES OF THE REGION'S INLAND CENOTES ARE AMONG THE ATTRACTIONS THAT DRAW DIVERS TO THE YUCATÁN PENINSULA, ONE OF THE MOST POPULAR DESTINATIONS IN THE CARIBBEAN.

 VISIBILITY

Cenotes: 180 ft (55 m) (may be affected by rainfall from June–Oct)

Cozumel: 100 ft (30 m) plus Oct–May, 60 ft (18 m) June–Sept

 MUST SEES

Cenotes

Palancar Reef

 DOWNSIDE

Busy

 GETTING THERE

International flights with a number of carriers from Miami through to Cancún.

 VISA

Visitors require a tourist card, available from Mexican consulates or embassies. The card is a single-entry document and is issued free of charge. A passport with a minimum of 6 months still to run is required, as well as a return or onward ticket and possibly proof of sufficient funds.

 MONEY

Currency is the Mexican peso. U.S. dollars are widely accepted, particularly in developed tourist areas. Major credit cards and traveler's checks are also accepted.

WATER TEMPERATURE

°C	°F	°C	°F
30	86	30	86
29°C			**26°C**
20 **84°F** 68	20 **78°F** 68
10	50	10	50
0	32	0	32
Summer		Winter	

▶ **TAJ MAHAL CENOTE**

The Yucatán Peninsula has more than 100 miles (160 km) of underground caves and sinkholes.

The prime dive sites of Mexico's Yucatán Peninsula are concentrated in the northeastern tip around Cancún and the island of Cozumel. Just a short distance inland from this small stretch of coastline, and less well-known, are the hidden treasures of the cenotes. These mysterious geological features are large sinkholes or caverns hewn out of the limestone bedrock of the peninsula as a result of erosion and sea-level change over millions of years. Deep pools at their bottom offer exciting cave dives in crystal-clear water.

GEOGRAPHY

The Yucatán Peninsula in southeastern Mexico separates the Gulf of Mexico, on the west, from the Caribbean Sea, on the east. Its northeastern tip also marks the northern end of a barrier reef that extends all the way along the coast of Central America as far south as Honduras. It is the longest such reef in the northern hemisphere.

The purpose-built resort of Cancún completely covers the shoreline of an 18-mile (29-km) sandbar just below the northeastern tip of the peninsula. It has become a popular diving center with a well-developed infrastructure catering for all needs.

A little way to the south of Cancún, arising out of the Caribbean Sea some 8 miles (13 km) offshore, is Cozumel Island. The island is 30 miles (48 km) long and 10 miles (16 km) wide at its broadest point. The most dramatic diving sites are located at the southwestern end of the island where the reefs plunge steeply toward the ocean depths.

A number of cenotes are located a little way inland to the south of Cancún. They are regarded by diving experts as being among the prime cave diving sites anywhere on Earth. Much of this underground system has yet to be fully explored and investigated.

MARINE LIFE

Although the reefs around Cancún are well dived, the marine life is still diverse and plentiful. Large schools of snapper and grunt swarm over healthy corals, and tremendous barrel sponges—some of them more than 100 years old and over 3 feet (1 m) high—are a particular characteristic of this area. Groups of eagle rays are commonly sighted at a number of popular sites, as well as large grouper.

The drop-offs and strong upwellings in the waters around Cozumel ensure that the marine life here is slightly wilder than off the mainland. Green, loggerhead, and hawksbill turtles nest on the island, and you may even get a sighting of the Caribbean manatee in the more sheltered bays and inlets. Cozumel is famous for its black corals, and it was declared a marine sanctuary in 1980. Its reefs and walls reflect this protected status in their abundance of marine life.

THE DIVES

The greatest downside to the diving at Cancún are the crowds. Nevertheless, the dives have much to offer with some fine wrecks (one sunk especially for divers) and bustling reefs. The Xcaret inlet provides a fine sheltered dive location, and as a general rule the reefs off Cancún are somewhat shallower than those further south, with more benign currents, so are particularly suitable for beginners and inexperienced divers.

Cozumel Island is the home of the dramatic wall and steep drop-off. Two of the most popular sites, Palancar and Colombia Reefs, are particularly impressive reef walls, plunging into abyssal depths. Much of the diving here consists of drift dives, and you must have appropriate experience and equipment to participate in them safely. However, the island offers a number of more sheltered areas such as Chancanab Lagoon, a fine site

Isla Mujeres

C 58 General Anaya

✚ ⟨⟩ Cancun

✈

Puerto Morelos

Tres Rios

MEXICO

San Miguel
deCozumel ⟨⟩

San Juan Reef

laya del Carmen

Xcaret

Cozumel

Paradise Reef

Tormentos

San Francisco Wall

Xpu-Há

Palancar Reef

Maracaibo Reef

Xel-Há

The Cenotes

Tulum

Boca Paila

7

0 — 14 km
0 — 10 mi

David Stephens

DIVE CENTERS

SCUBA DU S.A.
Hotel Presidente Intercontinental
Carr. A. Chankanaab KM 6.5,
Cozumel 77600, Mexico
Phone: +52-987-872-9505
E-mail: scubadu@usa.net
Web: www.scubadu.com

SCUBA COZUMEL
P.O.B. 11, Ave Rafael Melgar Prof. Sur 1251,
Cozumel 77600, Mexico
Phone: +52-987-872-0640
E-mail: scubacoz@scubacozumel.com
Web: www.scubacozumel .com

AQUAWORLD
Blvd Kukulcan 15100 al 15500, Interior
Marina Aquaworld, Cancún 77500, Mexico
Phone: +52-988-848-8327
E-mail: info@aquaworld.com.mx
Web: www.aquaworld.com.mx

SCUBACARIBE
Hotel Riu Cancún
Blvd Kukulcan, Lote 5A,
Cancún 77500, Mexico
Phone: +52-809-552-1435
E-mail: info@scubacaribe.com
Web: www.scubacaribe.com

DIVING ORGANIZATIONS

The Aquatic Sports Operators Association
(A.N.O.A.A.T.) in Cozumel has a list of
approved dive operators.
Phone: +52-987-872-0640
E-mail: anoaat@cozunet.finred.com.mx
Web: www.anoaat.com

RECOMPRESSION

Hiperbarica Cancún
Alcatraces L44, M10, SM 22
Cancún 77500, Mexico
Phone: +52-988-892-7680
E-mail: hiperbarica@prodigy.net.mx
Web: www.hiperbarica-cancun.com

Cozumel Hyperbaric Research Center
Clinica Guadelupe, Calle 2, Cozumel.
24hr emergency phone: +52-987-872-3070
E-mail: meditur@cozumel.czm.com.mx

HOSPITAL

Hospital Americano
Viento 15, SM 4, Cancún, Mexico
Phone: +52-988-884-6133

C.M.C. (Centro Medico de Cozumel)
50 Ave Sur, Cozumel, Mexico
Phone: +52-987-872-9400
This is Cozumel's newest hospital

CONSERVATION SOCIETY

One of the best sources for information on the
National Parks in Mexico is:
Mexico Affairs Office, 2455 Missouri Suite C,
Las Cruces, NM 88001, U.S.A.
Phone: +1-505-521-2689
Web: www.nmsu.edu/~nps/

▲ ANGELFISH
The reefs of Cozumel have an abundance of marine life.

for gentler, more meditative dives in the midst of a very healthy fish population.

Several of the cenotes that are readily accessible to the public can be dived without the need for specialist qualifications.

PALANCAR REEF

- **15 to 130 feet (5 to 40 m)**
- **beginner to intermediate depending on depth**

This is one of the most popular dives in Cozumel. The reef runs parallel to the southwest tip of the island for a length of 3 miles (4.8 km) and its sites range from shallow drifts to deep caverns and overhangs. White sand slopes leading to steep reef walls characterize the top of the reef. The reef is very convoluted, with a series of gullies, canyons, and caves providing hiding places for crayfish and morays. The most notable indentation in the reef, a craggy notch known as the Horseshoe, is home to several large French angelfish.

Divers have every chance of sighting stingrays, as

well as the odd passing turtle, on the sandy seafloor of a shallower section of the reef known as the Gardens. In the deeper sites, black coral is relatively common clinging to the steep walls of the reef and mixed in with large gorgonians and tube sponges. Snappers, Bermuda chub, and other species of angelfish appear to be ever-present.

WRECK OF THE C58 GENERAL ANAYA

- **75 feet (23 m)** • **beginner**

Located just off the coast of Cancún, this wreck was sunk deliberately in 2000 as an artificial reef. It is only 150 feet (46 m) long, which means that it can be comfortably explored in a single dive. The vessel sits upright on the seabed—indeed, her stern is actually proud of the seabed as she is perched on her rudders and stabilizers—and her superstructure is a mere 45 feet (14 m) below the surface. Perhaps the most impressive feature is the continuous presence of a school of eagle rays that glide around the wreck, as well as a large shoal of snapper occupying the bow. Numerous holes have been cut into the wreck to allow easy access and exit for divers,

Tony White   Tony White

making this shallow site an ideal site for a novice diver's first taste of safe wreck penetration.

THE CENOTES

• **Various depths** • **beginner to expert**

The journey from Cancún to the cenotes, though undeveloped tropical scenery, is almost as exciting as the dives themselves. To date, more than 100 miles (160 km) of these remarkable underground systems of caves and sinkholes have been explored and more than 50 cenotes charted, but there is still much to discover. The clear water and complexity of the larger cenotes make diving here a truly memorable experience. There are now several recognized sites where it is quite safe to explore large craggy caverns in crystal visibility surrounded by stalactites and exquisite rock formations.

OTHER ACTIVITIES

This part of the Mexican coastline is a very popular tourist destination. Cancún, in particular, has large modern hotels, bars, and nightclubs. You will find all the usual activities of a flourishing resort. At Xcaret Park

visitors can explore a beautiful lagoon complete with flamingos and encounter some of Mexico's more dramatic and colorful indigenous wildlife including scarlet macaws, tapirs, and jaguars.

For those interested in the region's cultural and historic heritage, the extensive Mayan ruins at Tulum, dating from about 1200 A.D., should not be missed. They are easily accessible from Cancún and make an impressive picture against the blue backdrop of the Caribbean. On Cozumel you can see jewelry and other items carved from the black corals of the island reefs.

☎ **TELEPHONE NUMBERS**

Recompression chamber	+52-988-892-7680
Hospital	+52-988-852-9884

💻 **WEBSITES & E-MAIL**

Mexico Tourism Board	www.visitmexico.com
Information on Travel in Mexico	www.mexonline.com
Online magazine on Mexico	www.mexconnect.com

▲ SPONGES

Large sponges, some over 3 feet (1 m) high, are a particular characteristic of the reefs around Cancún.

OTHER DIVE SITES

San Juan Reef
Paradise Reef
Tormentos
San Francisco Wall
Maracaibo Reef

DIVER'S TIP

Late August to early November is hurricane season, so book with caution during this period.

BELIZE

BELIZE BOASTS THE LONGEST BARRIER REEF IN THE NORTHERN HEMISPHERE AND THREE OUT OF THE CARIBBEAN'S FOUR ATOLLS. OFFERING A COMBINATION OF GENTLE INSHORE DIVING AND SOME WILDER OCEANIC SITES, BELIZE PROVIDES THE DIVER WITH A HEADY MIX OF REEF AND WALL, CAVERN AND CAY.

 VISIBILITY

100 to 150 feet (30 to 46 m) Feb–July
50 to 100 feet (15 to 30 m) Aug–Jan

✔ **MUST SEES**

Blue Hole
The Elbow

✖ **DOWNSIDE**

Reef lies offshore
Hurricane season mid-summer

 GETTING THERE

International flights to Belize City through Houston, Los Angeles, or Miami. Cheap flights to the cayes on Maya Airways, Tropic Air or Island Air depart from the main airport several times a day. They pass over some truly spectacular scenery and are worth the expense, but there is also a cheaper water taxi service to the cayes from North Front Street in Belize City.

VISA

U.S. and E.U. citizens do not require a visa. You may be asked to show you have sufficient funds for your stay, and the normal tourist limit is one month. There is a U.S.$10 departure tax.

$ MONEY

Currency is Belizean dollars, but they are very difficult to exchange outside the country. For tourists, U.S. dollars are the best currency.

There is a still a faintly buccaneering feel to Belize, a legacy of the piracy that flourished in these waters in bygone days when privateers attacked Spanish treasure ships from the Americas. Belize is pure Caribbean, not some sanitized tourist version, a mixture of cultures and sensations all the way from coastal mangrove swamp to inland mountain range. Such an eclectic mix of experiences is typified offshore in the Belize barrier reef, a glorious mixture of canyon and cavern, of strong currents, and secluded islands.

GEOGRAPHY

Tiny Belize lies on the Caribbean coast of Central America. It is only 8,866 sq miles (22,954 sq km) in extent. With a mere 200,000 inhabitants and more than 40 percent of the land area designated as a nature reserve of one kind or another, Belize is something of an ecological jewel.

▼ EAGLE RAY

Though the reefs of Belize may not have the diversity of marine life of other dive locations, they still have a lot to offer.

Linda Pitkin

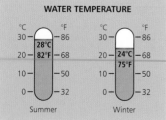

WATER TEMPERATURE

Summer: 28°C / 82°F
Winter: 24°C / 75°F

- Corozal
- Amergris Caye
- San Pedro
- Shark Ray Alley
- Caye Caulker
- Barrier Reef
- Caye Chapel
- St. George's Caye
- Belize City
- BELIZE
- BELMOPAN
- Turneffe Islands
- The Blue Hole
- Inner Channel
- Lighthouse Reef
- Long Caye
- The Elbow
- The Sayonara
- South Water Caye
- Dangriga
- Barrier Reef
- Glovers Reef
- Long Caye Wall
- Laughing Bird Caye
- Little Water Caye
- Sapodilla Caye

0 — 40 km
0 — 30 mi

▲ BLUE HOLE
The legendary Blue Hole is 410 feet (125 m) deep and has a resident population of bull sharks.

The land-based attractions of Belize are a compelling reason to visit the country, but just take a glance at the convoluted series of reefs and islands snaking up the coastline and you will quickly see why Belize is proving such a magnet for the global diving community. The Belize Barrier Reef is the longest in the northern hemisphere. It presents an array of diving possibilities to suit divers of all types and range of experience, from cautious beginners to hardened experts.

The reef itself is approximately 174 miles (280 km) in length, extending all the way along the coast from the Yucatán Peninsula in the north to Honduras in the south. Forming a band lying 9 to 19 miles (15 to 30 km) offshore, the reef creates a true barrier between the ocean and coast. Dotted along its length are coral islands, which are known in this part of the world as cays or cayes. Because the distance between the shore and reef is so great, most of the dive operations are based on these cayes, in particular Ambergris Caye and Caye Caulker.

Farther to the southeast, away from the main centers of diving, a large depression in the basin floor of the Caribbean Sea has created three atolls called Glovers, Turneffe, and Lighthouse. The Belizean atolls sit atop two parallel submarine ridges, unlike the atolls of the Pacific, which are built on volcanoes. The atolls rise close enough to the surface to allow the formation of massive coral and sponge growths. There are also fascinating reef complexes around the Pelican Cays, situated inside the barrier reef.

Such is the status of the Belizean reef, it has been declared a World Heritage Site. It has been the subject of intense conservation and research efforts supported by the activities of voluntary organizations such as the U.K.-based Coral Cay Conservation.

MARINE LIFE

Coral reefs in the Caribbean have a character all their own. They do not possess the extremely diverse systems of the Indo-Pacific reefs on the other side of the world, but they can lay claim to spectacular individual corals and sponges. The latter are some of the most dramatic to be found anywhere on Earth—some barrel

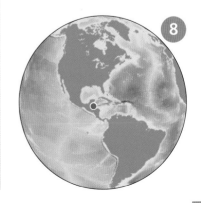

8

DIVE CENTERS

THE BELIZE ACADEMY OF DIVING
P.O. Box 69, San Pedro,
Ambergris Cay
Phone: +501-226-2873
E-mail: info@belize-academy-of-diving.com
Web: www.belize-academy-of-diving.com

GLOVERS ATOLL RESORT
P.O. Box 563, Belize City
Phone: +501-520-5016
E-mail: info@glovers.com.bz
Web: www.glovers.com.bz

DIVING ORGANIZATIONS

There are no official governing bodies for
diving in Belize.

RECOMPRESSION

Ambergris Cay. Located at the northern end of
the San Pedro Airstrip.
Always monitoring VHF 14.4600
Phone: +501-226-3195
Emergency phone: +501-226-2851

HOSPITAL

Belize City Hospital (Public)
Eve Street, Belize City
Phone: +501-227-7251

Belize Medical Association (Private)
St. Thomas Street, Belize City
Phone: +501-223-0302

CONSERVATION SOCIETY

Protected Areas Conservation Trust
2 Mango Street, Belmopan,
Cayo, Belize
Phone: +501-822-3637
E-mail: info@pactbelize.org

Coral Cay Conservation
The Tower, 13th Floor, 125 High Street,
London SW19 2JG, U.K.
Phone: +44-207-620-1411
E-mail: info@coralcay.org
Coral Cay Conservation no longer operates in
Belize, but it has a wealth of experience and
contacts for the conservation minded in the
country.

sponges are more than 100 years old and measure 6 feet (2 m) across. One of the undoubted attractions of diving in Belize is the contrast of marine habitats that the diver encounters at different points along the reef, ranging from bustling coral-reef communities on gentle sandy slopes to steep drop-offs patrolled by a number of large pelagic species.

The inshore reefs tend to be characterized by smaller coral communities supporting many of the 500 species of fish found in the region, including five separate species of butterfly fish. Large numbers of snappers, groupers, and barracuda patrol these reefs. Here, too, you may come across larger animals such as manatees. These are particularly abundant in the southern lagoon near Gales Point. Both on the barrier reef and on the atolls, divers can spot the larger residents of the reef. Among the animals providing chance encounters are jewfish up to 5 feet (1.5 m) long, wahoo, mantas, and a range of shark species including the whale shark.

THE DIVES

Dives in the vicinity of inshore sites such as Ambergris Cay tend to consist of gentle drifts along mildly sloping reefs and over patches of sugarwhite sand. The better diving is mostly concentrated at the southern end of the cay, also the site of the famous Shark Ray Alley, one of the more spectacular 10-foot (3-m) dives on Earth.

It is on the outer reaches of the reef that the drop-offs become more precipitous, and the reef assumes a classic spur and groove formation, resulting in over-hangs and caverns that can make for exciting dives. Some of these walls are truly spectacular, with one of the more well established—Half Moon Caye Wall—rising from an abyssal 3,281 feet (1,000 m) to a mere 32 feet (10 m) from the sea's surface.

One of the most compelling draws to Belize for the adventurous diver is the Blue Hole. This massive circular cavern in the reef is located roughly 50 miles (80 km) east

Naturalight Productions

◀ **YELLOW-TAIL SNAPPER**
Large numbers of snappers, groupers, and barracuda patrol the inshore reefs of Belize.

This is a moderately serious dive, and should not be undertaken lightly. The attractions of the Blue Hole lie deep underneath the overhangs amid the stalactites, and divers are required to hang over a blue water (or black water) drop of several hundred feet while at considerable depth. It is definitely not a dive for those susceptible to narcosis.

The dive begins on the gentle sandy slope that leads towards the stark lip of the hole itself. Most dive operators check their group at this point, at a depth of approximately 40 feet (12 m), to make sure that everyone is happy to proceed. From here the wall plunges sharply into the heart of the hole itself, and then begins to curve away at the start of a massive overhang. Following this overhang, you quickly discover stalactites, some as many as 10 feet (3 m) in length, twisted in the most beautiful formations. Looking down, you can clearly make out the lip of what appears to be the next stage of the hole where the shoulders of the bell begin their final plunge to the sea floor many hundreds of feet below.

Luckier divers may well find themselves being investigated by the hole's resident population of bull sharks during the course of the dive. Over recent years a trend has started of feeding these most charismatic of sharks. This practice is questionable, not only because many divers using the site are not directly under the supervision of the operators conducting the feed, but because of the extreme nature of the site itself.

As you return up the wall, you will find some interesting whip corals and tube sponges on the gentle slopes leading back to the surface. A gentle end to an exhilarating dive.

THE ELBOW

• **30 to 130 feet (9 to 40 m)** • **intermediate**

At the extreme southern end of Turneffe Atoll is the Elbow, which many experts regard as the finest individual dive in Belize. This wall dive with a 3,000-foot (900-m) drop below and an active drift along a beautiful coral slope is a particularly exciting way to explore the outer reef.

The coral in the area is liberally washed by nutrients and upwellings and is particularly abundant in animals. Patrolling close to the wall are thousands of dog snappers, horse eye jacks, and bermuda chubs. Drawn in by such bounty are several species of sharks, with the usual black tip and gray reef sharks mixed in with the occasional bull shark and school of great hammerheads. An added draw are the manatees sometimes to be seen grazing on the flats within the atoll itself.

of the Belizean coast at the heart of the Lighthouse Atoll. It has been an essential stop on the global diving circuit for more than 30 years, ever since French film maker and underwater explorer Jacques Cousteau brought it to international attention in 1972. Cousteau explored the seabed in a mini-sub, and the photograph of his vessel *Calypso* sitting in the very center of the hole is one of diving's iconic images. Stories abound of the subterfuge needed to get the vessel in the right position!

THE BLUE HOLE

• **130 feet (40 m)** • **advanced**

The Blue Hole is almost a perfect circle 900 feet (274 m) across and 410 feet (125 m) deep. The visible part of the hole is actually narrower than the main body, so that it is something like a vast bell sitting on the sea floor. Formed 15,000 years ago, the hole was plainly once above ground, as the shoulders of the bell are hung with beautiful stalactites.

OTHER DIVE SITES

Caye Chapel
Laughing Bird Caye
Sapodilla Caye
The Sayonara

DIVER'S TIP

Look out for huge aggregations of spawning snappers and feeding whale sharks at Gladden Spit after the full moon in April.

Monty Halls

▲ PERFECT VISIBILITY

The visibility in Belize is some of the very best in the world of diving.

LONG CAYE WALL, GLOVERS REEF

• **40 to 100 feet (12 to 30 m)** • **intermediate**

The reef that surrounds the five islands that make up Glovers Reef Atoll is designated as a Marine Nature Reserve. Located towards the southern end of the main barrier reef, it includes a number of high-quality dive sites dotted along the circular reef surrounding the islands. On the eastern edge of the atoll the reef drops off into 2,000 feet (610 m) of clear oceanic water, presenting opportunities for some tremendous wall dives, the most famous of which is Long Caye Wall. This dive allows divers to explore canyons and gullies leading into the drop-off itself, the sandy floors of which are home to massive fields of garden eels. Venturing into the blue water beyond the main reef face, there is the opportunity to see several shark species, king mackerel, tuna, dolphins, and mantas. Diving on the reef itself, you will be sure to come across large groupers, moray eels, and fine sponges, as well as a number of species of butterflyfish.

SHARK RAY ALLEY
• 10 feet (3 m) • snorkel

Located south east of Ambergris Caye, Shark Ray Alley is one of the more memorable large animal encounters to be found in Belize. For many years local fishermen cleaned their catch in this area, attracting large numbers of southern stingrays and nurse sharks to feed. As soon as the dive operators got wind of this activity, they moved in to develop the site. It is now a favorite with divers returning home at the end of a day's diving, or as a surface interval activity. The fishermen no longer clean their catch there, but doubtless they are doing so elsewhere, and helping to create another world-class site in the process.

The site is only 10 feet (3 m) deep, and is located above some beautiful seagrass beds. The minute the diving boat arrives, sharks and rays immediately crowd around it, eager for handouts. If these are not forthcoming the sharks move away very quickly, so it is best to enter the water swiftly to observe these beautiful animals at close range. They have completely lost their fear of humans, and the rays in particular will approach very close in search of tidbits.

OTHER ACTIVITIES

Away from the coast, Belize has a great deal to offer the ecologically minded visitor. Inland you will discover some of Central America's last remaining areas of pristine jungle, and a number of nature reserves have been established that cater for the tourist with a taste for adventure. One of the best contacts to access these reserves is the Belize Audubon Society, which was founded in 1981. The Society acts as a central management point for seven reserves covering 150,000 acres (60,705 hectares.)

The visitor to Belize should not overlook the opportunity to explore ruins from the Maya civilization dating back 1,500 years. The collapse and disappearance of this complex civilization within a relatively short period of time remain one of archaeology's enduring mysteries. There are some tremendous Maya ruins to be seen at Altun Ha and Lamanai, both of which are readily accessible through organized tours.

Belize also attracts vacationers in search of the simple pleasures of sea and sun. A number of well-established resorts on the mainland and the cayes cater for all budgets from backpacker to those craving five-star hos-

pitality. They offer a range of watersports and quality of service that stand comparison with any Caribbean resort.

☎ **TELEPHONE NUMBERS**

Recompression chamber	+501-026-2851
Hospital	+501-023-1542
Belize Tourist Board	+501-227-2420

💻 **WEBSITES & E-MAIL**

| Belize Audubon Society | www.belizeaudubon.org |
| Coral Cay Conservation | www.coralcay.org |

▼ **BRAIN CORAL**
A snorkeler hovers over one of the massive brain corals for which Belize is famed.

Naturalight Productions

DOMINICA

words by Arun Madisetti

👁 **VISIBILITY**

Summer 65 feet (20 m)

Winter 82 feet (25 m)

✔ **MUST SEES**

Frogfish

Crinoids and large sponges

Volcanic craters

✖ **DOWNSIDE**

Air transfers

✈ **GETTING THERE**

All U.S. arrivals fly via San Juan on American Eagle. International flights to Antigua, Barbados, St. Lucia then LIAT to Dominica (DOM). Air France to Martinique or Guadeloupe then LIAT or ferry to Dominica. New for 2008: St. Lucia to Dominica Canefield airport (DCF) on Caribbean Aviation.

🛂 **VISA**

American travelers are requested to hold a valid passport as no other document is acceptable. EU countries do not require a visa.

💲 **MONEY**

Currency is the Eastern Caribbean Dollar (XCD) and is fixed rate to the $US, which is widely accepted at all dive operations, hotels and for hikes and excursions. Credit cards are accepted in some locations.

▶ **A KALEIDOSCOPE OF COLOR**

Crinoids, sponges and clear water characteristic of Dominica

WATER TEMPERATURE

	Summer			Winter
°C	°F		°C	°F
30	86		30	86
29°C				
20	84°F — 68		20	26°C / 80°F — 68
10	50		10	50
0	32		0	32

EQUIDISTANT BETWEEN MARTINIQUE AND GUADELOUPE IN THE WEST INDIES SITS THE RELATIVELY UNDISCOVERED DESTINATION OF THE COMMONWEALTH OF DOMINICA. WITH GREAT DIVING, DOMINICA IS HOW THE CARIBBEAN USED TO BE DECADES AGO, BEFORE MASS TOURISM TOOK HOLD.

Images Dominica

Often confused with the Spanish-speaking island to the north, Dominica has for the most part been self-sufficient until recently, relying upon its abundant agricultural exports to support the economy. In the past two decades it has begun to open its doors to tourism and is garnering a list of eco-accolades to make the other islands blush. It was the world's first Green Globe 21 destination and is a benchmark for the region in ecotourism.

You will find no chain or high-rise hotels, no wild night life (unless during carnival or independence) and there is a scarcity of the sandy beaches that everyone equates with the Caribbean. What you will find here is great diving, friendly people, hiking and many other sporting and cultural activities.

GEOGRAPHY

It is said that Columbus scrunched up a piece of parchment and threw it on the table to describe Dominica to Queen Isabella. Deemed inaccessible, he never set foot there. It is the youngest island in the region at a mere 15,000 years old, and is mountainous. Dominica has an Eden-like quality, with an extensive range of terrestrial and marine biodiversity. Terrestrial flora is represented by 155 families, 672 genera and 1,226 species of vascular plants, a number of which are endemic to the island. There are seven distinct vegetation communities present from mountain rainforest to coastal scrub and dry woodland, in addition to fumarole vegetation associated with volcanic activity.

Dominica contains the most diverse stock of wildlife in the Eastern Caribbean. There are 175 species of birds, including the national bird, the endemic and extremely endangered Sisserou parrot (*Amazonia imperialis*). There are 18 species of wild mammals, 15 species of reptiles and amphibians, and various species of freshwater and estuarine fish and crustaceans and there are no poisonous animals at all. These facts have led to nicknames such as the "green gem of the region" and "nature island".

MARINE LIFE

Dominica has very little continental shelf along its (Caribbean) western diveable coast. The sand, being volcanic, is predominantly varying shades of tan to black, and this, where present, tends to absorb light and color. Because of the relative youth of the island the reefs are dominated by a profusion of sponges which, with crinoids, produce the kaleidoscopic arrays of color for which the island's diving is known. Coral growth is secondary and in very healthy condition due to the proximity of very deep water so close to shore.

Because of the lack of space for nocturnal creatures to hide, the island is known for the little and hard to find things, such as seahorses, frogfish, batfish and many species of shrimp. Rodale's polls have consistently rated Dominica in the top five destinations regionally every year since 1994. Diving Dominica is not about the big creatures; they do pass by but are not a reason to visit. The diving is slow and offers plenty of time to "stop and smell the crinoids." Dominica is host to three nesting species of turtles seen year round on the reefs.

THE DIVES

The island boasts three distinct types of diving. In the north there is reef slope and shelf around the Cabrits National Park. Diving in the central areas tend to follow a shelf to drop profile. In the south diving is situated around the rim of a submerged volcanic crater:

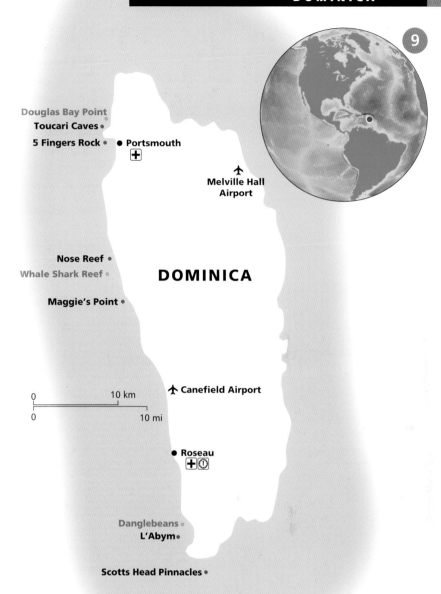

the Soufriere Scotts Head Marine Reserve. Also in the reserve is a unique site called Champagne where volcanic vents spew hot water and gases onto the reef, giving the effect that one is snorkeling or diving in a glass of champagne; it is a keynote site for the region. All dive sites along the coast have mooring balls. Unescorted diving is not permitted by law.

NORTH—CABRITS NATIONAL PARK
TOUCARI CAVES

• 20 to 80 feet (6 to 25 m) • beginner

The dive starts under the boat and heads off across what looks like a dump of old coconut husks (it is natural). This is a great spot for frogfish. Along rocky outcrops cloaked in sponges and soft corals then

DIVE CENTERS

All dive centers are covered under the Watersports Association: full information and packages may be found via the link below.

DIVING ORGANIZATIONS

Dominica Watersports Association is the governing body for watersports on the island.
Web: www.dominicawatersports.com

RECOMPRESSION

Princess Margaret hospital, Roseau.
Phone: +1-767-448-2231/ 5720
Almost every dive operator has a member of staff trained as a hyperbaric technician and there is a diving physician on the island.

HOSPITAL

Princess Margaret Hospital, Roseau.
Phone: +1-767-448-2231/ 5720

Portsmouth Hospital, Portsmouth
Phone: +1-767-448-5720

CONSERVATION SOCIETY

Cabrits National Park, Portsmouth
Soufriere Scotts Head Marine Reserve (SSMR)
Web: www.dominicamarinereserves.com

across a sandy bed, look out for shrimp and yellowhead jawfish. Eventually a lovely wall of exquisite color slopes out to sea; this is a good place for spotting mackerel and tuna passing by and is also home to a multitude of reef fish. In due course the shelf reappears and then it is on to the "caves". These are really swimthroughs of varying degrees of difficulty, cloaked in soft coral and filled with soldierfish and copper sweepers. The remainder of the dive is spent around the mooring area exploring the boulders and looking in among the crevices where you are likely to find seahorses.

5 FINGER ROCK

• **16 to 80 feet (5 to 25 m) • intermediate**

A beautiful but steep slope falls away from the headland and out to open sea, composed at depth of boulders from the peninsula all encrusted with life and cloaked in massive elephant ear, barrel, azure vase and branching sponges. There are many frogfish here, also scorpionfish and the occasional tuna, barracuda or mackerel swimming by. The site is named for the rock promontory resembling five knuckles near the surface. Sometimes there are currents, which accounts for the

prolific reef fish and size of the sponges. There is also amazing color and diversity here.

CENTRAL
NOSE REEF

• **33 to 100 feet (10 to 30 m) • intermediate**

Named for the two promontories sticking out from the reef into open water, this dive begins on the shelf then drops to a slope covered in deep water gorgonians heading southwest. Turtles and the occasional stingray are likely here. The "small nose" is apparent if you squint and use imagination, sitting in around 53 feet (16 m). The "big nose" is evident once you have gone past and are looking back. This is in around 100 feet (30 m) depth. Be careful: the area is deceptively deep and having meandered down to it, time is usually the defining factor. Expect to see huge schools of silversides, yellowtail snapper and creole wrasses out in the blue.

MAGGIE'S POINT

• **33 to 92 feet (10 to 28 m) • beginner**

Composed of the only spur and groove reef on the island, this is covered in predominantly finger coral.

Images Dominica

However this is the end point and under the boat. The reef extends out to sea then reaches a seamount rising from 80 feet (25 m) depth. This is where much of the interesting stuff lies: giant coral crabs; several species of eels; frogfish and beautiful bouquets of crinoids in varying colors on the sponges. The formation is also good for finding juvenile lobster; sleeping stingray are very often found lying on the sand. Back on the spur formation are schools of reef fish, azure sponges and sometimes several seahorses. This is also a good place to see both adult and juvenile spotted drum, goatfish, angels and schools of creole wrasse. Again this is a spot to watch depth and time; it is easy to get carried away fish watching.

SOUTH—SOUFRIERE SCOTTS HEAD MARINE RESERVE
SCOTTS HEAD PINNACLES

• 33 to 100 feet (10 to 30 m) • intermediate

Usually dived toward the end of a week-long trip, this site is a mixing zone for both Atlantic and Caribbean waters. The shelf lies in 33 feet (10 m) from which a series of rock lips rise, the largest accommodating a tunnel that takes you through the rim of the crater, diving from the Atlantic into the Caribbean. Inside the bay is essentially a bottomless pit of still unknown depth, a sloping lava chute not giving readings. The region of 16,000 feet (5,000 m) is usually quoted.

Being a mixing zone, currents can and do pick up, but the divemasters can read them very well. The nutrients being pumped from ocean to sea here create huge schools of smaller reef fish and larger ones to feed on them. The tunnel is cloaked in a variety of soft corals and the walls are packed with lobster as you swim through.

Once on the Caribbean side the rock face drops from as shallow as 6 feet (2 m) to around 150 feet (45 m) before sloping out to the black. Cloaked in an array of barrel sponges, gorgonians, sea rods, whip corals and black coral this wall is breathtaking, and on another day is sometimes ignored by divers as they drift by watching the show in the blue. Dives here are unforgettable for either the wall or the diversity of life in the blue.

LA BYM

• 16 to 100 feet (5 to 30 m) • beginner

La Bym, the French patois name means "the abyss", is the wall that is the eastern rim of the crater. It extends 1.5 miles (2.5 km) in length and forms a wonderful dive at whatever depth. In places it drops from the surface of the shelf to an extreme slope of below 1,310 feet (400 m), in others there is no shelf and the cliff reaches from the depths to over 2,000 feet (600 m) above sea level. Below is as sheer as glass with sponges and plate

Images Dominica

corals clinging to the sides. Numerous overhangs and gulleys provide opportunities for finding small creatures everywhere. Known for its schooling reef fish, seahorses, frogfish, shrimps, massive barrel sponges, black corals and resident turtles, dives here are an integral part of the Dominica experience.

OTHER ACTIVITIES

Dominica is known regionally as the place to go for hiking. Short hikes take the form of easy trails of about 45 minutes, and longer ones can take a whole day. Many trails pass a waterfall or other scenic spot. Alternatively, Dominica is the regional home of whale watching, with a resident population of sperm whales and 12 other marine mammals.

Other activities are bird watching, mountain biking, horseback riding, sport fishing, river tubing, wake boarding, water skiing, zip lining in the forest canopy, rappeling and canyoning, forest canopy Aerial tram, sea or lake kayaking, hanging out watching the sunset, lying by a river pool, meeting new people, or finding a secluded beach and being the only ones there for the day.

▲ SWIMTHROUGHS OF VARYING DIFFICULTY
A diver at Toucari Caves.

◄ A MIXING ZONE FOR ATLANTIC AND CARIBBEAN WATERS
Scotts Head Pinnacles.

☎ TELEPHONE NUMBERS

Recompression chamber	+1-767-448-2231/ 5720
Hospital (ROSEAU)	+1-7-448-2231/ 5720
Hospital (PORTSMOUTH)	+1-767-448-5720

🖥 WEBSITES & E-MAIL

Dominica Watersports Association	www.dominicawatersports.com
A Virtual Dominica	www.avirtualdominica.com
Discover Dominica	www.dicscoverdominica.com

OTHER DIVE SITES

Douglas Bay Point
Whale Shark Reef
Danglebens

GRENADA & THE BIANCA C

A MUST FOR DIVERS, THE MASSIVE HULK OF THE CRUISE LINER BIANCA C, KNOWN AS THE "TITANIC OF THE CARIBBEAN," LIES CLOSE TO THE HARBOR OF ST. GEORGE'S, GRENADA. BUT THERE IS MUCH MORE TO THIS SLEEPY CARIBBEAN ISLAND. OTHER WRECKS WITH A CHARACTER ALL OF THEIR OWN CAN BE FOUND BENEATH THE CRYSTAL WATERS.

On October 22, 1961, the Sunday morning calm of the colorful harbor town of St. George's, Grenada, was shattered by the repeated blasts of a ship's horn. The massive cruiser liner *Bianca C*, with 600 passengers and crew aboard, was ablaze as she lay at anchor. Minutes earlier a huge explosion had ripped through her port boiler, killing one crewman and mortally wounding two others. As the stricken liner's distress call echoed across the harbor, the people of St. George's hurried to her assistance. In a fleet of small boats they ferried the passengers to safety and towed the ship's lifeboats back to shore—the local customs officer won fame by jumping into the oil-covered water to secure a towline to a packed lifeboat. Once ashore, the people of St. George's took the shocked and traumatized

▼ BIANCA C
Even though the *Bianca C* has been on the seabed for over 40 years her size and grandeur can still be seen.

passengers and crew into their own homes. The cruiser's owners, the Costa Line, later showed their gratitude for what the Grenadians did that day by erecting a statue in the heart of the harbor.

As the paint boiled and crackled on her buckling hull, a British Royal Navy vessel, the *H.M.S. Londonderry*, attempted to tow the blazing ship to shallow water outside the harbor. The *Bianca C* was now in her death throes. About a mile off Grand Anse Beach her towlines parted, and she slipped beneath the surface, coming to rest on the seabed 150 feet (45 m) below. There she still sits, listing slightly, as though sailing through a sea of sediment.

GEOGRAPHY

Grenada is the most southerly of the Windward Islands of the Caribbean, lying roughly 100 miles (60 km) north of Venezuela on the South American mainland. The island, about 133 sq miles (344 sq km) in area, is 21 miles (34 km) long by 12 miles (19 km) wide, and has about 73 miles (117 km) of coastline. The western, leeward side of the island has more favorable weather conditions and deeper harbors for mooring. About 70 percent of the population of 90,000 lives on this side, with nearly 50 percent of them in the area between Grand Anse and the capital city of St. George's.

Grenada also has the distinction of being one of only a handful of islands that is surrounded by two major oceans. On the leeward side of the island is the Caribbean Sea, on the windward side the Atlantic Ocean. A few miles north of the island, an active underwater volcano called Kick'em Jenny is slowly making its way to the surface.

MARINE LIFE

The inshore marine life of Grenada is not overwhelmingly spectacular, as the reefs are subject to runoff from the mountainous main island. This is particularly true at the southwestern end of the island where the wrecks are concentrated. However, there are some good reefs with fine soft corals, sea fans and gorgonia on the Atlantic side. In terms of large animals, nurse sharks and eagle rays are particularly abundant at the inshore sites, and a number of wrecks and reefs have some very large Nassau groupers in residence. Generally, however, for really spectacular reef diving you will have to venture slightly farther afield to outlying sites such as the King Mitch and San Juan wrecks.

THE DIVES

Although the big draw is the *Bianca C*, it is sheer folly to ignore some of the other wrecks in Grenada. In particular, two spectacular recent discoveries, the *San Juan* and the *Shakem*, are rated as world-class sites.

Much of the diving is drift diving, with strong currents a real feature. The local operators are well set up to deal with this. You will find most demand that all divers have their own delayed S.M.B. and that the dive master has a large central buoy that is followed by the boat throughout. Diving is generally non-decompression. You may be frustrated by this on the *Bianca C* because of the wreck's depth and size.

THE BIANCA C

• 110 to 165 feet (33 to 50 m) • intermediate

The *Bianca C* has now been on the seabed for over 40 years and is beginning to show her age. But although her massive hull has started to collapse in places, it is still possible to get an impression of her size and grandeur, and there are a number of interesting sites to explore on the wreck.

Powerful currents sweep the wreck. This makes an ascent of the shot line desirable if you wish to surface next to a moored dive boat, but exhilarating if decompressing, as you flutter in the undersea gale while hanging on to the line. Use of a delayed S.M.B. is an option, but because much of the ascent may take place through blue water with no point of reference, this demands

OTHER DIVE SITES

Bucaneer
Windmill Shallow
Channel Reef
Runway
Grand Canyon
Shark Reef
Stingray Alley
Lighthouse Reef

Monty Halls

► THE SHAKEM
The bow of the *Shakem* still plows an imaginary course through the seabed.

►► SAN JUAN
The stern of the *San Juan* lies in 82 feet (25 m) of water and is home to a number of large animals such as nurse sharks and Nassau groupers.

 DIVE CENTERS

AQUANAUTS GRENADA
P.O. Box 1456, St. George's, Grenada
Phone: +1-473-444-1126
E-mail: aquanauts@spiceisle.com
Web: www.aquanautgrenada.com

CARRIACOU SILVER DIVING
Main Street, Hillsborough,
Carriacou, Grenada
Phone: +1-473-443-7882
E-mail: scubamax@spiceisle.com
Web: www.scubamax.com

DIVE GRENADA
P.O. Box 771, St. George's, Grenada
Phone: +1-473-444-1092
E-mail: info@divegrenada.com
Web: www.divegrenada.net

 DIVING ORGANIZATIONS

Grenada Scuba Diving Association.
A co-operative venture between various dive centers to ensure safety standards are maintained. Contact any of the above centers for details.

 RECOMPRESSION

None. However, there are recompression chambers in Barbados and Trinidad, both only 30-45 minutes away by low-flying aircraft (there is an air ambulance service on the island.)

HOSPITAL

There is a General Hospital in St. George's, a smaller hospital in Mirabeau on the east coast, and one on Carriacou. Clinics and doctors can be found throughout the islands. In addition, the islands have a number of district medical centers (small clinics.) Contact the Ministry of Health and Environment for more details.
Phone: +1-473-440-2649

 CONSERVATION SOCIETY

Ocean Spirits Inc
P.O. Box 1373, Grand Anse,
St. George's, Grenada
E-mail: info@oceanspirits.org
Web: www.oceanspirits.org
A voluntary organization running various programs in Grenadian waters.

that divers work in small groups and have good buoyancy skills. More pertinently, it can mean a struggle back along the wreck to the ascent line—something you should bear in mind when making your exploration of the site.

The stern of the *Bianca C* broke off when the vessel sank. It was this that collided with the seabed, and it is now a mass of twisted metal, so cataclysmic was the force of impact. The screwless underside of the overhanging stern is the deepest point of the dive.

Moving forward along the wreck, the swimming pool, lying at 130 feet (40 m), is the first vaguely recognizable feature you will see. One side of the pool has collapsed with the deterioration of the wreck, but you can still sit on the edge and dangle your feet over the side, imagining the time when this pool represented the height of luxury in sea cruises.

The main funnel has also collapsed. However, it is still possible to make out a huge embossed "C" on it, the mark of the Costa Line (whose ships, incidentally, still visit the port of St. George's). As you reach the bow, you cannot fail to be impressed by its unusual flared whaler design. Drop slightly deeper to observe the bow curving overhead—almost a wall dive in itself, and a really tremendous sight.

THE SHAKEM

• 100 feet (30 m) • intermediate

For the wreck enthusiast, the *Shakem* is a marvelous new addition to the dive scene in Grenada. She sank as

recently as May 30, 2001, within sight of the harbor, after her load of cement shifted. Unusually, given the manner of her sinking, she sits bolt upright on the seabed, and is in pristine condition. Curtains still billow from cabin portholes, and the ship's superstructure and machinery look as good as new. The *Shakem* is not a large vessel, and can comfortably be explored in a single dive. More adventurous divers may decide to explore the engine room, but this is a full penetration dive and should be treated with appropriate respect. A multitude of stinging hydroids now coat much of the superstructure, so take particular care when draping yourself over railings in quest of good photo opportunities (the voice of experience!).

THE SAN JUAN

• 80 feet (25 m) • intermediate

The *San Juan* is the wreck of a small inter-island fishing vessel that lies, listing slightly to starboard, 2 miles (3 km) offshore on an exposed shallow plateau, and is subject to the vagaries of the Atlantic weather. However, she is a diver's "must see" if conditions allow. The vessel itself merits a brief exploration, but it is the marine life, particularly the larger animals that have adopted the *San Juan* as their home, that make this wreck site truly exceptional. Scores of very large nurse sharks nestle around her hull, and two large Nassau groupers enthusiastically greet divers, following them around the wreck until they depart. If this is your first experience of a wreck dive, it is guaranteed to turn you into an instant wreck fanatic.

OTHER ACTIVITIES

Grenada, with the neighboring island of Carriacou, was directly administered as a British colony until 1958, and achieved full independence in 1974. The British heritage remains evident in these enchantingly beautiful Caribbean islands. Their mountainous interiors contain a number of exquisite nature reserves, ranging from the Grand Etang Forest Reserve to the tranquil intimacy of La Sagesse estuary, and you can explore cascading rivers, waterfalls, lush rainforest, and mountain lakes. The sandy beaches, especially Grande Anse Beach, are world-famous. You will find a wide range of accommodation options, as befits a popular Caribbean tourist destination, particularly around St. George's.

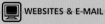 **TELEPHONE NUMBERS**

| Ministry of Health and Environment | +1-473-440-2649 |
| Grenada Board of Tourism | +1-473-440-2279 |

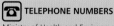 **WEBSITES & E-MAIL**

| Grenada Board of Tourism | www.grenada.org |
| Grenada Board of Tourism e-mail | gbt@caribsurf.com |

BONAIRE

words by Gillian McDonald

THE HOME OF DIVING FREEDOM, BONAIRE, WITH ITS PRISTINE REEFS, THE MOST DIVERSE FISH POPULATION IN THE CARIBBEAN AND CLEAR WARM WATERS IS A DIVING PARADISE.

Tucked away at the very southwestern tip of the Caribbean island sweep, this quiet, arid, rather austere little island could easily be overlooked in favor of its lusher and brasher neighbors. However, Bonaire has a great deal to offer both above and below the waves.

Bonaire has a turbulent history, having passed through Venezuelan Indian, Spanish, Dutch and, briefly, British hands—ceding to the Dutch again in 1816. The area was a center for the West Indies slave trade and the island was a notorious penal colony for over 300 years.

The word "salary" hails from the days of the Roman Empire, when soldiers were paid in salt (Latin name: *salarium*) such was its value as a commodity. Large scale salt production has existed on Bonaire for hundreds of years and although tourism has taken over as the primary source of revenue, the salt industry is still active today.

GEOGRAPHY

The second largest of the so-called ABC islands—Aruba, Bonaire and Curacao—Bonaire is crescent

 VISIBILITY

100–150 feet (30–55 m) year round

 MUST SEES

Seahorses
Tarpon
Diving freedom

 DOWNSIDE

Backlash of distant hurricanes can damage reefs

 GETTING THERE

Flamingo International Airport is served by several mainland U.S. airlines. KLM flies direct from Amsterdam. Sometimes connections are required from Aruba or Curacao which are 10–20 minute hops either on the serving airline or with Dutch Antilles Airlines.

VISA

Citizens of most countries do not need a visa for Bonaire. Outside of North America and Europe you may need one for a stay of more than 90 days. Check the website www.infobonaire.com

$ MONEY

Official currency is the Antillean Guilder, but U.S. dollars are widely accepted, as are credit cards.

▶ **CHRISTMAS TREE WORM**

These worms, which exibit in a dazzling array of color, live in tiny holes in hard coral.

WATER TEMPERATURE

°C	°F	°C	°F
30 — 86		30 — 86	
20 — **27°C 80°F** — 68		20 — **27°C 80°F** — 68	
10 — 50		10 — 50	
0 — 32		0 — 32	
Summer		Winter	

Gillian McDonald

shaped with its sheltered inner edge facing west and its windward eastern coast assailed by constant African trade winds. Most of the diving and other water sports take place on the protected, leeward side where there is little current or prevailing wind.

The island is just 27 miles (43 km) long and 5 miles (8 km) wide, lying 50 miles (80 km) north of Venezuela. The semidesert landscape of the hilly north is home to a 13,500 acre (5,500 hectares) nature reserve. The south is flat and exposed with sand dunes, mangroves and wildly colorful salt flats. Nestling in the curve of the main island is the tiny, uninhabited islet of Klein Bonaire and it is here the reefs are the most untouched and stunning.

While Bonaire is not directly on the hurricane belt it can occasionally feel the backlash of a passing storm and the coral can become damaged by wave action.

MARINE LIFE

The Bonaire Marine Park extends all the way around the island from the high water mark to 200 feet (60 m) depth and ensures the beautiful natural resources remain intact. Narrow, fringing reefs surround both Bonaire and Klein Bonaire and these are well preserved, incredibly diverse and support a spectacular array of reef fish. The shallow waters contain encrusting corals, growing low to avoid wave damage. These are very narrow in the north but can reach up to 220 yards (200 m) wide in the south. Sandy patches are scattered around where scorpionfish and lizardfish calmly pose for photographs. Peacock flounders glide below geometrically patterned flamingo tongue and fingerprint snails feeding on soft corals and numerous gorgonian fans. Here are stands of elkhorn and staghorn coral, sprinkled with fire coral, wafting clumps of soft coral and numerous patch reefs, all supporting a healthy community of colorful reef fish. Trumpetfish hang vertically among the flora, camouflaged among the coral branches.

Among the reefs slide moray and sharptail eels. You will also see many damselfish, tangs, parrotfish, butterfly, squirrel and angelfish and rag-tag goatfish stirring up the sand in their search for tasty tidbits. Anemones housing iridescent cleaner shrimps nestle in crevices.

Further down the drop-off are hard corals including large brain and mountainous star corals, home to tiny secretary blennies and multicolored Christmas tree worms. Here you will begin to see large parrotfish, snappers and schools of jacks cruising by.

A particular treat in this region are seahorses but you need to look carefully as they cleverly adapt their color to suit the surroundings among the soft corals, turning bright yellow, orange, pink, brown or black. Up to 6 inches (15 cm) long they cling to the coral with their curled tails, wafting in the gentle current. At the other end of the scale are tarpon. Shiny, silvery and prehistoric-looking they can surprise you in shallow waters by appearing over your shoulder. Fully grown at around 5–8 feet (1.5–2 m) and completely harmless, they can be seen both day and night. You will also observe turtles; there is an active organization, the Sea Turtle Conservation Bonaire, a nonprofit group dedicated to the protection and recovery of sea turtle populations.

THE DIVES

Once you have done a checkout dive, attended the marine park orientation talk and paid a nominal marine park fee you can dive wherever you want, whenever you want. Bonaire truly is the "home of diving freedom." You don't need to dive with a guide, you can set out alone or accompanied to any of the 60 or so shore dives at any time of the day or night. Car rentals are easy and there are also buses.

All dive sites are numbered and marked by the roadside with clearly visible yellow rocks, corresponding to a map received when you pay your fee. Most resorts provide a house reef with filled tanks available 24/7. There are also regular daily boat trips to all sites around the island, a few of which are only reachable by boat, and this is the only way to dive the lovely reefs on Klein Bonaire.

Boca Bartol

Boca Slagbaai

Nukove

Rincon

Karpata
La Daia's Leap
1000 Steps

BONAIRE

Captain Don's Habitat
Leonora's Reef
Yellowman
Klein Bonaire

Kralendijk

Rockpile

Town Pier

Hilma Hooker Wreck

Cai

Salt Pier
Pink Beach

Red Slave

Willemsoren Lighthouse

OTHER DIVE SITES

Something Special
Salt Pier
Joanne's Sunchi ("kiss")

Gillian McDonald

▲ AMAZING ADAPTION

Tarpon can breathe in air from the surface if the water is oxygen-poor.

DIVE CENTERS

CAPTAIN DON'S HABITAT

P.O. Box 88 Bonaire, N.A.

Phone: +599-717-8290

E-mail: bonaire@habitatdiveresorts.com

Web: www.habitatdiveresorts.com

BUDDY DIVE

Buddy Beach & Dive Resort

Kaya Gobernador Debrot

Kralendijk, Bonaire, N.A.

Phone: +599-717-5080

E-mail: info@buddydive.com

Web: www.buddydive.com

DIVING ORGANIZATIONS

The Bonaire Marine Park is managed by STINAPA, a non-governmental, not for profit organization run by a board of dedicated local professionals who donate their time to protect and conserve the island's natural flora and fauna.

RECOMPRESSION

Hospitaal San Francisco

Kaya Soeur Bartola #2, Kralendijk

Phone: +599-717-8187

HOSPITAL

Hospitaal San Francisco

Kaya Soeur Bartola #2, Kralendijk

Phone: +599-717-8900

E-mail: hospitaal@bonairelive.net

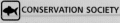CONSERVATION SOCIETY

Sea Turtle Conservation Bonaire

Web: www.bonaireturtles.org

Typically the reefs start right at the water's edge and gently shelve down to about 33 feet (10 m). The drop-off zone is 33–40 feet (10–12 m), and below this, the bottom descends sharply down the reef slope to the seabed at around 100–200 feet (30–60 m).

With its easy access, clear water and prolific life Bonaire is a mecca for underwater photography. Macro subjects abound and there are also wide-angle opportunities. Bonaire is not known for its wreck diving, however, there are a couple of attractions to keep wreck hunters busy.

PINK BEACH

• 0 to 90 feet (27m) • beginner to intermediate

A short stroll through coral rocks brings you to the white sands of the longest beach on the island. The reef crest is about 295 feet (90 m) from shore and it's a

Lesley Maw

pleasant swim over a sandy flat dotted with soft and staghorn corals with juvenile reef fish and goatfish all around. The drop-off is covered with lovely gorgonians and teeming with life. Seahorses live here alongside anemones and arrow crabs. Brightly colored vase sponges cover the wall and you will see stingrays, french grunts and occasionally turtles. Deeper around 90 feet (27 m), there may be schools of jacks and everywhere are scorpionfish, blue tang and pretty pufferfish.

LA DANIA'S LEAP

• 65 to 150 feet (20 to 45 m) • intermediate

So named for the 4-foot (1.2 m) leap from the volcanic rock if you approach from the shore, it's a whole lot easier by boat! This is a gentle drift dive north to the next dive site, Karpata, which is the only exit point if you are shore diving and takes about 30 to 40 minutes to reach. Here you can experience one of Bonaire's few vertical walls with numerous canyons and sand grooves. The shallow area teems with life with a pristine wall at 65 feet (20 m). If you head much deeper to 150 feet (45 m) straight after entry you will find caves with grouper, tarpon and occasional nurse sharks. A very large anchor at about 35 feet (10.5 m) signals your arrival at Karpata.

HILMA HOOKER WRECK

• 50 to 120 feet (15 to 36 m) • intermediate to advanced

When this steel-hulled freighter docked at the Town Pier for emergency repairs customs officers were suspicious. A search revealed a cargo of marijuana that was immediately burned. Rumors abound as to how the

Gillian McDonald

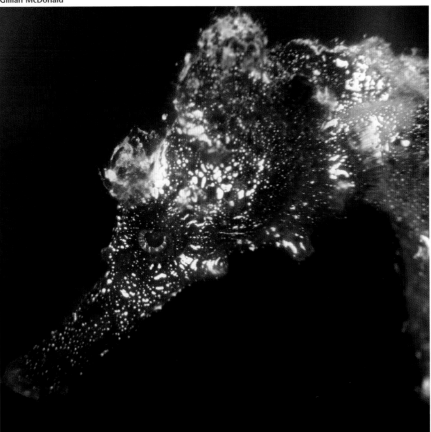

▲ HIDDEN BEAUTY
Seahorses adapt their color as camouflage as they hide among the flora along the reef.

freighter took on water, but ultimately it was towed to its present location just south of the main town of Kralendijk in 1984 and promptly sank to become an artifical reef. Lying on its starboard side on a double reef about 300–400 yards (275–365 m) offshore, the ship is intact with most of its running gear still in place. The bow lies in around 120 feet (36 m) with the stern around 50 feet (15 m) at its shallowest. There are still dangerous areas for advanced wreck divers only, but the outside can be easily enjoyed by most divers. Numerous moorings have been placed for dive boats. Photographic opportunities are endless including the large bronze propeller, passageways and engine room funnel. Many colorful fish have made this wreck their home.

TOWN PIER

- 30 feet (9 m) • all levels

For underwater photography, both day and night, Town Pier is unmissable. There are no beautiful reefs here—discarded tires lie alongside decaying car batteries. However, the coral encrustation and huge variety of life around the debris and on the pier legs provide a macro-photography heaven. Juvenile drumfish waft around arrow crabs and purple shrimps. Schools of French grunts glide around the pier legs, and at night there are beautiful, vivid bouquets of orange tubastrea and tiny red crabs on yellow sponges. Seahorses and octopus can be found in unexpected corners and eels are abundant, including the inquisitive sharptail eel, which sinews around the area and can surpise you by casually drifting over your shoulder. A special permit is required for the pier, which is obtainable from all dive shops, and it can only be dived when large vessels are not moored as it is still a working pier.

KLEIN BONAIRE—LEONORA'S REEF

- 20 to 80 feet (6 to 25 m) • beginner

About half a mile offshore this tiny islet has 24 dive sites at depths ranging from 20–130 feet (6–40 m). Leonora's Reef on the north side is typical of the area. An ideal site for novice divers, the currents are always light to moderate. There is a small tunnel that makes an ideal frame for a picture. Large groupers are generally seen in the deeper water, while parrotfish, yellowtail snappers, lizardfish, school masters and four-eye butterflyfish prevail in the shallows.

OTHER ACTIVITIES

The unusually steady trade winds provide world-class windsurfing and kitesurfing. Other sports include cycling, sea-kayaking, sailing, horseback riding and, of course, snorkeling.

The Washington Slagbaai Park in the hilly north is a 13,500-acre (5,500 hectares) nature haven covering almost one-fifth of the island. Here there are saline lakes, beaches, large areas of cacti and trees filled with exotic birds. Animals include iguanas, goats and wild donkeys. There is also excellent snorkeling. Ancient Indian rock and cave paintings are dotted around the northeast, and in the south, haunting and desolate slave huts flank the extraordinary landscape of the colorful salt flats and blinding white mounds of salt.

Pink flamingo colonies breed in only four places in the world and Bonaire is one of them. Pekelmeer, next to the salt pans in the south, is one of the largest flamingo sanctuaries in the western hemisphere, and here you can view spectacular flocks of lurid pink flamingos feasting on the brine shrimp and algae that are responsible for their vivid pink plumage. Pekelmeer is also populated by many other birds including osprey, heron, frigate birds and cormorants making it an excellent spot for birdwatching.

☎ TELEPHONE NUMBERS

| Recompression chamber | +599-717-8187 |
| Hospital | +599-717-8900 |

🖥 WEBSITES & E-MAIL

| Bonaire information site | www.infobonaire.com |
| Bonaire geographica | www.geographica.com/bonaire |

◄ FRAMED
Salt Pier provides fantastic wide-angle photographic opportunities.

ATLANTIC OCEAN

Covering 31.7 million sq miles (82 million sq km), and with an average depth of 2.5 miles (4 km), the Atlantic Ocean is the second largest ocean on Earth. It has a profound effect on every ocean throughout the world due to the influence of the Antarctic Circumpolar Current moving its oxygen and nutrient rich deeper water to other global regions.

In the North Atlantic the clockwise gyre, or circulation of surface waters, creates the Gulf Stream, an extremely significant current in terms both of marine life and environmental conditions. Flowing out of the Gulf of Mexico at a rate of up to 74 miles (120 km) a day, it travels northeast along the eastern seaboard of the United States before turning eastward and continuing toward the European coast as the North Atlantic Current. This great current moves up to 100 times more water than all the world's rivers combined. Due to its speed, the waters remain warm, a factor that profoundly affects the climate in certain areas of northwest Europe.

One of the largest mountain ranges on Earth, the Mid-Atlantic Ridge, formed by tectonic action and volcanic activity, runs north to south the length of the Atlantic Ocean. Molten rock rises up through the Earth's crust along the ridge, and as it cools and solidifies it lays down new ocean floor that spreads slowly east and west, pushing North America and Europe further apart, but only by about one inch (2.5 cm) each year. The abyssal plains thus created make up some 30 percent of the Atlantic seabed. Its deepest point is the Milwaukee Deep in the Puerto Rica Trench at 28,380 feet (8,650 m.)

Although some of the richest fishing grounds on Earth are found in the Atlantic, sustained and unregulated fishing has had severe impact on once abundant fisheries, such as the Grand Banks off Newfoundland, where cod have been fished to virtual extinction. Bordered on the east and west by industrialized landmasses, the Atlantic is heavily influenced by river run-off and exploitation by man.

Upwellings of cold waters rich in nutrients create bounteous areas for marine life in regions such as southwest Africa. The Atlantic also has gentler faces such as the warm waters at the eastern edge of the Caribbean and along the coast of southwest Europe, the latter influenced by the warm tongue of water seeping over the western sill of the Mediterranean Sea.

JP Trenque

◄ **BASKING SHARKS**
The cold waters of the northern Atlantic provide a rich bounty for giant filter-feeders such as the basking shark.

SCAPA FLOW

 VISIBILITY

40 to 60 feet (12 to 20 m) on blockship

10 to 60 feet (3 to 20 m) on German Fleet

 MUST SEES

World War I German wrecks

Blockships

 DOWNSIDE

Cold

Rough weather in winter

✈ **GETTING THERE**

Daily car ferry service from Scrabster on Scottish mainland. Regular flights to Kirkwall airport from Edinburgh, Glasgow, and Aberdeen. All of the latter are served by Gatwick and Heathrow airports.

VISA

E.U. citizens have free entry to the U.K. Citizens of the U.S., Canada, Australia, New Zealand, South Africa, Japan, and some other countries do not require visas if entering as visitors for a limited stay.

$ **MONEY**

Currency is pound sterling. A.T.M.s in Kirkwall and Stromness. Traveler's checks can be cashed at banks in all major towns. Most credit cards are accepted.

WATER TEMPERATURE

	°C	°F		°C	°F
	30	86		30	86
	20	68		20	68
18°C					
10	64°F	50		10	50
				8°C	
0		32		0	46°F	32
	Summer			Winter	

▶ **BIG GUNS**

Despite decades of salvage work, much of the armament remains on the vessels in Scapa Flow.

AN ANCIENT ANCHORAGE CONTAINING COUNTLESS WRECKS, SCAPA FLOW IN THE ORKNEY ISLANDS OFFERS EXCEPTIONAL DIVING. CONTRARY TO POPULAR MYTH, THE WRECKS ARE NOT ALL DEEP AND DARK, AND THE RANGE AND QUALITY OF THE DIVES MAKES SCAPA FLOW ONE OF THE PREMIER WRECK SITES IN EUROPE.

An indication as to the ancient importance of Scapa Flow comes from the name itself. A derivation of the Old Norse *Skalpeidfloi*, meaning "Bay of the Long Isthmus," the name dates back to Viking times when Norse seafarers beached their ships here on their long Atlantic voyages between Scandinavia, Iceland, and Ireland. Stromness was already a whaling and fishing center when, in 1670, it became a base for the Hudson's Bay Company trading between Britain and Canada. In 1813 the first substantial military bases were established here by the British to protect their commercial shipping in the North Atlantic during the wars with France. Today Scapa Flow houses a major oil terminal at Flotta.

The wrecks on the seabed of Scapa Flow span every period of European maritime history. But it is the ships from two world wars that give the Flow a special interest for divers. In 1919 the surrendered German Fleet consisting of some 79 ships was held in Scapa Flow by the Allies. On June 21, the German commander Rear Admiral von Reuter, wrongly believing that hostilities had been resumed, issued an order to scuttle the fleet rather

Dan Burton

than let it fall into enemy hands. Although the Royal Navy towed 22 of the ships to shallow water, and others were salvaged through the efforts of Messrs Cox and Danks (in itself an epic story), a large number of these magnificent wrecks still litter the seabed. During World War II Scapa Flow was once more an important British naval base. In 1939 a German submarine penetrated its defences and torpedoed *H.M.S. Royal Oak* while she was at anchor in the Flow. She lies there still, an official war grave, and is not accessible to divers.

GEOGRAPHY

Scapa Flow lies amidst the islands of Orkney, 16 miles (26 km) off the north coast of mainland Scotland. It measures approximately 15 miles (24 km) from east to west, and 10 miles (16 km) from north to south, and covers an area of 73 sq miles (189 sq km). In effect a huge flat-bottomed basin with a depth of between 60 and 150 feet (18 and 46 m), Scapa Flow is one of the largest natural harbors in the world. The islands that neatly encircle Scapa Flow are craggy, wild, and very beautiful. The capital of Orkney is Kirkwall on the northern side of the main island, a short overland drive away from the Flow. The main port on Scapa Flow itself is Stromness.

MARINE LIFE

The Flow is a classic coldwater European ecosystem. Cold tidal water, rich in oxygen and nutrients, washes over the shallower wrecks, while the deeper wrecks provide a less energetic environment for the larger inhabitants of the Flow. A staggering array of encrusting organisms covers the shallower wrecks; plumose anemones, jewel anemones, starfish, and urchins fight for space under swaying fields of kelp; the ballen wrasses are huge, in excellent condition, and extremely tame. Cuckoo wrasses, rare in British waters, are also abundant. Other creatures the sharp-eyed diver may see include beautiful nudibranchs, very large lobsters, octopuses, and conger eels. The Flow has one of the largest concentrations of gray seals found in northern Europe.

THE DIVES

Approximately 15 dive boats cater for the 20,000 divers who visit Scapa Flow each year—diving here is a thriving source of income for the local people.

The deep wrecks include 3 battleships, 4 light cruisers, 5 torpedo boats, a World War II destroyer, 2 submarines, and 16 charted British wrecks—riches indeed for the diver. In addition, the British Admiralty sank 22 vessels, 50,000 tons of shipping, in 1914 as blockships to close the four minor entrances to the North Sea to enemy shipping. These shallow wrecks are thumping good dives, swept by strong tidal currents and richly festooned with marine life.

It is often suggested that all diving in Scapa Flow is deep, dark, dangerous, and cold. If that were true, why do so many divers flock here year after year? To dive on the shallow blockships is to experience some of the best

OTHER DIVE SITES

Bayern
Kronprinz Wilhelm
Karlsruhe
Köln
Markgraf
König
Dresden
S36
V83
Vanguard
Prudentia
F2
S54
Roedean

Dan Burton

► **WRASSE**
Corkwing wrasse are present on the blockships in some numbers.

DIVE CENTERS

SCAPA FLOW DIVING
Polrudden House, Peerie Sea Loan,
Kirkwall, Orkney, KW15 1UH, U.K.
Phone: +44-1856-874-761
E-mail: john@scapaflow.com
Web: www.scapaflow.com

THE DIVING CELLAR
4 Victoria Street, Stromness,
Orkney, KW16 3AA, U.K.
Phone: +44-1856-850-055
E-mail: leigh@divescapaflow.co.uk
Web: www.divescapaflow.co.uk

 DIVING ORGANIZATIONS

All diving in the U.K. is overseen by the Health
and Safety Executive (H.S.E.):
H.S.E. Infoline
Caerphilly Business Park, Caerphilly,
CF83 3GG, U.K.
Phone: +44-(0)845-345-0055
E-mail: hseinformationservices@natbrit.com
Web: www.hse.gov.uk

 RECOMPRESSION

54" Twinlock Chamber
Orkney Hyperbaric Unit
Heriot Watt University, Old Academy,
Back Road, Stromness, Orkney, U.K.
Phone: +44-1856-885-400
24 hour cover

 HOSPITAL

Balfour Hospital, Kirkwall, Orkney, U.K.
Phone: +44-1856-888-000

 CONSERVATION SOCIETY

The Marine Conservation Society co-ordinates
a number of conservation projects throughout
the U.K.:
M.C.S., 3 Wolf Business Park, Alton Road,
Ross-on-Wye, Herefordshire, HR9 5NB, U.K.
Phone: +44-1989-566-017
E-mail: info@mcsuk.org

diving in U.K. waters. Indeed, Scapa Flow has a great deal to offer all levels of diving experience. Some of the dives are admittedly more demanding than others—the deeper battleships in particular demand a cool head and appropriate training. But to dismiss Scapa Flow as a place only for masochistic wreck fanatics is to ignore some of the best diving in Europe. A number of wrecks such the *James Barrie*, a trawler lying in deep, very clear water, have nothing whatever to do with the troubled military history of the Flow.

THE BRUMMER

• **100 feet (30 m)** • **intermediate**

The *Brummer* was a German mine-laying cruiser that worked in harness with her sister ship, the *Bremse*. A highly effective vessel of war, on October 17, 1917 she

took part in the sinking of 9 neutral and Allied merchant ships as well as their two destroyer escorts. Scuttled in 1919, she now lies on her starboard side in 100 feet (30 m) of water. Although time and wreck salvagers have taken their toll, she is still regarded by many as the best dive in Scapa Flow.

The shot line takes the diver down to a break in the hull made by salvagers over the engine room. Beneath this line is one of the ship's 5.9-inch (15-cm) guns, pointing toward the stern of the ship. It is open at the rear, allowing you to take a good look at the mechanisms and controls. From here you can move forward along the ship to explore the bridge and the armored conning tower, as well as the gun mounted on the bow itself. This is a good point to enter the wreck, should you wish to do so, and work your way back to the line, as much of the hull has corroded and allows reasonable passage with natural light and occasional points of exit. Moving back toward the stern, it is possible to find lumps of coal on the seabed as well as piles of coal in a bunker. Exploration of the stern section is somewhat confusing, however, as large parts of it are broken up, but there is still a nice swim-through past the stern gun under a large fallen plate.

GOBERNADOR BORIES

• 60 feet (18 m) • beginner

The *Gobernador Bories* is remarkably intact for a ship that was built 118 years ago and has lain on the seabed for more than 80 years after being sunk as a blockship in 1914. At only 2,332 tonnes she is not a large vessel, and it is easy enough to explore the whole wreck in a single dive. It is, however, a slack-water dive, and as such it is quite possible to enter the water with the tide running one way, and leave at the end of the long dive with it running the other.

Penetrations are not only possible on this wreck— when the tide is running they are virtually essential. The hull and superstructure are largely broken up, so there is plenty of natural light and easy exits and entrances. Although there are some interesting sections of vessel to view, such as the huge block of the steam engine and the largely intact stern, divers visit this wreck for the marine life. The *Gobernador Bories* has some huge wrasse in residence, and they have grown used to being fed by divers. Expect therefore to be bullied for tidbits throughout your dive. The encrusting growth on this wreck is spectacular, and lobsters peer from numerous nooks and crannies.

This is an excellent second dive or even a stand-alone dive in its own right, particularly for photographers. To drift through the spars of the hold in clear, cold water with strands of kelp waving overhead and multi-colored wrasses escorting you is one of the great sensations of British diving.

JAMES BARRIE

• 140 feet (43 m) • advanced

The *James Barrie*, a humble trawler with absolutely nothing to do with the German Fleet, has nonetheless become something of a classic wreck dive in Scapa. She was sunk in 1969, and lies leaning to her starboard side in 140 feet (43 m) of water. Her port rail amidships, the point where the shot line is secured, lies at about 100 feet (30 m). She is in superb condition, and at 180 feet (55 m) long is small enough to explore on a single dive. She lies in Hoxa Sound where the visibility tends to be better than elsewhere in Scapa Flow, although the currents can be strong on occasion. You can penetrate the wreck, and the main hold is particularly atmospheric

and easy to enter as the hold covers have completely rotted away. However, it is actually more fun to swim around the wreck and peer into the intact bridge and cabins at the stern than go for full penetrations. All in all, this is a fine wreck that offers a rewarding dive and can be used as a build-up dive for some of the more demanding deeper and larger wrecks in the Flow.

OTHER ACTIVITIES

The Orkney Islands are a beautiful part of Scotland with a rich heritage all their own, owing much to the Vikings. The Scapa Flow Visitors Center at Lyness on Hoy is worth a visit. It houses models of the German Fleet at anchor and exhibits of Scapa Flow in the 1940s, as well as exploring the history and heritage of the area.

The Ring of Brodgar lies on a promontory between two lochs close to Stromness. It has been described as the most significant prehistoric site in Scotland, and consists of a huge ring of stones set in a ditch 10 feet (3 m) deep and 30 feet (9 m) across.

Stromness has accommodation and food to suit most budgets, although there is little in the way of luxury hotels. There is a lively nightlife centered on a number of pubs, as befits a small bustling harbor.

☎ TELEPHONE NUMBERS

Recompression chamber +44-1856-885-400
Hospital +44-1856-885-436
Emergency services 999
Tourist Board +44-8452-255-121

💻 WEBSITES & E-MAIL

Tourism Board www.visitscotland.com
Orkney Tourism www.orknet.co.uk
Accommodation www.orkneyislands.com

▼ BLOCKSHIP
A diver explores under the stern of one of Scapa's famous blockships.

Dan Burton

PORTHKERRIS
& THE MANACLES

 VISIBILITY

Up to 15 feet (5 m) after storms or in rough weather

Up to 80 feet (25 m) on the Manacles in summer

 MUST SEES

Basking sharks in summer

Cuttlefish at Porthkerris

 DOWNSIDE

Cold

Crowded at peak times

 GETTING THERE

Fly to London Heathrow or Gatwick airports, then by rail to Truro or a 5-hour drive from London. You can fly to Exeter, Devon, on some European airlines, and from here it is only a two-hour drive to Porthkerris.

 VISA

E.U. citizens have free entry to the U.K. Citizens of the U.S., Canada, Australia, New Zealand, South Africa, Japan, and some other countries do not require visas if entering as visitors for a limited stay.

$ MONEY

Currency is the pound sterling. A.T.M.s are found in all towns, and credit cards are accepted by dive operators.

WATER TEMPERATURE

°C	°F	°C	°F
30 —	— 86	30 —	— 86
20 —	— 68	20 —	— 68
21°C			
10 — **69°F**	— 50	10 —	— 50
		9°C	
0 —	— 32	0 — **48°F**	— 32
Summer		Winter	

THERE ARE FEW FINER DIVING SPOTS IN THE U.K. THAN PORTHKERRIS COVE AND THE MANACLES ON CORNWALL'S RUGGED GRANITE COAST. THE COMBINATION OF A SHELTERED BAY AND A DRAMATIC OFFSHORE REEF IS A POWERFUL ONE, AND THERE IS THE ADDED DRAW OF ANNUAL CONGREGATIONS OF MASSIVE BASKING SHARKS, THE SECOND LARGEST FISH ON EARTH.

Linda Pitkin

► **CUSHION STAR**

A red cushion star stands out starkly against a heavily colonized reef wall.

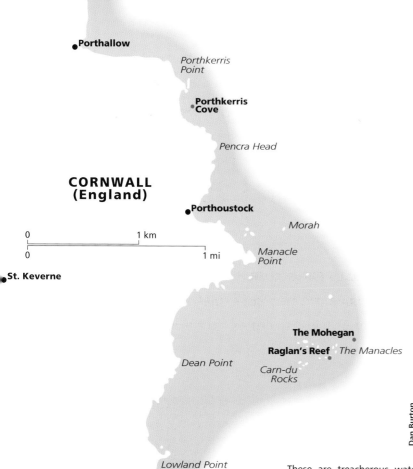

CORNWALL (England)

Porthallow

Porthkerris Point

Porthkerris Cove

Pencra Head

Porthoustock

Morah

Manacle Point

St. Keverne

The Mohegan

Raglan's Reef · The Manacles

Dean Point

Carn-du Rocks

Lowland Point

Dan Burton

These are treacherous waters, and many wrecks lie scattered along the shallow offshore reefs of this part of the coast. One of the most famous is the Manacles Reef, an outcrop of rock southeast of Porthkerris that rises precipitously from 195 feet (60 m) of water to within a few feet of the surface. Numerous ships have foundered on its craggy rocks, brought to grief while the captain hugged the lee of the Lizard in a violent storm or made a simple error of navigation on approaching the busy port of Falmouth.

MARINE LIFE

The combination of cold water and strong currents results in the Manacles being heavily colonized with kelp and temperate reef species. Sponges, tunicates, bryozoans, and sedentary mollusks all jostle for position on packed stone walls, while the crags and fissures of the reef are alive with crabs, conger, ling, and rockling. In the waters around the reef there are large pollack, several species of wrasse, including some impressive ballen wrasses, large schools of bass, and the occasional tope. In the sandy gaps between the rocky outcrops you sometimes encounter large anglerfish lying in ambush.

The area around the Lizard Peninsula has become one of the foremost sites in the U.K. for observing large congregations of basking sharks. They are attracted here by abundant plankton blooms, particularly in early summer, and reports have even been made of several hundred of these massive animals gathering together in the waters. In the height of the summer, dolphins are

▲ **SCORPIONFISH**
Close investigation of the reef at Porthkerris may well reveal a long spined scorpionfish lurking in ambush.

P rotected by tall cliffs, Porthkerris's shingle beach nestles in a cove cut into Cornwall's wild shoreline, and plunges into clear, calm water. It offers visiting divers easy access to the genteel charms of one of the best shore dives in the southwest of England, but it is also a launch point to a legendary reef only a few miles offshore. Each year the presence of large numbers of basking sharks in the area add to this mix of diving attractions. Porthkerris has something for everyone, be they a novice or expert diver.

GEOGRAPHY

The county of Cornwall, which occupies the extreme southwestern peninsula of England, has enjoyed a long association with the sea. Its rugged coast of cliffs, caves, and coves is studded with small fishing villages. On Cornwall's south coast lies the deep inlet of Falmouth Bay, with the large fishing harbor of Falmouth at its farthest end. Porthkerris Cove is at the seaward end of the bay, just east of the Lizard Peninsula, the southernmost point of the English mainland.

For centuries the Lizard has acted as a navigation marker for ships entering the Channel from the Atlantic.

13

DIVE CENTERS

PORTHKERRIS DIVERS
St. Keverne, Helston, Cornwall,
TR12 6OJ, United Kingdom
Phone: +44-1326-2860620
E-mail: info@porthkerris.com
Web: www.porthkerris.com

CORNISH DIVING
Bar Road, Falmouth, Cornwall,
TR11 4BN, United Kingdom
Phone: +44-1326-311-265
E-mail: info@cornishdiving.co.uk
Web: www.cornishdiving.co.uk

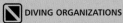
DIVING ORGANIZATIONS

All diving in the U.K. is overseen by the Health and Safety Executive (H.S.E.):
H.S.E. Infoline
Caerphilly Business Park, Caerphilly,
CF83 3GG, Wales, United Kingdom
Phone: +44-8701-545-500
E-mail: hseinformationservices@natbrit.com
Web: www.hse.gov.uk

RECOMPRESSION

Diving Diseases Research Centre
Research Way, Tamar Science Park, Derriford,
Plymouth, PL6 8BU, United Kingdom
Phone: +44-1752-209-999
Web: www.ddrc.org

Also call Falmouth Coastguard
Phone: +44-1326-317-575

HOSPITAL

Falmouth Hospital
Trevaylor Rd, Falmouth,
TR11 2LH, United Kingdom
Phone: +44-1326-434-700

Bideford Hospital
Abbotsham Road, Bideford, Devon,
EX39 3AG, United Kingdom
Phone: +44-1237-470-200

CONSERVATION SOCIETY

The Marine Conservation Society co-ordinates a number of conservation projects throughout the U.K.:
M.C.S., 3 Wolf Business Park, Alton Road,
Ross-on-Wye, Herefordshire, HR9 5NB, U.K.
Phone: +44-1989-566-017
E-mail: info@mcsuk.org

also regularly sighted by divers making their way by boat to the dive sites.

Porthkerris Cove offers more sedate pleasures, with gray mullet hunting in the shallows through beds of bootlace seaweed, and juvenile pollack stalking the colorful rocky walls and gravel seabed for fry and sand eels. Of particular note in early to mid summer is the presence of numerous common cuttlefish. They normally live in deep water, but come here to breed as the warm, sheltered waters of the bay provide perfect conditions, with plenty of rocky surfaces on which to secure their egg masses.

THE DIVES

There are excellent diving facilities to be found at both Porthkerris Cove and the Manacles. To dive at Porthkerris you have to do no more than walk a few yards from the car park by the beach and wade in from the shore. The Manacles Reef is only a short 15-minute boat-ride from Porthkerris, or you can find a place on one of the many dive boats organized by operators working out of Falmouth harbor.

Diving at Porthkerris Cove is simplicity itself. The protection afforded by the cliffs provides sheltered conditions from the prevailing southwesterly winds, and the gravel seabed ensures good visibility on most dives. All of the reefs in the cove are accessible from the shore, although the outer reefs are sometimes swept by strong tides and should be dived only at slack water. Depths do not exceed 70 feet (20 m).

The Manacles are a far more serious proposition. Be warned—several divers have lost their lives on this reef. The reason is the powerful tidal race, which produces currents of up to 5 knots and vicious swirling eddies at its height. Local knowledge is essential when diving these reefs, particularly as the top of some of the best sites lie several feet below the water's surface. They can only be located through the use of G.P.S., way points, and by studying the surface of the water for giveaway signs of disturbance.

THE MOHEGAN

• 50 to 95 feet (15 to 30 m) • intermediate

The *Mohegan* was a very large 428-foot (130-m) four-masted luxury liner that sank in 1898 under distinctly mysterious circumstances. After more than a hundred years on the sea bottom, she is now somewhat broken up. The remnants of the vessel start at 50 feet (15 m) and extend down to her large boilers at 80 feet (25 m). She has become a haven for marine life on the Manacles Reef.

The *Mohegan* has acquired something of a reputation among British divers, having claimed a number of lives over the years. But if the wreck is dived responsibly

Dan Burton

and in reasonable conditions, it is perfectly safe to do so.

PORTHKERRIS COVE

• 60 feet (18 m) • beginner

This is a busy small reef in sheltered water with easy access to the dive from the left-hand side of the beach close to the car park. The entry point slopes quickly down to 15 feet (4.5 m). Here, among bootlace seaweed and a gravel bottom, gray mullet and small pollack hunt. In the summer months cuttlefish also lurk here ready to ambush.

Move out on to the reef itself, about 300 feet (100 m) off the beach, and a series of small walls, gullies, and swim-throughs provides a great environment for several wrasse species, beautiful sponges, ascidians, and dense kelp. There are several options on this dive, which extends down to 60 feet (20 m) on the outer reef, and the site offers something for most levels of diver.

RAGLAN'S REEF

- 130 feet (40 m) • intermediate

The seaward-facing walls and pinnacles of an extensive reef system, Raglan's Reef is one of the most renowned sites in the Manacles group. It must be dived in the company of an experienced local skipper or divemaster. The reef proper does not break the surface and is subject to ripping tides that can sweep a diver off into open water. As a general rule, it should be dived at slack water. There are certain entry points that provide pockets of cover for divers when the tide is running, but only the local operators can be relied on to know them.

Kelp covers the shelving top of the reef down to about 20 feet (6 m), beyond which the walls are covered in plumose and jewel anemones. Colorful boring sponges also cloak the reef, mixed in with lightbulb seasquirts. In the deeper levels of the reef wall, large anglerfish lurk in sandy crevices and on the seafloor, while tope, bass, and pollack hunt for prey in the mid water. All in all, a wonderful example of British diving.

OTHER ATTRACTIONS

Porthkerris Cove is a family-run site, with a small restaurant and farm complementing the dive operation. Among the attractions are ostriches and pot-bellied pigs. North from Porthkerris, a short walk over the cliffs brings you to a small fishing village about 1 mile (2 km) away, with a pub that serves fantastic seafood.

☎ **TELEPHONE NUMBERS**

Recompression chamber	+44-1752-209-999
Hospital	+44-1326-434-700
Cornwall Tourist Board	+44-1872-322-900
Falmouth Tourist Information Center	+44-1326-312-300

🖥 **WEBSITES & E-MAIL**

Cornwall County Council	www.cornwall.gov.uk
Cornwall Tourist Board	www.visitcornwall.com

▲ **BASKING SHARK**
The waters around the Manacles are one of the top hotspots in the U.K. for encounters with majestic basking sharks.

LUNDY ISLAND

LUNDY ISLAND, A GRANITE OUTCROP OFF THE COAST OF NORTH DEVON WHERE THE ATLANTIC OCEAN MEETS THE BRISTOL CHANNEL, SITS AMIDST POWERFUL CURRENTS AND TIDES AND IS WASHED BY WATERS RICH IN NUTRIENTS AND OXYGEN. IT IS ENGLAND'S ONLY MARINE NATURE RESERVE AND HAS SOME OF BRITAIN'S BEST DIVING.

 VISIBILITY
30 feet (9 m) in summer
10 feet (3 m) in winter

 MUST SEES
Colorful and diverse reef life
Bird colonies
Rare species such as red-banded fish

 DOWNSIDE
Cold
Limited dive window

 GETTING THERE
International flights to Heathrow, Gatwick, or Birmingham airports. Three-hour drive to Covelly on the north Devon coast and from there by boat to Lundy.

 VISA
E.U. citizens have free entry to the U.K. Citizens of the U.S. and some other countries do not require visas if entering as visitors for a limited stay.

 MONEY
Currency is the pound sterling.

WATER TEMPERATURE

°C	°F	°C	°F
30	86	30	86
20	68	20	68
19°C			
10	**66°F** — 50	10	50
			8°C
0	32	0	**46°F** — 32
Summer		Winter	

▶ **BASKING SHARK**
Larger visitors to Lundy include the wonderfully impressive basking shark.

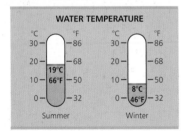

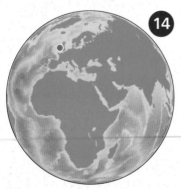 **14**

The name Lundy derives from the Norse word "lund-ey", meaning "puffin island", and Lundy Island is still celebrated for its wildlife today, particularly its breeding populations of seabirds and seals. There is also great biodiversity beneath the surface, thanks to the cold currents that strike the island from the Atlantic to the southwest and the contrasting warm tidal waters of the Bristol Channel, the inlet that separates the southwest peninsula of England from South Wales. As a result, Lundy offers some of the best diving in Northwest Europe.

GEOGRAPHY

Lundy Island is essentially a lump of granite that thrusts itself up out of the sea just 10 miles (16 km) north of Hartland Point on the north Devon coast. Some 3 miles (5 km) long by half a mile (0.8 km) wide, the island is oriented north to south, so that the wild coastline on the western side of Lundy is exposed to the prevailing Atlantic winds and is frequently battered by big swells; craggy cliffs, indented with bays and channels, rise to heights of 400 feet (120 m). The sheltered eastern coast is more benign, its southern end characterized by mud flats and sandy plains, whilst the northern end is more craggy and dramatic. The underwater topography includes crags, steps, kelp forests, sand-filled gullies, and steep walls. The northern and southern tips of the island are swept by powerful currents.

MARINE LIFE

The marine life on Lundy is truly exceptional for British waters, and diving here is invariably rewarding. The combination of dramatic underwater topography and powerful tides and currents has led to the creation of supremely rich cold-water reefs, and a number of

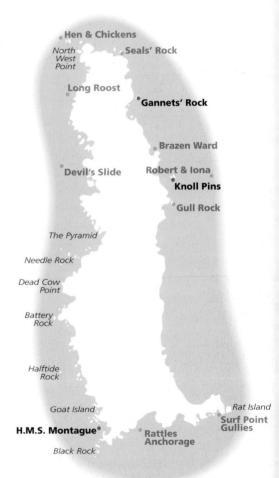

Hen & Chickens
Seals' Rock
North West Point
Long Roost
Gannets' Rock
Brazen Ward
Devil's Slide
Robert & Iona
Knoll Pins
Gull Rock
The Pyramid
Needle Rock
Dead Cow Point
Battery Rock
Halftide Rock
Goat Island
Rat Island
Surf Point Gullies
H.M.S. Montague
Rattles Anchorage
Black Rock

**LUNDY ISLAND
(England)**

0   1 km
0   1 mi

Malcolm Nobbs

▶ **COMMON LOBSTER**
The common lobster can live for over twenty years and can reach as much as 11 lb (5 kg) in weight.

 DIVE CENTERS

CLOVELLY CHARTERS
Clovelly, North Devon, United Kingdom
Phone: +44-1237-431-405
Phone: +44-7774-190-359 (daytime Apr-Oct)
E-mail: wrinkleberry@hotmail.com
Web: www.clovelly-charters.ukf.net

 DIVING ORGANIZATIONS

All diving in the U.K. is regulated by the Health and Safety Executive (H.S.E.):
H.S.E. Infoline
Caerphilly Business Park, Caerphilly, CF83 3GG, Wales, United Kingdom
Phone: +44-8701-545-500
E-mail: hseinformationservices@natbrit.com
Web: www.hse.gov.uk

 RECOMPRESSION

The Hyperbaric Medical Centre
Tamar Science Park, Derriford Road,
Plymouth, Devon, PL6 8BQ, United Kingdom
Phone:+44-1752-209-999
E-mail: enquiries@ddrc.org

✚ **HOSPITAL**

Ilfracombe Tyrrell Hospital
St. Brannocks Park Road, Ilfracombe, Devon,
EX34 8JF, United Kingdom
Phone: +44-1271-863-448

Bideford Hospital
Abbotsham Road, Bideford, Devon,
EX39 3AG, United Kingdom
Phone: +44-1237-472-200

 CONSERVATION SOCIETY

The Marine Conservation Society co-ordinates a number of conservation projects throughout the U.K.:
M.C.S., 3 Wolf Business Park, Alton Road,
Ross-on-Wye, Herefordshire, HR9 5NB, U.K.
Phone: +44-1989-566-017
E-mail: info@mcsuk.org

OTHER DIVE SITES

Hen & Chickens
Seals' Rock
Brazen Ward
Robert & Iona
Gull Rock
Surf Point Gullies
Rattles Anchorage
Devil's Slide
Long Roost

species found here are unique to the island, amongst them the red-banded fish, an eel-like fish about 3 feet (1m) long with a brick-red body and blue fins. All the five species of cup coral known to inhabit British waters are found here.

Jewel and, in shallow waters, snakelock anemones coat the rockfaces in sheltered areas on the east side of the island, together with huge numbers of beautiful sponges and rare sea fans. There are also quantities of urchins and starfish, as well as edible crabs, lobsters, cuttlefish, and common and lesser octopus, whilst cuckoo wrasses, goldsinny, and a number of very large ballen wrasses patrol the reefs and sand flats.

The deeper sites are home to conger eels and ling, as well as shoals of bib and pollack. Anglerfish are occasionally seen on the seafloor, while basking sharks and dolphins are frequent visitors to the island during the summer months.

The powerful currents at the northern and southern ends of the island keep the walls here almost entirely clean of encrusting colonies, and only particularly hardy species are able to survive.

THE DIVES

The diving around Lundy takes place from boats that sail out of Bideport and Ilfracombe on the Devon coast. It should be noted that suitable diving conditions exist only from May to September, so the window of opportunity is relatively brief. However, because of the way the island sits abeam powerful currents and tides, and

its widely contrasting underwater topography, the dives here are unusually varied, and Lundy has something for divers of all levels of qualification and experience.

H.M.S. MONTAGUE

• 15 to 45 feet (5 to 14 m) • intermediate

Lundy Island is situated in the midst of what was historically a very busy shipping channel, with ships returning to the prosperous port of Bristol from all parts of the globe. There are an estimated 137 wrecks around the island, the best known of which is the British battleship *H.M.S. Montague*.

This 14,000 tonne battleship, built in 1901, lies off the southwest tip of the island, having run aground on May 29, 1906. Although the wreck was extensively broken up during the huge salvage effort that followed, her armor plate is still several feet high in places, and the gun turrets are clearly visible; indeed, you can even see an occasional 12-inch (305 mm) shell in place. The marine life around the wreckage can be really tremendous, with large shoals of bib, wrasse, and pollack galore, as well as anglerfish and conger in the deeper sections.

GANNETS' ROCK

• 50 feet (15 m) • intermediate

This is a wonderful site when the conditions are right, with the steep faces of the rock continuing below the water until bottoming out at about 50 feet (15 m). The craggy nature of the rock surface gives plenty of secure points for sponges and small kelp beds to take hold, and a motley collection of wrasse, juvenile pollack, and the occasional bass moves through this tangled growth. Look into the darker recesses for swimming crabs or, if you are lucky, the very large edible crabs. In warmer conditions at the beginning of summer large cuttlefish are frequently encountered in the rough spoil and sand at the base of the rock wall. From the base of the wall of Gannets' Rock you can make your way directly to the base of Gannets' Rock Pinnacle.

KNOLL PINS

• 90 feet (27 m) • advanced

Located in the middle of the east coast, the stark pinnacles of the Knoll Pins can be a tremendous dive, but be wary of localized currents—numerous tales are told of divers failing to find the rockfaces after making their descent, or of being swept off them once they arrive. The trick is to enter the water as close to the rocks as possible, and to descend quickly.

There are two possible ways to conduct this dive—either maintain a shallow depth and contour around the rockfaces, or go deep and work your way upwards. The former is probably the better option, as the best marine life tends to be concentrated in the first 60 feet (18 m) or so. Keep an eye out for some hefty pollack and ballen wrasses, and peer into the nooks and crannies of the rock face for large bearded rockling and sometimes ling or conger.

OTHER ACTIVITIES

Lundy Island is owned by the National Trust, England's leading conservation body, and a landing fee is charged for all visitors. There is much here to attract outdoor enthusiasts, including rock-climbing and walking, but Lundy is above all a mecca for birdwatchers: puffins, fulmars, kittiwakes, manx shearwaters, and peregrine falcons all breed on the island. Stone Age flint tools and Bronze Age burial mounds are evidence of the island's long history of habitation, and there is a small village, complete with pub and church. Regular departures from the mainland and accommodation on the island are available for those wishing to explore it further.

TELEPHONE NUMBERS

Recompression chamber +44-1752-209-999
Hospital +44-1271-863-448
Emergency services 999
Lundy Shore Office +44-1271-863636

WEBSITES & E-MAIL

Lundy Island www.lundyisland.co.uk
Travel Information www.i-uk.com
English Nature www.english-nature.org.uk

DIVER'S TIP

In January 2003 an area off the coast of Lundy Island was designated Britain's first "no take zone", designed to protect the rare and delicate animals found there. So look but don't touch!

▼ CUP CORALS

The heavily colonized reef walls are home to sponges, anemones, sea squirts, and several species of cup corals.

Linda Pitkin

Linda Pitkin

ISLE OF MAN

words by Jane Burnett

THE DIVING IS AMONG THE MOST SPECTACULAR IN TEMPERATE WATERS, YET WHICHEVER DIVE SITE YOU PICK ON THE ISLE OF MAN YOU ARE LIKELY TO HAVE IT TO YOURSELF, IF YOU DON'T COUNT SHARING IT WITH SEALS, BASKING SHARKS OR GUILLEMOTS, THAT IS.

VISIBILITY

15 to 50 feet (5 to 15 m) is usual, but can be better or worse.

MUST SEES

The Burroo
Sugarloaf caves and cliffs
Diving guillemots
Basking sharks
Luxuriant walls of anemone

DOWNSIDE

Strong currents
Best sites are weather dependent

GETTING THERE

With Liverpool less than 60 miles away, it's easier than you might think. For many divers travelling with full gear taking a car may be the most convenient. Fast car-carrying ferries, run by the Isle of Man Steam Packet Company (www.steam-packet.com), travel regularly between Douglas and Liverpool, Heysham, Belfast and Dublin. However if that is too slow, there are flights to and from all major UK airports (1 hour 20 minutes from London City Airport, for example). Accommodation is good and plentiful. For diving, the south west of Man, Port Erin or Port St Mary are the best locations.

For tourist information, go to
www.visitisleofman.com,
www.gov.im/tourism
or www.isle-of-man.com

VISA

There is no need for a visa or passport if you are going to the Isle of Man through the UK, Republic of Ireland or the Channel Islands.

MONEY

UK money is accepted. The IoM does issue its own notes and coins, but spend them before you leave, as they are not legal tender outside the island.

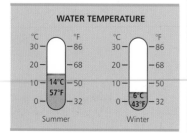

WATER TEMPERATURE

	Summer		Winter
	14°C / 57°F		6°C / 43°F

Jane Burnett

The Isle of Man is a rather different dive destination. With a distinctly exotic feel that starts with palm trees at the airport, it's hard to believe that it is geographically still within the British Isles. It is not part of the U.K. but a crown dependency with its own laws, government and parliament. It also boasts its own language, currency and stamps.

GEOGRAPHY

Measuring a mere 13 by 33 miles (20 by 50 km), the Isle of Man lies in the middle of the Irish Sea and has a population of 75,000. The island scenery is wonderful—a remarkable mixture for such a small space. From the rugged coastline with its many spectacular, secluded beaches and sand dunes to the mountains, glens and moorland, there is a fascinating view around every corner.

MARINE LIFE

The marine life is diverse and prolific. Whether you are looking for tiny organisms or large mammals, there will be something to hold your interest. The Isle of Man is a basking shark "hot spot" with late June/early July being the best time for spotting these amazing creatures—the second largest fish in the sea. If you do see one, please approach with care and consideration and report your sighting to the U.K. Marine Conservation Society (www.mcsuk.org).

Gray seals will often join divers. Fish life is varied and plentiful; all the British wrasses can be found here and some of the ballan wrasses are very large. Many different species of jellyfish may be encountered, from the large and sting-free barrel jellyfish (*Rhizostoma octopus*) to the lion's mane jelly (*Cyanea capillata*), which is best viewed from a distance. Demanding a little more from your powers of observation are the numerous nudibranchs; you may find species such as the diminutive *Diaphorodoris luteocincta*, the fried-egg sea slug, no bigger that the nail on your pinkie or the British Isles' largest nudibranch, *Tritonia hombergi*, which can be as large as your hand. Anemones — jewel, plumose, dahlia and more—spread over almost every rock surface. The intense colors are memorable.

THE DIVES

The best diving is in the south/southwest, particularly around the Calf of Man. There are a number of local dive clubs, but few dive operators. The island is subjected to a large tidal range and strong currents are the norm. Many sites should only be dived at slack water or on neap tides. Inshore currents do not always run in the same direction as offshore tidal streams. Unless you are very competent with charts and navigation, seek local knowledge.

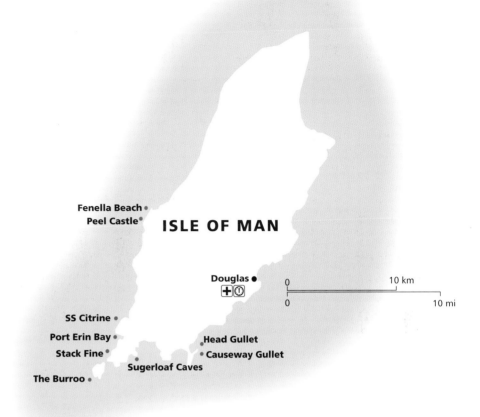

ISLE OF MAN

Fenella Beach
Peel Castle

Douglas

SS Citrine
Port Erin Bay
Stack Fine
The Burroo
Sugerloaf Caves
Head Gullet
Causeway Gullet

0   10 km
0   10 mi

THE BURROO

• 0 to 130 feet (0 to 40 m) • intermediate.

It is reputed to be one of the best dives in the Irish Sea, and some would say in the British Isles. The Burroo is the southwestern point of the Calf of Man. Best tackled at slack due to the strong currents, it can also be a great drift dive. Look out for basking sharks on the way to the site.

Almost invariably, seals will be hauled out on the rocks, resting, sunning themselves and watching divers with interest. If you're lucky, you will experience a close encounter underwater. If they come in, they come in very close, nibbling fins, maybe even letting you tickle their whiskers. Take care and remember they are wild animals.

Your entry point will be dictated by how the tide is running. Underwater, the seabed is varied with vertical cliffs, large boulders and deep gullies. Marine life is prolific due to the currents that converge on the headland. Kelp in the shallows gives way to beds of tubularia that in turn recede as the anemones take over. Carpets of plumose, dahlia and jewel anemones spread as far as you can see. So concentrated, it is impossible to find a space in which to place a finger to steady oneself. Good buoyancy control is essential.

Large quantities of fish give this site an almost

15

OTHER DIVE SITES

Gibdale Point
The Cletts
Carrick Ledges
Garden Rock
Culberry Bows
Creg Y Jaghee
Slea Ny Bery
Outer Bows

◄◄ **THE S.S. *CITRINE***
Although scattered, there is still enough wreckage of the S.S. *Citrine* to make an absorbing dive.

Jane Burnett

▲ CORYPHELLA LINEATE
One of the many types of nudibranchs found in the seas around the Isle of Man.

DIVE CENTERS
Isle of Man Diving Holidays
Web: www.isleofmandivingholidays.com
E-mail: mkeggen@manx.net
Phone: +44-1624-833133

Mann Scuba Divers
Web: www.mannscubadivers.co.uk
E-mail: manndivers@manx.net
Phone: +44-1624-835202

RECOMPRESSION
The Isle of Man Hyperbaric Facility is in Douglas: +44-1624-626394
In a diving emergency, phone the Coastguard – either a 999 call or Channel 16 on VHF radio

HOSPITAL
Noble's Hospital in Braddan is a modern hospital on the outskirts of Douglas. General +44-1624-650000
Accident & Emergency +44-1624-650040

CONSERVATION SOCIETY
Marine Conservation Society
Basking Shark Watch
C/o Marine Conservation Society
Wolf Business Park, Alton Road
Ross on Wye HR9 5NB
Phone: +44-1989-561594
Fax: +44-1989-567815
Web: www.mcsuk.org

Manx Wildlife Trust, Tynwald Mills
St. Johns, IM4 3AE
Telephone +44-1624-801985.
Fax: +44-1624-801022
Web: www.wildlifetrust.org.uk/manxwt

tropical feel. Very big ballan wrasses are usually present and occasionally ling may be seen. You can also expect to see large crabs and lobsters. There is some wreckage in the area but it is unidentifiable and very broken up.

SUGARLOAF CAVES

• **0 to 53 feet (0 to 16 m) • beginner**

In summer, the first thing you notice is the deafening noise. The Sugarloaf is bird paradise—a dramatic stack of weathered slate with every ledge packed full of nesting guillemots, razorbills, kittiwakes and other seabirds.

Next to the stack, a small cave system provides a relatively easy caving encounter for beginners and experienced divers alike. The main cave, "the Fairy Hall", is T-shaped. The left arm starts at the Sugarloaf itself, the upright exits to sea and the right arm leads to a small bay. Here is found a large rock known as the "Anvil" and the separate "Cave of the Birds." Both caves have clear surfaces. With the sun shining, this is a most beautiful dive with shafts of light illuminating the Fairy Hall or percolating through kelp in Anvil Bay. The direction of the current, if there is any, will determine your direction through the caves. Don't swim against it. If you end the dive by the stack, make like a sea otter: lie back quietly and watch and listen to the birds. It's fabulous!

In early summer, juvenile birds may even come to you. Settle down under the stack and wait. The young guillemots may come to investigate your bubbles. It is rather surreal to see seabirds flying past you underwater. Their familiar black feathers turn silver in a sheath of air, making them look coated in mercury—as if they have morphed into metallic sea creatures. A bizarre experience, but really special.

HEAD GULLET

• **0 to 50 feet (0 to 15 m) • intermediate**

This site must be dived on slack water. The strong currents guarantee abundant marine life, so be prepared for visual overload. The dive consists of swimming in and out of a series of gullies. Good buoyancy skills are essential as the spaces are tight and the wildlife does not appreciate being squashed. With so much to look at, the temptation is to remain in the first gully. Don't loiter too long, there's more to see. The plumose anemones are spectacular, the nudibranchs abundant. Conger eels, dogfish and lobsters like this area, and ling may be seen out in open water. For anyone interested in marine life this is a really excellent site.

S.S. *CITRINE*

• **0 to 53 feet (0 to 16 m) • beginner**

There are numerous wrecks around the island. One of the most accessible is the S.S. *Citrine*, a coaster that ran aground in 1931. Although very broken up and scattered, there are still many recognizable sections, though some are rather rusty. The boiler, engine, propellers, anchor and chains can be found. Visibility is generally good.

Most wreckage has a well-established cover of marine life with dead man's fingers and plumose anemones having a strong presence. Wrasses are here in large numbers with the ballans approaching close to divers in the hope of benefiting from the inevitable disturbance. This is also a good place to find corkwing wrasse as they like building nests in the wreckage. You might see them carrying seaweed they will use to line their chosen spots.

This is often a good dive on days when more exposed sites are ruled out.

Jane Burnett

Jane Burnett

SHOREDIVING

• 0 to 50 feet (0 to 15 m) • beginner

There are many great shore dives in the south/south-west. No visit to the Isle of Man is complete without a dive in Port Erin Bay. The best is the old breakwater, which can be swum around in one dive as long as you don't delay. Every type of wrasse is here and they will come in very close. Also look out for dogfish, topknots, pollack and congers. There are usually numerous types of jellyfish in this area, swept in by the currents. Within the bay, "Crab Row" is a brilliant night dive.

Causeway Gullet is accessed from Fort Island and has the only eel grass bed on the island. Seaweeds of different types and colors make this a very pretty dive. The gullies around Peel Castle just beg to be explored. Here you will find enormous dahlia anemones and you might even be joined by the resident seals.

STACK FINE IN BAY FINE

• 0 to 72 feet (0 to 22 m) • beginner

In the southwest corner of Bay Fine is the magnificent Stack Fine. The top of the pinnacle is at 15 feet (5 m) and, on a calm day, it can be seen from the surface. The north face is covered in plumose anemones—white, pink and green. Lots of friendly wrasse keep you company but you may also see ling, pipefish, tompot blennies, rocklings, edible crabs, lobsters, brittlestars and burrowing anemones. On a sunny day, the light on the kelp is fabulous.

OTHER ACTIVITIES

The Isle of Man has an intriguing past. Signs of the island's sometimes violent 10,000-year history and its fascinating culture can be found everywhere. There are medieval castles, Celtic crosses, Viking burial grounds— more than enough museums and heritage sites to keep you amused should the weather stop you from diving. There is also bird watching and riding on horse-drawn trams in Douglas.

The island is probably most famous as the host of the annual TT Races. They usually occur in early June so, unless motorcycles are another of your passions, this is a time best avoided.

Other pursuits include walking the coastal path "Raad ny Foillan"—the 90-mile (145 km) track that goes right around the island.

▲ PORT ST. MARY HARBOUR

Port St. Mary is a classic small harbor in a beautiful setting, popular with diving clubs and those seeking fishing excursions.

◄◄ WATCH ME FLY

Fascinated by the bubbles, young guillemots often investigate divers.

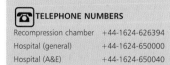 **TELEPHONE NUMBERS**

Recompression chamber	+44-1624-626394
Hospital (general)	+44-1624-650000
Hospital (A&E)	+44-1624-650040

ICELAND

words by Rebecca Corbally

 VISIBILITY

Excellent, and as much as one might be reluctant to say it, it truly is as far as the eye can see.

 MUST SEES

There are few places on earth with as much explosive scenery; desolate mountains, erupting geysers and eerie lava fields, but below the surface it is arguably to experience the spectacular of a dive between the tectonic plates.

DOWNSIDE

With its proximity to Scotland, the weather isn't too dissimilar, and if it's not on side it can be windy, wet and cold on the surface and, once under the water, it can be a fight not to let the near-freezing temperature distract you.

GETTING THERE

Iceland Air, and more recently Iceland Express run regular daily flights.
www.icelandair.co.uk from London Heathrow, Manchester and Glasgow.
www.icelandexpress.com from London Stansted and London Gatwick.

MONEY

The Icelandic Kroner. Take lots as the bottom line is everything in Scandinavia is expensive especially hotels, alcohol and food.

WATER TEMPERATURE

°C	°F		°C	°F
30	86		30	86
20	68		20	68
10 — **4°C 40°F**	50		10 — **2°C 35°F**	50
0	32		0	32
Summer			Winter	

▶ **I DON'T LIKE HEIGHTS!**
Snorkeling over the rift can be vertigo-inducing.

ICELAND HAS A DRAMATIC AND SURREAL LANDSCAPE THAT EXTENDS FAR BELOW THE SURFACE. THE UNDERWATER TOPOGRAPHY WILL CERTAINLY NOT DISAPPOINT WITH ITS CRAGGY BEAUTY, NOT LEAST BECAUSE IT OFFERS THE DIVER A CHANCE TO EXPLORE THE SPECTACULAR GEOLOGY OF THE EARTH'S TECTONIC PLATES.

Tobias Klose – DIVE.IS

Hrísey •

Strytan •

Stykkishólmur •

ICELAND

• Silfra

Gardur • • **Reykjavik**
✈ ✚ 🕐

Heimaey •

```
0          50 km
0          50 mi
```

Iceland straddles the point where two continental plates, the American and Eurasian, meet. This is the Atlantic rift, essentially a huge crack in the surface of the earth that is slowly widening by an inch or so per year. The position of Iceland straddling this rift has left the relatively large island a bit of a paradox. Green valleys and jagged mountains meet boiling mud pools and explosive geysers, and glaciers still cover over 10 percent of the country.

GEOGRAPHY

The volcanic eruptions have left behind curious rock formations—much as you would imagine on the Moon. In places you can see what were once molten waves of lava are now eerily frozen in time. In the summer months, the sun barely dips below the horizon, making it a great time to spend a long weekend here to enjoy a unique landscape in all its spectacular glory. Iceland has a distinctly otherworldly feel to it; the locals believe elves and trolls live in the valleys and mountains, and once you arrive here, the magical, ethereal quality of the landscape exerts an undeniable pull.

MARINE LIFE

As the water temperature never climbs much above about 4°C (40°F) in Thingvellir, regardless of the time of year, it doesn't make a great home for much marine life. In many ways this works in the diver's favor as the relative lack of life means there is very little particle life suspended in the water to interrupt the view, greatly adding to the water's clarity.

Stunning blasts of gold sea grass and a range of lime-green reed and weed cling to the shallows taking sustenance from the sun, but otherwise it's just you and the ever-so-slowly shifting tectonic plates.

On the chimney dive there is a mass of macro life clinging to the crusty limestone, and shoals of wild cod can be seen swirling in the chimney cavity itself.

THE DIVES

Diving is permitted in two submerged rifts in the national park of Thingvellir, Silfra and Davioshja. Silfra, the larger of the two, is a gigantic gully created by the

▼ THE WATER IS COLD
Laden with equipment and layers a diver sinks into the cold water ready to descend.

Tobias Klose – DIVE.IS

Alex Messenger

▲ LUNAR LANDSCAPE

The moonscape topography is as mesmerizing topside as it is underwater.

 DIVE CENTERS

There is only one PADI dive center in Iceland, but several tour operators run packages to dive the plates.

For those who don't want to dive, check out www.icelandexcursions.is if you want a snorkel trip at Silfra.

 DIVING ORGANIZATIONS

PADI Dive Centre:
The Dive Centre
Tobias Klose, Manager and Instructor
Phone: +354-663-2858

 RECOMPRESSION

The recompression chamber is at the hospital in Landspítali, details below.

 HOSPITAL

Landspítali
Hringbraut, 101 Reykjavik
Phone: +354-543-1000
Emergency phone: +354-543-2050
Web: www.landspitali.is

 CONSERVATION SOCIETY

Thingvellir National Park is a World Heritage site and as such divers have to fulfill all regulations and conditions regarding being adequately qualified and carrying the required equipment. Divers must abide by all rules concerning diving and agree to respect the national park regulations. It is prohibited to dive alone, to enter caves while diving and to dive to a depth greater than 100 feet (30 m), and as such diving here is entirely the diver's own responsibility and risk.

The Blue Army is a group of volunteers who painstakingly work to collect garbage from the coastline in Iceland and conserve the seas. Run vigilantly by Tomas Knutsson it celebrates its 10th anniversary in 2008.

split in the tectonic plates and, luckily for recreational divers, makes its way up into Iceland's freshwater lake—stretching its gaping jaws right up from the depths of the Atlantic where the other cracks sit out of reach.

The first thing that strikes you is the clarity of the water; it is so clear it can play tricks on your mind. Much like skiing in a white-out, where the snow becomes indistinguishable from your surroundings and motion sickness follows, the water becomes like glass and "invisible" thanks to its clarity, making the drop over the side of the crack down into the gully vertigo-inducing.

The dive starts with a 195-foot (60 m) trudge from your car along a footpath reminiscent of a Scottish heather-encased moor. Wearing a drysuit, balaclava and dry gloves in an effort to keep everything covered in the conditions, the walk can be quite exhausting. You can make a few trips for your tank and equipment if necessary, something that can turn what is essentially a short dive into an all-day affair.

There are three main segments to the dive: the Hall, the Cathedral and the Lagoon. After your eyes and brain have become used to the clarity of the water and you have finned the length of the Silfra Hall, where you are submerged in the belly of the deep crack, you rise up to almost knee-deep water to fin up and over a crag into the Cathedral. Disconcerting as it is, as you cruise back down into the depths of the crack again you have a whole new perspective. On a recent dive the sun momentarily emerged from behind the clouds sending dagger like shafts of light through the icy water that lit up the jaw of the enormous crack below.

Eventually, you fin through to the lagoon where you surface on your knees, a fitting posture for such majesterial and dramatic surroundings. As you sit after the dive in this isolated oasis you bask in the evening's warmth, shaking off the chill of the dive while letting the surreal environment, which only the more intrepid diver will ever experience, truly soak in.

OTHER DIVES

Although the tectonic plates are arguably the highlight of a dive trip to Iceland, there are other coastal and open sea dive experiences to be had. One that stands out is the impressive Strytan Chimney.

STRYTAN

- **0 to 165 feet (0 to 50 m)** • **advanced**

In the middle of the Eyjafjord in northern Iceland is a geothermal chimney open to recreational divers. At a depth of about 230 feet (70 m) a hot spring has burst the seams of the seabed and has been bubbling boiling-hot water up into the ocean for thousands of years.

At the place where this hot, mineral-rich water meets the ice-cold sea the particles coagulate and over time have formed an impressive limestone chimney. As many chimneys are buried deep below the surface and are out of the realm of most divers this is a rare treat.

Strytan protrudes up to just 50 feet (15 m) below the the surface and can be explored by experienced divers who will have a rare opportunity to study the unusual marine life that grows and lives here in these sea conditions. While you dive you will be immersed in the warm geothermal waters as they mix with the icy sea. Owing to the nature of this dive it is limited to experienced divers only; currents can be strong so you need to be physically fit and in excellent control of buoyancy.

OTHER ACTIVITIES

Once you have completed a dive and come down from the inevitable high, there is plenty to discover on your non-dive preflight day. You can jet-ski out to dolphin feeding grounds—an exhilarating experience in full drysuit and face helmets bouncing up and over the intimidating swell—or you can take the softer option of a boat trip to watch minke whales and dolphins.

If your stomach can handle the often boisterous seas you could try your hand at one of the many deep-sea fishing setups around. On the other hand, if you've had enough of the water by now you should go to see one of the steaming and abruptly exploding geysers, which send huge plumes of boiling water skyward. Or you could go horseback riding or hiking across the moonlike lava fields. If that all sounds too much like hard work, you can always have a dip in the surprisingly warm waters of the legendary blue lagoon geothermic spa, basting your skin with sulfur-rich creamy sand, which it is claimed, cures skin disorders and slows down the aging process. Magic.

Tobias Klose – DIVE.IS

◄ **MIND THE GAP**
A diver at the awe-inspiring gap between the Eurasian and American plates.

DIVER'S TIP

Get yourself familiar with drysuit diving to ensure you are totally relaxed in the environment and are able to get the most out of it. It's cold so you will need decent thermals and an effective layering system under your drysuit, as well as dry gloves and a balaclava to safely cover as much skin as you can. Most dives in Silfra are about 30 minutes, but the more covered and comfortable you can make yourself, the longer your dive experience will be.

📞 **TELEPHONE NUMBERS**

Recompression chamber	as hospital below
Hospital (general)	+354-543-1000
Hospital (emergency)	+354-543-2050

🖥 **WEBSITES & E-MAIL**

The Dive Centre	www.dive.is
Iceland Express	www.icelandexpress.com
Iceland Air	www.icelandair.co.uk
Blue Lagoon	www.bluelagoon.is
Whale watching	www.dolphin.is
Icelandic Tourist Board	www.visiticeland.com
Other activities:	www.adventures.is

SVALBARD

words by Jane Burnett

VISIBILITY

VISIBILITY

6.5 to 30 feet (2 to 10 m) in summer.

MUST SEES

Polar bears

Walrus

Icebergs

DOWNSIDE

It's very cold. In the summer, when diving occurs, the visibility is generally poor.

GETTING THERE

Regular flights from Oslo and Tromso

VISA

Not needed by nationals of all countries that signed the Spitsbergen Treaty, but they may be needed in mainland Norway as you travel to or from Svalbard. Citizens of the EU do not require visas in Norway.

MONEY

Norwegian krone (NOK)

ALTHOUGH PART OF NORWAY, SVALBARD IS SITUATED FAR TO THE NORTH OF THE NORWEGIAN MAINLAND. IT IS PROBABLY THE FURTHEST NORTH A DIVER CAN EASILY GO TO SEA DIVE. HOW DOES "80 DEGREES NORTH" SOUND AS A DIVE LOCATION IN YOUR LOG BOOK?

As tropical dive sites grow more crowded and divers seek new challenges, the polar regions can start to beckon. If you are looking for different, exciting diving and really do not want to meet hoardes of other divers underwater, a trip to the Arctic might be the answer. Over the summer months a number of operators lead trips to Svalbard, a small group of islands approximately 600 miles (965 km) from the North Pole. Trips balance diving with scenery and wildlife sightseeing. And what wildlife! In between diving around icebergs, you can get up close to polar bears, walrus and arctic foxes.

GEOGRAPHY

Although nearly as large as the Republic of Ireland, the Svalbard archipelago is virtually uninhabited. The total population is around 3,000. Covered in snow and ice for most of the year, this is true wilderness—real High Arctic. Gigantic glaciers, inching their way to the sea, nestle between towering mountains making the landscape inhospitable, treacherous and utterly beautiful.

The gap between Svalbard and the North Pole consists mainly of packed drift ice and it is only during summer that the ice recedes enough for passage around the top of the main island of Spitsbergen. Twenty-four hour daylight during the summer can be disconcerting, yet it is an amazing experience.

The main town of Longyearbyen, while not lacking in modern amenities, originally developed as a mining town and still has a slight "wild west" feel to it. With no roads between settlements, the main way to travel is by sea.

Today, tourism has replaced coal as the main industry. Much of the land and wildlife is now protected, tourism is tightly regulated and conservation is high on the political agenda.

MARINE LIFE

There is a popular misconception that cold water equals limited life, but this is not necessarily true. Even at temperatures of –1°C (30°F) or below, many species can be quite prolific. In contrast to the monotone landscape above, the marine environment can be very colorful. In Svalbard waters, you will need to get your macro eyes in focus as you are unlikely to see large mammals underwater. You may see bearded and ringed seals on the surface but they are shy of human contact. Atlantic walrus may also be seen on land or ice floes but are considered too dangerous and unpredictable to swim with. Moffen Island, north of Spitsbergen, is their summer stronghold. Almost exterminated in the 19th century, walrus are now protected and an obligatory 1,000 foot (300 m) minimum distance to their sanctuary is imposed on visitors. Fish numbers are few in the shallow coastal waters and the main catch in the fjords is shrimp. Of 60 possible species, sea scorpions, snailfish, lumpsuckers and snake blennies are the fish most likely to be seen by divers.

On reaching the seabed, the most obviously abundant animals are anemones. The colorful dahlia anemone will be familiar to temperate divers; its larger cousin, the horseman anemone, may be less so. Both are plentiful in Svalbard waters. Also common are species of *Hormathia* and *Sagartia* and the burrowing anemone *Cerianthus*. Sponges, sea squirts, soft corals and various filter-feeding worms are well represented. Crustaceans hold their own with numerous crabs, including the feisty "toad crab", and shrimps. Once your eye is in, amphipods provide serious and fascinating macro interest. The perennial favorite, the nudibranch, is also present and, if you're really lucky, you may come across a pteropod known as the sea butterfly. A minuscule but ferocious predator with pointy ears, it would look like the devil himself — were it not dressed in pale blue and pink.

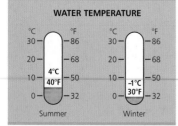

WATER TEMPERATURE

°C	°F		°C	°F
30	86		30	86
20	68		20	68
10	50		10	50
	4°C 40°F			–1°C 30°F
0	32		0	32
Summer			Winter	

17

SPITSBERGEN

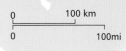

● **Longyearbyen**
✈ ✚

0   100 km

0   100mi

▼ ICEBERG SAFETY
Selecting the right iceberg before diving is crucial and takes time. To be safe it must be grounded.

Paul Biggin

DIVE CENTERS
None.

RECOMPRESSION
There is no recompression chamber in Svalbard. There may be a doctor on your boat, but medical facilities are very limited. You dive conservatively and at your own risk.

HOSPITAL
There is a small hospital in Longyearbyen but services are limited.

▼ NICE ICE
A diver marvels at a wall of ice.

THE DIVES

Theoretically you could dive the west coast of Spitsbergen all year round. The furthest reach of the Gulf Stream, the Spitsbergen current, brings a milder climate to the region than can be found in other areas on the same latitude. Generally this keeps the west ice-free for most of the year. In reality, the polar night and plunging air temperatures make this impractical. Most diving occurs in the brief summer from June to August.

You don't need huge amounts of experience or special equipment to dive here. You do need to be relatively fit, familiar with drysuit diving in cold seas and have ensured that your equipment is serviced and working properly. There is no dive shop so you must carry spares and be able to do basic repairs. Aside from your drysuit, the most vital pieces of equipment are your regulators—you'll need two—and they must be suitable for diving in icy conditions.

Water temperatures in summer can go down to –1°C (30°F). As seawater freezes around –1.8°C (28.4°F), it's about as cold as you can get in the liquid world—at least in the one that we inhabit. With few medical facilities within easy reach, the diving tends to be conservative with an enforced depth limit of 65 feet (20 m) and bottom time of 45 minutes (if the cold doesn't get you first).

The diving will include scenic, wall and iceberg dives. You are likely to clock up your coldest dive, most

Vicki Billings

northerly dive (just over the 80th parallel) and, possibly, shortest dive. The ability to dive any particular dive site will be determined by the weather and the state of the ice.

ICEBERG DIVES

Diving around an iceberg is a highlight of any Arctic trip and an experience that gives new meaning to the concept of "wall diving". Selecting a suitable 'berg is crucial. It must be a grounded—that is not moving—safe iceberg. Icebergs are large chunks of ice that have generally calved off glaciers and are, therefore, composed of freshwater. As freshwater freezes at a higher temperature than saltwater, icebergs usually take a long time to melt.

Their uneven surfaces tell the story of the trauma of their birth. The colors, shapes and textures are fabulous; the noise of the ice as it flexes and creaks fascinates. Depending on how tactile you are, you might find yourself just hanging next to the 'berg, stroking it. You may also hear the mournful "singing" of a bearded seal somewhere in the distance. The eerie beauty is guaranteed to make the hairs on the back of your neck stand on end.

SCENIC DIVES

Non-ice dives vary from shallow flat seabeds of gravel and shale—ideal feeding areas for walrus—to steep, pretty walls stuffed with all manner of marine life. With the visibilty limited to a few feet these tend to be "macro" dives for photographers. While much will be familiar to temperate divers, there are more than enough unusual creatures to maintain interest.

PACK ICE

Don't underestimate the dangers of the pack ice. It can look benign but the currents underneath can switch in an instant turning a seemingly clear stretch of water into compacting ice. It can move at a frightening speed. The dangers, if you have divers in the water, are obvious, and even a RIB will be little protection if trapped. Chose your icebergs carefully and keep an eye on the pack ice. Be prepared for instant recall if the ice starts to move.

OTHER ACTIVITIES

With few roads available, independent travel is quite restricted. Most tourists are likely to join a cruise ship or other organized tour. An interesting past provides numerous historical sites to visit in and around Longyearbyen and other settlements.

The main attraction, however, is the wildlife. Polar bears, walrus, reindeer, arctic fox and various seals can all be seen along with hosts of birds. Several species of

Jane Burnett

whales visit the area but you will be fortunate if you come across them at close quarters.

Whaling was a major industry from the 17th century, as was seal, walrus and polar bear hunting. Evidence of the whaling industry can be seen in Smeerenburg (Blubber Town) in the north of Spitsbergen. Gruesome though the industry was, it's impossible not to admire the hardiness of the people who lived and worked here in such tough conditions.

▲ NEXT STOP—THE NORTH POLE

Going around the top of Svalbard there is nothing between you and the North Pole but pack ice. Easily negotiated by a Russian icebreaker and while fascinating to see, it's best to seek out a dive site in a more sheltered area.

🖥 **WEBSITES & E-MAIL**

XO Holidays, c/o Asgeir Solli   www.xoholidays.com
Waterproof Expeditions   www.waterproof-expeditions.com
Ocean Adventures   www.oceanadventures.co.uk/arctic_OA_01.cfm

NEWFOUNDLAND
& LABRADOR

words by Gavin Parsons

WHEN IT COMES TO COLD-WATER DIVING, THE CANADIAN PROVINCE OF NEWFOUNDLAND AND LABRADOR IS A LEADER ON THE WORLD STAGE. IT HAS OUTSTANDING WRECKS, FASCINATING FAUNA, A MARINE LIFE SPECTACLE AND SOME OF THE FRIENDLIEST PEOPLE ON EARTH. IT IS A STUNNING CHALLENGE FOR ANY ADVENTUROUS DIVER.

Gavin Parsons

 VISIBILITY

Spring, autumn and winter 100+ feet (30+ m). Summer 33 feet (10 m) for the top 33 feet (10 m), 82 to 100 feet (25 to 30 m) below that.

 MUST SEES

Rose Castle Marconi room
PLM
Saganaga
Lord Srathcona
Caplin shoals
Icebergs

DOWNSIDE

Cold water, but that is also why it's good

 GETTING THERE

Air Canada (www.aircanada.com) International and domestic flights to St. John's, Newfoundland. Astraeus Airlines (www.flyastraeus.com) fly from Gatwick, UK to Newfoundland. Continental Airlines (www.continental.com) flies from U.S. to St. John's, Newfoundland.

VISA

Most visitors do not require a visa. A full passport is necessary.

MONEY

Canadian Dollar (CAD)

▶ **WELL PRESERVED**

Like the propeller on this whaling boat, many structures are well preserved in the cold water.

WATER TEMPERATURE

°C	°F	°C	°F
30	86	30	86
20	68	20	68
10	50	10	50
12°C		-1°C	
0 54°F	32	0 30°F	32
Summer		Winter	

GEOGRAPHY

The province comprises the Island of Newfoundland at the mouth of the Gulf of St. Lawrence on Canada's east coast, and the much larger territory of Labrador to the northwest on the Canadian mainland.

It sits within the Labrador current that runs southward from Greenland and brings icebergs, which make ideal novelty dives. Have you ever seen the bottom of an iceberg? Fishing was the major revenue earner for centuries and English, Irish, French, Portuguese and Spanish fishermen exploited the rich cod stocks around the island and out on the Grand Banks. In the early 1990s Canada had to close the commercial cod fishery due to serious declines in the stocks. The mainstay of Newfoundland's employment hemorrhaged jobs.

Oil and tourism are picking up where fishing left off, and diving is playing a part in that recovery, albeit a small part. Underwater there are hundreds of shipwrecks—some discovered, many not—and a plentiful supply of rocky reefs together with some beautiful shore dives. Most Newfoundland divers are hard core and know their stuff. Safety is paramount and technical disciplines are widespread, making all local divers extremely proficient.

MARINE LIFE

The cold North Atlantic supports a spectacular amount of marine life. The water is nutritious and while cod and other pelagic predatory fish are not in very large supply, there are numerous other species. Some, such as Atlantic plaice, are familiar to anyone who eats seafood. But there are also large numbers of lumpsuckers, eelpouts, sculpins and conners which are the resident species. In early summer the inshore bays fill with caplin (also spelt capelin)—a small member of the smelt family that come inshore in their billions, throwing themselves onto the beaches to breed — a marvelous marine spectacle.

Because food for their chicks is plentiful, millions of seabirds breed along the coast. Thousands of humpback and minke whales linger here, sometimes all summer, because caplin, sand lance and other staples of their diet are readily available. Tour boats take people to see whales and birds up close in their natural habitat, and while most people are content to watch, it is

possible to get in the water with the whales. People get in on the act, too, using casting nets from shore to scoop up the tiny fish for food or fertilizer. The caplin run is a wildlife attraction that is so far mainly undiscovered.

THE DIVES

Divers are well catered for. The main diving attractions are the WWII wrecks off Bell Island, with access from Conception Bay South, about 9 miles (15 km) from the capital of St. John's. All the vessels were once ore carriers waiting off the island to load with iron ore from the local mines. The wartime authorities thought protective cover should go to the shipping in St. John's harbor (forming up to become part of the famous north Atlantic convoys), leaving the ore carriers at anchor exposed. The guns on Bell Island that were supposed to defend them against U-boat attacks were ill-positioned and of the wrong type.

In 1942, on the nights of September 5 and November 2, the vessels in the bay were attacked by German U-boats, resulting in four shipwrecks. Today they are all within recreational diving depths. The cold water has preserved them wonderfully, and nutrient-rich water has covered their hulls in marine life. While the water temperature is certainly something to take into account, a good undersuit, drysuit and dry gloves will ensure that you will be warm enough.

S.S. *ROSE CASTLE*

• 88 to 164 feet (27 to 50 m) • advanced

This is the most intact of the Bell Island wrecks and, owing to its depth, the best preserved. Diving to the seabed is unnecessary. On the deck in around 100 feet (30 m) there is everything a diver needs to see. The most impressive part of the wreck is the Marconi radio room as all the valves and dials are still in place. Outside, all the deck machinery is present and shrouded in plumose anemones, seaweed and encrusting algae. Fish life is not as prolific as you'd expect, but at this depth, this is one of the few wrecks where large cod can still be found.

For more experienced divers happy to go inside, you will find the crew's artifacts still littered around (please leave it that way). On the seafloor at 164 feet (50 m) are the remains of a torpedo, and when the visibility is good, from this depth and from in front of the bow, the wreck can look uncannily like RMS *Titanic*.

S.S. *LORD STRATHCONA*

• 88 to 120 feet (27 to 37 m) • advanced

At 460 feet (140 m) long, the *Lord Strathcona* is a large wreck that has been colonized by seaweed and numerous, massive plumose anemones. It was struck

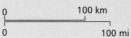

NEWFOUNDLAND AND LABRADOR

Conception Harbour Whalers
Holyrood Beach • **Dildo Whale Bones**
St. John's ●
● **S.S. *Rose Castle***
● **PLM 27**
● **S.S. *Lord Strathcona***
● **S.S. *Saganaga***

0 ——— 100 km
0 ——— 100 mi

▼ SAFETY FIRST
A male lumpsucker has selected one of the hundreds of wrecks as a protected place to tend his eggs.

Gavin Parsons

DIVE CENTERS

Ocean Quest Adventure Resort

17 Stanley's Road

Conception Bay south

NL, Canada

A1W 5H9

Phone: +1-709-834-7234

Web: www.oceanquestcharters.com

E-mail: online form

 RECOMPRESSION

The recompression chamber is at the hospital in St. John's, details below.

 HOSPITAL

St. John's Health Science Center

300 Prince Philip Drive

St. John's, Newfoundland

Canada

A1B 3V6

Phone: +1-709-777-6300

 CONSERVATION SOCIETY

Ocean Net

Web: www.oceannet.ca

E-mail: info@oceannet.ca

---

amidships by two torpedoes fired by U-513 during the morning of September 5, 1942. Loaded with iron ore its excessive weight and extensive damage meant it sank within 30 seconds. The wreck is bedecked with life and is often smothered in lumpsucker egg masses. The red-colored males are always present and provide divers with a good chance of seeing these slow moving fish up close. There is a plethora of boat paraphernalia still littering the deck and cargo holds.

S.S. *SAGANAGA*

• 72 to 115 feet (27 to 37 m) • advanced

A mid-sized ore carrier around 410 feet (125 m) in length, the wreck is at the perfect depth to explore easily, yet deep enough to have survived the ravages of winter. It has occasionally been struck by a passing iceberg, but damage is minimal. The torpedo that sent it to the bottom ripped a huge hole in its side and exposed a large section of the cargo hold. The wreck is full of swimthroughs and open companionways to explore.

During winter, spring and autumn almost the entire wreck is visible. Plankton blooms in summer are the only thing to reduce the visibility. Even with the damage it sustained, the superstructure is incredibly well preserved.

PLM 27

• 46 to 100 feet (14 to 30 m) • beginner

The shallowest of the Bell Island wrecks, PLM 27 was actually a Free French vessel with an international crew. It was waiting at anchor with the *Rose Castle* when her horrified crew saw the *Rose* go down, but couldn't react quickly enough to escape the U-518's next volley. One caught it amidships causing a devastating explosion that sent it to the bottom in less than a minute. The torpedo damage is most obvious on this wreck, but that doesn't mean the vessel is torn apart. To show just how well preserved it is, there is a wooden box still full of live rounds at the stern.

Off the stern, the rudder and propeller are popular destinations for divers. On the deck is a large deck gun and even a handheld machine gun that was discovered only a couple of years ago. The deck, machinery and other paraphernalia are covered in anemones, and life includes all the cold-water species such as Atlantic plaice, lumpsuckers, conners and eelpouts.

HOLYROOD BEACH—SHORE DIVE

• 0 to 40 feet (0 to 12 m) • beginner

The town of Holyrood on Route 60 is at the western end of Conception Bay. Along the beach are car parking bays and a new boardwalk and tables make kitting up easy. Local divers use the site as a training area. The marine life is prolific, it easily competes with other sites and is a great place to take a break from wreck diving. The beach consists of large pebbles and is easy to walk across. You simply pick a spot and head in. There is a small reef where divers find the odd wolf fish, but that's if you get that far. At around 20 feet (6 m) straight out from the beach is a weed line full of eelpouts, more Atlantic plaice than you can shake a snorkel at, plus sculpins and lumpsuckers. It is a favored spot for caplin during the spawning season (see below) and is also a great night dive location.

CONCEPTION HARBOUR WHALERS— SHORE DIVE

• 0 to 20 feet (0 to 6 m) • beginner

When whaling fell out of favor, three vessels were abandoned in an inlet at Conception Harbour. One is still exposed at the surface, but the other two sank and are slowly dying on the seabed. The site is easy to find; just off the coastal road you can see the surface wreck.

Enter the water just under the bow of the protruding wreck and submerge to find the first sunken ship. It is lying on its side facing the opposite direction, so the first thing you come across is the stern. All the deck gear has fallen down and is lying on the muddy seabed. Be careful not to kick up too much silt or the usually reasonable visibility will be reduced to zero.

As you swim around the wreck, keep an eye out for lumpsuckers, plaice and other fish species that abound here. The second wreck is covered in seaweed, but still has its harpoon gun intact at the bow. The dive exit is next to a small wooden wharf on this side of the wrecks, meaning you don't have to worry about retracing your fin kicks.

DILDO WHALE BONES

• 0 to 20 feet (0 to 6m) • beginner

As a shallow shore excursion in front of an old whale processing factory this is not, on paper, the most interesting of dives. The site is now a wharf for working fishing vessels. To many divers it feels odd to get in the water next to a ship being loaded or unloaded. In other parts of the world someone would call the police. Yet here it is different: a quick hello to the crew and you are treated as welcome friends thereafter.

The dive starts next to the wharf on a small pebble beach. As you descend the contour line into the bay, strange objects start to appear. These are the remnants of the whale processing factory. Vertebrae, skulls, ribs and other limb bones lie littered across the seabed. It's a macabre dive in a way, but fascinating for all that. Like everywhere else in the locality, the seabed is filled with life. Crustaceans, plaice, sculpins and lumpsuckers are ubiquitous.

CAPLIN MIGRATION

In mid-June to early July caplin migrate from the north Atlantic toward the shallow bays of Canada, Greenland and Iceland. Off Newfoundland they gather in their billions. They come here to spawn by throwing themselves onto the pebbly beaches in an attempt to ensure the next generation isn't eaten by other fish. For the majority of the adults it's a suicide mission; if they are not eaten by humpback and minke whales, seabirds or people, they die after copulation. Only a few females make it back to sea. The fish tend to spawn during the spring high tides mostly in the early mornings or evenings.

OTHER ACTIVITIES

Newfoundland is a wild and rugged place, ideal if you like outdoor activity. The climate is influenced by the cold Labrador current coming down from the Arctic, but that shouldn't stop visitors from enjoying the amazing scenery and wildlife.

Hiking the backwood trails in Gros Morne National Park is one of the more extreme walking activities, but there are also numerous walking trails suited to all levels of outdoor enthusiasts. The East Coast Trail on the Avalon Peninsula is one of the most popular.

Kayaking in the craggy bays is a joy and made immensely more enjoyable when humpback whales are around, feeding on caplin. These giants sometimes approach kayakers for a closer look. But if whale watching from a floating stick isn't your thing, there are several dozen dedicated whale watching boats operating along the coast.

Newfoundland and Labrador also has a rich history and plenty of places to discover it. Excursions of note include a visit to resettled communities such as Ireland's Eye, a visit to Cabot Tower where Marconi received the first trans-Atlantic wireless signal in 1901 and a wealth of local museums that offer an insight into the lives of Newfoundlanders and Labradorians. Their generous spirit lives on—the people here are warm and welcoming and their zest for life is highly infectious.

▲ **UNEXPLODED**
Live ammunition still sits in a box at the stern of PLM 27.

☎ **TELEPHONE NUMBERS**
Recompression chamber   +1-709-777-6300
Hospital   +1-709-777-6300

💻 **WEBSITES & E-MAIL**
www.newfoundlandlabrador.com
www.oceanquestcharters.com

NORTH CAROLINA
OUTER BANKS

 VISIBILITY

As low as 20 feet (6 m) after winter storms to 100 feet (30 m) on the right day in summer

 MUST SEES

Wrecks galore
Ragged tooth sharks Oct–Nov

 DOWNSIDE

Currents
Depth

 GETTING THERE

Raleigh-Durham International Airport is a 3-hour drive away from the Outer Banks, and is served by a number of international airlines. There are numerous internal flights to Raleigh-Durham from major North American hubs such as Washington D.C.

VISA

Canadians do not need a visa or passport to enter the U.S. Generally all other nationalities require a visitor's visa, though some 27 countries participate in the Visa Waiver Program. Check with a U.S. consulate or embassy.

 MONEY

Currency is the U.S. dollar

WATER TEMPERATURE

°C	°F	°C	°F
30	86	30	86
20	**25°C** 68	20	68
	77°F		
10	50	10	**12°C** 50
			53°F
0	32	0	32
Summer		Winter	

THE "GRAVEYARD OF THE ATLANTIC", THE OUTER BANKS HAVE BEEN CLAIMING SHIPS EVER SINCE SIR FRANCIS DRAKE RAN THE *TIGER* AGROUND THERE IN 1585. BUT IF THEY ARE A MARINER'S NIGHTMARE, THE OUTER BANKS ARE A DIVER'S DREAM—DRAMATIC SANDBARS, WARM CURRENTS, ABUNDANT MARINE LIFE, AND WRECKS GALORE.

www.Seapics.com

▶ **SAND TIGER SHARK**
The Outer Banks have become particularly renowned as a sand tiger shark hotspot.

NORTH CAROLINA (U.S.A)

0 ————— 30 km
0 ————— 30 mi

Nags Head
Bodie Island

Pea Island

Hatteras Island

Pamlico Sound

Cape Hatteras

Hatteras
Ocracoke Island
F.W. Abrams
Portsmouth Island

NORTH CAROLINA OUTER BANKS

British Splendour
Core Banks
Morehead City   Beaufort
The Proteus
Theodore Parker
Senateur   *Cape*   Caribsea
Duhamel   *Lookout*
Manuela
Malchace
Tamaulipas
Portland
W.E. Hutton   EA
Ashkhabad
Bedfordshire
Hardees's
U-352
The Papoose
Naeco-Stern
Cassimir

Courtesy of NC Division of Tourism, Film, and Sports Development.

▲ **CAPE HATTERAS LIGHTHOUSE**
The lighthouse at Cape Hatteras is the first sign of sanctuary for mariners navigating the rough waters of the Outer Banks.

N orth Carolina's Outer Banks have long been recognized as one of the most treacherous stretches of coastline in the United States. The combination of swirling tides and currents, big swells, rolling undersea sandbanks, and one of the largest estuary systems in the world have taken a terrible toll on ships and men through the ages. The wrecks strewn liberally along this tempestuous shore are representative of the history of American seafaring. There are thought to be anything from 1,500 to 5,000 shipwrecks here, only 200 of which have been clearly charted. Oregon Inlet, between Bodie and Hatteras Island, is the eastern seaboard's most notorious passage from the open sea to the safe haven of the North Carolina shore.

The fact that this coastline is washed by the warm waters of the Gulf Stream is a happy circumstance for divers as it extends the range of species usually found in subtropical and tropical waters and provides a rich environment for large pelagics and shoals of fish.

GEOGRAPHY

The Outer Banks are a chain of islands and sandbars that extend for 130 miles (210 km) along the North Carolina coast on the eastern seaboard of the United States. They are more sea than land, with 2.2 million acres (0.9 million ha) of water contained between the barrier islands and mainland. Some 15 billion gallons (56 billion liters) of tidal water flow in and out of several narrow channels and estuarine openings in the banks, creating a fragile wetland ecosystem that is a real ecological gem. Within the United States, only Alaska and Louisiana have greater areas of estuary.

Three currents—the Shelf Current, the Deep Western Boundary Current, and the Gulf Stream—meet offshore. They mingle to create warm water rich in nutrients, but also contribute towards the swirling tides and upwellings that make this area so notorious. The warm Gulf Stream in particular has a profound effect on the marine, and indeed terrestrial, environment of the Outer Banks.

MARINE LIFE

Strangely enough, the salt marshes and estuaries of the inner shore are probably more significant as a marine environment than the clear waters of the banks themselves. These sheltered inner coves and mudflats play a vital role as a nursery for juvenile fish—marine biologists estimate that 90 percent of the region's commercially significant fish spend at least part of their life cycle in these brackish waters.

For the diver, of course, the real thrills lie in the open waters of the Gulf Stream and great sand banks offshore. The Outer Banks are only 40 miles (64 km) away from the deep waters of the continental shelf, which are a source of nutrient- and oxygen-rich upwellings. The tepid waters of the Gulf Stream carry patches of Sargasso weed in which numerous small baitfish and

19

▶ SAND TIGER SHARK

The sand tiger sharks treat the wrecks of the Banks as they would natural reefs, with hulls doubling as reef walls, and holds as caverns.

OTHER DIVE SITES

F.W. Abrams
British Splendour
Manuela
Malchace
Theodore Parker
Caribsea
Senateur Duhamel
Tamaulipas
W.E. Hutton
Portland
EA
Ashkhabad
Bedfordshire
Hardees's
Naeco-Stern
Cassimir

 DIVE CENTERS

OUTER BANKS DIVING

57540 Hwy. 12, P.O. Box 453, Hatteras, NC 27943, U.S.A.

Phone: +1-252-986-1056

E-mail: outerbanksdiving@mindspring.com

Web: www.outerbanksdiving.com

DISCOVERY DIVING COMPANY

414 Orange Street, Beaufort, NC 28516, U.S.A.

Phone: +1-252-728-2265

E-mail: dive@discoverydiving.com

Web: www.discoverydiving.com

 DIVING ORGANIZATIONS

The U.S. Coast Guard is responsible for the safety of dive vessels:

Phone: +1-800-368-5647

E-mail: uscginfoline@gcrm.com

 RECOMPRESSION

Duke Medical Center, Duke University Hospital Erwin Road, Durham, NC 27710, U.S.A.

Phone: +1-919-684-8111

 HOSPITAL

Carteret General Hospital

3500 Arendell Street, Morehead City, NC, U.S.A.

Phone: +1-252-808-6000

 CONSERVATION SOCIETY

The National Parks Service run a number of reserves along this stretch of coastline:

National Parks Service

1401 National Park Drive, Manteo, NC 27954, U.S.A.

Phone: +1-252-473-2111

Web: www.nps.gov/caha/

---

juvenile turtles lurk. The threefold influence of warm water from the south, cold water from the east, and run-off from the land creates the perfect complex base for a rich ecosystem that supports a multitude of animals, large and small.

Enormous shoals of fish, including barracuda and jacks, are resident on the banks, and larger pelagic animals are never far away. Late in the year ragged tooth sharks move in, setting up territories around the many wrecks on the banks that act as natural reefs and caverns. Bull sharks are also present in considerable numbers, as are blue sharks. Loggerhead turtles are frequently encountered, and large crayfish live within many of the wrecks.

THE DIVES

There are riches indeed in terms of marine life, but it is the Outer Banks' well-founded reputation as the "wrecks capital" of North America that draws most divers to the area. The treacherous sandbanks have taken their toll of ships over the years, added to which, in 1942, during the Battle of the Atlantic, the German navy unleashed Operation Drumroll, sending wolfpacks of submarines to attack American shipping along the eastern seaboard. Caught unawares, the United States lost more than 300 ships before reacting to the threat. The evidence of this campaign now litters the seabed in the form of the wrecks of both merchant vessels and German submarines.

Many of the techniques of modern technical diving were developed here in order to cope with the problems of exploring deep wrecks in cool water, strong currents, and with occasional poor visibility. Diving here can be strenuous indeed, and a certain level of experience is required to dive the banks safely. It's a wise move to check this out with your operator before attempting any of the sites—there have already been too many diving dramas on the banks for comfort. Although diving on the banks is thrilling and dramatic, it may not be for everyone.

www.Seapics.com

THE PAPOOSE

• **80 to 125 feet (25 to 35 m)** • **advanced**

A casualty of the murderous U-boat killing spree of 1942, the *Papoose* now lies upside down on the seabed 30 miles (48 km) offshore. She still displays evidence of the torpedo strikes that sank her, but that is far from being her most dramatic feature. For some reason the *Papoose* attracts sand tiger sharks—also known as ragged tooth sharks—and divers almost invariably encounter several of them on a single dive. The trick with the raggies is to let them swim to you; they seem genuinely curious and will approach closely as long as you remain calm and still on the seabed. There are a number of cavernous openings and holds within the wreck itself, and within these there is every chance of encountering substantial groupers.

In the same area as the *Papoose* is the submarine wreck *U-352*, sunk in 1942 as the American navy found an answer to the attacks of the wolfpacks. The U-boat lies in 110 feet (33 m) of water, and is well worth exploring, although currents can be particularly intense in this area.

THE PROTEUS

• **80 to 125 feet (25 to 38 m)** • **advanced**

Another gathering point for raggies, the *Proteus* is a large steamship that sank after a collision in 1918. Her stern is mostly intact, with a number of small openings and swim-throughs that provide cover for a variety of local marine life. Look out for stingrays on the sand around the wreck, and of course aggregations of sharks toward the end of the year.

OTHER ACTIVITIES

This beautiful stretch of wild coastline extends for 130 miles (210 km), 70 percent of it protected by some form of legislation—there are six national parks and wildlife reserves within the Outer Banks. The highest sand dune on the Atlantic coast—so big you can hang-glide off it—is also here. All in all, a paradise for the wilderness and nature lover.

☎ TELEPHONE NUMBERS

Recompression chamber	+1-919-684-8111
Hospital	+1-252-247-1439
Tourism Organization	+1-800-847-4862

🖥 WEBSITES & E-MAIL

Tourism information	www.outerbanks.org
Government site	www.ncgov.com
Tourism Organization	www.visitnc.com

▼ SEA HORSE

Sea horses can be observed in some numbers in the shallow sheltered regions inshore, within the protection of the Banks system.

www.Seapics.com

GANSBAAI

ONE CREATURE ALONE, THE UNQUESTIONED TOP PREDATOR OF THE OCEANS, DRAWS DIVERS TO THE GANSBAAI REGION OF SOUTH AFRICA'S WESTERN CAPE, AND ESPECIALLY TO DYER ISLAND. GANSBAAI IS ONE OF THE GREAT WHITE SHARK CAPITALS OF THE WORLD.

 VISIBILITY

25 to 70 feet (8 to 20 m). Best from June–Sept

 MUST SEES

Great white sharks

Seal nursery

 DOWNSIDE

Cold water

Limited visibility

No guarantee star attraction will turn up

 GETTING THERE

Scheduled flight to Cape Town, then a leisurely 3-hour drive to Gansbaai, a distance of approximately 100 miles (160 km), taking in some of the most spectacular coastal scenery in South Africa en route. Most operators will arrange an airport pickup for groups.

 VISA

Visitors from the U.S., U.K., and most European countries do not need visas for holiday stays of up to 90 days; other nationalities may be limited to 30 days or require a visa. Check with a South African embassy before leaving.

 MONEY

Local currency is the rand. Changing money is not a problem in South Africa, and most towns have A.T.M.s that accept all major cards.

T he stretch of the South African Cape coastline where Gansbaai is located, washed by the cold, oxygen-rich waters of the Benguela Current, has beautiful reefs teeming with life. Such profusion of creatures sustains healthy numbers of large predators higher up the food chain, such as cape fur seals. But it is the great white shark, at the apex of the chain, that attracts divers here from all over the world.

GEOGRAPHY

The peaceful fishing village of Gansbaai lies in the Overberg region of Western Cape, some 2 hours' drive from Cape Town, 110 miles (180 km) away. The feature that makes this area of coastline a magnet for white sharks is Dyer Island, a long flat sandy island with occasional patches of grass and rocky outcrops. To the south is the stark Geyser Rock, a site favored by cape fur seals.

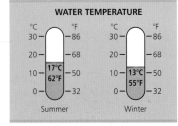

WATER TEMPERATURE

°C	°F	°C	°F
30 –	– 86	30 –	– 86
20 –	– 68	20 –	– 68
10 –	**17°C** – 50	10 –	**13°C** – 50
	62°F		**55°F**
0 –	– 32	0 –	– 32
Summer		Winter	

Monty Halls

► **BIG BITE**

The first sight of a great white taking a bait makes a lasting impression on the observer.

Mikayo Langhofer

WALKER
BAY

SOUTH AFRICA

Gansbaai ●   **Baardskeerdersbos** ●

Danger
Point

| 0 | 10 km |
| 0 | 7 mi |

Seal Alley ●   Pearly
Beach

Dyer
Island

Shell
Point

Quoin
Point

◄ **DYER ISLAND**
An ideal breeding ground for cape fur seals,
Dyer Island is a long flat sandy island with
many offshore rocky outcrops.

The waters around this island and rocky outcrop are the stage for a predatory relationship that has been played out for thousands of years. A significant feature of the underwater topography is a deep-water channel running to the north of the main island, while both the north and south coasts are areas of relatively shallow water cloaked by dense kelp beds. These gently sloping areas, particularly in the southwest of the island, act as nursery areas for the seal pups. Predating them are the great white sharks who use the deep-water channel to ambush unwary victims. Here they can gain the terrific momentum needed to surprise any seals that are inexperienced or sick enough to venture out into what local people have termed the "killing zone".

MARINE LIFE

Up to 10,000 cape fur seal pups are born late in the year on Dyer Island, turning the sloping coasts into a giant crèche, while the adults forage far from their island base for food, sometimes heading as much as 30 miles (50 km) out to sea. The great whites that cruise the waters around the islands are present all year round, but their numbers peak in the period from May to September.

Adult cape fur seals are huge animals, measuring up to 9 feet (3 m) in length and weighing 700 lbs (317 kg). Although the sharks do attack large adults, their main predatory activity takes place on the pups. Adult males sparring for territory frequently injure young seals, and these injured animals may well fall victim to the ever-watchful sharks. Other victims may simply stray into the killing zone through inexperience or foolhardiness. An explosive ambush follows, during which the shark sometimes leaps completely out of the water in its final lethal rush. Such scenes have made Gansbaai an iconic site for wildlife photographers.

The sharks around the island are mostly in the region of 6 to 12 feet (1.8 to 3.6 m) long, although larger individuals are occasionally sighted. The maximum size of the great white is subject to great conjecture and is prone to anecdotal evidence. Tales are told of 21-feet (7-m) monsters cruising these waters, and even of a 24-feet (8-m) specimen sighted in False Bay in 2002. What can be stated without shadow of doubt is that the sharks are present in these waters in very great numbers, making Gansbaai and Dyer Island one of the few areas in the world where divers are almost guaranteed a sighting of these awesome animals.

The rich waters around the island are also home to cat sharks and shy sharks, as well as sand tigers and bronze whalers. Butterfly rays are also occasionally seen in groups cruising the seafloor. On the island itself there are colonies of jackass penguins and extremely large numbers of cormorants.

THE DIVES

A lot of passion and debate is spent on the emotive issue of baiting for great white sharks. Does the act of using bait to draw them towards the boat and watching them from the safety of a cage change the behavior of the sharks? Does it lead to a natural association between boats and food? Does it show a lack of respect for this magnificent predator? Such questions are all perfectly valid, but what is undeniable is that the great white sharks of Gansbaai are safer now than they have ever been. They are a valuable resource, fiercely protected by a local population who are maximizing the potential of this international attraction found swimming off their shores.

South Africa was the first country to declare the great white shark a protected species in 1991, and the majority of operators around Dyer Island take a responsible attitude to the sharks, viewing them with enormous affection and pride. There are, however, a small number of less scrupulous operators, and divers are advised to take a little time to research their guides before committing themselves to any trip.

The area within 1,640 feet (500 m) of Dyer Island has been declared a Nature Reserve by the provincial government of the Western Cape. Baiting within this

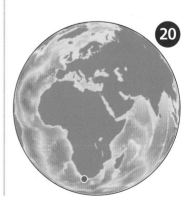

20

► GREAT WHITE SHARK
The unmistakable shape of a great white shark turning towards you is enough to make anyone's heart race.

 DIVE CENTERS

DIVE SOUTH
P.O. Box 38890, Faerie Glen 0043,
South Africa
Phone: +27-12-991-3134
E-mail: info@divesouthafrica.co.za
Web: www.divesouth.co.za

SHARK BOOKINGS
A co-operative booking site that gives access to all the major operators in Gansbaai. Of these, Marine Dynamics and the White Shark Diving Company are highly recommended.
Phone: +44-871-474-1821
E-mail: enquiries@sharkbookings.com
Web: www.sharkbookings.com

 DIVING ORGANIZATIONS
N.A.U.I. Services of Southern Africa
40 Gordonia Centre Beach Road,
Gordons Bay 7139, South Africa
Phone: +27-21-856-5184
E-mail: info@nauisa.org
Web: www.nauisa.org

 RECOMPRESSION
Cape Town National Hyperbarics operates a twinlock multiplace walk-in chamber at:
Cape Town National Hyberbarics
Kleinmont Hospital, Botrivier Road,
Cape Town, South Africa
Phone: +27-21-671-8655 (24 Hours)

 HOSPITAL
Hermanus Private Hospital
Hospital Street, Cape Town, South Africa
Phone: +27-28-313-0168

Hermanus Provincial Hospital
Hospital Street, Cape Town, South Africa
Phone: +27-28-312-1166

 CONSERVATION SOCIETY
The Shark Trust
National Marine Aquarium, The Rope Walk, Coxside, Plymouth, PL4 0LF, U.K.
Phone: +44-870-128-3045
Web: www.sharktrust.org

The Natal Sharks Board is an internationally recognized body that monitors shark diving in South Africa:
The Natal Sharks Board
1a Herrwood Drive, Umhlanga,
KwaZulu-Natal, South Africa
Phone: +27-31-566-0400
Web: www.shark.co.za

zone is strictly controlled, and the legislation permitting cage-diving activities within this area is extremely tight. There is a strong feeling among the more respectable operators that to allow persistent free-swimming activities with the great whites may well lead to a tragic incident in the near future, resulting in draconian measures being imposed by the South African government. Cage diving with great white sharks at Gansbaai may therefore have a limited future.

CAGE DIVING

• 6 feet (2 m) • beginner

It is best to make a whole day of the trip, as the sharks do not always co-operate and many tales are told of sitting in a rocking boat for days on end, the air heavy with the smell of greasy chum, and not a shark to be seen. After anchoring off the island, the operators throw out the chum (chopped up fish used for bait) to create a slick that stretches off into the current, and await the arrival of the main attraction.

The experienced shark boats lower the cage into the water before any animals arrive, as great whites are tremendously cautious and would possibly disappear should the cage hit the water after their arrival. Once a shark has made several passes at the bait, the divers are placed in the cage, most of the operators using hookah gear to supply air. Then it is simply a case of peering into the gloom, and waiting. No amount of research

Mikayo Langhofer

acrobatic young seals. David Doubilet, legendary underwater photographer, described this as the greatest seal dive on the planet, and the activity is indeed relentless. The young seals are completely fearless, mouthing the divers' equipment and pirouetting around them throughout the dive. The local operators are happy to dive this area as it is shallow, and the perceived wisdom is that the great whites do not hunt here. But it is a relatively new site, and the decision to dive may be easier for some to make than others!

OTHER ATTRACTIONS

Gansbaai itself is fairly sleepy, although quite charming in its own way. There are some lovely walks along this stretch of coastline, and the region is quite safe. Hermanus, a short drive west, is one of the whale-watching capitals of the world.

TELEPHONE NUMBERS

Recompression chamber	+27-21-671-8655
Hospital	+27-28-313-0168
Department of Environmental Affairs & Tourism	+27-12-310-3911

WEBSITES & E-MAIL

Tourist information	www.aboutcapetown.com
Travel information	www.go2cape.com

DIVER'S TIP

Make sure you explore the coast around Gansbaai for the beautiful cold water reefs in the area.

▼ SEAL PUPS
A diver is mobbed by seal pups in the kelp beds around Dyer Island.

Monty Halls

can prepare you for your first encounter with a great white shark underwater. The creature's massive bulk, the intelligence behind the dark eyes, the power, and easy elegance are all beyond words.

SEAL ALLEY

• 25 feet (8 m) • beginner

To the northeast of Dyer Island is a large flat area of sand covered in dense kelp forests. As soon as the dive boat drops anchor in this area, it is immediately surrounded by hundreds of juvenile fur seals. The divers enter the water and descend to the seafloor—a natural amphitheater with a white sand floor and walls of giant kelp stalks— where they are surrounded on all sides by

MEDITERRANEAN SEA

The Mediterranean Sea is in essence a vast bowl that plunges to depths of more than 3 miles (5 km) at its deepest point and stretches for 2,500 miles (4,000 km) from west to east. It is 11 million sq miles (29 million sq km) in extent, has an average depth of 4,700 feet (1,430 m), and contains 10 million cubic miles (42 million cubic km) of water. In the west, it is connected with the Atlantic Ocean by the Strait of Gibraltar, in the northeast with the Black Sea by the Bosporus, and in the southeast with the Red Sea by the Suez Canal.

The seafloor of the Mediterranean is by no means even and the basin falls into two distinct regions, divided by the Sicilian Channel. Large abyssal plains characterize the western half, and the Mediterranean Ridge System dominates the eastern half. The continental shelf extending from the shoreline to depths of 656 feet (200 m) and beyond is extremely narrow throughout the sea. Surface currents tend to originate from the inflow of cold water from the Atlantic through the Strait of Gibraltar, although the islands and rocky peninsulas of the Mediterranean create localized swirls and eddies.

Because of the Mediterranean's basin-like shape, the circulation of cold water from the Atlantic Ocean is limited. Warm salty water, created through evaporation and the lack of freshwater land run-off, sinks and creates deep layers upon which the colder, less saline water entering through the Strait of Gibraltar rests. The cold-water plume thus formed extends for a considerable distance, almost to the halfway point of the Sicilian Channel, and it is no coincidence that some of the sea's best diving sites lie in its path.

By and large, because of the lack of cold upwellings, the waters of the Mediterranean are low in nutrients and oxygen, and consequently lack plankton and plant life, the foundations of the food chain. Although the upside of this is crystal-clear water, the marine life is somewhat impoverished. Indeed, the Mediterranean has been described as a marine desert, largely because of its nutrient-poor waters, but also because the people living around its shores have drawn their livelihoods from it for thousands of years, and the sea is now sadly overfished.

All the same, all is not lost for divers. There are some long-established reserves, mostly those based around rocky islands or bays with ideal topography for encrusting organisms, that support a diversity of marine plants and animals. Scientific evidence is emerging to suggest that certain tropical species are entering the eastern Mediterranean through the Suez Canal, and over the last few years strong evidence has emerged of resident great white shark populations.

Tony White

◄ ANEMONE
The underwater topography of the Mediterranean has helped create a home for some colorful marine life.

MEDAS ISLANDS

AS ONE DIVING JOURNALIST MEMORABLY STATED "IF EVER ONE WONDERED WHERE ALL THE FISH IN THE MEDITERRANEAN HAVE GONE, WELL THEY ARE ALL HERE!" RUGGED TERRAIN, COLD WATER UPWELLINGS, NUTRIENT RICH WATER FROM A NEARBY RIVER, AND A PROTECTED STATUS SINCE 1983, MAKE THE MEDAS ISLANDS A CONTENDER FOR ONE OF THE BEST SITES IN THE MEDITERRANEAN.

 VISIBILITY

Up to 100 feet (30 m) in the summer months; affected by run-off from the River Ter

MUST SEE

Dolphin Cave

DOWNSIDE

Can be crowded in peak season

GETTING THERE

International flights to Barcelona or Gerona, and hire a car from there for the hour's drive to Estartit.

 VISA

Spain is a member of the European Union. Nationals of most countries do not need a visa for tourist visits of up to 90 days.

 MONEY

Currency is the Euro. Credit and debit cards are accepted at most hotels and restaurants.

WATER TEMPERATURE

°C	°F	°C	°F
30	86	30	86
20	68	20	68
25°C 77°F			
10	50	10	50
		13°C 55°F	
0	32	0	32
Summer		Winter	

▶ **DUSKY GROUPER**
Groupers are one of the larger residents of the Medas Islands and can be encountered in reasonable numbers.

Until the early 1980s it looked as if diving in the Medas Islands was going the same way as in so many other regions of the Mediterranean. Due to the combined efforts of local commercial fishermen and the scourge of unregulated recreational spearfishing, it was highly unusual to see any fish around the islands weighing more than 2.5 lbs (1 kg). Then, in 1983, the local people and regional government realized that they were watching the demise of a rare underwater ecosystem on their doorstep. With tremendous forethought, they set up a Nature Reserve and created a fishing preservation area around the islands which, to their credit, is supported by the local fishing community.

David Stephens

GEOGRAPHY

The Medas Islands (Islas Medas) are just 1 mile (1.6 km) from the holiday resort of Estartit on Catalonia's Costa Brava in northeastern Spain. They consist of two main islands—Meda Gran and Meda Petita—as well as numerous craggy outcrops, fissures, and pinnacles. On all but the sheltered western side the sea has eroded the limestone rock of the islands into numerous underwater tunnels, caves, and archways.

A combination of factors make the Medas Islands an outstanding species-rich environment. Firstly, the River Ter drains from the mainland into the sea close to the islands, creating a soup of organic run-off high in nutrients, added to which cold-water upwellings carry nutrients here from further afield—such as the River Rhône in southern France—and also lower the water temperature in the immediate vicinity of the islands, creating an oxygen rich environment.

MARINE LIFE

Justifiably famed as a haven of life in the Mediterranean, the marine life around the Medas Islands is very special indeed. This is one of the few places in Europe where the larger pelagic species are in residence as the foundation of the food chain. Bream and wrasse feed off the heavily colonized walls, drawing in predatory jacks, bonito, large groupers, and shoals of barracuda to circle the islands. Large groups of eagle rays may be seen here, and big Mediterranean moray eels lurk in numerous cracks and crevices.

The cliffs and rocky shelves are a glorious kaleidoscope of encrusting organisms, including multi-colored sponges, healthy red coral aggregations, and large gorgonians. Mixed in among these are some of the largest scorpionfish in the Mediterranean, together with healthy populations of octopus.

THE DIVES

There are five dive operations working on the islands, all strictly regulated by the rules that govern the reserve. A system of color-coded mooring buoys is in use, some for private vessels (which you have to pre-book), and some reserved for the individual dive operations. Divers on the reserve are limited to 400 a day, to a maximum limit of 60,000 a year. Despite these restrictions, this can still be a very busy dive site in the summer months. Rules are strictly enforced, and tales of divers having their equipment confiscated for breaches of regulations are not uncommon. A small fee is charged per dive for upkeep of the reserve and for maintenance of the local recompression chamber.

September is perhaps the best time to visit the Medas Islands, when conditions are still generally good, but towards the tail-end of the really busy diving period. Winds can blow up at any time—the Medas Islands are affected by two main prevailing winds, the Tramontana from the northwest and the Garbi from the southwest, and these can create difficult conditions, reducing visibility, and leading to considerable swells and choppy seas.

El Medellot

Pedra de Deu

El Salpatrot

Meda Gran

Punta de la Galeta

MEDAS ISLANDS
(Spain)

Dolphin Cave

Meda Petita

Tascons Grossos

Les Ferranelles

Carall Bernat

Tascó Petit

0   0.5 km

0   0.4 mi

▼ SCORPIONFISH

A scorpionfish is well disguised as it lurks among the colorful reef walls so characteristic of the islands.

John Bantin

► RED CORAL

Large clumps of red coral grow in the optimum low-light conditions created by overhangs and caves.

John Bantin

DIVE CENTERS

XALOC DIVING CENTER S.L.
c/o Eivissa 1, 17258 L' Estartit,
Gerona, Catalonia, Spain
Phone: +34-972-752-071
E-mail: info@xalocdive.com
Web: www.xalocdive.com

CALYPSO DIVING INTERNATIONAL
P.O. Box 148, 17258 L'Estartit,
Gerona, Catalonia, Spain
Phone: +34-972-751-488
E-mail: calypso@grn.es
Web: www.grn.es/calypso/english.html

DIVING ORGANIZATIONS

F.E.D.A.S. (Federación Española de
Actividades Subacuáticas)
c/o Santaló,15 301a, 08021 Barcelona, Spain
E-mail: fedas@fedas.es
Web: www.fedas.es/index.htm

RECOMPRESSION

Hospital de Palamós
36, 17230 Palamós, Gerona, Spain
Phone: +34-972-600-160

HOSPITAL

Hospital de Palamós
36, 17230 Palamós, Gerona, Spain
Tel: +34-972-600-160
or +34-972-600-620 (urgent enquiries)

CONSERVATION SOCIETY

Oficina del Área Protegida de las Illes Medes
Passeig del Molinet, s/n, 17258 L'Estartit, Spain
Phone: +34-972-751-103
This office must be contacted if you are
planning to dive the islands without using a
local operator.

OTHER DIVE SITE

Tascó Petit

Most of the dives are within the 30 to 80 feet (10 to 25 m) range, and are relatively benign, although one deep wreck a little way from the islands is by any standards an undeniably challenging dive. The islands' caves are what draws many divers to the site; however, once here, they will find so much more to enjoy as the dives provide a glimpse of what the Mediterranean Sea once had to offer in terms of marine life.

DOLPHIN CAVE

• 50 feet (15 m) • intermediate

The single dive for which the islands are particularly famed, the hugely impressive Dolphin Cave—named for the small statue of a dolphin that has been placed close to the entrance—runs all the way through Meda Petita for a distance of 150 feet (45 m) at a maximum depth of 50 feet (15 m). It has become something of a tradition with local divers that they stop to kiss the statue on passing.

In reality, Dolphin Cave is not so much a cave as a huge tunnel. Once the diver's eyes have adjusted to the initial gloom on entry, Dolphin Cave is well illuminated by light filtering in from either entrance. Despite this, if this is your first cave or cavern experience you may find it slightly disconcerting, and it is prudent to take a torch. Look out for the beds of red coral on the walls, thriving in the low-light conditions that are found around the cavernous entrances.

CARALL BERNAT

• 60 feet (20 m) • intermediate

This dive was highlighted by Mediterranean diving guru Egidio Trainito as one of the best in the region, and it fully lives up to his recommendation. Carall Bernat is the eastern of two small islets to the south of the main island group and sits on top of a large rocky platform that shelves gently from 30 to 60 feet (10 to 20 m). The divers circle this large rock during the course of the dive, which offers the opportunity to observe the densely colonized walls and boulder-strewn platform beneath. There is an interesting cavern on the southern edge of the rock, and the many crevices in the walls are inhabited by octopuses, groupers, and Mediterranean morays. Large shoals of bream and both painted comber and less flamboyant comber are present throughout the dive. You may also glimpse beautiful ornate wrasses in the shallower sections of the dive.

OTHER ACTIVITIES

Estartit lies at the northern end of the Costa Brava ("Wild Coast"), much visited by painters in the 1930s and still a popular holiday destination. The resort has a fine beach, charming restaurants, numerous bars, and lively nightlife, but gets rather crowded at the height of the season. Gerona, only 30 miles (48 km) away, is well worth a visit. This beautiful medieval city with a fine cathedral overlooking a winding river has survived a turbulent history. Further north there are Greek and Roman remains at Ampurias, and the Salvador Dali museum at Figueras is a shrine to this eccentric genius.

☎ TELEPHONE NUMBERS

Recompression chamber	+34-972-600-160
Hospital	+34-972-600-100
Tourist Office in Estartit	+34-972-751-910

💻 WEBSITES & E-MAIL

Tourist Office	www.spaintour.com/brava.htm
Tourist information	www.in-spain.info
Travel information	www.spain-info.com

▼ SEABREAM
Dense shoals of seabream offer a glimpse of how the marine life in the Mediterranean used to be.

John Bantin

SARDINIA

 VISIBILITY
60 to 100 feet (18 to 30 m) generally. Winter storms can cloud inshore areas to 20 feet (6 m) or less.

 MUST SEES
Caverns and tunnels at Nereo Cave
KT wreck

 DOWNSIDE
Limited pelagic activity
Some crowded sites

 GETTING THERE
Direct flights from London, Monaco, and Paris; many other major international airports have connecting flights to Sardinia. There are regular internal flights from airports throughout Italy.

 VISA
In general, no visa requirements for visitors entering as tourists for up to 3 months.

$ MONEY
Currency is the Euro. A.T.M.s are available in major towns, and credit cards and traveler's checks are widely accepted.

WATER TEMPERATURE

°C	°F		°C	°F
30 –	– 86		30 –	– 86
20 – **25°C 77°F**	– 68		20 –	– 68
10 –	– 50		10 – **14°C 57°F**	– 50
0 –	– 32		0 –	– 32
Summer			Winter	

▶ **RED CORAL**
Sardinia is renowned for its magnificent gardens of red coral.

THE RUGGED MEDITERRANEAN ISLAND OF SARDINIA IS SURROUNDED BY CLEAR WATER AND RIDDLED WITH A HONEYCOMB OF CAVES AND CAVERNS. MANY OF THE WRECKS THAT DOT ITS SHORES ARE ARCHAEOLOGICAL SITES, BUT SOME DATE FROM MORE RECENT TIMES AND CAN BE ACCESSED BY DIVERS.

Sardinia is a wild island of rugged cliffs, craggy mountains cloaked in thick scrub, and a stark shoreline pitted with caves and gullies. Its long history goes back to the Bronze Age, and it was invaded and ruled by many peoples in turn including Carthaginians, Romans, and Vandals. More recently, it played a central role in the creation of a united Italy in the 19th century. The wrecks scattered along the coast bear witness to its checkered past and tell the story of Mediterranean seafaring through the ages.

GEOGRAPHY

The second largest island, after Sicily, in the Mediterranean, Sardinia lies some 115 miles (185 km) west of the Italian peninsula. The island is 160 miles (257 km) long from north to south and 68 miles (109 km) across at its widest point, with a land area of 9,300 sq miles (24,090 sq km). Volcanic in origin, most of the interior is ruggedly mountainous, the highest point being Punta La Marmora at 6,017 feet (1,834 m). Large areas are sparsely inhabited, and more than half of the population of 1.65 million live in the few towns of the coastal region. Cagliari, the capital, is in the south.

The island's geological history is significant for divers. Until relatively recently much of the present seabed was above water, but as the sea level rose—by an estimated 395 feet (120 m) in the last 20,000 years—large caves and caverns carved out of the volcanic rocks through erosion disappeared beneath the water, and fossilized beaches were flooded to depths of 196 feet (60 m) and more. As a result, Sardinia enjoys some of the most dramatic underwater scenery in Europe.

MARINE LIFE

The marine life of Sardinia represents a fascinating mix of influences, reflecting the island's position in the middle of the Mediterranean. Cold-water species from the Atlantic share reefs with warm-water species from the Eastern Mediterranean and with immigrant species

from the Red Sea that are thought to have entered the Mediterranean through the Suez Canal. Divers therefore have the unusual experience of encountering tompot blennies and barracuda on the same dive, alongside conger and moray eels. This same mix of species is replicated on the reef walls, which are a dazzling mix of red coral (for which the island is famed), yellow, orange,

John Bantin

▶ GROUPER
The brown Mediterranean grouper can grow to 110 lb (50 kg) in weight, and is one of the rare large reef dwellers in the region.

 DIVE CENTERS

PRUETT SUB D.S.
c/o Calla Serena Village, Località Geremeas, Cagliari 09046, Sardinia, Italy
Phone: +39-339-218-0621
E-mail: arrigomarendino@hotmail.com

AIR SUB SERVICE
Via Balilla 24, Cagliari (Pirri) 09134, Sardinia, Italy
Phone: +39-070-506-863
E-mail: airsubsv@tin.it
Web: www.airsub.com

CENTRO SUB PORTO ROTONDO
Marina di Portorotondo, Porto Rotondo/Olbia (SS) 07020, Sardinia, Italy
Phone: +39-078-934-869
E-mail: patsub@tiscalinet.it

 DIVING ORGANIZATIONS

None. The Sardinia Tourist Board may be able to recommend reliable operators:
Assessorato al Turismo
Viale Trieste 105, I-09123 Cagliari, Sardinia, Italy
Phone: +39-070-606-280

 RECOMPRESSION

Ospedale Marino
Lungomare Poetto 12, Cagliari, Sardinia, Italy
Phone: +39-070-609-4430

Ospedale Civile P. Merlo
Via A. Magnaghi 67, La Maddalena (SS), Italy
Phone: +39-0789-791-200

A.M.I.
Strada Litoranea, Marina di Sorso, Sassari, Italy
Phone: +39-079-359-008

 HOSPITAL

Macciotta Hospital
Cagliari, Sardinia, Italy
Phone: +39-070-609-3414

Hospital-Accident & Emergency-24 hrs
(Ospedale Civile—Viale Italia)
Phone: +39-079-220-621

CONSERVATION SOCIETY

A special area of protected Mediterranean interest has been set up that covers north Sardinia.
International Cooperation
16, Boulevard de Suisse, MC-98000, Monaco
Phone: +377-9315-8148
E-mail: pvanklaveren@gouv.mc

and pink sponges, and red light bulb sea squirts, creating a gloriously rich habitat.

In common with many other sites in the Mediterranean, the waters around Sardinia have been severely overfished and certain areas are affected by pollution. Nonetheless, it retains an impressive range of marine species. There are six different species of wrasse, two species of comber, some large (but infrequently seen) amberjacks, two species of grouper, triggerfish, cuttlefish, and two species of octopus. Also present is the remarkable noble pen shell, a huge mussel that grows up to 3 feet (1 m) long and can live for 20 years. The island's huge beds of Neptune grass, a type of seagrass, act as a crucial nursery for juvenile fish species. These seagrass beds are generally disregarded by the island's diving community, but they would in all probability make a splendid muck dive, if time were taken to explore them in detail.

THE DIVES

Diving in Sardinia is well-established, and is centered around the caves, caverns, walls, and gullies of the dramatic undersea topography. The island's wrecks are also a great attraction. Much of the diving takes place on the sheltered eastern coast, as the west coast is exposed to the prevailing southwesterly winds. Most of the dives are dramatic caverns and overhangs on heavily colonized reef walls, and although the fish life is reasonable, it is unusual to see anything of any real size. Certain areas around the island are subject to military and archaeological restrictions, particularly off the southwest coast.

LA CITTA DELLE NACCHERE

• 30 feet (10 m) • beginner

As a dive, this actually has very little to recommend it aside from one remarkable feature. The dive site is close to a busy ferry port, and the seabed is scattered with nets, lines, and the detritus of modern man. Standing proud amidst this refuse is a field of fan mussels. This large bivalve, which is now increasingly rare, used to dot the seabed around Sardinia. Egidio Trainito, author of the excellent *Sardinia Diving Guide* describes fan mussels as looking like "the stones of an English cemetery", and the analogy is a good one. The strangely primeval scene that confronts the diver represents one of the largest colonies of fan mussels left on the island. Watch out for overhead boat traffic on this dive.

NEREO CAVE

• 100 feet (30 m) • intermediate to expert

This extraordinary cave, a short distance from Capo Caccia on the northwestern coast, is in fact a substantial network of caverns and tunnels that stretch for more than 1,150 feet (350 m), and demand a diver's respect. The more complex penetrations require appropriate levels of training and planning, but there is also some opportunity here for limited exploration by relative diving novices, with exits available a short distance in from a shallow entrance.

There are essentially three entrances to the cave. The first two are relatively shallow and take the form of cavernous, well-illuminated open areas. The third is at approximately 100 feet (30 m) and leads ultimately to the shallower exits through a series of channels, caverns, and tunnels.

A notable feature of this dive are the beautiful beds of red coral that coat the walls in certain areas. These beds have been extensively harvested to provide coral for the jewelry trade, but they must have presented an awesome sight in their original state.

THE KT

• 70 to 110 feet (20 to 35 m) • intermediate

Probably the best of the many wrecks around Sardinia, this 210-feet (65-m) small German fighting ship sits on the seabed in the Gulf of Orosei on the eastern coast. Sunk by a British submarine in 1943, she is remarkably well preserved, and despite being extensively looted in the past, still has a number of machine guns in place, as well as two large cranes that lie on the seabed alongside. Her stern, which is almost completely intact, pres-

ents a beautiful sight to the descending diver as the vessel sits perfectly upright on her rudder, with her two screws still in place.

Sadly, most of the forward sections are very broken up. However, it is still possible to penetrate the holds and superstructure aft safely, as long as it is done in the company of a knowledgeable local guide. Watch out for what can be a powerful current, particularly in the early stage of the descent and when decompressing at the end of the dive.

OTHER ACTIVITIES

Sardinia's rich history is evident in well-preserved examples of Roman architecture and the eclectic mix of later building styles in the larger towns. You can find out more by visiting the numerous museums dotted around the island. The beaches are justifiably famed; in particular, the Costa Verde resort area in the northeast is still relatively unspoiled if you want to bask and enjoy the Mediterranean sun and holiday lifestyle. For the more adventurous, four-wheel-drive trips can be arranged into the mountains of the interior.

☎ **TELEPHONE NUMBERS**

Recompression chamber	+39-070-609-4430
Hospital	+39-070-609-3414
Tourist office	+39-070-606-7005

💻 **WEBSITES & E-MAIL**

Tourism Organization	www.esit.net
Tourism Organization	www.comune.sassari.it
Travel information	www.discover-sardinia.com

▼ **WRECKS**

The wrecks that dot the coastline of Sardinia are an underwater record of trade in this part of the Mediterranean Sea.

John Bantin

USTICA
ISLAND

 VISIBILITY
Generally good at 60 to 100 feet (18 to 30 m). Winter storms can cloud inshore areas to 20 feet (6 m) or less.

 MUST SEES
The Colombara Bank
Red coral beds

 DOWNSIDE
Can be crowded in peak season
Lack of large pelagics

 GETTING THERE
Flights to Palermo, Sicily, or to Naples on the mainland from most major European hubs, then take a boat to the island (ferries operate from Naples only in summer.)

 VISA
In general, no visa requirements for visitors entering as tourists for up to 3 months.

 MONEY
Currency is the Euro. A.T.M.s are widely available in Italy. Credit cards and traveler's checks are accepted widely around the island.

THIS TINY ISLAND OF RUGGED BAYS AND INLETS, ONCE DESCRIBED BY JACQUES COUSTEAU AS THE MOST BEAUTIFUL ISLAND IN THE MEDITERRANEAN, IS THE SPIRITUAL HOME OF ITALIAN DIVING AND AN ESSENTIAL STOP FOR ANY MEDITERRANEAN DIVING ENTHUSIAST.

John Bantin

WATER TEMPERATURE

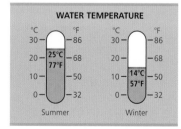

Summer	Winter
25°C / 77°F	14°C / 57°F

▶ **RED CORAL**
Red coral is found in caverns and under overhangs at depths down to 325 feet (100 m).

Ustica Island, northwest of Sicily, was a penal colony until 1950 and housed political prisoners under the Mussolini regime—a grim fate for a beautiful craggy island that is now one of the iconic sites of Italian diving. The island is the home of Italy's Academy for Underwater Sciences and Techniques and is a Marine Reserve. Washed by cold currents flowing from the Atlantic, it has much to offer the visiting diver, including an interesting underwater archaeological trail.

GEOGRAPHY

Lying in the Tyrrhenian Sea some 40 miles (66 km) off the north coast of Sicily, Ustica is tiny, with an area of 3.3 sq miles (8.6 sq km) and a population of only 1,370. There are daily ferries between the Sicilian port of Palermo and Ustica, and during the summer ferries depart three times a week from Naples on the Italian mainland. Part of the outer Sicilian archipelago, the island is the summit of an ancient volcano, its dramatic origins only too plain to see in the dark rocks for which it is named (Ustica derives from the Latin *usta*, meaning a burnt-red color) and in its convoluted coastline of bays, caves, and caverns. This tortuous topography extends some way beneath the surface of the water to create a fascinating marine environment.

MARINE LIFE

Ustica's dramatic underwater topography alone makes for exciting diving, but the excellent marine life around the island is an added bonus. This includes large dusky groupers—the presence of which is an indication that the local ecosystem is particularly healthy according to a recent scientific paper about the area. Turtles and sunfish are sometimes seen, and resident schools of barracuda swirl around local pinnacles and walls.

The colonization of reef walls is very impressive, with beautiful fields of red gorgonians a particularly striking feature at a number of sites. Mixed in with these is the normal range of brightly colored encrusting organisms. Some clue as to how glorious these reefs look in reality can be gleaned from the very names of the sponges— gold sponge, pink tube sponge, orange encrusting sponge, and yellow clathrina among them. Huge meadows of Neptune grass extend down to 130 feet (40 m). These seagrasses are known locally as the "lungs of the sea" because they oxygenate the water.

THE DIVES

The Marine Reserve around Ustica extends seaward for nearly 3.5 miles (5.6 km) and is divided into three separate zones of protection. Zone A in the southeast is the most strongly protected; no fishing and only limited diving activity can take place within an area extending for 1,150 feet (350 m) from the shore. Zones B and C

23

The Colombara Bank

Faraglioni

The Medico Tunnel/
Doctor's Rock

USTICA
(Italy)

Ustica

0   1 km

0   1 mi

John Bantin

► HERMIT CRAB
Large hermit crabs up to 2 inches (6 cm) in length can be found on the reefs around Ustica.

 DIVE CENTERS

BARRACUDA
c/o Lirial Club Punta Spalmatore,
Ustica (PA), Italy
Phone: +39-392-338-6426
E-mail: barracuda.ustica@email.it
Web: www.barracudaustica.com

ALTA MAREA
Località San Ferlicchio,
c/o Hotel Grotta Azzurra, Ustica (PA), Italy
Phone: +39-091-625-4096
E-mail: info@altamareaustica.it
Web: www.altamareaustica.it

 DIVING ORGANIZATIONS

Scuba Schools International Italy
Via Bergami, 40133 Bologna, Italy
Phone: +39-051-383-082
E-mail: info@ssi-italy.org
Web: www.ssi-italy.org

 RECOMPRESSION

Hyperbaric Center A.S.L.
6 Via Petriera, Ustica, Italy
Phone: +39-091-844-9380 or 844-9369

 HOSPITAL

Civico Regionale Generale
Via Carmelo Lazzaro, Ustica, Italy
Phone: +39-091-666-1111

CONSERVATION SOCIETY

Riserva Marina "Isola di Ustica"
c/o Comune di Ustica
Ustica (PA), Italy
Phone: +39-091-844-9456

extend much further from the shoreline, and provide graduated protection. Virtually all fishing activities are allowed in Zone C.

The undersea topography displays a range of caves and craggy reefs typical of a volcanic island. Visibility is generally good, and the walls and platforms around the island give the opportunity for varied dives, from gentle overhangs right through to some true overhead environments. Below the headland at Punta Gavazzi an undersea archaeological trail is clearly marked with buoys, allowing divers to view an interesting variety of artefacts such as anchors and Roman amphorae scattered about the seafloor.

THE MEDICO TUNNEL/DOCTOR'S ROCK

• 100 feet (30 m) • intermediate

Situated approximately 1,640 feet (500 m) off the northwestern coast of Ustica, this dive is immediately next to Zone A, the most heavily protected part of the Marine Reserve, and is one of the most popular dives around the island. The site itself is a stark rocky pinnacle, yet what draws divers in particular is the spectacular tunnel passing through it. This tunnel is approximately 70 feet (21 m) wide, bottoms out at 60 feet (18 m), and runs for at least 150 feet (45 m). It is a spectacular feature, well illuminated by light streaming in at either end, and acts as a perfect site for red gorgonians and coral in the limited light of the entrance caverns. Look out for some large dusky groupers in the

vicinity, vying with barracuda and amberjacks for the baitfish swirling over the busy reef walls. This site undoubtedly benefits from its proximity to Zone A. The spillover of large healthy fish populations is most obviously evident when contrasted with the marine life on dives on the more heavily exploited southern coast.

THE COLOMBARA BANK

• 100 feet (30 m) • intermediate

To the north of the island, about 2,296 feet (700 m) off-shore, is the large shoal that is the Colombara Bank. This site has long been a favorite with visiting divers, and its rich walls and sloping reefs provide the best that Ustica has to offer in terms of variety. Dives traditionally take place on the western and southern edges of the shoal, which rise to within 10 feet (3 m) of the surface. It drops away to the west through a series of steps and mini walls, disappearing off into the gloom at 130 feet (40 m) and beyond. Much of the real action on this dive takes place in the 30 to 60 foot (10 to 20 m) range, beyond the influence of the swells that occasionally batter the rocks, and within the reach of the powerful Mediterranean sunshine.

There are some quite beautiful and very extensive fields of red gorgonians. Their branches held at 90 degrees to the prevailing currents stand out in sharp contrast to the low-lying sponges, sea squirts, and urchins. Wrasses and painted combers move through this dense multicolored forest, while Mediterranean morays lurk within. European barracuda gather here in large shoals, and scorpionfish sit in ambush above crevices that sometimes conceal octopuses. Tuna, turtles, and sunfish have also been observed at this site from time to time.

OTHER ACTIVITIES

Accommodation on the island ranges from hotels and apartments to B&Bs. There is a good choice of restaurants and cafés. To best appreciate the dramatic nature of the coastline you can hire a boat locally that will take you to the more remote caves and small beaches around the island. The Grotta delle Barche can be reached on foot, a beautiful walk through pine forests and hedges of prickly pears.

The archaeological museum on the island has a fascinating range of relics from the island's past, including items from a Bronze Age settlement at Il Faraglioni, excavated about 20 years ago, and objects found in Greek and Roman tombs at Capo Falconiera. On Capo Falconiera itself there are remains of cave settlements dating from the 3rd century B.C., and a stepped path leads up to the ruins of a Spanish Bourbon fortress.

☎ TELEPHONE NUMBERS

Recompression chamber	+39-091-844-9380
Hospital	+39-091-666-1111

🖥 WEBSITES & E-MAIL

Tourist board	www.enit.it
Tourist information	www.italiantourism.com
Dive information	www.sportesport.it
Local information	www.isole-sicilia.it

▼ **AMBERJACK**
Amberjacks are one of the larger fish that can be found swimming the waters around Ustica.

John Bantin

CROATIA

words by Rebecca Corbally

WITH SURPRISINGLY GOOD VISIBILITY THE ADRIATIC IS LITTERED WITH RELICS OF WAR AND TRADE AS WELL AS A MYRIAD OF CAVERNS, MAZES AND CAVES TO KEEP DIVERS OCCUPIED.

VISIBILITY

Surprisingly clear and in good conditions it can be up to 130 feet (40 m), but can close in.

MUST SEES

Wrecks and caves abound here so get to one.

DOWNSIDE

Transport links aren't the best, especially in the south

GETTING THERE

www.aircroatia.com

VISA

No

MONEY

Kuna (HRK)

► **FOLLOW ME**

Descending into the Blue Hole.

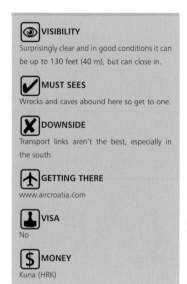

Croatia Divers

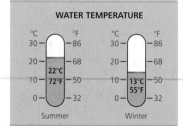

WATER TEMPERATURE

°C	°F		°C	°F
30 —	— 86		30 —	— 86
20 —	— 68		20 —	— 68
22°C			**13°C**	
10 — **72°F**	— 50		10 — **55°F**	— 50
0 —	— 32		0 —	— 32
Summer			Winter	

Croatia is located in the western Balkans between Bosnia, Herzegovina and Slovenia. It borders the Adriatic Sea and as such the coastal areas have a distinctly Mediterranean climate, while most inland areas experience short, cool summers and long, severe winters. The local terrain is quite diverse given the size of the country and there are flat plains along the Hungarian border where much of the farming goes on. Low rolling mountains climb to the highlands near the Adriatic coastline giving it a dramatic and somewhat desolate beauty.

GEOGRAPHY

Its geographical location gives it control over most land routes from Western Europe to the Aegean Sea and the Turksish Straits, and for centuries the Adriatic provided the most obvious and direct route from the Croatian Med through to the more populated northern and central European mainland for traders and cargo ships.

As a result of wars and the ancient trading routes, the sea is littered with relics of a bygone age; large cargo ships with scattered cargo, fighter planes, torpedo carriers, and a mass of broken pottery being fairly easy finds. As well as this treasure trove of twisted metal, it's common to stumble across a diver maze made from an often intricate design of natural caves, caverns, rocky outcrops and shelves as well as large boulders that have crashed to the seabed leaving gaps and channels to explore. Despite the sometimes spartan marine life, there is always a lot to see.

After the wars calmed in Bosnia and Croatia in the late 1990s, diving these waters reappeared on the more intrepid diver's hit list and rightly so. With over 3,100

CROATIA

Cres and Kvarner Bay

Istra •

✈
☩⊕
Split
•

Blue Hole •

24

miles (5,000 km) of coastline and 1,000 islands, this is arguably one of the finest of the Mediterranean waters for wrecks and visibility.

MARINE LIFE

The underwater environment is typically Mediterranean, composed of intimidating walls, striking drop-offs, caverns, crevices and wrecks, all holding a certain craggy beauty awash with marine life. There is often great visibility for the Mediterranean, and many of the walls are bursting with magenta and fawn-colored gorgonians and wafting anemones. Shrimps, nudibranchs, octopus and large grouper are common sights as are conger eels hiding deep in wrecks, moray eels and the more unusual fork beard. There are turtles and scorpionfish if you're lucky, and some impressive and territorial lobster can be seen on most dives.

The larger of the grouper and other pelagic fish are more regularly seen just off the lip of a drop-off around the 65 foot (20 m) mark. Occasionally you will also spot hunting shoals of great amberjack and tuna.

THE DIVES

Easily one of the most indented coastlines in the world with the largest island being Cres, the largest peninsulas Istria and Peljesac, and the largest bay is Kvarner Bay. There are thousands of dive sites now established and in active use, many including wrecks with often harrowing stories to tell. There is an abundance of deeper wrecks—over 130 feet (40 m)—for the more experienced diver, as well as some technical diving opportunities on the deeper accessible wrecks.

THE NORTH
CRES AND KVARNER BAY

• 0 to 180 feet (0 to 55 m) • intermediate to advanced

Lina is a 230-foot (70 m) Italian merchant ship. One night in 1912, while transporting wood from Rijeka to Sicily, the ship cruised silently into deep fog, hit a shallow reef and went down. It now lies conveniently by

Croatia Divers

◀ **A DECAYING WRECK**
One of the many relics that litter the seabed and are symptomatic of more turbulent times.

DIVE CENTERS

There are over 120 dive centers and a full list can be found at www.diving-hrs.hr. Many dive centers won't run without a certain number of divers, and some aren't open all summer. Check out www.croatiadivers.com and www.korcula-diving.com

DIVING ORGANIZATIONS

It is recommended to dive with a professional outfit as some areas are under the supervision of the Ministry of Culture and the National Parks of Brijuni, Kornati and Mljet, and centers are required to have appropriate permits.

You'd be advised to check the dive center is a well run and reputable operation that adheres to standards and offers quality and service. Without correct permits, the tourist diver could be in real difficulties with the authorities.

In addition to areas requiring special permits, there are no-diving zones, including those around anchored warships and near guarded military facilities on the coast. Always check before diving.

RECOMPRESSION

Hyperbaric chambers are located in Split, in Pula and Zagreb. Rescue services are linked with helicopter units in the event of an emergency.

In the event of a diving accident contact should be made with the Centre for Search and Rescue at Sea in Rijeka, free-phone 9155, and follow the instructions.

CONSERVATION SOCIETY

There are eight national parks with more in the pipeline; included are coastline, sea and reefs, and it is estimated that 9 percent of the entire country is now under protection.
Many dive sites featuring wrecks are protected as cultural heritage sites under the watchful eye of the Ministry for Culture, and to dive here you must dive with a licensed and official dive center.

OTHER DIVE SITES

Cathedral, Vela Luka
Bijelac, Lastovo
Susac, Lastovo
B-72 The Flying Fortress, Vis
U-57

the shore facing the land, and though its bow is at an accessible depth of 90 feet (28 m), its stern is right down at 180 feet (55 m). With clear water it's important you aren't seduced out of your depth.

The hull is well preserved, but predictably all wooden structures including the decks have completely decayed revealing cavernous cargo holds that are now empty but easy to imagine packed full of goods. Still in an impressive state decades on, its location and depth means it can often be found in waters of excellent visibility. Even the novice diver can enjoy the thrill from relative shallows.

ISTRA

• 0 to 130 feet (0 to 40 m) • intermediate to advanced

Another impressive site in the Northern Adriatic is the wreck of the Austro-Hungarian passenger ship, the *Baron Gautsch*. It met its doom in a minefield in 1914 taking many innocent lives down with it.

Its final voyage—ferrying passengers between Dalmatia and Trieste—came to a terrifying and tragic end in the waters west of the Brijuni islands in a freshly laid minefield designed to defend the naval port of Pula. Lying now immediately before Rovink, the 275-foot (84 m) long bulk was scarred and damaged by the blow and, subsequently, by irresponsible divers scavenging for trophies and souveniers.

Thankfully today it is protected by the Ministry of Culture and diving is possible with a reputable center organizing specific trips. The upper deck sits at an accessible depth of 90 feet (28 m) while the lower deck is at 120 feet (36 m) and the hull is around 140 feet (42 m), so the wreck in its entirety is within most fairly experienced divers' grasp. The wreck is rated as one of the finest by dive centers operating in the area and is suitable for those with some experience.

THE SOUTH
BLUE HOLE, KORCULA

• 30 to 115 feet (9 to 35 m) • beginner

Situated on the west side of Korcula Island close to the town of Vela Luka sits this stunning spot, arguably one of the best dives in the south. The dive begins by dropping down to a wall that starts around 30 feet (9 m), continuing to 115 feet (35 m), and is full of red gorgonians covered in smatterings of mermaid's purses. It's common to see hunting tuna here and the crevices are alive with lobsters.

As you make your way through the dive you come across a cave at 52 feet (16 m), which is about 13 feet (4 m) across and 10 feet (3 m) high. You fin inside and move along the tunnel toward the light streaming down from above. All the while you are flanked by caverns full of small shrimp dancing on anemones and on the walls above your head the langoustines and slipper lobster dash away from your exploding bubbles. Scanning with your flashlight you'll see the encrusted walls bright with an explosion of red soft coral, so watch your buoyancy here.

In the very center of the cave you can see the swollen boulders lying in a heap—evidence of the collapsed roof. At the back of the cave there is another tunnel entrance, but this one sits in complete darkness hiding a giant grouper and many more excitable shrimp. It is best to go in two at a time for reasons of space. Once the dive is over you make your way out at the cave's exit, which sits directly above the entrance in 15 feet (5 m) of water. This is an exceptional dive, well worth tracking down.

OTHER ACTIVITIES

Among the other usual activities available most notably sailing, the advice is to take the non-adrenaline option of visiting the Plitvicka Jezera (Plitvice Lakes) which is in the UNESCO Register of World Natural Heritage and, as such, is a suitably impressive and popular non-dive day out.

Sixteen peculiar little lakes are interconnected with waterfalls made largely from deposits of an indigenous local limestone. It is all shrouded in a dense virgin forest of beech, fir and spruce that is inhabited by brown bears. Panoramic trains and electric boats cruise around transporting visitors throughout its surreal and delightful borders.

☎ **TELEPHONE NUMBERS**

Recompression chamber	FREEPHONE 9155

🖥 **WEBSITES & E-MAIL**

Croatian National Tourist Board	+385-1-4699-333
E-mail: info@htz.hr, www.croatia.hr	
Diving Tourism Group	+385-(0)21-321-118
E-mail: ikulis@hgk.hr	
Croatian Diving Association	+385-1-4847-582
E-mail: info@diving-hrs.hr	
Institute for Maritime and Hyperbaric	+385-(0)21-354-511
Chambers Seat, Split	
Polyclinic for Baromedicine OXY	+385-(0)1-2902-300
Pula Seat: Zagreb	
E-mail poliklinika.zg@oxy.hr	
Centre for search and rescue at sea Seat, Rijeka	+385-9155
E-mail	mrcc@pomorstvo.hr
Dive insurance and advice	www.daneurope.org

▲ **COLORFUL LIFE**
Macro life on most dives is rife and for the observant, vibrant colorful nudibranchs can often be spotted.

DIVER'S TIP

Every diver must purchase a diving card, which is issued by the Croatian Diving Association and obtained through diving clubs and centers along the coast. The card is issued to those with valid qualifications and is current for 365 days from the date of issue for a fee of 100 Kuna.

Individual diving is carried out on the basis of obtaining permission from the port authorities and costs 2,400 Kuna for one year. The individual must hold a valid qualification as well as a valid diving card.

THE ZENOBIA

TAKE A LOOK FROM THE LEFTHAND WINDOW OF YOUR AIRPLANE AS IT COMES IN TO LAND AT LARNACA INTERNATIONAL AIRPORT. IF IT IS A CLEAR DAY, YOU MAY BE LUCKY ENOUGH TO CATCH A GLIMPSE OF A MASSIVE PASSENGER FERRY LYING ON ITS SIDE ON THE SEABED. THIS IS THE ZENOBIA, A WRECK THAT DRAWS DIVERS TO CYPRUS FROM ALL OVER THE WORLD.

The *Zenobia*, a newly-built roll-on, roll-off truck-carrying ferry, was on its maiden voyage from Kopor, Sweden, to Cyprus in June 1980 when disaster struck. As the ship was making its way toward Larnaca harbor in the small hours of the morning, one of the officers demonstrated the autopilot to a passenger. The ship's officers had already raised concerns about the vessel's stability and the reliability of the autopilot—fears that proved all too correct as the ferry keeled over and ended up at an angle of 40° with her starboard propeller completely clear of the water. Frantic efforts to right her over the course of the next few days failed, and on June 7th she sank beneath the waves even as a pilot boat was racing toward her to tow her to shallow water. More than 100 trucks still remained on board.

GEOGRAPHY

The wreck of the *Zenobia* lies just outside the harbor entrance to the ancient port of Larnaca on the southeastern coast of the popular holiday island of Cyprus in the east Mediterranean Sea. Although Cyprus has a good number of dive sites, with clear water, mild temperatures, and some interesting caverns and reefs, the *Zenobia* is the only one that that merits the description of world-class. The cavernous holds and mazelike passageways of this large vessel, 541 feet (165 m) long, 75 feet (23 m) wide, and displacing 10,528 tonnes, make her one of the finest wreck dives in Europe.

MARINE LIFE

Marine life is sparse in the waters around Cyprus, although the *Zenobia* acts as a beacon for what little there is in the area off Larnaca harbor. Barracuda and

Dan Burton

groupers are frequently sighted around the wreck, as well as smaller species of multicolored wrasse. Marine growth on the wreck seems to consist entirely of a coating of fibrous brown and green algae.

THE DIVES

The *Zenobia* offers a complete range of dives suitable for all levels of experience, from gentle exterior explorations on the top of the wreck at 59 feet (18 m) through to technical penetrations of the lower hatches that lie close to the seabed at 141 feet (43 m).

Some of the dives on the *Zenobia* are a great draw for those wishing to try penetration diving for the first time in the company of suitably qualified guides. The penetration dives include the cavernlike spaces of the main vehicle deck, long passages and cluttered smaller spaces such as the bridge and accommodation area, and finally some tricky overhead environments like the engine room, requiring complex penetration techniques.

0   60 km
0   40 mi

CYPRUS

NICOSIA
Baths of Aphrodite
Devil's Head
Famagusta
Larnaca
The Zenobia
Achileas
Mismayola Reef
Limassol
Aphrodite Park
Jubilee Shoals
Twin Rocks
Shark Cove

DIVER'S TIP

Take a redundant air system when diving the *Zenobia*. Out-of-air situations due to equipment failure in the heart of this wreck are no fun!

◄ **LIFEBOAT**
A diver drifts over one of *Zenobia's* lifeboats, still hanging from the davits.

Dan Burton

► **THE BRIDGE**
A diver emerges from the *Zenobia* with the bridge towering above him.

 DIVE CENTERS

VIKING DIVERS
Ithakis 2, 6500 Larnaca-Dekelia Road
P.O. Box 42589, Larnaca, Cyprus
Phone: +357-24-644-676
E-mail: vdivers@spidernet.com.cy
Web: www.viking-divers.com

EASY DIVERS (AYIA NAPA & PROTARAS)
P.O. Box 30459, 5344 Ayia Napa, Cyprus
Phone: +357-121-288-2850
E-mail: Dive@EZDivers.com
Web: www.EZDivers.com

SUNFISH DIVERS LTD
P.O. Box 30274, 5342 Agia Napa, Cyprus
Phone: +357-23-721-300
E-mail: sunfish@cytanet.com.cy
Web: www.sunfishdivers.com

ALOHA DIVERS
Georgiou A' 4E, Potamos Yermasoyia,
3820 Limassol, Cyprus
Phone: +357-25-313-208
E-mail info@alohadivers.om
Web: www.alohadivers.com

 DIVING ORGANIZATIONS
None

 RECOMPRESSION
There are two recompression chambers on the island, one in Limassol in the British Forces Hospital, and the other in Larnaca General Hospital, where they offer free diving accident treatment.
Phone: +357-24-800-500

 HOSPITAL
Lefkosia General Hospital
Phone: +357-22-801-400
or +357-22-806-680 (Emergency)

Lemesos General Hospital
Phone: +357-25-801-100

Larnaca General Hospital
Phone: +357-24-800-500

 CONSERVATION SOCIETY
Cyprus Conservation Foundation
P.O. Box 50257, 3602 Limassol, Cyprus
Phone: +357-25-358-632
E-mail: info@terracypria.org
The Cyprus Conservation Foundation is a charitable trust incorporated in 1992. It aims to promote environmental and conservation education and awareness among today's decision-makers and young Cypriots.

After a series of tragic incidents, the *Zenobia* is now well buoyed with three shot lines, and also has a number of decompression trapezes. In addition, most operators hang a decompression cylinder beneath their boat as a standard precaution. If you are penetrating the wreck and this cylinder is not present, don't hesitate to point it out to the operator.

VEHICLE DECK ONE

• **70 to 90 feet (20 to 27 m)** • **intermediate**

This is the upper vehicle deck on the *Zenobia* and is best entered through the huge stern doors, still hanging on their hinges, close to the central shot line. You enter the hold to find yourself swimming above the tangled remains of the trucks, lying with their loads spewed out all around, just as they fell in 1980.

This is a genuine overhead environment dive, albeit a relatively safe one as the divers are never out of sight of the exit point, even if it is a considerable distance away for much of the dive. However, it should be stressed that there is no clear line to the surface at any point along the deck. The exit point is a small hatch located in the far bulkhead and it draws the divers along like a beacon as they travel the length of the vehicle deck, some 245 feet (75 m) long—a considerable distance to be under overhead cover.

VEHICLE DECK TWO

• **72 to 98 feet (22 to 30 m)** • **advanced**

This dive is considerably more demanding than the upper vehicle deck, and should only be undertaken by appropriately qualified divers. The entry point is a relatively small hatch on the port side of the vessel about 164 feet (50 m) back from the bow. On entering this hatch be aware of the large pool of oil that has collected in the top of this small compartment—many a diver has come up with a neat plimsoll line of vintage 1980 diesel across his or her kit.

Turn left after squeezing through this hatch, and descend through the gap between the bulkhead and the ladder in front of you. You are now in the lower vehicle hold. You must make sure to tie off at this point, as well as marking the exit with a strobe or light stick. The hold itself is completely contained—this small gap is the only entry and exit point—and it is an elephants' graveyard of jumbled trucks with the occasional poignant small personal possession scattered among the wreckage. Turn for home with ample air—exiting through the gap can be tricky, and you should aim to find yourself outside the wreck with enough air remaining for a leisurely ascent.

THE BRIDGE

- 60 to 130 feet (20 to 40 m) • beginner–advanced

Descend on the bowline, and then work your way over to the upper (starboard) side of the bridge. This is a relatively easy dive as the exit and entry points are the main windows of the bridge, and most of them have been pushed out to allow divers access. As the *Zenobia* is lying on her port side, the diver effectively drops down the length of the bridge floor on the descent and must take care to avoid cables and jumbled wreckage. Divers have the option of descending to considerable depth on this dive as the port side of the bridge lies almost on the sea floor.

THE ACCOMMODATION

- 70 to 85 feet (18 to 25 m) • intermediate

This is another relatively safe dive, although there are places during the diver's progress through the passenger accommodation areas where there is no direct line to the surface. These are not of long duration, however, as most of the windows overhead have been broken to allow exit at various points along the route. It is worth noting that some of these windows are relatively small, so they can be something of a tight squeeze for anyone wearing a twin set.

To reach the accommodation, you descend the amidships shot line, and then swim toward the bow, where you make your way in through a large U-shaped passageway. Your journey toward the stern takes you through the jumbled remains of soft furnishings—you can make out the large prints still fastened to what used to be the lounge walls. Watch out for the presence of silt and loose debris, which may be unstable.

THE ENGINE ROOM

- 125 feet (38 m) • expert

This is a serious dive. The entry point is a small hatch located at 125 feet (40 m), and the engine room itself is a complex, silty, pitch-black space. For safe penetration, you must lay lines and use lights to clearly mark the entry and exit point.

Enter the first car deck and head towards the stern. After traveling 165 feet (50 m) or so you will see a small hatch 5ft x 4ft (1.5 x 1.2 m) on the lefthand side. This gives you access to the engine room, where you will observe the port engine. To explore the more interesting aspects of the engine room, such as ladders, pipes, generators, and so on, you have to ascend within a very confined space. You then have to descend again to exit the engine room at the original entry point. This complex multi-level dive takes place in a completely sealed environment. It requires expert diving skills, and should not be lightly undertaken.

OTHER ACTIVITIES

Larnaca is a lively holiday port, with a good range of hotels offering watersports and other activities. For the young at heart, the nearby town of Aiya Napa is one of the party capitals of Europe. The island of Cyprus itself is a well-established holiday location. It has a rich cultural heritage dating back to Greek and Roman times. It is well worth taking advantage of your time here to visit some of the fascinating sites of the interior. A trip to the beautiful pine forests of the Troodos Mountains is strongly recommended. This is an area of considerable religious significance, and nine Greek Byzantine churches in the mountains are included in the official U.N.E.S.C.O. list of cultural treasures of the world's heritage.

☎ **TELEPHONE NUMBERS**

Recompression chamber +357-24-304-300
Hospital +357-22-801-400
Emergency services +357-22-806-680
Tourism Organization +357-24-643-576

🖥 **WEBSITES & E-MAIL**

Tourism Organization www.visitcyprus.org.cy

OTHER DIVE SITES

Baths of Aphrodite
Devil's Head
Achileas
Mismayola Reef
Jubilee Shoals
Twin Rocks
Shark Cove
Aphrodite Park

▼ **EGG CARGO**
The *Zenobia* contained a cargo of eggs, now strewn over the sea floor.

John Bantin

RED SEA

The Red Sea, the long thin body of water separating Africa from the Arabian Peninsula, runs approximately 1,180 miles (1,900 km) southeast from the Gulf of Suez to the narrow mouth at Bab El Mandeb that connects it to the Gulf of Aden, and thence to the Indian Ocean. The width rarely extends beyond 186 miles (300 km), and the depth varies from an average of 410 feet (125 m) at the southern sill at Bab El Mandeb to the deeper waters of the central regions, which plunge to abyssal depths of just under 10,000 feet (3,000 m). The Red Sea is the submerged section of the rift valley system that extends from the Dead Sea through to the Great Rift Valley in southeast Africa, a great crack in the Earth's crust formed millions of years ago by violent volcanic action. The Red Sea's turbulent geological past is still evident in pockets of high temperature at extreme depth.

Due to the enclosed nature of the Red Sea, tidal movement is minimal, although there are localized currents. The terrain surrounding the sea is on the whole arid and harsh, with Saudi Arabia dominating the eastern shoreline and Egypt and Sudan the west. Also abutting the Red Sea are Jordan and Israel to the north, and Eritrea and Yemen to the south.

One of the characteristics of the Red Sea is very high salinity. This is because more water is lost through evaporation than enters the Red Sea as freshwater precipitation or run-off from the land. The result is a very warm body of water that extends a salty tepid deep-water plume into the Indian Ocean from its southern tip.

The prevailing winds on the Red Sea blow from the north in the northwestern section and from the south in the southeastern section. This made navigation extremely difficult for sailing vessels at least until the problem was solved by the development of the dhow with its characteristic triangular sail that could be sailed almost directly into the wind.

The Red Sea has truly exceptional marine life. There are more than 400 recorded species of coral, and several hundred fish species, 20 percent of which are endemic. Although the more popular reefs and wrecks have undoubtedly felt the impact of heavy diver traffic over the last few years, the sea's more remote areas are still justifiably famed for the presence of large shark populations and encounters with roaming pelagics.

The dive industry in the Red Sea is extremely well established. When diving first took off in the region some decades ago, resorts in Egypt and Israel were the most popular destinations, but recently Jordan and Sudan have begun to make an impact. The latter in particular has become an essential stop for the modern adventure diver seeking encounters with big animals and relatively pristine reefs.

Mikayo Langhofer

◄ **SERGEANT MAJORS**
A school of sergeant majors moves through the crystal-clear shallows of the reef top.

THISTLEGORM

A LEGEND IN THE DIVING WORLD, THIS WRECK REALLY DOES HAVE IT ALL. SADLY, MANY THOUSANDS OF DIVERS SWARM OVER HER HULL AND INSIDE HER HOLDS AND PASSAGEWAYS EVERY YEAR, AND SHE IS NOW SHOWING UNMISTAKABLE SIGNS OF WEAR AND TEAR. NONETHELESS, AN UNMISSABLE WRECK THAT IS AN ESSENTIAL STOP ON ANY VISIT TO THE RED SEA.

The location of the *Thistlegorm*, a World War II supply ship sunk in 1941, was first identified by Jacques Cousteau in the 1950s. Nevertheless, her whereabouts remained a tantalizing rumor until her rediscovery in October 1992. Now divers from all over the world are drawn to the *Thistlegorm*, irresistibly attracted by her amazing cargo of military hardware.

In the fall of 1941, the British Eighth Army was fighting a desperate campaign against Rommel's forces in North Africa. On the night of October 6, the freighter *S.S. Thistlegorm*, carrying much-needed supplies from England, lay at anchor at Sha'ab Ali only a day away

WATER TEMPERATURE

Summer: 29°C / 84°F
Winter: 20°C / 68°F

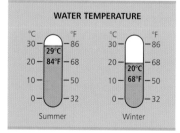

▶ **BROKEN STERN**
The stern of the *Thistlegorm* lies on her starboard side and has broken away from the rest of the wreck.

Gulf of
Aqaba

Gulf of
Suez

SAUDI
ARABIA

SINAI
PENINSULA

Tiran

Sinafir

• El Gouna

✚ 🕐 • **Sharm el Sheikh**

Thistlegorm •

Gezr
Qeisum

• **Shag Rock**

Bluff Point

Ras Muhammad

S.S. Rosalie Muller • **Malek**

Gezr
Tawila

• **Sha'ab Abu Nuhas**
Yellowfish Reef

RED
SEA

Gezr
Shadwan

EGYPT

• **Hurghada**

Gifatin Islands

Abu Ramada

0 ——————— 40 km
0 ——————— 30 mi

John Bantin

▲ **LEAVING A MARK**
The pointless desire of some divers to leave their mark has hastened the deterioration of this magnificent wreck.

from Suez at the end of her long voyage around the southern cape of Africa. Alongside her was her escort, the battlecruiser *H.M.S. Carlisle*. The stationary vessels were spotted by a German plane, and immediately two bombers were dispatched from a base on the German-held island of Crete. Low on fuel, the bombers attacked the first target they saw—the hapless *Thistlegorm*. A bomb struck the fourth hold, which was packed with ammunition, causing a huge explosion that set the ship ablaze. As the fires spread, she was rocked by further explosions, blowing the stern midsections apart and sending her to the bottom. Nine of her crew died.

GEOGRAPHY

The Red Sea is an enormous inland sea extending for 1,200 miles (1,930 km) from north to south, and with a maximum width of 190 miles (350 km). The salinity of its water is much higher than that of any ocean. No rivers empty into it, annual rainfall averages less than 1 inch (3 cm), and in this desert region it loses the equivalent of about 6 feet (2 m) of water each year through evaporation. Water to replace this loss flows in from the Indian Ocean through the shallow Bab al Mandab, the strait at the southern end that connects with the Arabian Sea. This strait is just 300 feet (91 m) deep. It effectively isolates the Red Sea from the current systems of the Indian Ocean, so it is virtually tideless.

The Red Sea has borne this name since antiquity. It may refer to the occasional red algal bloom in the sea, or to the reflection of the sun off the reddish deserts that border it. Its coastline is shared between the countries of Egypt, Sudan, Eritrea, Djibouti, Yemen, Saudi Arabia, and Jordan. The *Thistlegorm* dive site is located in the northernmost part of the Red Sea west of

the Sinai Peninsula, just to the northeast of Shag Rock, and west of Ras Muhammed. It is about a 5-hour boat journey from the busy Egyptian port of Sharm el Sheikh.

MARINE LIFE

Despite the very large number of divers crawling all over the wreck of the *Thistlegorm*, the marine life is excellent. The Red Sea is spectacular in its species diversity, with an estimated 1,000 species of fish—up to 17 percent of which may be unique, or endemic to the area—some 2,000 species of invertebrates, and 180 species of coral. Look out for large lionfish on the *Thistlegorm*, particularly during evening dives when they emerge to hunt great shoals of glassy sweepers. Jacks, snappers, banner fish, and barracuda are a perpetual presence, and you may get a glimpse of the occasional large grouper. Lujtan and angelfish inhabit the clusters of gorgonians, sea fans, and soft corals that cling to the wreck itself.

DIVER'S TIP

To dive the *Thistlegorm* without the crowds is a great experience. You can avoid the rush by getting there at dawn if you find a skipper willing to steam there overnight.

DIVE CENTERS

POSEIDON DIVING CENTER
Crazy Camel Camp, Dahab,
South Sinai, Egypt
Phone: +20-69-364-0091
E-mail: info@poseidondivers.com
Web: www.poseidondivers.com

M.Y. JULIET LIVEABOARD
Sharm el Sheikh, Egypt
Phone: +20-10-121-7030
E-mail: info@julietdivers.com
Web: www.julietdivers.com

DIVING ORGANIZATIONS

Association of Egyptian Travel Businesses on
the Internet (A.E.T.B.I.) provide information on
registered dive operators:
E-mail: contact@touregypt.net
Web: www.touregypt.net

RECOMPRESSION

Hyperbaric Medical Center
Sharm el Sheikh, Egypt
Phone: +20-69-660-922/3

HOSPITAL

Sharm el Sheik International Hospital
Hai el Nour, Sharm el Sheik, Egypt
Phone: +20-69-366-1624

OTHER DIVE SITES

Shag Rock
Ras Muhammed
Bluff Point
Malek
S.S. Rosalie Muller
Sha'ab Abu Nuhas
Yellowfish Reef
Giftun Islands
Abu Ramada

► B.S.A. MOTORCYCLE

One of the famous B.S.A. motorcycles,
destined for the British army in North
Africa, still looks complete after sixty years
beneath the sea.

THE DIVE

The notable drawback to diving the *Thistlegorm* is not the current (generally low), the visibility (generally high), or the depth (generally safe). It is the crowds. It is not at all unusual to see more than 20 dive boats moored above the wreck, and you can be sure of the company of scores of other divers during the course of a single dive. This can be quite a problem, particularly on the surface where many dive operators appear to have a distinctly cavalier approach to safety. As the large vessels jostle for position, they frequently collide, while a cat's-cradle of shot lines greets the unwary diver on ascent.

One very regrettable aspect of all this activity is that shortly after the wreck was rediscovered, the removal of countless priceless artifacts began on a scale not short of looting and plundering. The sheer mechanical impact of such repeated diving is also damaging. This is now a very tired, old wreck, and it is only a matter of time before the holds and bulkheads start to cave in.

THE THISTLEGORM

• 55 to 100 feet (17 to 30 m) • beginner.

The *Thistlegorm* was only 413 feet (126 m) long and can therefore feasibly be explored on a single dive, particularly if you use a nitrox mix to extend bottom times. But it is well worth taking your time to really appreciate the wreck. She lies straight on the sand, except for her stern, which is broken from the rest of the hull, lying on her starboard side. The midsection is extensively broken up, a legacy of that bomb blast so many years ago, although her stern is relatively intact. Her forward holds contain riches indeed.

Most dives begin either on the bow section or, more commonly, directly above the forward holds, where the cargo is a cross between a military surplus store and a museum. Penetration of the holds is relatively easy. Number One hold contains in its lower levels crates of Lee Enfield Mk.III rifles, aircraft spares, and a large number of rubber boots. Deeper down in this hold are two large Rolls Royce armored cars, badges long gone.

John Bantin

On the upper level are British-manufactured Morris cars and the famous B.S.A. W.D.M.20 motorcycles, specially made for military use.

The starboard side of Number Two hold, entered through Number One hold or from above, contains many large Bedford trucks in its lower sections, some of them loaded with motorbikes. Also in this hold are portable generators, trailers, and more motorcycles. On the seabed at 100 feet (30 m), just forward of Number Four hold and a distance of about 65 feet (20 m) from the main wreck lies one of the two 0-2-0 steam locomotives the *Thistlegorm* was carrying.

It is possible to swim through any of the doors in the wheelhouse to access the chart room, the officers' mess, and the bathroom saloon. One of the most famous sights of the *Thistlegorm* is the skipper's bath, now partly filled with silt and neatly planted with tube-worms. The ceilings in all these areas frequently have a glassy finish, caused by a film of air trapped from the steady stream of divers as they process through these spaces in their numbers. The stern is also worth investigating if time permits, if only for the massive propeller, still in place and well preserved. There are also crew quarters, and a 4.5-inch (7-cm) gun on deck.

OTHER ACTIVITIES

Despite its history as a simple fishing village, Sharm el Sheikh has now grown into a completely modern resort. Banks, car rentals, bars, restaurants, and desert safaris—all are available here. Perhaps the only complaint is a lack of real budget accommodation. Much of the attractions of the town actually lie in the desert nearby, with Wadi Kid and a number of oases all within easy reach. Nearby is the Greek Orthodox monastery of St. Catherine's, dating from the 6th century A.D.

☎ **TELEPHONE NUMBERS**

Recompression chamber	+20-69-660-922/3
Hospital	+20-69-660-893/4/5
Sharm el Sheikh, Sea Search and Rescue	+20-12-3134-158
Pharmacy	+20-62-600-388

🖥 **WEBSITES & E-MAIL**

General Information on Red Sea   www.spotredsea.com

▼ LONGNOSE HAWKFISH
The extended jaws of the hawkfish are perfect for probing nooks and crannies in a reef or wreck.

Linda Pitkin

THE BROTHERS

VISIBILITY

70 feet (20 m) plus year round
Peaks at 100 feet (30 m) plus

MUST SEE

Range of shark species

DOWNSIDE

Rough seas
Currents

GETTING THERE

Scheduled flights to Cairo, Egypt, from most parts of the world connect with domestic flights to Sharm el Sheikh or Hurghada on the Red Sea coast, but specialized packages direct to these holiday resorts are usually a better deal and include hotel vouchers. From North America it may work out cheaper to fly to Europe and pick up a deal there.

VISA

All visitors to Egypt must have a visa and a passport valid for six months. Visas can be arranged through Egyptian embassies worldwide. Visitors from the U.S., E.U. and Commonwealth countries may be able to purchase a visa stamp upon arrival. One-month visitor's visas can be extended.

MONEY

Currency is the Egyptian pound. It is advisable to take U.S. dollar traveler's checks.

WATER TEMPERATURE

°C	°F	°C	°F
30 —	— 86	30 —	— 86
20 — 29°C / 84°F	— 68	20 —	— 68
10 —	— 50	10 — 20°C / 68°F	— 50
0 —	— 32	0 —	— 32
Summer		Winter	

WITH BIG SHARKS AND SWEEPING CURRENTS, THESE TWO ROCKY ISLANDS RISING OUT OF THE RED SEA HAVE EARNED A REPUTATION FOR ADVENTUROUS DIVING. THEIR RIOTOUS REEFS ARE AN OASIS OF LIFE IN THE SURROUNDING DEEP WATER, AN IRRESISTIBLE DRAW FOR ANY DIVER.

The two remote, flat-topped islands known as the Brothers (El Akhawein in Arabic) are about a mile apart. In common with so many of the world's best dive sites, they are steep-sided rocks surrounded by swirling tides and upwellings. This creates a dramatic collection of precipitous reefs, drawing in rich fish communities and large predators.

The islands, uninhabited except for a small Egyptian garrison, are a long-established diving location. The Egyptian government recognized the unique quality of

John Bantin

► **OCEANIC WHITE TIP SHARK**
The waters around the Brothers attract a wide range of shark species.

the site's marine life by declaring it a National Marine Park in 1998. Since then, it has been closed from time to time to divers. Even when open, visiting divers are required to pay a fee of U.S.$5.

GEOGRAPHY

The Brothers are located off-shore 36 miles (58 km) northeast of the town of El Quseir on the Egyptian Red Sea coast. They are the remnants of two massive volcanic cones rising from the seabed, formed during the upheavals that created the Red Sea rift. The largest of the two (named Big Brother) is about 980 feet (300 m) long and 130 feet (40 m) wide. A 100-foot (30-m) high lighthouse built by the British in 1880 stands on Big Brother, but aside from that both islands are practically featureless. All the action here takes place in the swirling currents beneath the waves. Of the two, Little Brother is generally acknowledged as having the better diving, but really there is very little in it!

MARINE LIFE

As its status as an officially designated Marine Park indicates, this has to be one of the best sites for marine life in the Red Sea, with tremendous coral communities hanging in rich currents patrolled by large pelagics. The walls are covered in huge sea fans and some of the best soft coral you will see anywhere in the Red Sea. At greater depth on the walls are large colonies of black coral. There are millions of orange anthias swirling around the reef walls, with schools of trevally, blackfin barracuda, and large individual napoleon wrasse a permanent fixture.

One of the real draws for the diver is the shark population around the Brothers. The sharks move in from May onwards, and in the right conditions a tremendous range of species can be observed prowling around the walls and reefs. Alongside the more frequently encountered species such as gray reef there are also scalloped hammerheads and—most exciting of all, perhaps—the

DIVE CENTERS

SEA QUEEN FLEET
Hadabet Um El Seed, Sharm el Sheikh,
Sinai, Egypt
Phone: +20-12-218-6669 or
+20-12-100-3942
E-mail: info@seaqueens.com
Web: www.seaqueens.com

EMPEROR DIVERS
Hurghada Hilton Resort, Safaga Rd,
Hurghada, Egypt
Phone: +20-65-345-0537
E-mail: info.hurghada@emperordivers.com
Web: www.emperordivers.com

TONY BACKHURST SCUBA TRAVEL
Smithbrook Kilns, Cranleigh,
Surrey GU6 8JJ, U.K.
Phone: +44-800-0728221
E-mail: travel@scuba.co.uk
Web: www.scuba.co.uk

 DIVING ORGANIZATIONS

Association of Egyptian Travel Businesses on
the Internet (A.E.T.B.I.) provides information
on registered dive operators:
E-mail: contact@touregypt.net
Web: www.touregypt.net

 RECOMPRESSION

Hyperbaric Medical Center
Sharm el Sheikh, Egypt
Phone: +20-69-660-922/3

 HOSPITAL

Sharm el Sheikh International Hospital
Sharm el Sheikh, Egypt
Phone: +20-69-366-1624

OTHER DIVE SITES

Panorama Reef
Sha'ab Shear
Hyndman Reefs
Beit Goha

► **NUMIDIA**
One of the unidentified spoked wheels
lying in the wreckage field of the *Numidia*.

occasional large thresher. Divers around the Brothers may also be lucky enough to encounter the oceanic white tip shark, a distinctly ominous fish that is one of the great opportunistic predators of the open ocean.

THE DIVES

This is liveaboard diving country only, with most of the boats visiting the Brothers operating out of Hurghada. Good weather is a key requirement to dive this site, as it is completely exposed to the worst the elements can throw at it. Anchoring is not permitted, so the boats tie up to mooring buoys, but in rough weather the buoys can be pulled under. Many horror stories are told of close shaves around these islands as wide-eyed skippers, unfamiliar with the area, grapple with their wildly pitching boats. Choose an operator who visits the islands regularly and knows the vagaries of the local conditions.

The best time to visit the Brothers is at full moon, when the winds are weakest, during the months of June to August (although the heat can be fairly oppressive at this time). The diving itself is nearly all wall and drift diving.

BIG BROTHER SOUTHEAST TIP

• 130 feet (40 m) • advanced

This is the side of Big Brother that is most exposed to the open ocean, and consists of a steep wall cloaked in dense coral growth. The soft coral is the most impressive found anywhere on the Brothers—on some sections of the upper wall it is so thick as to look like a deep patchwork carpet.

Most dives start at the eastern edge of the wall, with the drift taking the diver around to the west for pickup at the southwestern tip. After entering at the reef wall, the diver has a steady drop down the wall. A large ledge encoutered at 130 feet (40 m) acts as a good reference point.

Dazzling though the display of life on the reef undoubtedly is, it is well worth looking into open water regularly throughout this dive. Tuna, big sharks, and eagle rays all patrol this wall, and a sighting of at least one large pelagic visitor is virtually guaranteed at some point during the dive.

THE AIDA II AND THE NUMIDIA

• 30 to 130 feet (9 to 40 m) • intermediate

Both of these wrecks are located on the northwest side of Big Brother, and are about 330 feet (100 m) apart. It is a bit much to try to do both in a single dive, and you will be better off taking time to explore each one on separate dives.

Located at the western tip of the island, the *Aida II* was an Italian troop-carrying ship that sank in 1957 after striking the reef. She is a large wreck and is virtually intact. Her shallowest point at 50 feet (15 m)

John Bantin

John Bantin

stretches off to a deepest point of 130 feet (40 m). She is heavily overgrown and is swept by powerful currents. A useful tip on this dive is to observe where the resident schools of jacks and barracuda are hanging in the current, and make for that spot! The currents swirl and eddy around this wreck, and the fish tend to make for the calm areas.

The wreck of the *Numidia* lies north of the *Aida II*. She appears to be a 19th-century British cargo ship. After more than 100 years on the bottom she has broken up, with wreckage lying from 30 feet (9 m) down to 130 feet (40 m). Some heavy iron wheels with large spokes are scattered on the reef. There is some doubt as to what they are, but they may possibly have been part of a locomotive.

OTHER ACTIVITIES

Very few—this is strictly a dive site only! Both islands are essentially flat-topped featureless lumps of rock, making you feel rather sympathetic towards the unfortunate Egyptian soldiers stationed on Big Brother.

TELEPHONE NUMBERS

ecompression chamber	+20-69-660-922/3
Hospital	+20-69-660-893/4/5
Sharm el Sheikh, Sea Search and Rescue	+20-12-3134-158
Pharmacy	+20-62-600-388

WEBSITES & E-MAIL

General Information on Red Sea   www.spotredsea.com

▲ SCALLOPED HAMMERHEAD
The Brothers are a beacon for most shark species encountered in the Red Sea.

DIVER'S TIP

Look away from the reef very regularly while diving at the Brothers. This site draws some tremendously impressive visitors from the open ocean, but don't rely on your guide to point them out!

DAHAB

THE SMALL TOWN OF DAHAB IN SOUTHERN SINAI STILL HAS A PIONEER FEEL TO IT. THE DIVE SITES THEMSELVES—A COLLECTION OF WALLS, CORAL CAVES, AND CAVERNS—ONLY HEIGHTEN THOSE FEELINGS. ONE OF THEM, THE INFAMOUS BLUE HOLE, HAS GAINED A LEGENDARY REPUTATION AMONG THE DIVING FRATERNITY.

 VISIBILITY
100 feet (30 m)

 MUST SEES
The Canyon
The Bells

 DOWNSIDE
Entry points at popular sites

GETTING THERE
Scheduled flights to Cairo, Egypt, from most parts of the world connect with domestic flights to Sharm el Sheikh, but specialized packages are usually a better deal and include hotel vouchers. From North America it may work out cheaper to fly to Europe and pick up a deal there. Most visitors to Dahab fly into Sharm and are picked up by their operator for the drive to Dahab itself.

 VISA
All visitors to Egypt are required to have a visa and a passport valid for six months. Visas can be arranged through Egyptian embassies worldwide. Visitors from the U.S., and E.U. countries may be able to purchase a visa stamp upon arrival at many large airports. One-month visitor's visas can be extended.

 MONEY
Currency is the Egyptian pound. It is advisable to take traveler's checks with you.

Dahab lies 49 miles (80 km) north of the bustling dive community of Sharm el Sheikh on the Gulf of Aqaba. Until relatively recently all that was here was a Bedouin settlement beside a number of large oases, providing crucial shelter on this stretch of barren coastline where stark mountains plunge into the clear waters lapping the rocky shore.

The once tranquil Bedouin settlement is now a bustling tourist haven, and yet it still retains the feel of a frontier settlement. Dusty narrow streets are packed with colorful stalls and traditional coffee houses, and contrast with a seafront lined with bars and restaurants. The reason for Dahab's rapid growth over the last decade is simple—the diving off the shores of this special stretch of the Sinai coastline.

GEOGRAPHY

The Egyptian shore of the Gulf of Aqaba, the northeast branch of the Red Sea, runs from Taba on the Israeli border down to the northern section of the Ras Mohammed National Park at Nabeq. Dahab is about one-third of the way along this coast, and is reached by a two-hour vehicle ride over the craggy coastal road from Sharm el Sheikh. The area is less developed than the Red Sea coastline farther south. It has become increasingly attractive to divers in recent years as the southern sites feel the impact of excessive diver numbers.

MARINE LIFE

The geology and tremendous reef formations are the main attraction of Dahab's dive sites. The marine

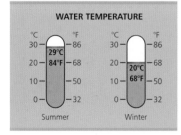

WATER TEMPERATURE

	Summer			Winter	
°C	°F		°C	°F	
30	86		30	86	
20 — **29°C**	68		20 —	68	
84°F			**20°C**		
10	50		10 — **68°F**	50	
0	32		0	32	

▶ **GLASSFISH**
Large shoals of glassfish can be seen in the larger gullies of the reefs around Dahab.

Dan Burton

life, although very pleasant, is actually less spectacular than in many other areas of the Red Sea, particularly as certain of the sites here are dived fairly heavily in peak season. That being said, some of the caverns and over-hangs have immense shoals of glassy sweepers, beloved of many an underwater photographer. Snappers, pufferfish, groupers, parrotfish, and triggerfish are present in some numbers on the reef walls.

THE DIVES

The key characteristic of the diving in the Dahab region is that it is shore-based. All local operators either dive house reefs or run vehicles out to the popular nearby sites. Once there, the operations are generally very slick. Large tarpaulins are laid out to prevent sand clogging gear, and refreshments are on hand in the baking heat. There is even a large encampment beside the famous Blue Hole site, complete with restaurant and hire shop.

Just because the diving is shore-based, it does not mean it is free of danger. Some of these sites have been responsible for a large number of deaths, and have a fearsome reputation. Avoid the temptation to dive beyond your experience and qualifications, particularly as there is a tremendous range of sites to suit all levels of diver; you need not partake in dangerous diving to experience the best these sites have to offer.

THE BLUE HOLE

• 165 feet (50 m) plus • expert

This site is famed for its habit of killing divers! The reason is simple enough—divers overextend themselves when attempting a dramatic swim through the arch at the seaward side of the Blue Hole that leads to the outer reef wall. This arch is at a depth of 165 feet (50 m), and extends for 100 feet (30 m) until exiting in the wall, a very tall order indeed in conventional dive gear, as many divers have discovered to their cost. A number of memorial plaques set in the northern cliff face at the site should remind anyone considering this swim-through to treat it as a technical penetration. In fact it is now perceived wisdom that this portion of the dive should not be attempted without technical gear.

The entry point is at the southern end of the tented encampment. The site is not actually a blue hole but the top of a huge shaft in the reef that extends for over 900 feet (274 m). The immediate blue water phase of the dive ends when you sight the inner reef wall after about 150 feet (45 m). This wall is topped by a shelf at 15 feet (5 m), which leads to the outer reef, where the action in terms of marine life really starts. Although pelagics are rare in this heavily dived area, the reef fish are fairly abundant, with plenty of triggerfish, angelfish, and some respectably sized groupers.

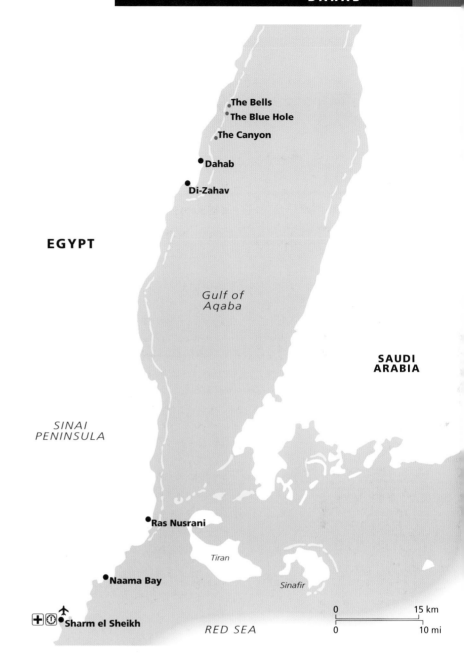

Most guides combine a nearby site such as the Bells with the Blue Hole, and exit through the lagoon.

THE BELLS

• 100 feet (30 m) plus • intermediate

This site is a steep wall with many overhangs and swim-throughs, mostly occupied by glittering shoals of glass-fish. The dive begins at the entry point about 328 feet (100 m) north of the main lagoon over sharp rocks and edges, which can make entering quite tricky when the swell is up. It is important to remember that this dive, like all the dives in the area, takes place over an abyssal drop—this is a true continental wall—and buoyancy needs to be spot on.

After entering, the diver drops almost immediately down to maximum depth, then works back up the wall towards the Blue Hole lip, and exits across the lagoon.

John Bantin

 DIVE CENTERS

POSEIDON DIVING CENTER
Crazy Camel Camp, Dahab,
South Sinai, Egypt
Phone: +20-69-364-0091
E-mail: info@poseidondivers.com
Web: www.poseidondivers.com

SINAI DIVERS
Naama Bay, Sharm el Sheikh, Egypt
Phone: +20-69-640-100
E-mail: dahab@sinaidivers.com
Web: www.sinaidivers.com

 DIVING ORGANIZATIONS

Association of Egyptian Travel Businesses on
the Internet (A.E.T.B.I.) provides information
on registered dive operators:
E-mail: contact@touregypt.net
Web: www.touregypt.net

 RECOMPRESSION

Hyperbaric Medical Center
Sharm el Sheikh, Egypt
Phone: +20-69-660-922/3

HOSPITAL

Sharm el Sheik International Hospital
Hai el Nour, Sharm el Sheik, Egypt
Phone: +20-69-366-1624

DIVER'S TIP

Plan the dive, dive the plan! Many a
spontaneous narcosis-induced decision to
push too deep into the Blue Hole has
resulted in disaster.

► **DROP-OFF**

Despite the dives being from the shore, it
is only a short swim to busy drop-offs,
glorious corals, and gorgonians.

David Stephens

Once again large pelagics are not overly abundant, and it is well worth sticking close to the reef throughout the dive to investigate the numerous overhangs and crags. Look out for parrotfish and shoals of glassfish in the larger gullies, which are frequently patrolled by opportunistic lionfish at dawn and dusk.

THE CANYON

• 100 feet (30 m) • intermediate

This site is located short of the Blue Hole, approximately halfway along the road from Dahab. It is an exquisite canyon that runs from the edge of the shore to a depth of 165 feet (50 m). A large coral mound approximately 40 feet (12 m) from the shore marks the entrance to the canyon. The shaft itself is a wonderful convoluted passage twisting into the depths, illuminated throughout by an eerie light filtering down from the opening overhead. Unfortunately, this opening is too narrow to allow a diver to exit. The first point it is possible to squeeze through appears at about 100 feet (30 m). This dive should again be taken very seriously, as many less

experienced divers have felt rather claustrophobic in the canyon's confined space.

OTHER ACTIVITIES

Dahab has developed into a lively night-spot while retaining its traditional feel, so there is plenty to amuse the diver in the evenings or lazy afternoons. A camel safari with the Bedouin from a local oasis may be somewhat contrived but is nonetheless a great experience. Kite and wind surfing are also very popular off the main beach in Dahab.

☎ **TELEPHONE NUMBERS**

Recompression chamber	+20-69-660-922/3
Hospital	+20-69-660-893/4/5
Sharm el Sheikh, Sea Search and Rescue	+20-12-3134-158
Pharmacy	+20-62-600-388

💻 **WEBSITES & E-MAIL**

General Information on Red Sea	www.spotredsea.com

▲ **YELLOW-MOUTHED MORAY**
The caverns and overhangs of Dahab are home to a number of species of moray eels.

JACKSON REEF

words by Gillian McDonald

IT IS EASY TO DISMISS JACKSON REEF AS BEING OVER-BUSY, OVER-DIVED AND RUINED BY DECADES OF UNDERWATER TRAFFIC. HOWEVER, LOOK AGAIN. JACKSON STILL STANDS OUT IN THE NORTHERN RED SEA AS A BEAUTIFUL, HEALTHY DIVE LOCATION OFFERING FANTASTIC VARIETY BOTH IN WILDLIFE AND DIVING OPPORTUNITIES.

 VISIBILITY

70 to 100 feet (20 to 30 m)

 MUST SEES

Schooling scalloped hammerhead sharks
Stunning soft corals and reef life

 DOWNSIDE

Busy from a day boat

GETTING THERE

Scheduled flights to Cairo, Egypt, from most parts of the world connect with domestic flights to Sharm El Sheikh. Charter flights operate from main European hubs. Specialized packages are usually a better deal and include hotel vouchers. From North America it may be cheaper to fly to Europe and pick up a charter flight deal there.

 VISA

All visitors to Egypt must have a visa and a passport valid for six months. Visas can be arranged through Egyptian embassies worldwide. Visitors from the U.S., Canada, EU and GCC countries can purchase a visa stamp upon arrival at Cairo or Sharm el Sheikh for around 15 USD.

 MONEY

Currency is the Egyptian pound, although the Euro is also used in many stores. There are ATM machines in the main areas of Na'ama Bay and Old Sharm, including some hotels. It is advisable to take traveler's checks with you.

WATER TEMPERATURE

	Summer		Winter	
°C	°F		°C	°F
30	86		30	86
20	68		20	68
10	50		10	50
0	32		0	32

Summer: 29°C / 84°F
Winter: 20°C / 68°F

Anthony Holley

▲ **STILL GOING STRONG**

Jackson Reef is remarkably colorful and still teems with life despite decades of busy dive traffic.

Jackson is the most northerly reef in the Strait of Tiran which is a strategic channel providing narrow passage for shipping traveling from the Red Sea to the Jordanian port of Aqaba and the Israeli port of Eilat. Jackson and nearby neighbors Woodhouse, Thomas and Gordon reefs, all named after British cartographers, ascend from the depths of the Gulf of Aqaba right up to the surface. At the north end of Jackson, and the south end of Gordon, the most southerly reef, perch the distinctive rusted husks of two shipwrecks, Lara and Loullia, respectively, demarking the outer limits of the reef system. The location is a pleasant one—a half-hour boat ride out of Na'ama Bay, often accompanied by bow-riding dolphins and, if you are lucky, the occasional whale shark.

GEOGRAPHY

Washed by the currents flowing through the Gulf of Aqaba, the reefs are the peaks of submerged mountains. The Strait of Tiran is the westernmost channel between Egypt and the barren island of Tiran. The strait has two passages deep enough for large ships, the Enterprise passage next to the Egyptian side at 950 feet (290 m), and the 240-foot (73 m) deep Grafton passage to the east. The reefs sit between these passages, descending almost vertically to a depth of at least 200 feet (60 m) reaching 650 feet (200 m) in

Million Hope
NABQ ●

Straits of Tiran

Woodhouse Reef ● **Jackson**
● Lagoona
Thomas Reef ●
● **Gordon Reef**

EGYPT

● Ras Nasrani
● Ras Bob
Sharks Bay ● **White Knights**

ma Bay ● ● The Gardens

— The Tower
● Pinky's Wall
● **Amphoras and Turtle Bay**
HARM EL SHEIKH
● Ras Umm Sid

— Temple

Tiran

Sanafir

0 — 5 km
0 — 5 mi

29

▼ **EMPEROR ANGELFISH**
An emperor angelfish swims among vibrant soft coral and ubiquitous orange anthias fish.

places, before plunging down into the abyss.

Because the strait is narrow but deep, strong currents can occur. These result in a bottleneck that funnels rich nutrients to the upper level plankton, thus supporting a food chain that attracts a diversity of marine life, allowing healthy coral growth. They can also provide exciting and spectacular drift dives.

Each of the four reefs has its own characteristics, with Jackson being the most likely location to see both large and small creatures in one place. Jackson and Gordon are both a large, rounded shape with Thomas and particularly Woodhouse forming a long, thin connection between them. On Jackson the reef sides give way at the southwest and northeast ends to shallower coral zones, while walls full of life stretch along the southeasterly and northwesterly sides of the reef.

MARINE LIFE

Scalloped hammerhead sharks, hawksbill turtles, eagle rays, barracuda and large schools of snapper are found here. Not to mention blue-spotted rays and crocodile fish quietly observing you as they lie gently on the sand, while masked puffer fish whir by and giant squirrelfish eye you warily as they hang stationary under shelves of coral. Colorful nudibranchs, tiny banded pipefish and the floaty, spiral egg lace of a Spanish dancer greet more careful eyes in the nooks and crannies of the reef. This great diversity of life is surrounded by beautiful red, purple and yellow soft corals swaying along the edge of the walls, rooted around hard corals and sandy patches above luxuriant gorgonian fan corals and absolutely everywhere are the orange anthias fish.

Anthony Holley

Gillian McDonald

 DIVE CENTERS

CAMEL DIVE CLUB & HOTEL
Centre of Na'ama Bay
Sharm el Sheikh, South Sinai, Egypt
Phone: +20-69-3600-700
E-mail: info@cameldive.com
Web: www.cameldive.com

RED SEA DIVING COLLEGE
Sultana Building
Na'ama Bay, PO Box 67, Sharm el Sheikh
South Sinai, Egypt
Phone: +20-69-3600-145
E-mail: info@redseacollege.com
Web: www.redseacollege.com

SHARKS BAY UMBI DIVING VILLAGE
PO Box 275
Sharm el Sheikh, South Sinai, Egypt
Phone: +20-69-3600-942
E-mail: info@sharksbay.com
Web: www.sharksbay.com

 DIVING ORGANIZATIONS

Association of Egyptian Travel Businesses on
the internet (A.E.T.B.I.) provides information
on registered dive operators:
E-mail: contact@touregypt.net
Web: www.touregypt.net

 RECOMPRESSION

Hyperbaric Medical Center
Sharm el Sheikh, Egypt
Phone: +20-69-660893

HOSPITAL

Sharm el Sheikh International Hospital
Hai el Nour, Sharm el Sheikh, Egypt
Phone: +20-69-366-1624

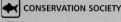 **CONSERVATION SOCIETY**

HEPCA
Hurghada Environmental Protection and
Conservation Association
PO Box 104, Hurghada, Red Sea, Egypt
Phone: +20-65-344-5035
E-mail: info@hepca.com
Web: www.hepca.com

The calmer south side is sheltered from the weather, while if swells permit, the northern point is the place most likely to present sharks. Drop to around 60 to 100 feet (20 to 30 m) deep and head out into the blue and you are often rewarded with schools of scalloped hammerhead sharks in the summer months, around June to November. White tip reef sharks can also be seen around the reef.

THE DIVES

There is no getting away from it, Jackson Reef is busy. By far the best way to experience it is from a liveaboard, dropping into the clear, crystal water soon after dawn before the day boats arrive from the south. However, it is still well worth a day-boat journey, especially since the overloaded and noisy snorkel excursion hoards have been banned from Jackson since 2005. North, south, east and west there is truly something for everyone on this wonderful reef.

Most boats moor around the middle of the sheltered south side from where wall dives either to the east or west, depending on the current, provide wonderful vistas and often large animals out in the blue. Alternatively to the north, weather permitting, there is much more chance of seeing sharks and also a deep wreck with part of its broken structure visible on top of the reef. The high nutrient content feeding the plankton here keeps the reefs teeming with smaller fish life, which draws in the big stuff to gorge.

SOUTH WALL TO THE AQUARIUM— MOORING DIVE

• 0 to 90 feet (0 to 28 m) • beginner

Gently descend the wall as you head southwesterly, keeping the reef to your right. Look out for turtles, barracuda and many bannerfish and butterflyfish fluttering all around. Toward the corner, the reef levels out to a gentle slope and you will see a stunning red anemone and luxuriant gorgonian fan corals where pretty long-nosed hawkfish regularly perch. Here, as you approach the saddle between Jackson and Woodhouse reefs at about 92 feet (28 m), the current can start to pick up strongly so you need to turn round as you feel the movement; otherwise, you can be swept around the southwest corner into the channel between the reefs, from where it is much more difficult for boats to pick you up thanks to the swell. You need to carry a DSMB just in case the current catches you unawares. As you turn back from the current, the bottom slopes upward to a superb coral garden known as the Aquarium where you will find giant porcupine fish resting on the sand, vibrant, healthy corals and heavily camouflaged stonefish lying in wait for unwary, tasty morsels. Your safety stop can be spent on an enjoyable and leisurely waft back to the boat along the gorgeous garden and absolutely vibrant reef wall.

SOUTH WALL, EAST—DRIFT DIVE

• 0 to 60 feet (0 to 20 m) • intermediate

As you descend the wall this time turn right with the reef on your left. Further down are sandy gullies and out in the blue a high chance of spotting schools of jacks or snapper and sometimes an eagle ray cruising by. Stunning red and purple soft corals hug the vertical wall and all manner of Red Sea life can be seen in and around the cracks and crevices. As the dive progresses toward the northeast again a current is usually felt. Around the 16 to 20 foot (5 to 6 m) mark there is a cave where snoozing white tip reef sharks can often be found. Relax, all you have to do here is float, observe and soak in the multicolored, busy splendor as the current carries you along the beautiful coral garden teeming with life. It's one of the best safety stops imaginable as you fly along the reef at 16 feet (5 m) until eventually surfacing by the light beacon where the boat will be waiting to pick you up.

A word of caution: there can be quite a swell at this pickup point so exercise care when getting back on to the boat.

NORTH WALL

• 50 to 80 feet (15 to 25 m) • advanced

While spectacular schooling scalloped hammerhead sharks are not guaranteed here, there is a very high chance of encountering them in the summer months between June and November. You may also find tiger sharks and even the occasional oceanic white tip shark. The swell and general sea conditions can get heavy around the north side of Jackson, so this can only be attempted in calm weather. If it is viable, drop in on the north wall somewhere between the beacon and the topside remains of the Lara. Descend down the beautiful wall, then at around 60 feet (20 m) head straight out into the blue. Visibility is excellent in these waters, so you can keep the reef easily in sight while still being around 80 feet (25 m) away from it. Keep one eye on your depth and air, and the other on the blue, as chances are the hammerheads will be around. It is an awesome privilege to spend a little time in this silent, blue world with these incredible creatures and is a dive you will certainly never forget.

LARA WRECK

• 148 to 197 feet (45 to 60 m) • very advanced

The fate of the Lara remains a mystery, but that merely increases its appeal for serious wreck divers. It was a Cypriot freighter built in Germany and launched in 1956. In November 1982 it set sail from Aqaba in Jordan and drove hard on to the top of Jackson Reef, where some remains can still be seen today. Many rumors have circulated since, including the idea that it only had enough fuel on board to reach Jackson and no farther, and that people remained onboard for over two years after it grounded, providing a useful drug smuggling location. All very James Bond, but nothing has ever been proved. However, the freighter does have a rather strange appearance as the only topside wreck where the steel plates have been removed and different very large sections have been cut off and pushed over the reef.

The submerged part of the wreck is the main superstructure from midsection to stern at around 197 feet (60 m), with the bridge and richly encrusted mast rising to 148 feet (45 m). Soft and hard corals cover the wreck in a myriad of colors and large hawksbill turtles can often be seen here. On your relaxed journey back to the surface keep your eyes out for the schools of hammerhead sharks often seen in this area. This is an extremely advanced wreck dive only suitable for divers with the necessary qualifications and deep wreck experience.

OTHER ACTIVITIES

Decades ago Na'ama Bay was a simple edge of desert fishing community. Now, however, it is a vibrant, bustling, light-filled mini-metropolis crammed with shops, restaurants, bars, hotels, banks and even casinos. You can certainly find a huge variety of good food and interesting entertainment here. Alternatively, stay at Sharks Bay north of Na'ama, which is an altogether less hectic environment with local restaurants offering simple yet delicious food. In the desert there are camel rides and safaris, quad-biking and horseback riding, all arranged from kiosks in Na'ama Bay or through your travel representative.

☎ **TELEPHONE NUMBERS**

Recompression chamber	+20-69-660893
Hospital	+20-69-366-1624

◄◄ **CROCODILE FISH**
A well-camouflaged crocodile fish waits for its next meal to swim by.

▼ **GORGONIAN FAN CORAL**
Exquisite gorgonian fan corals lean out into the current to feed on plankton.

Anthony Holley

GULF OF AQABA

 VISIBILITY

Average 60 feet (18 m). Up to 100 feet (30 m)

 MUST SEES

Amazing coral cover
Healthy reef fish populations

 DOWNSIDE

Lack of really impressive pelagics

 GETTING THERE

Some airlines fly directly to Aqaba from North America, Europe, and the Far East, but most visitors arrive at Queen Alia International Airport in the Jordanian capital, Amman, and connect to Aqaba from there.

 VISA

All foreigners need a visa to enter Jordan, purchased at the border or airport on arrival, or from consulates in your country of departure. Visas are valid for two weeks from entry, but can be easily extended for up to three months. The cost for all nationalities is JOD10 (single entry visa.)

$ MONEY

Currency is the Jordanian dinar. Money changing is relatively easy, and traveler's checks and credit cards are widely accepted.

AFTER YEARS OF OBSCURITY, JORDAN HAS RECENTLY EMERGED AS ONE OF THE LEADING DIVING DESTINATIONS IN THE NORTHERN RED SEA. WHAT SETS IT APART IS THE QUALITY OF THE CORAL COVER, WITH GAUDY REEFS FESTOONED WITH DENSE BEDS OF HARD AND SOFT CORALS SUPPORTING HEALTHY POPULATIONS OF REEF FISH.

Jordan has only a tiny section of coastline at the northern end of the Gulf of Aqaba on the Red Sea. It sits in the shadow of the popular Israeli dive resort of Eilat—so close to Jordan's port of Aqaba, it is visible across the bay that separates them—and for many years it was considered off limits to much of the international diving community. Momentous changes in the political stability of the troubled Middle East have since brought Jordan into the diving limelight. Its reefs have escaped the damage wrought by the advent of

John Bantin

WATER TEMPERATURE

°C	°F	°C	°F
30 — — 86		30 — — 86	
20 — **26°C / 78°F** — 68		20 — **20°C / 68°F** — 68	
10 — — 50		10 — — 50	
0 — — 32		0 — — 32	
Summer		Winter	

▶ **ANTHIA**

Several species of anthia add yet more color to the already vibrant inshore reefs.

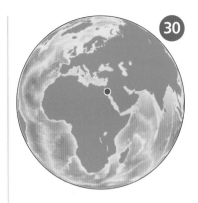

mass diving tourism elsewhere in the region, and Jordan is now regarded as one of the few places where it is possible to drift over beautifully healthy reefs and savor the Red Sea experience of old.

GEOGRAPHY

Jordan is a small Middle Eastern country with a land area of only 34,442 sq miles (89,206 sq km) and a population of only 4 million. Its entire coastline amounts to a stretch of 15 miles (24 km) at the top of the Gulf of Aqaba at the north end of the Red Sea. Aqaba, the country's only port at the very head of the gulf, now acts as the launch point for the bustling dive industry that serves this narrow strip of Red Sea coastline.

MARINE LIFE

Although there is absolutely nothing wrong with the abundance and variety of the reef fish that inhabit the reefs off Jordan, it is the coral itself that has assured the region's fame among the diving community. The gently

sloping topography of the coastline, generally benign water conditions, lack of river run-off from the land, and intense sunlight have combined to create perfect conditions for both hard and soft corals. Several of the sites along the coast owe their attraction entirely to their remarkable coral cover.

It is true that this part of the Red Sea tends not to see the really spectacular pelagic species found farther south; all the same, many of the reefs are regularly visited by hawksbill turtles and have large napoleon wrasses and groupers in residence. Also expect the occasional encounter with dolphins. Large shoals of barracuda and jacks stalk the more precipitous reefs, and the range of smaller reef species throughout this part of the coast is splendid.

THE DIVES

Diving in Jordan is now very well established, with modern centers catering for an international clientele, and professional instruction and equipment readily

▶ PARROTFISH

These brightly colored fish owe their names to their mouths, which look like parrot's beaks.

David Stephens

DIVER'S TIP

Take care when entering the water at many of these sites. Damage to the reef can be avoided by gently finning over the top of inshore corals (as opposed to stamping through them!) so put your fins on in shallow water, establish positive buoyancy, and swim as soon as possible.

 DIVE CENTERS

ROYAL DIVING CLUB
Jordan Projects for Tourist Development
Amman Head Office, P.O. Box 941299
Amman 11194, Jordan
Phone: +962-3-201-7035
E-mail: info@rdc.jo
Web: www.rdc.jo

SEASTAR WATERSPORTS
Alcazar Hotel, P.O. Box 392,
Aqaba 77110, Jordan
Phone: +962-3-201-4131
E-mail: alcsea@alcazar.com.jo
Web: www.seastar-watersports.com

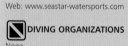 **DIVING ORGANIZATIONS**
None

 RECOMPRESSION
Princess Haya Hospital, Aqaba, Jordan
Phone: +962-3-201-4111

 HOSPITAL
Princess Haya Hospital, Aqaba, Jordan
Phone: +962-3-201-4111

 CONSERVATION SOCIETY
Jordan Royal Ecological Diving Society
P.O. Box 831051, Amman 11183, Jordan
Phone: +962-6-567-6173
E-mail: information@jreds.org
Web: www.JREDS.org

OTHER DIVE SITES

Black Rock
Cedar Pride
Hussein Reef
Gorgonian II
Russian Tank
Blue Coral
Moon Valley
Long Swim

available. Most of the dive operators working along this stretch of coastline are based in Aqaba, although one notable center (the Royal Diving Center) has set up operations farther south, offering doorstep access to some of the best reefs in Jordan.

Because the Jordanian coastline is so short and the sites themselves are invariably close inshore to take advantage of the shallow reefs, most of the diving is done from shore. The standard way of accessing the sites is by vehicle from Aqaba, but it is also possible to arrange boat dives through a number of the centers, should you prefer to do so.

This is a splendid region for newcomers to the sport to learn to dive, offering abundant coral, shallow dives of real quality, low currents, and good visibility.

GORGONIAN 1

• 20 to 130 feet (6 to 40 m) • beginner

Everything that makes diving in Jordan so special is at this site. On entering the water, divers are confronted by a glorious patchwork of hard and soft corals covering a shallow, gently sloping reef that disappears into the depths before them. Moving among the beds of branching hard corals and stout bommies is a tremendous array of reef fish—lionfish, scorpionfish, glassfish, morays, wrasses, triggerfish, surgeonfish, anthias, and damselfish; these reefs are very busy indeed. Don't forget to look out for stingrays in the sandy patches between the coral.

One of the real joys of this reef is that it holds attractions for all levels of diver. The more experienced diver will appreciate the incredible coral cover and fish life, whilst the novice has the chance to explore a world-class reef in relatively benign conditions.

SAUDI BORDER

• 130 feet (40 m) • intermediate

This is a slightly more dramatic reef at the southern end of Jordan's shoreline. Here the inshore waters start to veer away from the gently sloping reefs farther north, and the first hints of precipitous walls begin to appear. Once again there is magnificent coral cover on this dive, with the added bonus of the occassional encounter with passing pelagic species. The dive starts on the reef top leading from the shoreline to a shelf at 20 feet (6 m). From this point on there is a distinct wall that drops to deep water far more quickly than at sites farther north, bringing the chance of encounters with jack and barracuda, often present in considerable numbers, while large napoleon wrasses patrol the mid water.

AQUARIUM

• 20 to 130 feet (6 to 40 m) • beginner

There is always a slight sense of trepidation when diving any site called "Aquarium"—and most resorts have at least one! Fortunately this Aquarium lives up to its name. You'll find a stunningly beautiful cross-section of northern Red Sea coral and fish species here.

The reef has the classic Jordanian underwater profile, sloping gently from the water's edge down to 130 feet (40 m) and beyond. There is a pleasant mix of delicate soft corals, patchlike bommies of plate and brain coral, and forests of branching acropora. Swarming over these dense coral beds are pufferfish, triggerfish, some medium-sized groupers, and an array of smaller species such as anthias and damselfish. A very pleasant dive indeed.

OTHER ATTRACTIONS

The hospitality of the Jordanians is in the finest traditions of the Arab people, and you will find a genuine sense of live Arab culture here, something that has become somewhat diluted in the diving hotspots farther south along the Red Sea.

Aqaba has been a key strategic port at the head of the Red Sea for generations, a fact highlighted by the presence of a 14th-century fort in the town. Despite this remarkable history, the town itself has limited attractions, apart from an excellent range of traditional restaurants. Jordan's real treasures lie nearby in the desert, with two world-renowned sites within a day's drive. The extraordinary remains of Petra, an ancient city carved out of a red rockface, and the canyons of Wadi Rum are both considered to be wonders of the Arab world. There is a well-organized tourist infrastructure to both these sites, and the opportunity to visit them really shouldn't be missed.

☎ TELEPHONE NUMBERS

Recompression chamber	+962-3-201-4111
Hospital	+962-3-201-4111
Jordan Tourist Board	+962-6-567-8444

💻 WEBSITES & E-MAIL

Jordan Tourist Board	uk.visitjordan.com
Travel information	www.mideasttravelnet.com

▼ **HAWKFISH**
Blackside hawkfish spend many hours resting on top of the reef, lying in wait for passing baitfish.

John Bantin

SHA'AB RUMI

 VISIBILITY
80 feet (25 m) plus year round

 MUST SEE
Precontinent II experiment wreckage

 DOWNSIDE
Lack of tourist infrastructure

 GETTING THERE
International flights from Europe into Khartoum or Port Sudan. Sudan Airways operate domestic flights to major towns, but planes are sometimes grounded and in need of repair. There is a twice-weekly air-taxi service from Khartoum to Nyala. Your operator should meet you at your destination airport.

VISA
All visitors to Sudan require visas. Passports must be valid for at least six months and not contain any Israeli stamps or visas. Israelis are not permitted to enter the country.

 MONEY
Currency is the Sudanese dinar. American Express is widely accepted but other credit cards are not much use. Traveler's checks and cash are best taken in U.S. dollars. Outside Khartoum you will find it difficult to exchange traveler's checks.

WATER TEMPERATURE

°C	°F		°C	°F
30 —	— 86		30 —	— 86
	30°C			**27°C**
20 —	**86°F** — 68		20 —	**80°F** — 68
10 —	— 50		10 —	— 50
0 —	— 32		0 —	— 32
Summer			Winter	

▶ **SILVERTIP REEF SHARK**
The silvertip reef shark is one of the bolder shark species and should be treated with respect.

WITH VERY LIMITED INFRASTRUCTURE AND FACILITIES FOR THE TOURIST OR DIVER, SUDAN REPRESENTS THE WILDER SIDE OF RED SEA DIVING, BUT THOSE BRAVE ENOUGH TO FACE THE CHALLENGE ARE IN FOR A RARE TREAT: SHA'AB RUMI IS ONE OF THE LEGENDARY SITES OF UNDERWATER EXPLORATION.

Sudan is not for the faint hearted. This is not some bustling tourist trap with sleek hotels and air-conditioned shopping. A potent combination of political instability and limited infrastructure means that this is genuine adventure diving. The entire southern region of the country is engaged in a bitter civil war, and is completely off limits to foreigners. Indeed, visiting divers may need to call upon considerable reserves of patience and resourcefulness even to get as far as the arrivals lounge at Port Sudan! Once there, most divers are whisked to their liveaboards, and have no opportunity to experience the land-based side of Sudan—something of a shame as the Sudanese are a wonderfully warm and hospitable people.

Sha'ab Rumi is famous throughout the diving world as the scene of a remarkably bold experiment. In 1963 Jacques Cousteau established his research station *Precontinent II* here in a visionary and successful attempt to show that divers could live underwater for sustained periods. The resultant documentary film was a massive international hit, and the ghostly remains of his undersea community can still be dived on the flat shelf surrounding the reef.

GEOGRAPHY

Although Sudan is the largest country in Africa, its share of the Red Sea coastline is relatively small at 404 miles (650 km). Most of the well-known Sudanese dive

John Bantin

sites are located within easy sailing distance of Port Sudan, although some, including Elba, Pfeiffer, and Abington Reefs, lie some distance to the north.

Sha'ab Rumi is an offshore reef 22 miles (35 km) to the north of Port Sudan. A broad flat-topped undersea mountain with a large lagoon at its center, the reef does not break the surface and—with the exception of the highly significant shelves to west and south—plunges into water more than 2,300 feet (700 m) deep.

MARINE LIFE

Diver after diver, guidebook after guidebook, have enthused about the incredible range of marine life on Sha'ab Rumi and other reefs in these waters, although local and visiting spearfishermen have had considerable impact on the more accessible reefs. However, the richness of life of those in more remote areas remains almost unparalleled in the Red Sea. Of particular note are the sharks, in particular giant and scalloped hammerheads, both present in some numbers—this is one of the few places on Earth where these magnificent animals can be seen in large groups.

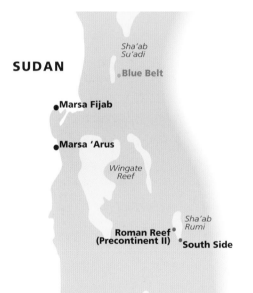

SUDAN

Sha'ab Su'adi

Blue Belt

Marsa Fijab

Marsa 'Arus

Wingate Reef

Roman Reef (Precontinent II)

Sha'ab Rumi

South Side

Sanganeb Reef

Silayet

Umbria

Port Sudan

| 0 | 60 km |
| 0 | 40 mi |

John Bantin

▲ UNDERSEA COMMUNITY
The remains of Cousteau's Precontinent II experiment are an evocative monument to a genuine diving pioneer.

Jane Morgan

▶ **COUSTEAU'S GARAGE**

This unusual structure, built to resemble the body of a sea urchin, was used by Jacques Cousteau as a garage for his submersible vehicle during the Conshelf Two experiment.

DIVER'S TIP

Carry a spare everything. Don't get bent!

OTHER DIVE SITES

Blue Belt
Umbria

🏠 **DIVE CENTERS**

PLANET DIVE
11 Jew Street
Brighton, East Sussex
BN1 1UT, U.K.
Phone: +44-870-749-1959
E-mail: enquiry@planetdive.co.uk
Web: www.planetdive.co.uk

RED SEA DIVERS
19 Westfield Road, Cupar KY15 5AP
Scotland, U.K.
Phone: +44-1334-656-577
Web: www.redseadivers.com

 DIVING ORGANIZATIONS
None

🕐 **RECOMPRESSION**

The only chamber in Sudan is on one of the larger liveaboards, "The *Don Questo*". For further information contact:
Acqua Action for Water Sports
Via Borodin, 19, 56122 Pisa, Italy
Phone: +39-333-643-3254
E-mail info@sudandiving.it

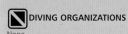 **HOSPITAL**

Your best bet in Sudan is to arrange insurance cover that includes rapid evacuation in the event of an incident. Ensure your operator has adequate first aid facilities.

THE DIVES

Although foreign vessels may register within Sudan to dive these waters, most of the diving is in the hands of a number of tenacious operators working out of Port Sudan. The diving is all done from liveaboards, and conditions are basic compared to those provided by the more established and well-equipped operators on the Red Sea coast to the north in Egypt. All "luxury" items have to be imported into Sudan at considerable cost and difficulty, so you should expect a slightly different diving experience from the usual pampered one of the Red Sea diver.

Much of the diving at Sha'ab Rumi and other reefs in the area is along steep walls, with the characteristic strong currents and upwelling associated with this type of formation. Normal safety measures strictly apply, with one added warning— Sudan is possibly one of the less desirable diving locations in the world to get bent, as it could take a very long time to evacuate you to the nearest recompression facility in Egypt. Dive extremely cautiously, observe decompression limits to the letter, and add extra safety stops. Your safety when you dive in Sudan is your responsibility. The consequences of a bend or an embolism could be extremely complex.

SOUTH SIDE SHA'AB RUMI

• 30 to 65 feet (10 to 20 m) • intermediate

Although the western edge of Sha'ab Rumi is more famous as the scene of Cousteau's Precontinent II habitat experiment, the south side is the best site for marine life. The dive vessel enters the lagoon through a pass on the western edge and makes its way to the southern edge where the water deepens. Here the boat's tender must be used to take divers through the shallow water at the edge of the drop-off, and the dive begins.

The initial drop-off is a sedate wall leading the diver down to a large shelf that extends south for approximately 330 feet (100 m), sloping slowly as it does to a maximum depth of approximately 100 feet (30 m) at its southern lip. Although this gentle wall is cloaked in soft corals and sea fans, it is the vertical walls plunging to more than 2,300 feet (700 m) on either side of the shelf that give this dive genuine world-class status.

The reefs here are exceptionally rich, and the ardent fish enthusiast can find almost every Red Sea species somewhere on these walls or on the shelf itself. But it is the big sharks, most notably the hammerheads, that draw in the divers. These giants may be seen off the edge of the shelf at 100 feet (30 m) and deeper, or occasionally shallower. It is best to sit tight and let the sharks come to you; they don't take kindly to being chased, and will swiftly disappear into the deep water surrounding the walls, and that will be the end of the shark encounter for that particular dive. At the right time of year, as many as 20 or 30 hammerheads may be seen in majestic formations at this site, an increasingly rare encounter in the world of diving.

ROMAN REEF (WEST SIDE)

• 30 to 130 feet (9 to 40 m) • intermediate

Not up to the standard of the South Side dive in terms of marine life, but a must see as one of the iconic sites in dive adventure. The remains of Cousteau's experiment are located just outside the southern entrance to the west of the lagoon on a shelf at 30 feet (9 m). The most dominant feature is the garage that housed the submarine used by the aquanauts. Now largely overgrown by corals and sea fans, it is nonetheless possible to swim beneath it and enter the main bubble. Here the exhausts of divers' bubbles have created an air pocket, and it is possible (but not overwhelmingly advisable) to remove your regulator and exchange a few words with your buddy. Do this for too long and you will pass out due to the high concentrations of CO_2 in the exhaled air that makes up the air space, so replace the regulator in reasonable time!

North from the garage is the remains of the tool shed and some fish pens. These are loosely moored to the seabed and roll around in high currents or strong swell. At 90 feet (27 m) are the remains of a shark cage, heavily overgrown with gorgonias and corals.

OTHER ACTIVITIES

The tourist infrastructure of Sudan is very limited, and the attractions are really based around the diving. Whilst in the country do try to dive the *Umbria*, a freighter scuttled in June 1940, which is stacked with explosives and vehicles. She lies close to the entrance of Port Sudan, and is an easily accessible world-class wreck. It is also worth visiting the ancient town of Suakin, 40 miles (64 km) south of Port Sudan, to see the ruins of what was once a great trading port and major hub of the slave trade in the 19th century.

TELEPHONE NUMBERS

Recompression chamber +39-333-643-3254

WEBSITES & E-MAIL

Travel information   www.sudan.net
Tourist information   www.sudani.co.za

▼ BUMPHEADS
Large schools of bumphead parrotfish can have a significant impact on areas of hard corals.

John Bantin

INDIAN OCEAN

The third largest ocean in the world, the Indian Ocean, known to the ancient world as the Eritrea Sea, was extensively navigated long before the Atlantic or the Pacific. It differs from both of these oceans in that the vast majority of its 28.4 million sq miles (73.6 million sq km) lie within the southern hemisphere. Surrounded by 25,685 sq miles (66,526 sq km) of mainly tropical coastline, the Indian Ocean has an average depth of 2.5 miles (4 km), its deepest point being the Java Trench, which descends to 24,440 feet (7,450 m). The Mid-Indian Ridge, starting close to the Arabian Peninsula, runs down the center of the ocean before dividing southeast of Madagascar into the Southwest Indian Ocean Ridge and the Southeast Indian Ocean Ridge, ending south of Australia. The Ninety East Ridge has the distinction of being the straightest ridge in any of the world's oceans.

The Indian Ocean is land-locked from the north, with salty, warm bodies of water such as the Red Sea and Persian Gulf creating pulses of tepid water that reach far into the main ocean. The major cold-water inputs come from the circumpolar Antarctic Current. Winds profoundly influence currents. In the monsoon zone, northward from 10° S, winds blow from the northeast from November to April, causing a weak counterclockwise gyre to develop in the Arabian Sea and a strong clockwise gyre in the Bay of Bengal. From May to October the monsoon winds reverse to blow from the southwest, and the currents also reverse direction. A north-flowing current develops off the Somali coast, causing upwellings of cool water. South of the monsoon zone the anticlockwise gyre produces the Mozambique and Agulhas Currents.

Although Indian Ocean coral reefs do not have the diversity of the Pacific systems, they support an outstanding range of associated fish species, both large and small. Unfortunately, extremely destructive fishing techniques have had an adverse impact on many inshore reefs, driving a number of species, including dugongs and seals, to the brink of extinction. Ocean-going fishing fleets have had a similar effect on a number of whale species and, more recently, sharks.

Diving in the Indian Ocean offers a huge variety of experiences ranging in character from swimming with giant whale sharks off Ningaloo Reef in Western Australia to classic atoll diving in the scattered coral islands of the Maldives and Seychelles, not to speak of wild surf launches and adventure diving off the southeastern coast of Africa.

◀ **GRAY REEF SHARK**
A gray reef shark glides over a classically rugged volcanic reef off East Africa.

Linda Pitkin

ALIWAL SHOAL

ALIWAL SHOAL ENCAPSULATES ALL THE EXCITEMENT OF SOUTH AFRICAN DIVING. EXPERIENCE IT FOR THE SAKE OF THE LAUNCH INTO THE TEETH OF THE DRAMATIC SURF THAT POUNDS SOUTH AFRICA'S "WILD COAST", BUT THERE ARE ALSO UNFORGETTABLE ENCOUNTERS WITH RAGGED TOOTH SHARKS, AND MUCH, MUCH MORE.

The thrill of diving Aliwal Shoal starts in the mouth of the Umkomaas River, where the experienced local skippers launch their high-powered dive boats, outboards roaring, out to sea. It continues with your first encounter with the magnificent ragged tooth sharks that lurk within the dark recesses of the Shoal, and ends with the boat's thunderous charge up the beach at the completion of the day's dive.

GEOGRAPHY

The Umkomaas River enters the Indian Ocean some 30 miles (48 km) south of Durban in KwaZulu-Natal. A small town, also named Umkomaas, has grown up at this point. Three miles (5 km) off the coast a mountain of sandstone juts into the underwater highway of the warm Agulhas Current that sweeps down the southeast coast of Africa from Mozambique. This is Aliwal Shoal.

 VISIBILITY

75 feet (23 m) plus Feb-Apr
30 to 75 feet (9 to 23 m) May-Jan

 MUST SEES

Surf launch
Ragged tooth sharks
Migrating whales

 DOWNSIDE

Strong currents
Limited visibility

 GETTING THERE

International flights to Durban via Johannesburg or Cape Town. 30-mile (48-km) drive down coast road to Umkomaas. Most dive operators will arrange pickup from Durban Airport.

 VISA

Visitors from the U.S., U.K., and most European countries do not need visas for holiday stays of up to 90 days; other nationalities may be limited to 30 days or require a visa. Check with a South African embassy before leaving.

 MONEY

Local currency is the rand. Changing money is not a problem, and most towns have A.T.M.s that accept all major cards.

WATER TEMPERATURE

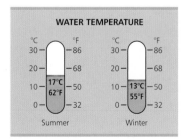

Summer 17°C / 62°F
Winter 13°C / 55°F

▶ **RAGGED ENCOUNTER**
Aliwal Shoal offers guaranteed close encounters with large ragged tooth sharks.

Dan Burton

Dan Burton

MARINE LIFE

The warm waters that swirl around the Shoal extend the southern range of many species of tropical fish, while several cool-water species are at the northern end of their range during the winter. The reefs of Aliwal Shoal therefore display a diversity of marine life almost unmatched in South Africa as the mingling of species creates a glorious tapestry of color and interest.

But there is really only one reason why divers from all over the world are drawn to Aliwal Shoal—for the annual migration of large numbers of ragged tooth sharks, affectionately known as "Raggies" by the South African diving fraternity, that move into the area from their feeding grounds to the south, attracted by the warm water at the tail end of the current. The sharks arrive in July and over the course of several months they feed in the gullies, caves, and overhangs of the Shoal, before moving away in October, the end of the Raggy season.

Ragged tooth sharks are magnificent animals. Measuring up to 10 feet (3 m) and weighing an impressive 660 lbs (300 kg), they are a deep-bodied shark with dark-brown to olive-gray coloration. The underbelly is pale, and the upper part of the body is dappled with large dark spots that fade with age. The shark uses its catlike eye to seek prey, a lightning sideways strike sweeping its victims into a mouth crammed with needlelike teeth that slope backwards in the classic overbite of the habitual fish-predator. Raggies are one

▲ SARDINE RUN

The sardine run is one of the great natural spectacles, with shoals of up to 1,000 tons of fish, extending like a black cloud for 3 miles (5 km) or more.

Umkomaas

Umkomaas●
    The Nebo●
    ●**The Produce**
The Pinnacles● ●**Raggy Cave**
The Cathedral *Aliwal*
      Shoal
Scottburgh●

●**Landers Reef**

SOUTH AFRICA

0   15 km

0   10 mi

Port Shepstone ●

    Protea Banks
    Protea
    Banks
Margate ●

32

DIVE CENTERS

DIVE SOUTH
P.O. Box 38890, Faerie Glen 0043,
South Africa
Phone: +27-12-991-3134
E-mail: info@divesouthafrica.co.za
Web: www.divesouth.co.za

ALIWAL DIVE CHARTERS
Reynolds Rd, Umkomaas, South Africa
Phone: +27-39-973-2233
E-mail: dive@aliwalshoal.co.za
Web: www.aliwalshoal.co.za

DIVING ORGANIZATIONS

N.A.U.I. Services of Southern Africa
40 Gordonia Center Beach Road,
Gordons Bay 7139, South Africa
Phone: +27-21-856-5184
E-mail: info@nauisa.org
Web: www.nauisa.org

RECOMPRESSION

Eugene Marais Hyperbaric Therapy Centre
Eugene Marais Hospital, 696 5th Avenue,
Les Marais, Pretoria, South Africa
Phone: +27-12-334-2567

HOSPITAL

Addington Hospital
Erskine Terrace, South Beach, Durban,
South Africa
Phone: +27-31-327-2000
E-mail: jill.hurst@kznhealth.gov.za

Randles Road Medical Center
468 Randles Road, Sydenham 4091,
South Africa
Phone: +27-31-207-5252
E-mail: rrmc@ion.co.za

CONSERVATION SOCIETY

Environmental Justice Networking Forum
P.O. Box 32184, 184 Smit Street,
Bloemfontein 2017, South Africa
Phone: +27-331-949-073
Society established by Andy Cobb, founder of
shark diving in Aliwal, in order to protect the
reef and its inhabitants.

The Natal Sharks Board
1a Herrwood Drive, Umhlanga, KwaZulu-
Natal, South Africa
Tel: +27-31-566-0400
Web: www.shark.co.za
Internationally recognized body monitoring
shark diving in South Africa.

OTHER DIVE SITE

Landers Reef

of the few sharks that can actively pump water over their gills. They therefore possess the remarkable ability to hover motionless in the water. If divers are patient and are prepared to sit quietly on the bottom in one of the classic shark locations on the Shoal, the Raggies will gradually sweep closer and closer until they come within touching distance—an unforgettable encounter.

As well as Raggies, the Shoal also has populations of tiger, bull, and white sharks. Whales move into the area in great numbers on their annual migrations, and dolphins are very common feeding over the Shoal. Notable fish species on the Shoal include large brindle and potato bass, kingfish, and other predatory species. Some very large scorpionfish may be seen blending with the multicolored overgrown rocks of the reef. Hard corals are not present. However, there are beautiful soft corals and sponges, including thistle and feather coral.

The other great biological event in Aliwal is the world-famous Sardine Run. This takes place between May and July, when huge shoals of sardines move north into these warmer waters for the southern winter. The mass of fish in one of these great shoals can weigh as much as 1,000 tons and darken the water like a great black cloud extending 3 miles (5 km) or more. As the shoals move north, they are accompanied by vast numbers of predators, including an estimated 20,000 common dolphins and 2,500 bottlenose dolphins, as well as copper, dusky, black tip and spinner sharks, and various species of game fish such as shad and garrick. The result is one of the greatest marine bonanzas on the planet. As the vast shoals of sardines are attacked from above and below they split up into boiling bait balls that thrash the surface of the water to foam.

The exact dates of the run are impossible to predict with any degree of accuracy. Therefore to be sure of experiencing the melee of the run you must be ready to move into the area at very short notice.

Aliwal Shoal has been declared a Marine Protected Area (M.P.A.) by the South African Government.

THE DIVES

Although depth is not a major issue at any of the dives around Aliwal Shoal, it should be noted that all of them are frequently accompanied by strong currents and limited visibility. It is important that divers prepare well before attempting them and make sure that they possess the required level of experience and qualifications indicated for each dive.

THE CATHEDRAL

• 92 feet (28 m) • intermediate

The most famous site on Aliwal Shoal, the Cathedral is a huge triangular cavern over a white patch of sand on the southeast side of the main reef. On entering the cavern, take up a position resting on the sand on the seafloor. At the height of the season from July to October, the Cathedral almost always has a number of Raggies in residence—indeed the only reason they may be absent is the activities of other divers. Watch out for what seems to be a consistently large population of scorpionfish on the rocks leading to the entrance to the cavern. Also found in the vicinity of the Cathedral are kingfish, potato bass, moorish idols, and the occasional passing turtle.

RAGGY CAVE

• 45 feet (14 m) • beginner

The aptly named Raggy Cave is one of the other key locations on the Shoal where you can be pretty certain of seeing Raggies at the right time of year. A large overhang next to a smooth white amphitheatre of sand, the cave is located on the eastern bank of the main reef. The best strategy for observing the Raggies is to settle on the sand next to the main ledge. The sharks are constantly on patrol, moving in and out of the cave, and if you remain quiet and calm, they will in all probability approach close to the ledge to investigate your presence. The view you then have of these creatures swimming in open water is truly magnficent. You are also virtually guaranteed an encounter with large stingrays at Raggy Cave.

THE PINNACLES

• 15 to 100 feet (5 to 30 m) • beginner

Rising to within 15 feet (5 m) of the surface, the Pinnacles are located on the northern edge of Aliwal Shoal and are normally dived when the current is weak or there is little surge. The Pinnacles themselves—stark angular rock features—make a great backdrop for underwater photography on days when the sun is in the right position and visibility is good. Kingfish and other predatory fish frequently patrol the Pinnacles, and it is an excellent site to finish a dive after exploring other areas of the reef.

THE PRODUCE & THE NEBO

• 55 feet (17 m) & 100 feet (30 m) • intermediate

These are the only two diveable wrecks in the area of Aliwal Shoal. Both are located 0.6 miles (1 km) north of the main Shoal and lie a similar distance apart from each other. The *Produce* sank as recently as 1974 and is still largely intact. Divers can have an interesting dive exploring around the hull and stark superstructure, but unfortunately this wreck experiences very low visibility when the Umkomaas River is in spate, so be prepared. The top of the wreck lies at 55 feet (17 m) and the seabed is at 100 feet (30 m).

Tony White

Sunk after striking the Shoal in 1884, the *Nebo* lies hull up in about 100 feet (30 m) of water. Kingfish can be found on this wreck, as well as large groupers, scorpionfish, and trumpetfish.

PROTEA BANKS

• 100 feet (30 m) plus • advanced

Located south of Aliwal Shoal, Protea Banks is essentially a wilder version of the Shoal, and at the right time of year actually surpasses it in terms of adventurous diving. Protea Banks is deeper than the Shoal, while sharing many of the same characteristics. Dives involve vigorous drifts over caves and caverns, and during October through May some very large specimens of bull sharks as well as hundreds of ragged tooth sharks can be encountered in this area, particularly in the South Pinnacles site.

Protea Banks requires more complex dive skills than Aliwal Shoal, and is considerably deeper and more unpredictable. Although a magnificent site at the right time of year, it should only be explored by those with an appropriate level of experience.

OTHER ACTIVITIES

Nightlife in Umkomaas is somewhat limited. However, the beautiful Empisini Nature Reserve, only 10 miles (16 km) away, offers safari accommodation at bargain prices. Among the local wildlife to be seen here are monkeys, mongooses, bushbucks, blue duikers, otters, bushpigs, and bats. The Natal Sharks Board is also a short drive away.

Further along the coast is Durban. This vibrant city and holiday resort offers a variety of attractions, and is particularly noted for the fine surfing to be found along its long beach.

☎ **TELEPHONE NUMBERS**

Recompression chamber	+27-12-335-1577
Hospital	+27-31-327-2000
Tourism KwaZulu-Natal	+27-31-366-7500
Department of Environmental Affairs & Tourism	+27-12-310-3911

💻 **WEBSITES & E-MAIL**

Aliwal Shoal	www.aliwalshoal.com
Africa Guide	www.africaguide.com
Tourism KwaZulu-Natal	www.kzn.org.za

▲ BLACK TIP SHARK

The blacktip shark is rarely found in water deeper than 100 feet (30 m). This is a very active, fast-swimming species that often occurs in large schools at the surface.

DIVER'S TIP

When diving at Aliwal, instead of facing inwards and exploring the classic sites of the reef, spend at least one dive on the margins of the Shoal, facing outwards into open water. At the height of the season you will almost certainly be rewarded with the sight of great white sharks passing in the far distance.

SODWANA

 VISIBILITY

50 to 65 feet (15 to 20 m), with reports of up to 130 feet (40 m), Apr–May

75 feet (23 m) plus Feb–Apr

 MUST SEES

Surf launch

Seven Mile Reef

Hluhluwe-Umfulozi National Park

 DOWNSIDE

Very crowded at weekends

 GETTING THERE

International flights to Durban via Cape Town or Johannesburg. There is a four-hour drive to Sodwana (four-wheel-drive vehicle strongly recommended.)

 VISA

Visitors from the U.S., U.K., and most European countries do not need visas for holiday stays of up to 90 days; other nationalities may be limited to 30 days or require a visa. Check with a South African embassy before leaving.

 MONEY

Currency is the rand. Changing money is not a problem in South Africa, and most towns have A.T.M.s that accept all major cards. Facilities at Sodwana are very limited though.

WATER TEMPERATURE

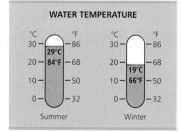

Summer — 29°C / 84°F

Winter — 19°C / 66°F

THE QUINTESSENTIAL AFRICAN DIVING EXPERIENCE—CLASSIC WILD DIVING THAT STARTS WITH A WHITE-KNUCKLE LAUNCH RIDE FROM A REMOTE SHORE, BLASTING THROUGH THE POUNDING SURF TO REACH THE DIVERSE REEFS BEYOND, WHICH ARE PATROLLED BY SERIOUSLY LARGE PREDATORS.

Sodwana Bay lies just south of the Mozambique border and is the only truly tropical dive site in South Africa. It was relatively untouched until the early 1970s, when the civil war in Mozambique barred access to that country and its miles of beaches and reefs. Divers were forced to seek sites farther south, and as Sodwana Bay already had a reputation as one of the premier big game fishing sites in South Africa, it was a natural progression to explore its diving potential. Today it is one of Africa's most popular dive locations, drawing thousands of divers to the drama and beauty of its reefs. It is one of the most species-rich sites in southern Africa, with an estimated 1,200 different fish species swarming over healthy reefs.

GEOGRAPHY

Sodwana is in northern KwaZulu-Natal, approximately a four-hour drive from the capital, Durban. An idea of how remote the site is can be gleaned from the name itself—Sodwana derives from a local term meaning "Little One On Its Own". The whole of the bay area, extending from Cape Vidal in the south to the border

Dan Burton

▶ **SURF LAUNCH**

The big surf launch at Sodwana is possibly the most exciting start to a day's diving anywhere on earth.

with Mozambique in the north is a National Park, and within this the dive area itself is actually quite small. There is only one launch point for dives, just south of the mouth of the small creek in the bay that enters the sea beside a sheltered headland. The area around it is relatively wild bush, and it is closely monitored by the Natal Parks Board. To reach the site demands a bumpy drive over dust roads—fairly hairy in the wet season!

MARINE LIFE

Since the Sodwana National Park was established in 1950 the reefs have enjoyed more than 50 years of protection. The marine life is extraordinary. Due to the influence of the warm Agulhas Current traveling south from Mozambique, there is tremendous biodiversity, with an estimated 1,200 fish species present on and around the reefs and new ones continually being added to the list. Marlin, sailfish, and dolphins can be seen throughout the year, and large sharks are also a constant presence. Whale sharks move in from October to February, and other seasonal visitors include humpback whales, ragged tooth sharks, and manta rays. The discovery of a healthy population of coelocanths in the area has only added to Sodwana's mystique as an adventurous diving location.

Manzenowenya
Lake Sibaya
•Nine Mile Reef
•Seven Mile Reef
Mbazwana•
•Five Mile Reef
•Two Mile Reef
Sodwana Bay•

SOUTH AFRICA

0   20 km
0   15 mi

Red Sands Reef

Leadsman Shoal

Lake St. Lucia

THE DIVES

There are tight constraints on the commercial exploitation of this pristine area, and only three dive centers are allowed to operate in Sodwana at any one time. This doesn't stop the site from being ridiculously crowded at weekends and in the holiday season, with fleets of four-wheel drive vehicles arriving from all over South Africa. The narrow launch site becomes something of a bottleneck and long delays are inevitable, so it's best to avoid these times.

The classic sites in Sodwana are a series of reefs named for their distance from a lighthouse on the headland. The four most popular—Two, Five, Seven and Nine Mile Reefs—have characters all their own. Diving access to Nine Mile Reef is limited to minimize impact on its delicate soft corals, found here in abundance.

The trek to Sodwana is worth it just for the launch itself. All the dive operators are expert at charging the

33

DIVE CENTERS

DIVE SOUTH
P.O. Box 38890, Faerie Glen 0043,
South Africa
Phone +27-12-991-3134
E-mail info@divesouthafrica.co.za
Web: www.divesouth.co.za

CORAL DIVERS
Private Bag 310, Mbazwana 3974,
South Africa
Phone: +27-33-345-6531
E-mail: info@coraldivers.co.za
Web: www.coraldivers.co.za

SODWANA BAY LODGE SCUBA CENTRE
Private Bag 317, Mbazwana 3974,
South Africa
Phone: +27-83-229-0318
E-mail: sblsc@icon.co.za
Web: www.sodwanadiving.co.za

 DIVING ORGANIZATIONS

N.A.U.I. Services of Southern Africa
40 Gordonia Centre, Beach Road,
Gordons Bay 7139, South Africa
Phone: +27-21-856-5184
E-mail: info@nauisa.org
Web: www.nauisa.org

 RECOMPRESSION

Eugene Marais Hyperbaric Therapy Centre
Eugene Marais Hospital, 696 5th Avenue,
Les Marais, Pretoria, South Africa
Phone: +27-12-334-2567

 HOSPITAL

Addington Hospital
Erskine Terrace, South Beach,
Durban, South Africa
Phone: +27-31-327-2000
E-mail: jill.hurst@kznhealth.gov.za

Eshowe Hospital
Kangela Street, Eshowe, South Africa
Phone: +27-35-473-4500
E-mail: zandile.jaffe@kznhealth.gov.za

 CONSERVATION SOCIETY

Natal Parks Board
P.O. Box 662, Pietermaritzburg 3200,
South Africa
Phone: +27-33-147-1961
Web: www.kznwildlife.com
E-mail: webmail@kznwildlife.com

KwaZulu Dept., Nature Conservation
Private Bag X98, Ulundi 3838, South Africa
Phone: +27-35-870-0552

▶ **BIODIVERSITY**
Due to the influence of the Agulhas
Current you can find a tremendous range
of fish species in the waters off
Mozambique.

Indian Ocean swell, but the ride through the serried ranks of huge breakers, any one of which is capable of flipping the boat over, is still a heart-stopping experience, especially for the uninitiated. The surge can be felt beneath the surface, particularly on the shallow sections of Seven and Nine Mile Reefs.

The variety of reefs means that divers can explore caves and overhangs, walls, or more benign sloping reefs in relatively shallow water. Each reef is sub-divided into individual sites, all offering a slightly different diving experience. You can also explore some very exciting deeper reefs, although appropriate training and equipment may be required.

TWO MILE REEF

• **Up to 80 feet (25 m) • beginner**

The most popular site in Sodwana, but still providing some tremendous dives. The reef itself is approximately 1.3 miles (2 km) long and half a mile (1 km) wide, and is characterized by convoluted coral formations with numerous crags and outcrops. The evocative names of the sites speak volumes for the nature of the dives—The Pinnacles, Chain Reefs, Cave and Gullies, and Overhang. The diving is relatively shallow, with a number of the sites in the region of 45 feet (13 m).

Two Mile Reef provides the opportunity to observe the smaller marine life of the area, with dense shoals of big eyes, goatfish, and snappers in evidence. Large lone potato bass are also frequently sighted on this reef. Within the folds and overhangs of the reef are honeycomb morays and scorpionfish, while marbled rays are often seen above the sandy patches between coral formations. In the reef's shallower sites such as Caves and Gullies you will find a good range of invertebrates hiding within the complex coral formations, enjoying the consistent strong light conditions.

FIVE MILE REEF

• **70 feet (20 m) • advanced**

Paradoxically, given its name, this reef is only three-quarters of a mile (1.2 km) offshore as the distance is measured from the launch point, not in a straight line out to sea. Its underwater topography differs slightly in character from that of Two Mile Reef. Five Mile Reef is large and flattened, and is formed by a range of rather delicate corals. The most impressive of these are tiny staghorn corals, which are beautifully intact. Mushroom and plate corals are also present on the reef, and frequently provide shelter for juvenile scorpionfish and paper fish. Five Mile Reef is only suitable for divers with excellent buoyancy skills, and the site is vigorously policed by rangers from the Natal Parks Board. Over the years it has become known as an excellent spot to encounter dolphins.

Linda Pitkin

Dan Burton

SEVEN MILE REEF

• 55 to 75 feet (17 to 23 m) • intermediate

If Two Mile Reef is the most popular dive site in Sodwana, Seven Mile Reef is probably the best all-round dive. Despite the fact that it is only half a mile (0.8 km) offshore, this reef offers steep walls and drop-offs. The corals are characterized by a number of mushroom-shaped formations, and the marine life is a heady mix of reef fish and open ocean species. Turtles and rays are frequently seen here, and it is also home to large numbers of anemone and skunk clownfish.

NINE MILE REEF

• 40 to 70 feet (12 to 20 m) • intermediate

This is a protected site, rarely dived due to park restrictions and powerful surge. The most famous feature on the reef is the "Green Tree", a spectacular coral tree standing 10 feet (3 m) high, surrounded by clouds of goldies. Continue south of the Green Tree and there is a beautiful series of swim-throughs, gullies, and caverns, where sleeping sharks may sometimes be encountered.

OTHER ACTIVITIES

Where to begin! This is a beautiful, wild area of South Africa, and a number of game parks and reserves are within easy striking distance of Sodwana.

Hluhluwe-Umfulozi National Park, once the hunting ground of Zulu warrior kings such as Dingiswayo and Shaka, was established as a game reserve in 1895. It is only a short drive away from Sodwana, and is home to southern Africa's "big five"—lion, black and white rhino, elephant, and Cape buffalo. Viewing hides overlook pans and waterholes, enabling visitors to see these game animals at close range.

☎ **TELEPHONE NUMBERS**

Recompression chamber	+27-12-335-1577
Hospital	+27-31-327-2000
Tourism KwaZulu-Natal	+27-31-366-7500

💻 **WEBSITES & E-MAIL**

Tourism KwaZulu-Natal	www.kzn.org.za
Africa Guide	www.africaguide.com

▲ RAGGED TOOTH SHARK

Ragged tooth sharks are only one of a number of shark species that hunt around the reefs of Sodwana.

DIVER'S TIP

Only dive with established dive operators. There are numerous stories of weekend visitors getting it wrong in the surf launch.

INHACA ISLAND
& BAZARUTO

RAVAGED BY CIVIL WAR FOR OVER TWO DECADES, MOZAMBIQUE WAS THE FORGOTTEN LAND OF DIVING. THE GRADUAL REVIVAL OF TOURISM SINCE THE END OF THE CONFLICT IN 1992 HAS LED TO MOZAMBIQUE'S DIVING LEGENDS BEING REBORN. FOREMOST AMONG THESE ARE INHACA AND THE BAZARUTO ISLANDS.

When Portuguese navigator Vasco da Gama sailed around the Cape of Good Hope to become the first European to visit Mozambique in 1498, he found Arab and Swahili Indian Ocean traders already making use of its natural harbors. Mozambique has had a checkered history since then as a slaving center, a Portuguese colony, and, most recently, a country torn asunder by independence wars and vicious civil conflicts. What has always been present is mile after mile of beautiful reef and large marine animals traveling in the warm waters of the Agulhas Current. With the re-establishment of the tourist and diving industry, Mozambique is once again taking its rightful place on the international diving scene, as new sites are opened up and old areas re-discovered.

GEOGRAPHY

Mozambique is a country of some 308,640 sq miles (799,379 sq km) on the east coast of southern Africa facing the island of Madagascar on the other side of the Mozambique Channel. Its coastal plains are cut by a number of great rivers including the Limpopo and the Zambezi, two of the most evocative names in African geography. Most of the population of more than 17 million lives in Maputo Province and the capital Maputo in the extreme southeast.

Mozambique has seen some savage civil conflicts since winning its independence from Portugal in 1975, and at one time it was officially declared the poorest country on Earth. Things have improved since the fighting ended in 1992, though devastating floods in 1999 and 2000 brought renewed suffering.

Diving is a major factor in Mozambique's reviving tourist industry. The country has 1,500 miles (2,413 km) of coastline. Running north from Maputo for approximately half of its length is a landscape of estuaries, sandbars, and mangrove swamps. The northern coastline consists mostly of sandy beaches and cliffs. The

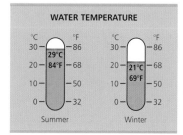
WATER TEMPERATURE
Summer 29°C/84°F · Winter 21°C/69°F

Andrew Pugsley

► RAGGED TOOTH SHARK
A close-up view shows unmistakable evidence of why this shark acquired its name.

John Bantin

▲ BULL SHARKS

As well as abundant and reliable aggregations of ragged tooth sharks, encounters with bull sharks are also a feature of diving in Mozambique.

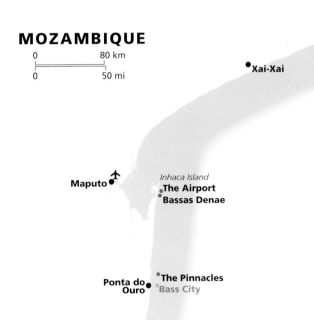

MOZAMBIQUE

0 — 80 km
0 — 50 mi

- Inhassoro
- *Ilha do Bazaruto*
- *Ilha Benguéhua*
- **Cabo San Sebastian**
- **Inhambane**
- Xai-Xai
- Maputo
- *Inhaca Island*
- **The Airport**
- **Bassas Denae**
- **The Pinnacles**
- Ponta do Ouro
- Bass City

small islands off this stretch of coastline are a mix of rolling sand and limestone, creating on the one hand gentle white sandy beaches, and on the other craggy caverns, overhangs, and numerous caves.

MARINE LIFE

The warm waters of the Agulhas Current passing through the Mozambique Channel are the key to Mozambique's abundant marine life. Unexploited during the long years of the civil war, its reefs are amazingly healthy, having largely escaped the ravages of El Niño. Many are rich in the larger animals of the East African coast. Although becoming rare, it is still possible to sight dugongs in some estuaries and shallow bays, and humpback whales migrate along the coast in great numbers. Whale sharks and dolphins are also regulars at some sites, particularly around the celebrated Bazaruto Archipelago in the north. Very large potato groupers are common in the south, and marlin and sailfish sightings are recorded at some of the wilder walls and reefs with access to the open sea.

The shark population is also healthy. Some Mozambican sites even challenge the famed dive sites of South Africa for the sheer quantity of ragged tooth sharks they attract, while others boast bull, black tips, tigers, and—in the south—what is reported to be a year-round population of great whites.

THE DIVES

Tourist facilities in grindingly poor Mozambique are pretty basic by the standards of most western travelers. The small number of dive operators here have however been catering for the South African market for many years and they are mostly professionally run and organized. Nonetheless, the healthcare infrastructure of Mozambique is very rudimentary. Adequate planning and care when diving is essential, and it is a wise precaution to take out an insurance package that includes evacuation to South Africa should a hyperbaric emergency occur.

34

 DIVE CENTERS

DIVE SOUTH
P.O. Box 38890, Faerie Glen 0043,
South Africa
Phone: +27-12-991-3134
E-mail: info@divesouthafrica.co.za

SIMPLY SCUBA DIVE CHARTERS
Ponta do Ouro Campsite,
Ponta do Ouro, Mozambique
Phone: +27-11-678-0972/3 (South Africa)
E-mail: info@simplyscuba.co.za
Web: www.simplyscuba.co.za

DIVERSITY SCUBA LDA
T12 Praia do Tofo, P.O. Box 194,
Inhambane, Mozambique
Phone: +258-232-9002
E-mail: info@diversityscuba.com
Web: www.diversityscuba.com

 DIVING ORGANIZATIONS
None

 RECOMPRESSION

Eugene Marais Hyperbaric Therapy Centre
Eugene Marais Hospital, 696 5th Avenue,
Les Marais, Pretoria, South Africa
Phone: +27-12-334-2567

 HOSPITAL

Maputo General Hospital
Maputo, Mozambique
Phone: +258-925-420-448

CONSERVATION SOCIETY

The World Wildlife Fund's Conservation Action
Network has information on conservation
activities in Mozambique:
Web: takeaction.worldwildlife.org

OTHER DIVE SITES

Bass City

DIVER'S TIP

Ensure you have adequate funds and/or
insurance to get you out of the country if you
have an accident. Medical facilities are limited,
and evacuation almost essential in a serious
incident.

The dive sites are concentrated in two main areas: Inhaca Island, some 21 miles (35 km) east of Maputo; and around the famous Bazaruto Archipelago in the far north. The diving around the islands tends to be quite sedate. However, there are some challenging dives on the outer reefs, and you will more than likely be repaid with some thrilling encounters with the larger pelagics for which Mozambique is justifiably famed. Other important sites are Ponta do Ouro in the south, and Inhambane Bay. The diving off Ponta do Ouro is very similar to Sodwana in South Africa, including the dramatic surf launch from the beach.

INHACA ISLAND

• **100 feet (30 m)** • **intermediate**

Inhaca Island lies only 21 miles (35 km) east of Maputo across the bay and yet it is a world away from this busy capital city. The island was declared a Nature Reserve in 1976 and its combination of reef, wreck, and big animal diving is absolutely world-class.

A dive known as "The Airport" is a particular favorite. It owes its name to the large numbers of ragged tooth sharks that are constantly passing back and forth above the sand runways. Bassas Denae is a large reef about 7 miles (12 km) off the island where you can expect to see migrating humpback whales and also access a number of wrecks.

Dives on the inshore reefs of Inhaca Island are excellent for less experienced divers. Although the visibility may lack the crystal clarity of the outer reefs, there is some tremendous marine life, and gentle drifts on the turn of the tide offer a chance to explore long sections of reef. There is a maximum depth limit of 100 feet (30 m) when diving off the island, although the average depth is well above that at about 60 feet (18 m).

CABO SAN SEBASTIAN

• **100 feet (30 m)** • **intermediate**

Cabo San Sebastian lies off the southernmost tip of the Bazaruto Archipelago, which many people judge to contain the best dive sites in the entire country. An area covering 540 sq miles (1,400 sq km) around the four main islands in the Bazaruto group was designated a Marine National Park in 2002, one of the largest in the whole of Africa. The archipelago is home to dugongs, sawfishes, and several species of turtle. Migrating humpback whales pass through in great numbers during the summer months.

You need local knowledge backed up with a little G.P.S. technology to locate Cabo San Sebastian. This deep reef offers the classic range of large animal encounters—mantas, whale sharks, turtles—as well as busy reef communities of snappers, barracuda, jacks, and several species of moray.

THE PINNACLES

• **120 feet (37 m)** • **advanced**

A classic adventure dive. It's all here—the reasons why Mozambique has gained a reputation for epic dives and dramatic encounters with large animals. The Pinnacles dive is located 2 miles (3 km) off the coast at Ponta do Ouro, just within the Mozambican border with South Africa, and is one of the most popular sites in the country. It is a deep dive over craggy terrain, but the rewards are immense. Hammerhead, tiger, bull, white tip, silver tip, dusky, and leopard sharks cruise along the flanks of a ridge running at 120 feet (37 m); in a single week 10 different species of shark were recorded at this one site alone. Look out into the blue for the passing shadows of marlins and sailfish, and remember to glance upwards for cruising whale sharks.

OTHER ACTIVITIES

The legacy of Mozambique's civil war is ever-present in the shape of more than a million land mines strewn across the countryside and along the coast. The attractions of the wildlife and the remote regions of this large country are immense, but the dangers mean that much of it will be strictly off-limits for some considerable time to come.

It is possible to visit the Lago de Cahora Bassa dam about 300 miles (482 km) inland on the Zambezi River, and to take a tour around the dam itself, which is one of the most impressive in Africa. Tofu and Barra beaches, legendary in their time, are once again starting to cater for tourists—Barra is the more developed and easily accessible, Tofu is more remote but all the more attractive for it. You should also visit Maputo Elephant Reserve, a short drive north of the capital, which contains about 400 elephants that migrate through the rolling dune country between Mozambique and South Africa.

Many South Africans drive up the coast to enjoy Mozambique's big game fishing. Dive operators in both South Africa and Mozambique are able to organize combined safari and fishing tours.

☎ **TELEPHONE NUMBERS**

Recompression chamber	+27-12-335--577
Hospital	+258-925-420-448

🖥 **WEBSITES & E-MAIL**

Tourist information	www.mozambique.mz
Travel information	www.africaguide.com/country/mozamb

▲ **GIANT GROUPER**

Years of civil war and an absence of large-scale commercial fisheries have allowed fish such as this giant grouper to grow unmolested by divers or fishermen

WATAMU
MARINE PARK

WATAMU, KENYA'S EARLIEST MARINE PARK, IS AN ECOLOGICAL JEWEL OF RARE DELIGHT, FAMED FOR ITS DESERTED STRETCHES OF WHITE SANDY BEACHES AND GENTLE LAGOONS. ITS CORAL FRINGING REEFS HAVE PROSPERED UNDER THEIR PROTECTED STATUS, CREATING ONE OF THE FINEST DIVING EXPERIENCES ON THE COAST OF EAST AFRICA.

 VISIBILITY

30 to 70 feet (10 to 20 m) depending on season

 MUST SEES

Whale sharks

Mantas

 DOWNSIDE

This is a poor country, and tourists are frequent targets for crime

 GETTING THERE

You can fly direct to Nairobi's Jomo Kenyatta International Airport from many U.S. and European cities. Airport departure tax for international flights is U.S.$20 but is usually included in the cost of your ticket. Your operator should arrange transport from Nairobi Airport to Malindi.

 VISA

All visitors except East African citizens require a visa. Apply for your visa well in advance, especially if doing so by mail.

 MONEY

Currency is the Kenyan shilling. Most operators will accept major credit cards or cash payment in U.S. dollars.

Kenya's coastline extends for only 310 miles (500 km) from Somalia in the north to Tanzania in the south, and for the most part it is densely colonized and heavily exploited as the result of mounting population pressure. Watamu's protected status therefore allows the visiting diver to experience Indian Ocean reefs in a pristine state that has long disappeared from the rest of the Kenyan coastline, offering a tantalizing glimpse of how things must once have been.

GEOGRAPHY

Fringing reefs are the predominant feature of the south coast of Kenya, and there is less sediment and land run-off than occurs farther north. Located on the southern coast, some 74 miles (120 km) north of Mombasa, is Malindi National Marine Reserve, which extends for 18 miles (30 km) from Malindi town to beyond the entrance to Mida Creek. It protects a complex of coastal and marine habitats within a total area of 82 sq miles (213 sq km). Two National Marine Parks, Malindi and Watamu, lie within this larger conservation area. Watamu National Marine Park encompasses the mangrove forest at the entrance to Mida Creek, a large, almost land-locked lagoon of saline water, as well as the coral reefs, platforms, and cliffs, and the sandy beaches that lie along its seaward side.

The East African Coastal Current flows from the south along this stretch of coast. During the summer months, southwesterly monsoon winds create the Somali Current, which moves water down the coast from the north. The meeting of these two large ocean currents is highly significant for the diversity of marine species at Watamu.

MARINE LIFE

There are four National Marine Reserves and four National Marine Parks in Kenya, two of which have been designated as U.N.E.S.C.O. Biosphere Reserves. Watamu has held this status since 1979, in recognition of its immense importance in the ecology of the surrounding coastline and reef systems.

Although the official number of fish species for the region is around 200, the real number is thought to be much higher, probably around 500. This motley collection of fishes swarms over reefs made up of 140 different species of hard and soft corals. The mangroves around the mouth of Mida Creek are a crucial nursery for juvenile reef fish species that develop here in relative safety among the roots of the trees before taking their place on the reefs themselves. The mangroves also provide a rich habitat for crabs, insects, and birds.

Some of the smaller residents of the reefs include several species of nudibranch, frogfish, and leaf fish, the latter being particularly abundant. Look out for octopus, frequently encountered in the nooks and crannies of the shallower reefs. Titan triggerfish breed on the reef in January, the cause of many an exhilarating dive as they furiously defend their territories from divers who encroach too close.

Whale sharks are particularly abundant from October through to February, while humpback whales pass through the area from June to September. The latter are frequently seen breaching beyond the outer reefs. One of the great experiences at Watamu is to wander the beaches at dusk when there is a high tide and watch juvenile black fin reef sharks feeding in the shallows. These young sharks come right to the very

---

WATER TEMPERATURE

	Summer		Winter	
°C	°F	°C	°F
30 —	— 86	30 —	— 86
30°C			
20 — **86°F**	— 68	20 —	— 68
		20°C	
10 —	— 50	10 — **68°F**	— 50
0 —	— 32	0 —	— 32

Linda Pitkin

edge of the beach, and if you are feeling brave enough, you can wade out into the shallows to watch them swirl around your feet. Of the seven sea turtle species in the world, five have been encountered at Watamu, the most common being green and hawksbill turtles.

The park is under the management of Kenya's Wildlife and Conservation Department, who do a good job of protecting the reef with limited resources. The greatest threat to the reefs comes from the activities of souvenir hunters and from collectors of coral to make craft objects for sale to tourists. Increasing siltation from the nearby Sabaki River is also something of a problem. All visitors are charged U.S.$5 to enter the park. Most dive operators incorporate this cost in their booking fee.

THE DIVES

The dives at Watamu are all within a 10 or 20 minutes' boat-ride from the beach, and range from sheltered gentle inner reefs to more dramatic drop-offs and drift dives on the outer reef walls. The dive sites are buoyed to prevent diving boats causing damage to the reefs by dragging their anchors. There are several very interesting inshore sites such as Tewa Caves, home to some massive groupers, and a number of spectacular snorkeling sites.

THE CANYON

• 80 feet (25 m) • intermediate

This site is named for a long sandy channel bordered by reef walls. Look out for stingrays on the floor of the channel, and also for species of pelagic ray in the blue water above the walls. Halfway through the dive there

▲ FLATWORM

Smaller residents such as nudibranchs, leaf fish, and frogfish are a real draw to Watamu's reefs.

WATAMU MARINE PARK (Kenya)

0 ——————— 3 km
0 ——————— 2 mi

Watamu Village ●

The Canyon
Brain Coral ● ● Moray Reef
WATAMU
MARINE PARK

35

Jeremy Stafford-Deitsch

▶ WHALE SHARK

The confluence of two major ocean currents can bring the large visitors from the open ocean.

▶▶ BLACK-SPOTTED GRUNTS

Black-spotted grunts form large shoals during daylight hours at the edge of the reef.

DIVER'S TIP

Personal security is a real issue when traveling through Kenya to Watamu, so do take precautions when out of the resort.

 DIVE CENTERS

AQUA VENTURES DIVE CENTRE
P.O. Box 275, Watamu, Kenya
Phone: +254-42-32420
E-mail: scubav@diveinkenya.com
Web: www.diveinkenya.com

SCUBA DIVING KENYA
P.O. Box 160, Watamu, Kenya
Phone: +254-122-32099
E-mail: skriedl@swiftmalindi.com
Web: www.scuba-diving-kenya.com

 DIVING ORGANIZATIONS

None. See P.A.D.I. website for status of dive operators in the area: www.padi.com

 RECOMPRESSION

Kenya Navy Headquarters
P.O. Box 95350, Mombasa, Kenya

 HOSPITAL

The Mombasa Hospital
P.O. Box 90294, Mombasa, Kenya
Phone: +254-113-12191
E-mail: info@mombasahospital.com
Web: www.mombasahospital.com

Nairobi Hospital
Argwings Kodhek Road, Nairobi, Kenya
Phone: +254-284-5000

 CONSERVATION SOCIETY

Kenya Wildlife Service,
P.O. Box 40241, Nairobi, Kenya
Phone: +254-260-0800
E-mail: kws@kws.org
Web: www.kws.org

---

is a beautiful natural arch festooned with gorgonians and soft corals. Flying over the top of the canyon is a good way to spot resident shoals of snappers, sweetlips, and rock cod.

MORAY REEF

- 80 feet (25 m) • intermediate

The main feature of this site, apart from a giant moray called George, is an impressive overhang leading to a white sandy platform at 80 feet (25 m). Out in the blue water off the overhang keep a watch out for schools of barracuda and jacks, as well as fusiliers and banner fish closer to the wall. Huge groups of sergeant majors seem to hang around the reef crest, along with the occasional angelfish and tang.

You'll find George, the star attraction, under the overhang at about 70 feet (20 m). He is now thoroughly accustomed to divers invading his privacy, and provided he is in the right mood, you should be able to get the moray photos of your diving life.

BRAIN CORAL

- 70 feet (20 m) • beginner

A wonderful shallow dive where the smaller residents of the reef take center stage, although rumor has it that dolphins are sometimes encountered here.

The buoy line runs down to approximately 30 feet (10 m) to bring you among some complex coral structures that are home to leaf fish, small lionfish, octopus, and the ubiquitous clownfish. The reef slopes

away on either side from this central coral area, reaching a depth of 70 feet (20 m) on the seaward side. To the north there are some extensive colonies of garden eels, and it is possible to spot blue spotted stingrays buried in the sand. South of the buoy several overhangs and crags swarm with glassfish, with prowling schools of trevally in constant attendance. You may even sight large napoleon wrasses or passing turtles in the blue water off the reef.

OTHER ACTIVITIES

This is one of the better locations to be a non-diver, or to mix a little local exploration with your diving. There are a number of sites of great interest locally, including the 12th-century Gede Ruins, where it is possible to encounter Syke's Monkeys, as well as the splendidly named Golden Rumped Elephant Shrew.

The bird life of the region is truly spectacular, with three species of plover, sanderlings, and a number of species of terns and gulls. Local wildlife includes giant monitor lizards, dik dik, antelope, mongoose, and various species of monkey.

 TELEPHONE NUMBERS

| Recompression chamber | +254-114-51351 |
| Hospital | +254-113-12191 |

 WEBSITES & E-MAIL

Kenya Tourist Board	www.magicalkenya.com
Kenya information	www.kenyaweb.com
Travel information	www.africaonline.com

ZANZIBAR

words by Mark Evans

THE ISLAND OF ZANZIBAR, LYING JUST OFF THE COAST OF TANZANIA, IS A LITTLE GEM IN THE INDIAN OCEAN OFFERING PRISTINE CORAL REEFS SWARMING WITH MARINE LIFE AND CLOSE ENCOUNTERS WITH LARGER SPECIES SUCH AS TURTLES, SHARKS, GROUPER AND RAYS.

 VISIBILITY
65 to 100 feet (20 to 30 m)

 MUST SEES
Huge green turtles

 DOWNSIDE
Can lack infrastructure and facilities.

 GETTING THERE
At present, Gulf Air, Ethiopian Airlines and KLM (together with Kenya Airways) offer international scheduled flights to Zanzibar. Several large carriers fly into Dar es Salaam, which is only a short trip by air or sea from Zanzibar. Amongst them are British Airways, Emirates Airlines and Swiss.

 VISA
Visas are required by nationals from most countries. Travelers are advised to obtain visas in advance but they can be issued on arrival for the relevant fees. Alternatively, check if there is a Tanzanian Consulate in your country of origin. The island of Zanzibar is part of the United Republic of Tanzania, so there is no need to obtain a second visa if your itinerary will include both Tanzania and Zanzibar or Pemba Island.

 MONEY
Tanzanian Shilling (Tsh)

► A STAR IS BORN
The prolific hard and soft corals smothering the reef are rich habitats for all manner of marine life.

Mark Evans

WATER TEMPERATURE

°C	°F		°C	°F
30 —	— 86		30 —	— 86
20 —	— 68		20 —	— 68
27°C **80°F**			**21°C** **70°F**	
10 —	— 50		10 —	— 50
0 —	— 32		0 —	— 32
Summer			Winter	

Nankivell •

• Mbwangawa
• Kichafi
Leon's Wall

• Cave 20

• Pale Pale Reef

• Ukweli Reef

• Blue Wall
• Clupis Sponges

• Zanzibar

TANZANIA

✈ **ZANZIBAR**

0   10 km

0   10 mi

Zanzibar is relatively unknown in the diving world, often overlooked in favor of its near-neighbors Mozambique, South Africa and Kenya. But this is a crying shame, as the island offers unspoiled reef diving, thrilling drift dives and a high chance of big animal encounters. Best of all, head for the southeastern coastline and the only other divers you are likely to see are the ones joining you on your boat!

GEOGRAPHY

Zanzibar is an archipelago made up of Zanzibar and Pemba islands, and several islets. It is located in the Indian Ocean about 25 miles (40 km) from the Tanzanian coast and 6° south of the equator. Zanzibar island (known locally as Unguja, but as Zanzibar internationally) is 60 miles (96 km) long and 20 miles (32 km) wide, occupying a total area of approximately 650 square miles (1,680 sq km). The island itself is made up of ancient coral and is characterized by beautiful sandy beaches with fringing coral reefs.

Zanzibar's local people are an incredible mixture of ethnic backgrounds, indicative of its colorful history. Islam is the dominant religion, and practised by most Zanzibaris, although there are also followers of Christianity and Hinduism. Zanzibaris speak Swahili (known locally as Kiswahili), a language that is spoken extensively in East Africa. Many believe that the purest form is spoken in Zanzibar, as it is the birthplace of the language.

Fishing and agriculture are the main economic activities of the local people. Zanzibar was once the world's largest producer of cloves, and its economy was based on large incomes thus derived. Although cloves are still a major export, along with coconut products and spices, tourism has been earmarked as the primary foreign exchange earner, with more visitors coming to Zanzibar each year. At this stage, the numbers are still

▼ **HERE'S LOOKING AT YOU**
A white mouth moray eel meanders in and out of crevices along the reef.

Mark Evans

Mark Evans

▲ SIZE IS EVERYTHING
Adult turtles can reach the size of a small car.

DIVE CENTERS
RISING SUN DIVE CENTER
Breezes Beach Club & Spa
Zanzibar
Phone: +255-747-415-049
E-mail: bookings@risingsun-zanzibar.com
Web: www.risingsun-zanzibar.com

HOSPITAL
Mnazi Mmoja Hospital
PO Box 338
Zanzibar
Tanzania
Phone: +255-54-31-071

low (less than 100,000 annually) and the potential for tourism is relatively untapped, so my advice is get in now before the masses arrive.

MARINE LIFE

The prolific hard and soft corals smothering the reefs along the southeastern coastline of Zanzibar are rich habitats for all manner of marine life, from fish such as parrotfish, bannerfish, butterflyfish, moray eels, wrasse and grouper to invertebrates like crabs, lobsters and shrimps. The deeper walls and sandy slopes, complete with seagrass beds, are popular hangouts for green turtles, which can attain a quite monstrous size. Other large species likely to be encountered on the deeper sites include various rays, giant grouper, Napoleon wrasse and sharks such as bull and blacktip. Fish traps are in use, but sustainably so; and spearfishing, for which you need a permit, is only allowed on breath-hold.

THE DIVES

The underwater topography of the region means that the deeper reef wall does not lie miles offshore, so the majority of the main dive sites along the eastern coastline are within a 30-minute boat ride. Experienced divers will love the free descents, strong currents and deeper walls and reefs, while newly qualified divers will feel equally at home on the shallower reefs that teem with marine life and rarely drop below 65 feet (20 m).

For those with a thirst for exploration, dive centers often venture to new areas to sample the diving in the hope of finding new regular sites. These can be a gamble. You might drop in and be on a relatively sparse, boring location, but on the other hand, you could find something out of the ordinary—and you'll have the satisfaction of knowing you were among the first group ever there. There are also several dive sites located off the north and northeast coast.

BLUE WALL

• **120 to 165+ feet (36 to 50+ m)** • **expert**

This is not a dive for the faint-hearted. You roll off the boat and do a free descent through endless blue water until the 118- to 125-foot (36 to 38 m) bottom comes into view. There is usually a strong current running and, as you near the seabed, it just drops away from sight. This is the top of the wall. As you go over the edge and allow the current to carry you along, the bottom of the wall can be seen below at 230 to 245 feet (70 to 75 m). You need to have good air consumption, good buoyancy skills and be comfortable deep and in a current. However, for experienced divers, this is a thrilling dive, offering high chances of pelagic encounters with large rays, giant grouper and various species of shark.

UKWELI REEF

• **80 to 105+ feet (25 to 32+ m)** • **intermediate**

The reef starts relatively deep, meaning you don't get a huge amount of time at depth, but what time you do have will seem to fly past at a rate of knots thanks to all the marine life going about its daily business in front of you. The sloping reef plays host to large shoals of snapper and fusiliers and, in certain areas, it is deeply undercut, creating small caverns and overhangs, which are popular with large grouper and, occasionally, green and hawksbill turtles.

CLUPIS SPONGES

• **65 to 75 feet (20 to 23 m)** • **intermediate**

A desolate sandy seabed covered in swathes of seagrass and dotted with the odd dark barrel sponge doesn't sound like the world's most exciting dive site. Closer inspection reveals each and every sponge outcrop is a veritable treasure-trove of small critters, from juvenile reef fish to various species of crabs, shrimps and lobsters. However, while these little fellows are interesting in their own right, the main reason for diving here is the better-than-average chances of encountering feeding green turtles. And these are proper adult turtles, some getting up to the size of a small car! Because there is usually a current running over the site, it is often difficult to get up close and personal with the turtles—you tend to see them as you drift past—but if you spot them in time and are able to make a slow, stealthy approach where they can see you coming, they will generally allow you to get within a few yards—perfect for those close-up photographs.

CAVE20

• 82 to 115+ feet (25 to 35+ m) • intermediate

A sloping reef gives way to an area of coral deeply cut through with gullies, overhangs and small caverns—hence the name Cave20. As you sweep along in the current, keep an eye out for the horde of large grouper wallowing on the seabed in the vicinity. This must be a prime hunting ground as they are reluctant to leave, and if a passing diver does venture close enough to make one stir, it doesn't swim far before settling back down on to the bottom. There are plenty of reef fish, including shoaling snapper, surgeonfish, parrotfish, wrasse, butterflyfish and trumpetfish.

PALE PALE REEF

• 65 to 82 feet (20 to 25 m) • intermediate

Another top turtle-spotting location. Again, a sandy seabed with large patches of seagrass and the odd coral and sponge outcrop awaits descending divers. As well as the turtles, the sandy areas also play host to monster rays and, occasionally, guitar sharks. Spotted eagle rays will sometimes glide past, coming in to rummage around on the bottom for food.

OTHER ACTIVITIES

When you visit Zanzibar you must take time out from the diving to explore the island, which boasts many cultural and natural attractions.

First port of call should be Stone Town, the cultural heart of Zanzibar, which has changed little in the last 200 years. In fact it was recently declared a World Heritage Site by UNESCO. It is a place of winding alleys, bustling bazaars, mosques and grand Arab houses boasting magnificent brass-studded carved wooden doors. You can spend many idle hours just wandering through the fascinating labyrinth of narrow streets and alleyways; remember though that there are some "must-see" locations including the House of Wonders, Livingstone's House and the Arab Fort.

The spice plantations to the north of Zanzibar are worth a look, if only to try and guess what products come from what trees, bushes and vines. The island is also home to the endemic endangered Zanzibar red Colobus monkey, also known as Kirk's red Colobus after Sir John Kirk, the British President of Zanzibar, who first brought it to the attention of zoological science.

TELEPHONE NUMBERS
Hospital   +255-54-31-071

WEBSITES & E-MAIL
Zanzibar commission for tourism
Web: www.zanzibartourism.net
E-mail: marketing@zanzibartourism.net

▼ **JUST HANGING AROUND**
Large schools of colorful reef fish can often been seen hanging in the currents.

GRANDE COMORE

VISIBILITY

50 to 130 feet (15 to 40 m) depending on location and season

MUST SEES

Banc Vailheu

Masiwa wreck (just to tell the story afterwards!)

DOWNSIDE

Poor tourist infrastructure

Reef degradation

GETTING THERE

Getting there can be difficult. Air France operates two flights a week from Paris to Moroni on Grande Comore. Emirate Airlines also flies into Moroni from Dubai.

VISA

Passport and onward/return ticket required. Visas for more than a 24-hour stay must be bought on arrival.

MONEY

Comoran franc. The Banque Internationale des Comores (B.I.C.) will exchange all currencies, but the best currency to carry with you is the Euro. Credit cards and traveler's checks are usually accepted at resorts.

WATER TEMPERATURE

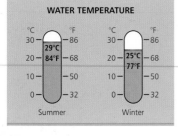

Summer: 29°C / 84°F
Winter: 25°C / 77°F

TIME WAS WHEN NO SERIOUS DIVER WOULD BOTHER WITH THE COMOROS ISLANDS, SO BAD WAS THE DEGRADATION OF THEIR REEFS. BUT THINGS HAVE MOVED ON AND THE REEFS HAVE IMPROVED DRAMATICALLY. TODAY GRANDE COMORE, THE LARGEST ISLAND, AND ITS NEIGHBORS MOHÉLI AND ANJOUAN, HAVE DIVES THAT WILL SATISFY ANY TRAVELING DIVER.

This tiny group of islands was for a long time overlooked by the world's travelers and tourists, who considered them a poor alternative to the attractions of Mozambique or the Seychelles. The islands' main claim to fame was that it was in their waters that the so-called "living fossil" fish, the coelacanth, was first discovered in 1938. Described as the equivalent of finding a dinosaur while strolling through a jungle village, news of this event rocked the world and put the islands on the map. Another coelacanth was found here in 1952, no great surprise to the local fishermen who had been catching them for centuries. The Comoros Islands, a fascinating mixture of craggy volcanic reefs, caves, and overhangs, are a perfect environment for this living relic, and have much to offer the diver of today.

GEOGRAPHY

The Comoros Islands lie at the northern end of the Mozambique Channel midway between the African mainland and the northwestern tip of Madagascar. The islands are not large, with a total land area of only 758 sq miles (2,034 sq km). But what they lack in size, they make up for in dramatic scenery. They are unmistakably of volcanic origin, with stark peaks rising from a rugged shoreline. The highest peak in the Comoros, at 7,743 feet (2,360 m), is the active Le Kartala volcano.

The Republic of Comoros is made up of three small islands—Grande Comore (Ngazidja), Mohéli (Mwali), and Anjouan (Nzwani). A fourth island in the group, Mayotte, remains a French overseas territory. After gaining independence in 1975, the Comoros Republic acquired a reputation for political instability, with 19 coups in 25 years. In 2000 agreement was reached on a new confederal constitution, and in 2002 each island elected its own president under these new arrangements, bringing hopes of a more secure future. But the country remains one of the poorest in the world.

MARINE LIFE

The islands' reefs have long suffered the scourge of blast- and cyanide-fishing, damage made worse in recent years by an increase in fertilizer run-off from cultivated land. But there have been some environmental success stories. The Mohéli Marine Park was set up in April 2001 with strong local involvement—ten of the 16 board members are local villagers. It has established a 150-sq mile (400-sq km) protected area policed by local people. Tourist numbers to this region have increased by 100 percent in the last two years, creating 30 new jobs. Visitors come to see reefs that already show a 35 percent increase in healthy coral cover, and have turtles nesting on more beaches. The Comoros story is a shining example of what can be achieved with the intelligent inclusion of local people.

A total of 475 species of fish have been recorded in the waters that surround the Comoros Island reefs. The smaller residents of the reef include leaf fish, frogfish, starry dragonets, and Spanish dancers, while unicornfish, soldierfish, and groupers are frequently to be seen patrolling the coral. Larger animals are often encountered on the outer reefs, including humpback whales as they pass through the Mozambique Channel on their annual migration in August, as well as mantas, some very large green morays, and marlin. The islands' famous coelacanths are undoubtedly present in some numbers here. However, they lurk in caves beyond the reach of most recreational divers.

Linda Pitkin

▲ CORAL GROUPER
A coral grouper enjoys the close attentions of a
cleaner shrimp.

THE DIVES

The most popular dive area within the island group is
off Grande Comore—indeed the vast majority of diving
activity in the Comoros used to take place from just one
hotel, Le Galawa Beach, and used one operator. (Of the
12,000 annual visitors to Grande Comore, 11,000 stay in
this single resort.) Most of the diving takes place on the
western coast. There are, however, other sites sprinkled
around the islands that are worth noting, and quite possibly some undiscovered areas that could hold some real
diving gems. One quite spectacular site is the tiny island
of Chissioua Ouenefou, just off the south coast of
Mohéli, within the marine reserve.

There are, loosely, two types of diving in the
Comoros Islands. The first is shallow dives on fringing
reefs, offering a range of encounters with smaller reef
species in a classically jumbled volcanic topography. The
second type invariably involves longer boat-rides and
takes in the walls off the edge of the outer reef. Here

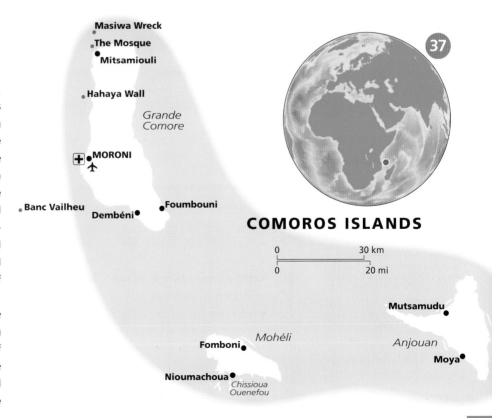

Masiwa Wreck

The Mosque
Mitsamiouli

Hahaya Wall

*Grande
Comore*

✚ MORONI
✈

• Banc Vailheu
Dembéni • • Foumbouni

COMOROS ISLANDS

0   30 km
0   20 mi

Mutsamudu •

Mohéli   *Anjouan*
Fomboni •
                                        Moya •
Nioumachoua •
*Chissioua
Ouenefou*

37

▶ VOLCANIC PINNACLES

Certain areas of inshore reef show stark evidence of the islands' volcanic origins in craggy rocks and abrupt pinnacles.

 DIVE CENTERS

No recognised or sanctioned dive operators in the location at present. It is well worth searching some South African diving websites for information on operators to the islands, as South Africa provides 70 percent of diving visitors to the Comoros.

 DIVING ORGANIZATIONS

None

RECOMPRESSION

None on the islands. Call Divers Alert Network (D.A.N.) Southern Africa, based in South Africa for assistance and advice in a diving emergency:
Phone: +27-112-541-112 (24-hour hotline)
D.A.N. accepts collect calls on the hotline

 HOSPITAL

Hospital El Maarouf,
Moroni District, Grande Comore, Comoros
Phone: +269-730-624

 CONSERVATION SOCIETY

Mohéli Marine Park is a fine example of a modern reserve utilizing the skill of local people. Contact the park for details of conservation around the islands:

the diving becomes altogether more spectacular, with every chance of encountering large pelagics such as tuna, sharks, mantas, and—if the diver is particularly lucky—whale sharks or humpback whales. The months of May to October are the best time for these dives.

BANC VAILHEU

• **30 to 130 feet (9 to 40 m)** • **intermediate**

The top of an undersea mountain that rises from the seabed a mile (1.6 km) below, Banc Vailheu will one day be another island in the Comoros archipelago. For now it offers one of the best dive sites in the islands, and indeed the wall dive is noted as one of the best of its type in the Indian Ocean. There are a number of dives along this wall, which stretches for several miles and is renowned for great visibility and visiting pelagics. Look out into the blue for sightings of wahoo, rainbow runners, kingfish, dogtooth tuna, barracuda, hammerhead sharks, mantas, and, at the right time of year, whale sharks. The wall also has some fascinating mini

caves, caverns, and overhangs, which are home to very large green morays.

MASIWA WRECK

• **110 feet (35 m)** • **intermediate**

One of those wrecks where the story behind it is almost as good as the dive on it! This 200-foot (60-m) long trawler was used by a French mercenary called Bob Denard to smuggle himself and 12 men onto the island in 1978, whereupon they shot dead the president and took the reins of power behind a new puppet leader. For 11 years Denard ruled the islands before being deposed by the French, and two years later the trawler was towed to its present site on the northwestern tip of Grande Comore and sunk as an artificial reef by a local resort owner.

The *Masiwa* is 80 feet (24 m) long and weighs 2,500 tonnes, and sits upright on a sandy seabed with her mast rising to 35 feet (10 m). She is in good shape, and it is possible for divers to enter her superstructure, as

Linda Pitkin

electric rays, and tiger snakes, as well as some particularly beautiful nudibranchs.

OTHER ACTIVITIES

The Republic of Comoros is a very poor country, a fact that is brought home to you immediately on leaving the comfort of your western-style resort. Moroni, the capital, is fairly unprepossessing and is probably worth avoiding unless you have a particular interest in the islands' colonial past. On the north side of Moroni lies Isandra, the former capital of Grande Comore, where you will find the Sultan's Palace, built during the 15th century when the islands were under Arab rule.

Also worth a visit is the village of Domoni where, amongst old forts and Portuguese graves, you will find Lac Salé, a salt lake surrounded by luxuriant vegetation. It is possible to visit the rim of the Kartala volcano if you are willing to camp overnight, and the rainforest on the islands is home to some spectacular tropical species, including 500 species of plant, 21 different types of bird, and nine reptile species. The giant fruit bat on the islands has a wingspan of more than 3 feet (1 m), and is found nowhere else on Earth.

☎ **TELEPHONE NUMBERS**

Recompression chamber	+27-112-541-112
Hospital	+269-730-624
Director General of Tourism	+269-744-242

🖥 **WEBSITES & E-MAIL**

| Comoros Islands info: | www.personal.ksu.edu/~omar/comoros |

▼ ORIENTAL SWEETLIPS
Sweetlips generally lurk in small groups under overhangs or areas of table coral.

long as they proceed with caution. Aside from good diving protocol, another sensible reason for moving carefully is the presence of "Bob", a large and ill-tempered potato bass, as well as a number of Grande Comore's impressive green morays.

HAHAYA WALL

• 100 feet (30 m) • intermediate

After an hour's boat-trip, this dive offers the opportunity to explore a precipitous wall cloaked in amphora sponges and large gorgonians. Look out for emperor angelfish, while off the wall you have a good chance of spotting marlins and sailfish in the blue water.

THE MOSQUE

• 35 feet (10 m) • beginner

A great night dive, the Mosque is a small coral structure close to shore that shelters an array of spectacular smaller reef inhabitants. You may see green and honeycomb morays, together with Spanish dancers, lionfish,

Linda Pitkin

MAURITIUS
& RODRIGUES

THE POPULAR HOLIDAY ISLAND OF MAURITIUS TOGETHER WITH RODRIGUES, MAY NOT FIGURE AMONG THE CULT SITES OF THE INTERNATIONAL DIVING WORLD, BUT FOR RELAXING DIVING FROM EXCELLENT FACILITIES WITH FRIENDLY GUIDES, THEY HAVE FEW RIVALS. THE TRAVELING DIVER WILL FIND PLENTY OF ATTRACTIONS AMONG THE RUGGED CORAL REEFS THAT COMPLETELY ENCIRCLE THE ISLANDS.

 VISIBILITY

100 feet (30 m) plus on the outer reef of Rodrigues Island
Only 40 to 60 feet (12 to 18 m) in shallow reefs around Mauritius

 MUST SEE

The Rempart Serpent reef for morays

 DOWNSIDE

Impact of tourism
Overfished reefs

 GETTING THERE

Most flights from the U.S. to Mauritius go via France. You can also fly there from Australia and several hubs in Africa and Asia. You must have a return or onward ticket before arriving in Mauritius. The departure tax is roughly U.S.$10. You can get to Rodrigues only by domestic flight from Mauritius.

 VISA

All visitors are required to have a passport and onward ticket in order to enter the country. Most visitors do not require visas for stays of up to 90 days.

$ MONEY

Currency is the Mauritius rupee. Traveler's checks in any major currency are easily exchanged in Mauritius and bring a better rate of exchange than cash. Credit cards are widely accepted.

Mauritius is famous for the warmth of the welcome it lays on for tourists and it is this, in combination with the low diver numbers on many of the sites, that sets it apart as a dive destination. Not deserving of the low regard held by some veterans of world diving, with some 250 miles (330 km) of coral-fringed coastline to explore, Mauritius has much to offer visiting divers, with many fine sites worthy of exploration.

GEOGRAPHY

The island of Mauritius lies about 500 miles (800 km) east of Madagascar, and with two smaller island groups, Rodrigues to the east and Agalega some way to the north, forms an independent state some 772 sq miles (2,000 sq km) in area. The islands are unmistakably volcanic in origin, and Mauritius is dominated by three rugged peaks, the tallest of which, Piton de la Rivière Noire, reaches an impressive 2,717 feet (828 m).

Discovered by the Portuguese in 1505, Mauritius was later held by the Dutch (who named it in honor of Prince Maurice) and then by the French, who developed sugar-cane production, still the mainstay of the island's economy. It passed into British hands in 1810, becoming independent in 1968. The population of around 1.2 million lives mostly in the north and west.

MARINE LIFE

Approximately 200 species of coral make up the reefs around the island, which are patrolled by the usual range of reef-dwelling fishes—the number of fish species in Mauritius is "officially" estimated as 430 by a major environmental monitoring organization, but the actual figure is probably slightly higher. Some of the dives in the islands on the north side of Mauritius are developing a reputation for rarely seen pelagic action, with reported encounters with species such as tuna, marlin, and wahoo off the drop-offs on the wilder

dives. Eagle rays and green turtles are present at most of the popular dive sites, and there are also a number of smaller reef species that are well worth looking out for. Leaf fish are frequently spotted, and one dive is notable for the staggering array of moray eels, lionfish and stonefish clustered together on a single small reef.

It is sad to note that many sites around the island are anything but pristine, and many of the operators report significant falls in fish stocks in the last few years, the result of illegal fishing methods and of mounting pressure on the reefs from continuing tourist development on the island.

THE DIVES

The dives on Mauritius cater for every level of diving experience from beginners all the way up to advanced. The reefs are predominantly rugged in nature, with crags, overhangs, caverns, and gullies a common feature on most dives. The main diving season is from October through to May.

Most of the diving on the island tends to be concentrated on the sheltered west coast, particularly the southern and northern ends. Because the east coast is exposed to powerful currents and the battering of the southeasterly trade winds, diving opportunities are more limited here. But the presence of these powerful currents means that some of the east coast dives are among the most dramatic in Mauritius. Round Island to the north of Mauritius is the place to see the larger pelagics off the reef walls.

The Mauritius Scuba Diving Association (M.S.D.A.) regulates diving operators in Mauritius. The dives themselves are on the conservative side, and no-decompression diving is actively encouraged. Although the majority of operators (particularly those associated with the M.S.D.A.) are usually very professional, there are one or two rogue operators at large so it is advisable to pick your operator with care.

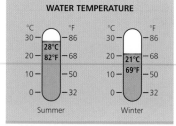

WATER TEMPERATURE

	Summer		Winter
°C	°F	°C	°F
30	86	30	86
20 — 28°C / 82°F	68	20 — 21°C / 69°F	68
10	50	10	50
0	32	0	32

Dan Burton

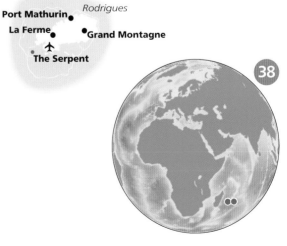

▲ TURTLE
Turtles are frequently encountered on the shallow sloping reefs off Mauritius. They should be allowed to proceed unharrassed by divers.

Flat Island
Gunner's Quoin *Gabriel Island*

The Silverstar
Wreck *Gunner's Quoin*
●Tortoise

Stella Maru *Ile D'Ambre*

Goodlands●

Port Mathurin● *Rodrigues*
La Ferme● ●Grand Montagne
✈
The Serpent

MAURITIUS

PORT LOUIS ●

Point Petite Rivière

0		15 km
0		10 mi

Please note that the distance between the two island groups has been reduced and is not to scale.

Centre de Flacq●

Flic-en-Flac
The Cathedral ● 🕐
Vacoas● ●Curepipe
The Rempart
Serpent

Ile aux Cerfs

Ile aux Bénitiers

Rose Belle●

✈
Colorado

Pointe Sud Ouest

Chemin Grenier●

DIVE CENTERS

SUN DIVER DIVING LTD
La Pirogue–Sugar Beach Resorts, Wolmar,
Flic-en-Flac, Mauritius
Phone: +230-453-8441
E-mail: sundiver@intnet.mu
Web: www.sundiversmauritius.com

DIVING ORGANIZATIONS

Mauritius Scuba Diving Association (M.S.D.A.)
36 bis, Meldrum Street, Beau Bassin, Mauritius
Phone: +230-454-0011
E-mail: msda@intnet.mu
Web: www.msda-cmas.org

RECOMPRESSION

c/o Special Mobile Force, Vacoas, Mauritius
Phone: +230-686-1011

HOSPITAL

Sir Seewoosagur Ramgoolam
National Hospital,
Pamplemousses, Mauritius
Phone: +230-243-4661

A.G. Jeetoo Hospital
Volcy Pougnet Str., Port Louis, Mauritius
Phone: +230-212-3201

CONSERVATION SOCIETY

The Mauritius Marine Conservation Society
E-mail: mmcs-ngo@intnet.mu
Web: pages.intnet.mu/mmcs/

OTHER DIVE SITES

Gunner's Quoin
Tortoise
Stella Maru
Colorado

► EAGLE RAY

Eagle rays are one of the great sights of
diving, the epitome of graceful
underwater flight.

THE CATHEDRAL

• 75 feet (23 m) • intermediate

Situated off the west coast, this dive is one of the most popular on the entire island, and is a large cavern that is entered through a small crack in the reef, leading to an open space about 40 feet (12 m) high. The cavern is lit by an eerie glow filtering through the entrance. The touch of drama this adds compensates for the somewhat limited marine life, although a number of small cracks and crevices in the wall may hide morays, pufferfish, and soldierfish. The floor is silty, and over-zealous finning can cut visibility drastically, so take care.

THE REMPART SERPENT

• 70 feet (21 m) • beginner

The Rempart Serpent is something of a biological one-off! It is a small nondescript reef about 300 feet (90 m) long, a scattered mass of coral boulders on a relatively featureless seabed. For some reason, this rather dull-looking reef hosts extraordinary collections of moray eels, lionfish, and stonefish. The numbers really are quite without precedent—it is rumored (somewhat improbably) that 32 separate species of moray have been identified at the site. The reason could well be that baitfish cluster around the boulders, but whatever

Linda Pitkin

Linda Pitkin

draws these species in to the area in such numbers, it makes for a site that is quite unique in Mauritius, and possibly the entire underwater world.

THE SILVERSTAR WRECK

130 feet (40 m) • advanced

The *Silverstar*, a former fishing vessel that was sunk to create an artificial reef, lies at some depth and for this reason the wreck has escaped many of the ravages that are the downside of frequent diver visits. The vessel is coated in impressive soft corals and gorgonians, her masts being particularly densely colonized. Some exceptionally large morays have taken up residence in the *Silverstar*'s holds and cabins.

RODRIGUES ISLAND

• 50 feet (15 m) • intermediate.

Rodrigues Island lies some 250 miles (330 km) east of Mauritius, an isolated volcanic peak in the midst of the Indian Ocean. Diving here offers a glimpse of how the reefs around Mauritius must have looked before they were damaged by the impact of destructive fishing and tourism some decades ago. The Serpent, in the channel leading out of the island's main lagoon, is a shallow site on a jumbled reef that just positively buzzes with life. Octopus, big-eye trevallies, kingfish, eagle rays,

groupers and many more species of fish benefit from the nutrient-rich water in this channel.

OTHER ACTIVITIES

Mauritius was once covered in rainforests, but the majority were cleared long ago to make way for sugarcane plantations, and now a scant 3 percent of the original cover remains. This is an absolute tragedy as Mauritius used to be home to a number of extraordinary mammals and birds, including the world's rarest parrot (the echo parakeet), pigeon (the pink pigeon), and kestrel (the Mauritius kestrel). Dedicated conservation programs are currently in force to re-introduce each of these to the island.

The island's capital, Port Louis, has a fantastic open-air market as well as a fine aquarium and some good shopping for those who enjoy the activity. The Green Island Rum factory is also worth a visit.

☎ TELEPHONE NUMBERS

Recompression chamber	+230-686-1011
Hospital	+230-243-4661

🖥 WEBSITES & E-MAIL

Mauritius Tourist Board	www.mauritius.net

▲ CORAL GROUPER

The coral grouper lurks in ambush in crevices in the reef, hunting small fish and crustaceans.

DIVER'S TIP

Enjoyed your diving in Mauritius? Let someone know! Many of the prime sites and reefs are under threat from development, and every letter, e-mail, and fax adds grist to the conservation mill.

SEYCHELLES

words by Tony Baskeyfield

THE SEYCHELLES ISLANDS SPARKLE LIKE JEWELS IN THE WESTERN INDIAN OCEAN. THIS IS ONE OF THE WORLD'S GREATEST UNDERWATER ADVENTURE PLAYGROUNDS, WHERE YOU CAN SWIM WITH WHALE SHARKS, TURTLES, RAYS AND SWIRLING SHOALS OF FISH IN CLEAR TURQUOISE WATER. FORGOTTEN FOR CENTURIES BEFORE BEING REDISCOVERED BY THE MOST FEARLESS OF SAILORS, THE SEYCHELLES STILL CONJURE UP VISIONS OF LOST PIRATE TREASURE.

The Seychelles are a year-round destination. The islands' equatorial location means there is always hot weather with some rainfall. May to October are the driest months with temperatures at a fairly constant 30°C (86°F) and more than seven hours of sunshine a day. October to April are the more humid months when rain falls in short, heavy bursts but the skies generally clear rapidly. December, January and February tend to be the wettest months.

Seychelles is a comparatively young nation that can trace its first settlement back to 1770 when the islands were settled by the French. The islands remained in French hands until the defeat of Napoleon at Waterloo, evolving from humble beginnings to attain a population of 3,500 by the time Seychelles was ceded to Britain under the treaty of Paris in 1814. Seychelles achieved independence from Britain in 1976 and became a republic within the Commonwealth.

Diving is possible all year round but best conditions around the inner islands are March to May and October to November when the water temperature can reach 29°C (84°F) and visibility is 100 feet (30 m). The southerly islands are close to the cyclone belt, so during the months of December and January there can be

 VISIBILITY
60 to 120 feet (18 to 36 m)

 MUST SEES
Whale sharks
Mahe: large marble rays
Silhouette: Spanish dancers
Praslin: turtles
Denis: manta rays

☒ DOWNSIDE
Expensive

 GETTING THERE
The main international airport is on Mahe. All flights within the Seychelles arrive and depart from here. Air Seychelles runs an efficient inter-island service using twin otter planes. The airport on Praslin is currently being expanded. Helicopter Seychelles (Phone: +248-373900) flies to Denis, Praslin, Frigate, Cousine and Silhouette islands. Transfers are expensive and not included in accommodation prices. Travel Services Seychelles (Phone: +248-322-414) can organize all flights, as well as accommodation and excursions. There is also a motor-schooner ferry service (Phone: +248-234-013) that operates between all the islands. There is a departure tax of US$40, payable at Mahe airport.

 VISA
Most nationalities do not require visas to enter Seychelles. However, you need a valid passport, return or onward ticket, proof of accommodation and sufficient funds for the duration of your stay.

$ MONEY
Although the Seychelles Rupee is the official currency, most businesses prefer to receive hard currency, with the Euro and US Dollar being the most favored. Credit cards are accepted at most restaurants and hotels and the ATM coverage is almost non-existent.

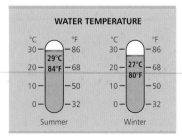

WATER TEMPERATURE

Summer	Winter
29°C / 84°F	27°C / 80°F

Tony Baskeyfield

extremely rough conditions. However, due to their remoteness, marine life around these islands tends to be even more prolific than the inner islands.

GEOGRAPHY

Of the 115 Seychelles islands there is a nucleus of 42 spectacular granite land masses including the major islands of Mahé, Praslin and La Dique and a further 73 outlying sand cays and atolls. The Seychelles lie 620 miles (1,000 km) off the East African coast and are 7° south of the equator.

At 59 square miles (155 sq km) Mahé is, by far, the largest island. It is home to the capital, Victoria, and also to the international airport, fishing and commercial ports and most of the nation's population.

MARINE LIFE

Every October there is an up-welling of currents that bring nutrients from the deep ocean that feed the plankton close to the surface of the Seychelles plateau. At the same time each year migrating whale sharks feed on this plankton. So, if you want guaranteed whale sharks, time your arrival for October.

The Marine Conservation Society Seychelles (MCSS) track the whale shark migration, using a microlight to locate the animals and guide their boats into position. A team of scientists then document precise facts about each passing creature, noting the size, number of remora and pilot fish, sex, identifying marks, scars and any previous tag number. You can hook up with the dive center based in Beau Vallon that is run by the MCSS and swim alongside marine biologists as they document the world's biggest fish. With the combined skill and knowledge of the MCSS team, the Seychelles in October has got to be the best place in the world to observe whale sharks.

The Seychelles' inner islands, with their huge granite rocks, have beautiful white sand beaches bathed in clear blue waters. The underwater topography is very similar. The boulders are covered with sponges and soft and hard coral, hosting all kinds of creatures crawling, walking, resting, feeding and hunting surrounded by clouds of multicolored reef fish of all sizes and shapes. The rocks have a lot to offer for both fish and divers with holes, caves, overhangs and swimthroughs, beautifully built by nature and used by the local marine community. This life owes its great diversity to the richness of plankton hereabouts.

There are a host of tiny creatures including nudibranchs, shrimps, blennies, gobies and pipefish. There are plenty of big creatures too. Stingrays, turtles, white tip and nurse sharks and groupers seeking "granite houses" to rest in during the day. But don't forget to raise your head and look all around, because you might see a group of batfish or shoal of barracuda in the blue.

Tony Baskeyfield

▲ **WHALE SHARK**
A free diver with a juvenile whale shark.

◀◀ **GOING DOWN**
Divers decend into the warm clear blue waters of Denis Island.

39

Bird Island

Denis Island

Praslin

La Dique

Silhoutte Island

Shark Bank •

• I'ILot

VICTORIA ●

✚ ◻

✈
Mahé

0   20 km

0   20 mi

Tony Baskeyfield

The inner islands provide a diversity of diving rarely found anywhere in the world. With pure coral reefs, rocky walls, gullies and wrecks, there are dive sites to suit everyone. All manner of reef life can be seen, from soldierfish to napoleon wrasse and giant grouper. For even bigger thrills there are reef sharks and eagle rays. Add to this heady mix the invertebrates such as octopus, spiny lobsters and Spanish dancers and you have a marine ecosystem to entertain and surprise divers of all levels.

THE DIVES
MAHÉ—L'LLOT

• **0 to 65 feet (0 to 20 m)** • **beginner**

L'llot is a tiny granite outcrop, a 20-minute boat ride from Beau Vallon Bay, Mahé. It resembles a kind of cartoon desert island with granite boulders and palm trees. This dive involves swimming around the island in a clockwise or counterclockwise direction, depending on the current.

Whatever level of diver you are, L'llot will offer something of interest to make it a memorable dive and there is always the chance of encountering a whale shark anywhere in Seychelles.

A constant current passing through the narrow passage between the island and shore ensures a high concentration of marine life. The coral garden on the east side is one of the finest soft coral sites in Seychelles. The east and west sides are spectacular and the north, with its enormous boulders, is incredible. Large bump head parrotfish scrape at the coral and bigeye are in abundance.

MAHÉ—SHARK BANK

• **62 to 148 feet (19 to 45 m)** • **intermediate**

Shark Bank is a set of deep-water granite rocks 5 miles (8 km) west of Beau Vallon Bay. It is renowned for huge marble stingrays and a large number of gorgonian fan corals. Small barracuda and batfish are seen in large schools. As with most offshore sites, almost anything big can cruise by from whale sharks to enormous grouper, making this a dramatic dive site.

There is a majesty about Shark Bank, with its inky blue water swirling with shoals of blue lined snapper, marble rays, eagle rays and turtles all to be seen in one dive.

From the boat, you descend the anchor rope to around 65 feet (20 m) then, depending on the current, swim around the granite rocks to the deepest point of your dive, usually around 100 feet (30 m). Here you may see the huge marble rays about 6.5 feet (2 m) wide. They usually hover on the current as it flows up and over the rocks. Do not chase them and they will swim around and back toward you to their original position. If you are lucky they will swim right over you and make contact. As you return to the anchor line there are massive shoals of blue lined snapper that you can swim right through as they part and close up around you; it's a fantastic experience. Finally as you ascend the anchor rope there are several large inquisitive batfish that come very close.

SILHOUETTE ISLAND

• **0 to 65 feet (0 to 20 m)** • **beginner**

The island of Silhouette is a one-hour boat ride from Mahé. The dive center has its own decompression unit that can accommodate up to three patients in the main chamber.

Diving is excellent all around Silhouette Island. The steep, granite rocks and boulder-strewn sandy bottom are a particular feature with glassfish festooned swimthroughs surrounded by lionfish waiting in the shadows to hunt. Watch out for the urchins as their long spines can penetrate your suit and are very painful. In the middle of the day, Spanish dancers and turtles swim here and there are often sightings of jumping sailfish from the boat.

PRASLIN ISLAND

• **0 to 65 feet (0 to 20 m)** • **intermediate**

Most of Praslin's dive sites are around 65 feet (20 m) deep and between 5- and 50-minute boat ride from the dive center. Huge, spectacular granite rocks rise out from a sandy plateau with a profusion of life on the currents, which can be very strong depending on the tides. The topography is slightly different from Mahé. Here, it is flatter both on the bottom and atop the granite rocks and the visibility is usually better, making the scenic dives a fantastic experience. You can expect to see eagle rays, napoleons curiously checking you out and humphead parrotfish passing by.

DENIS ISLAND

• 0 to 65 feet (0 to 20 m) • beginner

Denis Island is 3° south of the equator and an hour's flight north from Mahé. This island is truly a paradise, with the most beautiful white coral sand beaches surrounding 350 acres (140 hectares) of untouched foliage, exotic flowers and rare and endangered species unique to these islands. Situated at the edge of the Seychelles bank the Indian Ocean descends here to 6,500 feet (2,000 m). The island is 3,000 feet (900 m) long with a runway through the middle.

The protected underwater zone around Denis ranks as one of the finest in this part of the world. There are a number of dive sites allowing sightings of turtles, sharks, stingrays, sailfish, tuna and dolphins, with whale sharks often sighted from September to November. There are shoals of barracuda, bigeye and snapper, and you may be lucky enough to snorkel with a manta rays in the shallow water.

OTHER ACTIVITIES

Once you are in Seychelles there are so many things to do. Island hop by air or charter yacht where each of the 115 islands has something to offer. There are many exotic flowers and rare and endangered species of birds.

You can also find golf, horseback riding and guided nature tours. Don't miss the mellow Seychelles nightlife where you can take in some local bars and fine restaurants offering unforgettable Creole and international cuisine.

☎ **TELEPHONE NUMBERS**

Recompression chamber	+248-224-400
Hospital	+248-224-400
Emergency services	999

💻 **WEBSITES & E-MAIL**

Seychelles Tourist Office	www.seychelles.com

◀ **MARBLE RAYS**
Two marble rays with approximately 30 eagle rays hovering overhead.

▼ **AWE INSPIRING**
Whale sharks have poor eyesight and will swim right up to snorkelers to have a closer look.

ALDABRA & AMIRANTES

THESE REMOTE CORAL ATOLLS BELONG TO THE SEYCHELLES, A SPRINKLING OF TINY ISLANDS IN THE VAST EXPANSE OF THE INDIAN OCEAN. WITH WILD DRIFTS AND BIG ANIMALS, ALDABRA AND THE AMIRANTES OFFER TRUE ADVENTURE DIVING, WHILE THE REEFS AROUND MAHÉ AND THE INNER ISLANDS ARE GENTLER.

 VISIBILITY
Over 100 feet (30 m) in offshore sites

MUST SEE
Aldabra Atoll

DOWNSIDE
Expensive

GETTING THERE
Many international airlines fly direct to Mahé from European, Australian, and South African hubs. Air Seychelles offers an additional 22 lbs (10 kg) kit allowance for divers. There is a U.S.$20 departure tax.

VISA
Visas are not required for visitors to the Seychelles, but you'll need to show an onward ticket, booked accommodation, and sufficient funds for your stay on arrival. A one-month visitor's permit (extendable on application) will then be issued.

$ MONEY
Currency is the Seychelles rupee. Major credit cards and traveler's checks are accepted by reputable dive operators and resorts. This is not a cheap destination, with prices somewhat inflated by the top-end tourism of the main islands.

WATER TEMPERATURE

°C	°F		°C	°F
30 — — 86			30 — — 86	
20 — **29°C** — 68			20 — **27°C** — 68	
84°F			**80°F**	
10 — — 50			10 — — 50	
0 — — 32			0 — — 32	
Summer			Winter	

▶ **GLASSFISH**
Large swarms of glassfish can be seen at most of the dive sites around the Seychelles.

Visitors to the Seychelles, true tropical paradises with swaying palms and sugarwhite sands, will find a glorious patchwork of people and languages. Although known to Arab traders, and to Portuguese seafarers after 1505, the islands were uninhabited until the 18th century when they were colonized by the French, who introduced slavery and plantations. With neighboring Mauritius, the islands passed into British hands during the Napoleonic Wars and remained British until 1976, when they became an independent republic. However, the French influence in the Seychelles remains strong. Although there are three official languages—English, French, and Creole—you are most likely to hear the last two being spoken by the islanders. These beautiful islands even have the obligatory buried treasure—the famous French pirate Olivier de Lasseur is said to have concealed a fortune on the main island in 1721, still sought by treasure hunters.

GEOGRAPHY

The Seychelles consist of approximately 115 islands, islets, and reefs scattered across a vast expanse of the Indian Ocean, divided between the inner and outer islands. The inner granite islands are situated about 620

Linda Pitkin

Linda Pitkin

miles (1,000 km) northeast of Madagascar. They cluster around the main island of Mahé, their craggy contours outlined against the sparkling blue of the surrounding ocean. The outer islands consist essentially of four widely separated groups of low-lying atolls: Amirantes, Alphonse, Farquhar, and Aldabra. The latter, some 715 miles (444 km) southwest of Mahé, is one of the world's largest atolls.

The total land area of this constellation of islands, large and small, is only 175 sq miles (453 sq km). Some 17 miles (27 km) long and 5 miles (8 km) wide, Mahé is the largest island in the Seychelles. It is home to 80 percent of the population of just over 80,000, most of whom live in the capital, Victoria.

MARINE LIFE

Marine biologists estimate that there are about 900 fish species in the waters of the Seychelles, 85 percent of which are common reef species of the Indian and Pacific Oceans. There are only some 50 coral species in the islands, although the calm shallow waters around the islands of the Seychelles, combined with powerful sunlight for much of the year, create ideal conditions for impressive reef formations.

The reefs of the inner islands are constantly busy with large schools of reef fish such as snappers, chromis, and fusiliers, while eagle rays cruise off the reef walls and above the occasional wreck on the seafloor. The many overhangs and small caverns in the reefs are occupied by swarms of glassfish and rolling balls of tightly bunched striped eel catfish. The white sand between the reefs are feeding grounds for stingrays and white tip reef sharks.

For more impressive encounters, however, divers will find it necessary to travel further afield to sites some distance from the main island group, or to the outlying coral atolls. Of these, the jewel in the Seychelles' crown is undoubtedly faraway Aldabra, where you are likely to encounter mantas, gray reef sharks, and whale sharks in addition to the more traditional reef species. Shortfin pilot whales and sperm whales are also occasionally seen around the islands.

▲ **ISLAND PARADISE**
Tropical beaches and palm trees are the characteristic scenery of the 115 islands that make up the Seychelles.

SEYCHELLES

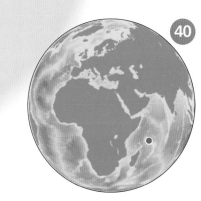

John Bantin

▶ **STRIPED EEL CATFISH**
Large aggregations of striped eel catfish
are frequently seen on the reefs. They rely
on safety of numbers as well as their
venomous fin spines for protection.

 DIVE CENTERS

EPSEY ROYAL WATERSPORT
Alphonse Island, Seychelles
Phone: +248-229-040
E-mail: seydive@seychelles.net

ISLAND VENTURES DIVE SEYCHELLES
Berjaya Beau Vallon Bay Beach Resort, Victoria,
Mahé, Seychelles
Phone: +248-247-845
E-mail: info@islandventures.net
Web: www.islandventures.net

SEYCHELLES UNDERWATER CENTER
Coral Strand Hotel, Beau Vallon Beach,
P.O. Box 384, Victoria, Mahé, Seychelles
Phone: +248-345-445
E-mail: divesey@seychelles.net
Web: www.diveseychelles.com.sc

 DIVING ORGANIZATIONS

The Association of Professional Divers
(A.P.D.S.) in the Seychelles
Phone: +248-345-445

 RECOMPRESSION

Victoria Hospital
Sans Souci Rd., Mont Fleuri, Mahé, Seychelles
Phone: +248-224-400
All doctors speak English and/or French. The
physician in charge of the chamber is Dr.
Masoni.

 HOSPITAL

Victoria Hospital
Sans Souci Rd., Mont Fleuri, Mahé, Seychelles
Phone: +248-224-400

 CONSERVATION SOCIETY

There is a dedicated Marine Conservation
Society in the Seychelles, also incorporating a
Shark Research Institute. Contact:
E-mail: info@mcss.sc
Web: www.mcss.sc/about.htm

OTHER DIVE SITE

Shark Bank

THE DIVES

The inner islands of the Seychelles stand atop a large
platform rising from the ocean floor, so the majority of
the diving is in the 30 to 100 feet (9 to 30 m) range.
Diving here is usually mellow, with calm waters, good
visibility, shallow lagoons, abundant reef life, and
blazing sunshine. The outer edges of the platform rise
from a depth of 3 miles (2 km), and present altogether
more demanding diving conditions.

At one or two sites within the vicinity of the inner
islands the granite rock of platform forms interesting
arches and caverns within the reefs, and these dives
may prove quite challenging. Within this same area, the
large wreck of the *Ennerdale*, a short boat-ride from
Mahé, is a good dive for intermediates.

The diving on the outer coral islands is of a different
nature, for here cuts in the reefs create impressive tidal
races and busy walls. Unfortunately, the logistics of
getting to these outer islands, particularly the rarely
visited islands of Aldabra, can be quite considerable,
but it is certainly worth the effort.

The Association of Professional Divers in the
Seychelles (A.P.D.S.) is responsible for seeing that its
members observe high standards of operations. All
visiting divers are recommended to use an A.P.D.S.
approved operator.

THE ENNERDALE

• **60 to 100 feet (18 to 30 m)** • **intermediate**

The *Ennerdale* foundered after striking an uncharted
rock in the waters north of Mahé in June 1970. It was
later sunk by the British Royal Navy as she represented
a hazard to shipping. She now lies in three distinct
sections on the seabed at 100 feet (30 m).

The most frequently dived section of the wreck is
the stern, which has remained intact. The bridge was
completely blown off the superstructure during the
violent final sinking of the vessel, and now lies on the
seabed next to the stern. Some large groupers and
moray eels have made this section of wreck their home.
As happens so commonly on wrecks in warm-water
regions of the world, small schools of batfish will stick

closely to individual divers throughout the dive, following them loyally as they make their way around. Look out for nurse sharks within the wreckage, but take care—the tangled edges can be sharp and present a hazard for the unwary diver.

ALDABRA ATOLL

• **30 to 130 feet (9 to 40 m)** • **beginner to expert**

Aldabra Atoll is a World Heritage Site and is uninhabited except for a few park rangers for part of the year only. Not without reason, the atoll's four islands—Picard, Polymnie, Malabar, and Grand Terre—are often referred to as the Galápagos Islands of the Indian Ocean; they have a population of more than 150,000 giant tortoises, and thousands of green turtles come here to breed each year. The bird life is remarkable, too: there are huge breeding colonies of frigate birds, boobies, and terns, as well as the last flightless bird of the Indian Ocean, the white throated rail.

Aldabra Atoll has steep walls, racing tidal cuts, and wonderful fish life. Manatees have been sighted in the shallow lagoon, and reef shark and stingrays lurk in the channels. Yet this wonderful atoll is virtually undived, due to its remoteness. To get there, you have to fly from Mahé to the small airstrip on the island of Assumption, some 20 miles (32 km) southeast of Aldabra, and then board a liveaboard. Most operators visit the island of Astove and Cosmoledo atoll as well as Aldabra.

AMIRANTES

• **30 to 130 feet (9 to 40 m)** • **beginner to expert**

This island group of three atolls is 146 miles (235 km) from Mahé. The most frequently dived is Desroches, where a precipitous wall known as the Desroches Drop is famous for its tremendous abundance of reef species and attendant large pelagics. A lodge with twenty tourist chalets on Desroches offers easy access to the sites around the island.

OTHER ACTIVITIES

Early settlers likened the famous Vallée de Mai on Praslin to the Garden of Eden, and it is one of the Seychelles' two World Heritage Sites, with 28 endemic species of plants, 5 of reptiles, and 5 of birds. The best-known plant of the Seychelles, the Coco de Mer palm, is here in profusion. Weighing 48 lbs (22 kg), the nut of this palm is the largest in the world and has a famously erotic shape! Look out for the black parrot, the national bird of the Seychelles, while exploring the valley.

In the capital, Victoria, you'll find a fascinating mix of cultures despite the inroads of tourism. For example, the traditional weekly open-air market still takes place against a backdrop of modern hotels and holiday apartments. Beau Vallon Beach nearby is well worth a visit.

John Bantin

▲ **JELLYFISH**
Large jellyfish are truly oceanic creatures, drifting for many hundreds of miles in great ocean currents.

☎ **TELEPHONE NUMBERS**

Recompression chamber	+248-224-400
Hospital	+248-224-400
Emergency services	999

💻 **WEBSITES & E-MAIL**

Seychelles Tourist Office   www.seychelles.com

DIVER'S TIP

Try to get off the beaten track if possible. There are still bargains to be had in terms of accommodation in the Seychelles. If you must go through the bigger hotels, it's worth getting an all-in package deal.

LHAVIYANI & FELIDHOO ATOLLS

THE MALDIVES—A UNIQUE COLLECTION OF ATOLLS RISING FROM DEEP BLUE WATER IN THE INDIAN OCEAN—OFFER A RANGE OF UNFORGETTABLE DIVING EXPERIENCES FROM STEEP WALLS AND WRECKS TO SHALLOW LAGOONS OF SUGAR-WHITE SAND AND EXHILARATING DRIFTS OVER EXQUISITE REEFS.

 VISIBILITY

65 feet (20 m) in tidal channels

130 feet (40 m) on walls

 MUST SEES

The Shipyard

Thilas

 DOWNSIDE

Remote

Expensive

GETTING THERE

There are regular flights from Colombo (Sri Lanka), Dubai (United Arab Emirates), and Kuala Lumpur (Malaysia), as well as many charter flights from European centers. Malé International Airport is the only international gateway; departure tax is U.S.$10.

 VISA

Visas are required for most nationalities, but are free and can be obtained on arrival for a maximum stay of 30 days.

MONEY

Currency is the rufiyaa. Money can be exchanged at banks, hotels, island resorts, and leading stores. The U.S. dollar is the most common foreign currency. Most hotels will accept major currencies, traveler's checks, or credit cards as payment.

The Maldives came to the attention of the diving fraternity in the early 1970s, and swiftly rose to become one of the world's premier dive locations. In the succeeding years the discovery of hundreds more world-class dives in the island chain reinforced this initial promise, and although the coral reefs were affected by the El Niño event of 1997–98, the archipelago has remained a beacon for the diving aficionado eager to swim with big pelagic animals or to explore complex reef formations. The scattered atolls and sandbars of the Maldives now have a well-established dive industry catering for divers from all over the world who make the pilgrimage to this, the most popular of the Indian Ocean's dive destinations.

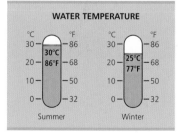

WATER TEMPERATURE

°C	°F		°C	°F
30	86		30	86
30°C / 86°F			**25°C / 77°F**	
20	68		20	68
10	50		10	50
0	32		0	32
Summer			Winter	

▶ **THOUSAND ISLANDS**

There are over a thousand islands in the Maldives, presenting an array of diving possibilities.

John Bantin

GEOGRAPHY

There are more than 1,000 islands in the Maldives archipelago, extending over 475 miles (764 km) from north to south and 80 miles (128 km) from east to west. Only 200 of the islands are inhabited. Some idea of how isolated they are in the midst of the vast expanse of the encompassing Indian Ocean can be gained from the fact that while the island chain covers an impressive 38,000 sq miles (98,382 sq km) of ocean, their total land mass is a mere 115 sq miles (298 sq km).

The islands are the tops of an undersea mountain range that extends out from the west coast of India for more than 1,000 miles (1,600 km) in a line running to the southwest. Loosely grouped in 26 atolls, they are classic examples of the form, with the rounded tops of the mountains reflected in the reefs that have slowly formed as the mountain peaks have gradually subsided below the surface of the water.

This is a significant factor in terms of diving in the Maldives, as the visible islands, sandbars, and reefs represent only a fraction of the diving available. Beneath the surface are the ridges and plateaus of the

DIVE CENTERS

ONE & ONLY KANUHURA
Lhaviyani Atoll, Maldives
Phone: +960-664-88-00
Web: www.oneandonlyresorts.com

MALDIVES LIVEABOARD
Amr Nour Consulting Co Pte Ltd., 20 Cecil
Street, 14-01 Equity Plaza, Singapore 049705
Phone: +66-987-15124
E-mail: info@amrnour.com
Web: www.amrnour.com

Information on ten different liveaboards
operating in the islands can be found at:
www.maldivesliveaboard.net

 DIVING ORGANIZATIONS

None. However the Maldives Tourism
Promotion Board will offer advice on suitable
dive operators. Diving in the Maldives is on the
whole well regulated and run.
3rd Floor, H Aage 12, Boduthakurufaanu
Magu, Malé, Republic of Maldives
Phone: +960-323-228
E-mail: mtpb@visitmaldives.com.mv
Web: www.visitmaldives.com

 RECOMPRESSION

Bandos Medical Clinic and Hyperbaric Centre
Bandos Island Resort, Republic of Maldives
Phone: +960-440-088

 HOSPITAL

The Maldives has limited medical facilities.
Some medicines are not available. The capital
has two hospitals, one private and one
government owned.

Indira Ghandi Memorial Hospital Malé
Phone: +960-333-5336

Alternatively contact the Ministry of Health for
information on atoll hospitals and clinics:
Ministry of Health
Ameenee Magu, Malé 20-04,
Republic of Maldives
Phone: +960-332-8887
E-mail moh@dhivehinet.net.mv
Web: www.health.gov.mv

 CONSERVATION SOCIETY

Banyan Tree Maldives Vabbinfaru
North Malé Atoll, Republic of Maldives
Phone: +960-664-3147

Marine Environment Consultant:
Mr Abdul Azeez Abdul Hakeem
E-mail: marine-maldives@banyantree.com

undersea mountains' shoulders and faces, dropping off
into the abyssal waters that surround them.

The islands are extremely low-lying and many are
threatened by rising sea level as the result of climate
change. The only human settlement of any size is the
capital Malé, on the atoll of the same name, the other
inhabited islands having only small fishing villages or
tourist resorts. Tourism is highly controlled, and
freedom to travel outside the tourist atolls is limited.

MARINE LIFE

The atolls of the Maldives not only shelter thriving
reef communities, they also play host to some extremely
impressive pelagic visitors. The combination of rich
reefs and open ocean creates a system swarming with
more than a thousand fish species. There are now 25
officially protected marine areas within the Maldives.

The El Niño event of 1997–98 had considerable
impact on the hard corals of the Maldives, when a rise

John Bantin

in sea temperature caused coral bleaching on a wide scale. There was some concern for the long-term health of these reefs at the time, but in the intervening years they have proved to be more resilient than was feared might be the case. The idea that coral communities in the Maldives were "wiped out" by El Niño is unfounded, and some of the reef systems here are truly spectacular, with soft corals particularly abundant and colorful. Some sites have uniquely pigmented soft coral; a classic

example being the walls at Felidhoo Atoll which are covered in beautiful white gardens much loved by visiting photographers.

The fish life around the archipelago is equally spectacular. Most reef walls are not without their attendant shoals of big eye jacks and barracuda, while sweetlips and fusiliers swarm under and around larger coral formations. Three species of moray, including some very large giant morays, inhabit dark lairs within the reef,

▲ FUSILIERS
A school of blue and gold fusiliers stay in tight formation as a protection from predators.

Jane Morgan

▲ MANTA RAY

Breathtaking encounters like this are common off the walls or in the channels between reefs.

while brightly colored scorpionfish lurk in ambush. Large shoals of glassy sweepers occupy dark overhangs and the holds of wrecks, making for truly spectacular evening dives as lionfish and jack ambush these shoals at high speed.

Sandy patches within the lagoons and tidal channels attract colonies of black spotted garden eels as well as large stingrays, with mantas and eagle rays in attendance in mid water. Among visiting shark species to the reefs are white tip reef sharks, present in considerable numbers, gray reef sharks, and nurse sharks. Whale sharks are also a noteable feature of the Maldives, and on rare occasions hammerheads may be encountered in deep water.

THE DIVES

As a rule, diving in the Maldives is well run and professional. The diving here has grown out of a tourist trade that caters for the quality end of the market and has demanded high standards from its inception. Resorts have grown up around their diving facilities,

and there are now more than 80 diving resorts in the Maldives, each of them having access to many hundreds of dive sites. Equipment is generally of a high standard, boat operators are used to catering for the unique demands of divers, and their familiarity with the local diving conditions and individual reefs is impressively sound. Such local knowledge is very important, because although there are numerous truly world-class sites in the Maldives, there are also hundreds of miles of relatively featureless reef. Local laws prevent divers venturing deeper than 100 feet (30 m).

Much of the diving on the outer atoll walls is drift diving, and the local dive industry is well set up to support groups of divers gliding along reef walls in the teeth of currents. Though not obligatory, most operators insist on the use of a surface marker buoy, with individual divers recommended to use marker flags.

As in other world-class sites, much of the large animal action takes place in the channels and gaps between the individual islands of the atolls, with strong tidal streams drawing filter feeders such as mantas and whale sharks. These channels are dotted with bommies that act as cleaning stations and natural focal points for local marine life, large and small.

A feature of the undersea terrain in the Maldives are the large coral-covered platforms that rise gently from the deep sea. These are known locally as *thilas*, which can be loosely translated as "submerged reef". Many of them do not break the surface, and local expertise is required to locate them in the expanses of the open sea between islands.

The island resorts are invariably well appointed and comfortable, offering convenient hassle-free diving on local sites. However, the ultimate way to enjoy the Maldives' experience is on a liveaboard, which will allow you to access many spectacular sites beyond the range of the day boats that strike out from the island resorts, including the open ocean reefs where large pelagic animals are more frequently encountered.

THE SHIPYARD

• **100 feet (30 m)** • **intermediate**

The Shipyard is made up of two wrecks located within a few yards of each other on the western section of Lhaviyani Atoll. One of the wrecks is lying on its port side flat on the sea bottom at 100 feet (30 m), while the other sits vertically against the reef wall, its bow standing 15 feet (4.5 m) proud of the water's surface. The picture of this rusting bow reaching for the sky, with the small island of Gaaerifaru behind it, has made itself famous as one of the great iconic images of diving in the Maldives.

The stories behind the sinking of the two wrecks are somewhat confused. It is rumored that both were deliberately sunk in 1980 for insurance purposes, while another tale relates that the deeper wreck was a fishing vessel that caught fire after having been caught fishing illegally. She is said to have drifted for several days

▼ **REDMOUTH GROUPER**
One of the Maldives' many residents, seen here with a cleaner shrimp.

Linda Pitkin

before coming to grief on the reef and settling in her present position.

What is undeniable is that both vessels now offer a magnificent dive site for the wreck fanatic, the photographer, and the wildlife diver alike. They sit in the tidal channel between Gaaerifaru and Felivaru, and are subjected to swirling localized currents. They are probably best dived at slack water, although some operators choose to place their divers in the water up-current so as to allow them to drift gently onto the wrecks from the open sea. Whichever of these two methods is followed, it should be possible to cover both wrecks on a single cylinder dive.

The vessels both have a healthy covering of soft corals and gorgonians, and are populated by a wide range of fish species. In the holds are massive schools of sweepers, prey for the jacks and lionfish that prowl the superstructure of the vessels.

Depending on the currents, it is possible to start the dive by moving down the superstructure of the larger vertical vessel, 120 feet (36 m) long, and then down the reef wall towards the second smaller wreck, lying about 330 feet (100 m) away, This latter wreck is in an excellent state of preservation, and offers some splendid opportunities for wide-angle photography. Look out in the dark holds and crevices for some impressive giant morays, while overhead you can always be sure of sighting large batfish moving in sedate shoals.

Make your way back to the vertical wreck, where it will be possible to pass between the hull and the reef wall before ascending the superstructure to the safety stop. This is very often the best part of the entire dive, because here the glassy sweepers are caught between the lionfish below and jacks above, and if you make the dive in the evening you will find yourself surrounded by frantic predatory activity.

FELIDHOO ATOLL

• **100 feet (30 m)** • **advanced**

Felidhoo Atoll has a number of steep walls interspersed with deep cuts, overhangs, and swim-throughs. This potent combination has created a number of extremely dramatic individual dive sites, with Foththeyo and Rakeedhoo two of the most spectacular.

▼ **MAORI WRASSE**
These large fish get their name from the elabrate swirled marking on their heads.

John Bantin

Linda Pitkin

Foththeyo is located on the outer reef wall on the east side of Felidhoo Atoll, and is a combination of steep drops-off and busy *thila* coral communities. This is an advanced dive due to the strong currents that may be swirling around the site. You begin the dive by descending a deep cut in the reef wall, ending in a magnificent arch at 130 feet (39 m). Moving gradually up the reef, you then pass a number of deep horizontal channels in the reef wall cloaked in increasingly dense growths of soft corals. Look out for eagle rays and gray reef sharks in the blue water off the reef wall, as well as stingrays in the bottom of the channel towards the tail end of the dive. Albino alcyonians are one of the noteworthy features of this site, and make for eerie photographs when taken against the dark blue background of the open sea.

Rakeedhoo is located on the southern tip of a small sub-atoll just south of the main Felidhoo island group. This dive is essentially on two large steps in the reef wall, the deepest of which is at 120 feet (36 m). Below this second step the reef wall drops away into the dark blue of truly deep water. The reef represents the corner of the outer reef and the channel, and splits the local currents neatly in two, creating an eye of relatively still water in the tidal stream.

This is a thrilling dive due to the presence of large pelagic animals in the blue waters off the reef. Several species of shark will be present, and you may also spot mantas and eagle rays in the strong currents surrounding the site. Watch out for the massive school of trevally that seems to be permanently in residence in the channel mouth towards the tail end of the dive.

OTHER ACTIVITIES

In the early days, couples would visit the Maldives, one to dive and the other to enjoy the pure white beaches of these tropical islands. The diver would wax lyrical about his or her stay, while all too often the non-diver would slowly go stir crazy as island fever took hold. In those days the islands, while ideally set up for divers, could be somewhat limiting for their non-diving companions! Things have moved on since then, and most resorts now cater for every kind of watersports activity, while several offer a full range of health spa facilities. Malé is a bustling town, but does not really typify the island experience for most visitors. If the aim is peace and quiet or pampered island life in the quintessential tropical paradise, then the Maldives has much to offer. But it does not come cheaply.

☎ TELEPHONE NUMBERS

Recompression chamber	+960-440-088
Hospital	+960-333-5336
Maldives Tourism Promotion Board	+960-323-228

🖥 WEBSITES & E-MAIL

Maldives Tourism Promotion Board	www.visitmaldives.com
Travel information	www.maldives.com
Travel information	www.islandsmaldives.com

▲ BUSY REEFS

Although the hard corals of the Maldives were undoubtedly affected by El Niño they are still home to wide variety of fish species, like these powder-blue surgeon.

OTHER DIVE SITES

Fehigili
Express
Fushifaru Thila
Kakani Thila
Famimi Kuda Thila
Horubadhoo Thila
Finger Point
Boduhithi Thila
Rasfari
Lion's Head
Maldives Victory
Lankanfinolhu Faru
Girifushi Thila
Fairytale Reef Blue Caves
Trixie's Caves
Madivaru
Ukulhas Thila
Maaya Thila
Orimas Thila
Mushimasmigili
Kalhuhadhihuraa Thila
Kalhuhadhihuraa Faru
Hukuruelhi Faru
Kudarah Thila
Broken Rock Thila
Medhu Kandu
Miyaru Kandu
Dharaboodoo Point

SIMILAN
ISLANDS

THESE REMOTE UNINHABITED ISLANDS COULD WELL BE LOCATION OF THE FINEST DIVING IN THAILAND. THEY OFFER TWO COMPLETELY DIFFERENT DIVING EXPERIENCES ON THE SAME TINY ARCHIPELAGO—GENTLY SLOPING CORAL REEFS TO THE EAST AND DRAMATIC BOULDERS AND CRAGGY WALLS TO THE WEST.

 VISIBILITY
90 to 140 feet (27 to 43 m) Oct-May
60 to 100 feet (18 to 30 m) May-Oct

 MUST SEES
Fantasea Reef
Elephant's Head

 DOWNSIDE
Journey out can be long and rough

 GETTING THERE
Most international flights to Thailand arrive at Bangkok's Don Muang International Airport. Phuket's airport is served by only a few international flights during the peak season.

 VISA
Passports must be valid for at least three months. Visitors of most nationalities do not need a visa for a 30-day stay. Tax of 500 baht, payable on departure, is only accepted in baht.

$ MONEY
Currency is the Thai baht. Currency exchange is possible in most resorts. Major credit cards and traveler's checks are widely accepted.

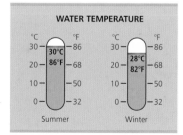

WATER TEMPERATURE

°C	°F		°C	°F
30	86		30	86
20	**30°C 86°F** 68		20	**28°C 82°F** 68
10	50		10	50
0	32		0	32
Summer			Winter	

▶ **SEA FANS**
Sea fans tend to grow perpendicular to the prevailing currents, indicating that this wall is swept by lateral water movement.

John Bantin

Christmas Point

Island 9
Koh Bangu

Fantasea Reef

Island 8
Koh Similan

Elephant's Head

Beacon Point

Island 7
Koh Pabu

East of Eden

Island 4
Koh Miang

*Similan
Islands*

Island 3
Koh Payan

Island 2
Koh Payang

Shark Fin Reef

Boulder City

Island 1
Koh Huyong

*ANDAMAN
SEA*

THAILAND

*Phuket
Island*

Phuket

The Similan Islands are a line of nine harsh granite outcrops cloaked in dense undergrowth rising from the depths of the Andaman Sea. Some of the larger islands have the most exquisite beaches on their eastern shores, which have the added advantage of being relatively deserted. The islands have become a magnet for divers only in the last decade and are now regularly visited by liveaboard vessels. Encounters with pelagic species in crystal-clear water over dramatic reefs make it obvious why.

GEOGRAPHY

The nine islands run north–south in a 15-mile (24-km) long chain some 40 miles (64 km) from the mainland of Thailand and more than 70 miles (112 km) from Phuket, the main point of departure for dive vessels visiting the islands. All the islands are uninhabited. They have individual names, but each is generally known simply by its number in the chain, starting from Island 1 in the south to Island 9 in the north. The largest island is Koh Similan (or Island 8). It has a small ranger station, although the headquarters of the Similan National Park is sited on Koh Miang (Island 4) and constitutes the only significant human presence on the islands.

The islands perch on the eastern edge of large sandbanks, and this is reflected in their underwater topography, with steep precipitous cliffs to the west, and more gentle slopes to the east.

MARINE LIFE

Although there was a considerable amount of dynamite fishing in the past, the Similan Islands achieved National Park status in 1982, and are now a particularly healthy example of a rapidly recovering Asian Pacific reef system. Although the marine life on both sides of the islands is prolific, the boulders to the west of the islands have the added bonus of being colonized by particularly dramatic congregations of soft corals and gorgonians.

The staggering range of reef fish swarming over the coral and crags of the islands includes butterfly fish, several species of clownfish, angelfish, sweetlips and anthias. Banded sea kraits may be encountered around the islands, and there is also the possibility of encountering larger animals such as whale sharks and manta rays at the right time of year (peak season is October through to May).

THE DIVES

The real attractions of the Similan Islands is the variety of diving available and the accessibility of good sites even in rough weather—this is due to the numerous bays and coves within the island group, one of which is always bound to be in the lee of prevailing conditions. However, although the islands themselves offer shelter, the trip out to them can be very exposed, particularly in the low season lasting from May through to October.

The only way to dive the Similans is from a liveaboard. Most depart from Phuket, although a few operate out of Ko Phi Phi and Thap Lamu. In peak season something in the region of 70 boats regularly visit the islands, and the sites can become very busy. It is also possible to take day trips to the Similans out of Phuket, although this round trip of 130 miles (209 km) plus is not for the faint-hearted!

▶ BLACK-TIP GROUPER

The black-tip grouper is a visual predator, relying on large well-developed eyes to seek out prey.

Linda Pitkin

 DIVE CENTERS

FANTASEA DIVERS

219 Rat-U-Thit 200 Yr Road, Patong Beach, Phuket 83150, Thailand

Phone: +66-76-340-088

E-mail: info@fantasea.net

SUNRISE DIVERS

589 Patak Road (Karon Beach),

Phuket 83100, Thailand

Phone: +66-76-398-040

E-mail: info@sunrise-divers.com

Web: www.sunrise-divers.com

DIVING ORGANIZATIONS

The Tourism Authority of Thailand (T.A.T.) has a list of registered dive operators. The terms of registration include a financial bond against insolvency or malpractice.

Check the T.A.T.s website to see if your liveaboard is listed.

Tourism Authority of Thailand

1,600 New Phetchaburi Road, Makkasan, Ratchathewi, Bangkok 10400, Thailand

Phone: +66-22-505-500

E-mail: center@tat.or.th

Web: www.tourismthailand.org

RECOMPRESSION

Hyperbaric Services Thailand

233 Rat-U-Thit 200 Pee Road,

Patong Beach, Phuket, Thailand

Phone: +66-76-342-518

E-mail: sssphk@loxinfo.co.th

 HOSPITAL

Phuket Adventist Hospital

4/1 Thepkrasattri Rd., Phuket 83000, Thailand

Phone: +66-76-212-386

Phuket Ruam Paet Hospital

340 Phuket Road, Ampur Muang, Phuket 83000, Thailand

Phone: +66-76-211-578

 CONSERVATION SOCIETY

The Thai Parks website has information on how to book accommodation in the parks:

Web: www.amazing-thailand.com/parks

More general conservation information can be found on World Wide Fund for Nature:

Web: wwf.org.uk

The diving reflects the terrain of the islands. To the east are hard coral gardens that slope down to 130 feet (40 m). These are interspersed with large bommies at depth that act as beacons for marine life. To the west, large boulders are the dominating feature of the topography, creating tremendous caves, caverns, and swim-throughs, around which powerful currents swirl.

FANTASEA REEF

• 20 to 130 feet (6 to 40 m) • intermediate

This dive typifies all that is best about the Similan Islands. Throughout this large reef there are dramatic gullies, swim-throughs, arches, and caverns, all coated with beautiful soft corals, crinoids, and gorgonians. It is probably best to split the reef into two dives, as there is so much to see.

There is a large underwater valley called the Bronx, which has a reputation as a gathering point for shovel-nose rays and is dotted with impressive giant clams. Strong currents are not at all unusual on this site, although the ragged underwater topography makes it possible for divers to dart into the numerous folds and cuts in the reef—to simply drift with the flow would make for a very short dive indeed as the reef disappears behind you!

The fish life on this reef is particularly garish and approachable. Coral groupers, sweetlips, snappers, blue triggerfish, fire gobies, and lionfish all prowl the busy reef walls, while jacks and mackerel hover in the blue water making opportunistic dashes into splintering shoals of baitfish closer to the reef. Whale sharks are occasionally sighted at this site in peak season.

ELEPHANT'S HEAD

• 20 to 120 feet (6 to 36 m) • intermediate

In terms of dramatic underwater scenery, this site is the most spectacular in the Similan Islands. It owes its name to the top of a granite pinnacle that protrudes from the water's surface before plunging 20 feet (6 m) to the seafloor. The dive is a steady series of arches, passages, and shelves, all coated with gorgonians and hard and soft corals.

Traditionally, this dive moves to the deeper areas first. Divers generally enter the water to the west of the granite rock above the surface and move down the steep walls and steps to the sloping bottom at 90 feet (27 m). Look out for blue-spotted stingrays in this region, as well as flagtail gobies. Traveling around the rock, the divers gradually ascend, moving through some dramatic outcrops and smaller pinnacles, an excellent spot to observe the smaller inhabitants of this reef, including some iridescent blennies and colorful purple dragon nudibranchs.

OTHER ACTIVITIES

There is some excellent snorkeling to be had around the islands, particularly at sites such as Donald Duck Bay, and of course the beaches are among the most beautiful in Thailand.

It is well worth taking time away from diving to explore the land-based wonders of the National Park if your stay here is long enough. The Similan Islands are rich in flora and fauna, and are home to 27 species of mammals, 22 species of reptiles, and at least 4 species of amphibians. The Park also has a visitors' center on the mainland.

A limited number of tourist bungalows are available on Koh Miang (Island 4) and Koh Similan (Island 8). Camping facilities are also available on both these islands, which can be reached by a fast boat-trip out from Phuket.

▼ COLLARED BUTTERFLYFISH

In common with many species of butterflyfish, collared butterflyfish are frequently observed in pairs.

OTHER DIVE SITES

Christmas Point
Beacon Point
East of Eden
Shark Fin Reef
Boulder City

DIVER'S TIP

Currents can be strong to the west of the islands at the best of times, but there are reports of real snorters when the moon is full, so try to avoid visiting the islands then.

 TELEPHONE NUMBERS

Recompression chamber	+66-76-342-518
Hospital	+66-76-212-386

WEBSITES & E-MAIL

Tourism Authority	www.tourismthailand.org
Travel in Thailand	www.thailand-travel.net

Linda Pitkin

KOMODO

 VISIBILITY

40 to 120 feet (12 to 36 m) depending on location

 MUST SEES

Night dive at Cannibal Rock
Komodo dragons

 DOWNSIDE

Remote
Strong currents

 GETTING THERE

From Jakarta or Denpasar, Bali, fly to Bima, Sumbawa, or Labuan Bajo, West Flores, and from there take a boat to Komodo. Alternatively, ten-day liveaboard cruises from Bali visit Komodo.

 VISA

No visa required for stays of up to 60 days for most countries.

$ MONEY

Currency is the rupiah. Traveler's checks and credit cards are accepted at most major resorts in Indonesia. Bank opening hours make it difficult to change money, but A.T.M.s can often be found.

WATER TEMPERATURE

°C		°F		°C		°F
30		86		30		86
20	29°C / 84°F	68		20	24°C / 75°F	68
10		50		10		50
0		32		0		32
	Summer				Winter	

▶ **VOLCANIC ISLANDS**

The stark outline of Sangeang, the northernmost island in the Komodo National Park.

KOMODO REPRESENTS ONE OF THE WORLD'S TRUE ADVENTURE DIVING LOCATIONS, WITH LARGE AREAS OF UNEXPLORED REEF, FABULOUS MARINE LIFE, AND CHALLENGING TIDES AND CURRENTS TO CONTEND WITH.

The arid island of Komodo and its neighbor Rinca are famed as the home of the remarkable and unique Komodo Dragon, the world's largest monitor lizard, which was discovered by scientist J.K.H. Van Steyn in 1911 (and what a day that must have been!). Much more recently, only about 20 years or so ago, divers and naturalists began to realize the tremendous quality of the reefs around this scattered group of tiny islands and exposed rocks, and the National Park originally set up to protect the Komodo Dragon was extended to cover the marine environment, many areas of which remain unexplored. As more was learned about the reefs, U.N.E.S.C.O. was moved to declare the park a region of global conservation significance and in 1986 it became a World Heritage Site.

GEOGRAPHY

Lying between Sumbawa and Flores, the largest of the Lesser Sunda Islands, Komodo National Park covers an area of 700 sq miles (1,817 sq km) in the Wallacea biogeographical region of southern Indonesia. The three largest islands within the park—Komodo, Rinca, and Padar—together with numerous smaller islets and protruding rocks have a total land area of 233 sq miles

John Bantin

(603 sq km), representing only 33 percent of the park's complete coverage, the rest being reef and open sea. The location of the islands is significant, being positioned between two contrasting bodies of water—the cold upwellings of the Indian Ocean and the warm waters of the Flores Sea.

The areas of open sea within the park are between 300 and 600 feet (90 and 180 m) deep, whilst at 90 to 200 feet (27 to 60 m) the straits between the islands are relatively shallow. This creates swirling tides and challenging currents within the island group that in turn provide an ideal nutrient-rich environment for bustling marine communities. There are essentially three main marine ecosystems within the National Park—seagrass beds, mangrove swamps, and coral reefs— each playing a separate and key role in the overall marine ecology.

MARINE LIFE

As in other areas of Indonesia, the range of marine species encountered is tremendously impressive. A recent survey of the park counted 260 species of reef-building coral, 70 species of sponge, and more than 1,000 species of fish, but as with many such surveys, the actual number of species is probably considerably higher. Larger residents include dolphins and turtles, and at certain times of the year minke whales pass

through the area on their annual migration. But it is the smaller members of the reef community that are particularly impressive. Pygmy sea horses, skeleton shrimps, leaf scorpionfish, ghost pipefish—all of the myriad tiny creatures beloved by underwater macro-photographers can be found within the park's confines. Indeed, so great is the profusion of life, a well-known reef biologist has been heard to declare that every reef species of Indonesia is represented here.

THE DIVES

Although some dive operators on Flores offer excursions to Komodo National Park from Labuan Bajo, this is something of a trek even by speedboat (and a voyage of true epic proportions when undertaken by traditional smaller boat). Many liveaboards offer regular trips to the islands, and while this is not necessarily a cheap option, it is certainly the best and most convenient way to enjoy the numerous dive sites.

Tides and currents are an issue here, although there are sheltered areas within the park. Get it right, however, and the currents can be used to create some tremendous drift dives with periodic pauses in the lee of coral heads or on the reef top.

The following description by underwater photographer Teresa Zubi on www.starfish.ch gives an idea of just how impressive these dives can be (her excellent website also offers some useful tips on diving Komodo in general): "At the aptly named dive site 'Current City' we hung onto the peaks of the underwater mounds with both our hands (no camera), barely daring to look over the edge to the schooling mackerels, sweetlips, and snappers below. Our masks were wobbling and the

Mikayo Langhofer

This mantis shrimp represents a typically garish smaller reef resident of Komodo.

 DIVE CENTERS

DIVE KOMODO
Labuan Bajo, Flores, N.T.T.,
Indonesia
Phone: +62-385-41354
Email: info@divekomodo.com
Web: www.divekomodo.com

REEFSEEKERS FLORES
Labuan Bajo, Flores, N.T.T.,
Indonesia
Phone: +62-385-41443
E-mail: reefseekers_diving@mataram.wasan
tara.net.id
Web: www.angelisleflores.com

TAUCH TERMINAL RESORT TULAMBEN
Jl. Danau Tamblingan X / 40-42,
80000 Jimbaran, Bali, Indonesia
Phone: +62-361-774504
E-mail: resort@tulamben.com
Web: www.tulamben.com

 DIVING ORGANIZATIONS
None

 RECOMPRESSION
U.S.U.P. Sanglah Denpasar Jl.
Diponegoro, Denpasar 80114 Bali, Indonesia
Phone: +62-361-227911

 HOSPITAL
There is a basic clinic on the hill above Labuan Bajo's town center, however evacuation is probably going to be your best option in serious medical emergency. Rumah Sakit Umum Mataram Hospital in Denpasar, Bali is a short flight away. Phone: +62-361-621345

 CONSERVATION SOCIETY
Komodo National Park
Head Office (Balai Taman Nasional Komodo)
Labuan Bajo, Flores Barat, N.T.T. 86554,
Indonesia
Phone: +62-385-41448
E-mail: info@putrinagakomodo.com

DIVER'S TIP

Currents are tricky here. Look out for what the reef fish are doing. Their body orientation is a good indicator of the current you are about to enter. If the fish are pointing directly up or directly down, think very carefully about sharing the same piece of water!

Don't get bent or injured! It's a long haul to the nearest recompression chamber or major hospital on Bali. Take responsibility for your own safety when diving in the park.

---

regulator was trying to escape sideways from our mouths. The air from our regulators was sucked straight down and out, forming a cloud of bubbles below us!"

Such conditions create the rich reefs and wonderful species diversity of the area. Diving them demands discipline and planning. However, with 36 recognized dive sites within the boundaries of the park, there are of course a number of alternatives to such adrenaline-charged experiences, particularly some wonderfully relaxing night dives.

CANNIBAL ROCK

• **30 to 130 feet (9 to 40 m)** • **intermediate**

Made famous by underwater photographers Burt Jones and Maurine Shimlock, this is a large pinnacle of rock in the channel between Kode and Rinca Islands. A visiting camera crew witnessed a large Komodo Dragon devouring another of its kind (a particular habit of the species) near this site, and gave it its name.

Cannibal Rock is known for being a magnificent night dive, made on the sandy slope on the northern side of the island starting at about 70 feet (21 m). But it is a particularly fine dive at any time of day. The rock walls are coated with sea whips, sponges, and soft corals. Mixed in with this busy patchwork of colonial and encrusting life is a myriad of the smaller inhabitants for which the Komodo reefs are famous. These include decorator crabs, Spanish dancers, bumblebee shrimps, frogfish, and pygmy sea horses. Larger members of the reef community here include big schools of red snappers and surgeonfish, as well as scorpionfish and octopuses within the nooks and crannies of the reef wall.

TATAWA KECIL

- 15 to 100 feet (5 to 30 m) • advanced

This small rocky islet lying southwest of Tatawa Besar Island is an egret nesting site. Because powerful currents roar through the area, it is an advanced dive, but less experienced divers will find they can dive it at slack in the company of an experienced guide.

Tatawa Kecil is a wonderfully varied site, with boulders, gullies, and small caverns festooned with coral growth in the nutrient-rich tidal streams. Although there is the normal range of fascinating smaller reef inhabitants here, the site's real reputation is for encounters with larger animals. Mantas, dugongs, and white tip sharks are frequently seen here (particularly on the south side of the island) as well as large bumphead parrotfish and napoleon wrasses.

OTHER ACTIVITIES

It would be madness to come all the way to dive the Komodo National Park and not take the opportunity to experience the wonders of its terrestrial wildlife. The obvious attractions are the dragons themselves. Once brought close to extinction through the activity of collectors and now highly protected, these carniverous lizards measure up to 10 feet (3 m) in length and can weigh in at 300 lbs (135 kg). Their name of dragon is well-deserved; they run swiftly and as well as eating carrion and smaller, weaker members of their own species, they are also known to attack and kill people (according to legend, the islands' original human inhabitants, the Ata Modo, were immune from their attacks.) For $5 a day a local guide will take you to the best spots to see the dragons, something not to be missed.

In addition to the dragons, the Komodo National Park also boasts 12 species of snake. The mammals at home in these islands include the rare Timor deer, wild boar, water buffalo, palm civets, long tailed macaques, and fruit bats.

☎ TELEPHONE NUMBERS

Recompression chamber	+62-361-227911
Hospital	+62-361-621345
Komodo National Park	+62-385-41448

💻 WEBSITES & E-MAIL

Komodo National Park	www.komodonationalpark.org
Indonesian Tourist Authority	www.indonesia-tourism.com
Travel Information	www.komodotours.com
Dive tips	www.starfish.ch

OTHER DIVE SITES

Tondok Rasa
Galley Rock
Batu Toko-Toko
Toro Moncong
Tatawa Besar
Batu Samsia
Chinese Mound
Batu Tiga
Pulau Damar
Three Sisters
Manta Valley
Tanjung Lelok Sera
Colleen's Corner
End of the World
Crynoid Point
Kerita Tol

▼ FEATHER STARS
Feather stars stretch filamentous arms into the rich currents and upwellings of a classic Komodo reef.

John Bantin

BALI

THIS POPULAR HOLIDAY ISLAND AT THE HEART OF THE INDONESIAN ARCHIPELAGO IS A MECCA FOR DIVERS. LOCATED ON THE WALLACE LINE, THE BOUNDARY BETWEEN THE SOUTH ASIAN AND AUSTRALIAN BIOGEOGRAPHICAL REGIONS, IT LIES AMIDST THE MOST DIVERSE MARINE SYSTEM ON EARTH.

 VISIBILITY
Up to 130 feet (40 m)

 MUST SEES
Sunfish
Pelagics off Nusa Penida

 DOWNSIDE
Dive sites some distance from tourist facilities
Strong currents

 GETTING THERE
Flights direct to Denpasar Airport on Bali from many large hubs in the U.S., Australia, and Europe. A change in Jakarta may be required depending on your airline or airport of origin.

 VISA
No visa required for stays of up to 60 days for most countries.

$ MONEY
Currency is the rupiah. Traveler's checks and credit cards widely accepted. Bank opening hours make it difficult to change money and complete your diving schedule, but you will find A.T.M.s in Kuta and Denpasar.

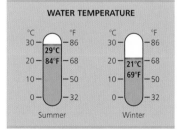

WATER TEMPERATURE

°C	°F		°C	°F
30	86		30	86
20 — 29°C 84°F	68		20 — 21°C 69°F	68
10	50		10	50
0	32		0	32
Summer			Winter	

▶ **STAGGERING REEFS**
The reefs around Bali are home to an astounding number of marine species.

Mikayo Langhofer

The Indonesian archipelago is the largest in the world, with a total area of 741,000 sq miles (1,919,440 sq km), 35,907 sq miles (93,000 sq km) of which are ocean. Although Indonesia is the fifteenth most populated country in the world, most of its population of more than 230 million are crowded onto the island of Java and a few more islands. Some 6,000 of its 17,000 islands are uninhabited.

Indonesia is home to 10 percent of the world's mammal species and 17 percent of all bird species. From 1853–61 British biologist Alfred Russel Wallace, a contemporary of Charles Darwin, explored the islands of the archipelago and studied the distribution of its rich flora and fauna. As a result of his investigations, Wallace established that the animals of Indonesia fall into two distinct groups. East of an imaginary line running through the Lombok Strait they belong to the Australasian biogeographical region, and west of this line (known today as the Wallace Line) they are Asian. There is some overlap between the two faunas in the islands immediately either side of the line. The small island of Bali, east of Java and immediately west of the Wallace Line, consequently boasts one of the most staggeringly diverse marine environments on Earth, an irresistible draw for divers.

GEOGRAPHY

Bali lies almost at the center of the long chain of Indonesian islands that stretches from Sumatra in the northwest to Irian Jayan, the western end of New Guinea, in the southeast. The unique overlapping of biogeographical regions in Bali is neatly summarized in the fact that the island's northern coast abuts the Java Sea, while the south is on the northeastern edge of the Indian Ocean. It measures only 50 miles (80 km) by 35 miles (56 km) at its widest point, and is home to more than 2 million people, most of whom live in the southern part of island in and around the small capital city, Denpasar. Bali's long-established and well-developed tourist infrastructure—attracting visitors from Australia and Japan in particular—is centered on Kuta Beach, also on the south coast. Most of the good dive sites are located on the east and west coasts, well away from these crowded areas.

MARINE LIFE

There are riches indeed in the waters around Bali. Heavily dependent on tourism as it is, many of its reefs have escaped the scourge of dynamite fishing that has so direly affected other parts of Indonesia. There seem to be as many estimates of numbers of species as there are species themselves—a conservative estimate speaks of 1,200 species, while the more exuberant talk breathlessly of more than 3000! The staggering diversity is best conveyed by breaking down the mind-blowing totals into specific genus of fish or crustaceans: for example, 21 different species of scorpionfish, 14 species of pufferfish, 20 species of seahorse and pipefish, and 75 species of prawn and lobster including 9 different types of mantis shrimp. The list goes on and on.

For many divers, the real attraction of Bali is the additional presence of large pelagic species, particularly in the cold upwellings around the small island of Nusa Penida. Here barracuda, sharks, tuna, and bonito share the water with dolphins, manatees, three species of turtle, and the (very) occasional blue and sperm whale.

DIVE CENTERS

BALI INTERNATIONAL DIVING PROFESSIONALS
Jl. Danau Poso No.26, Sanur,
Bali 80228, Indonesia
Phone: +62-361-285065
E-mail: info@bidp-balidiving.com
Web: www.bidp-balidiving.com

ENA DIVE CENTER & WATER SPORTS
Jalan Tetra Ending No. 1, Denpasar,
Bali 80227, Indonesia
Phone: +62-361-288829
E-mail: ena@indo.com
Web: www.indo.com/diving/ena/

SEA LOVERS
Rai No. 82C Kedonganan, Tuban,
Bali 80362, Indonesia
Phone: +62-361-703263
E-mail: marketing@balisealovers.com

DIVING ORGANIZATIONS

None, however the Bali Tourism Authority
recommends a number of operators:
Bali Tourism Authority, Denpasar,
Bali, Indonesia
Phone: +62-361-222387
E-mail: webmaster@balitourismauthority.net

RECOMPRESSION

U.S.U.P. Sanglah Denpasar Jl.
Diponegoro, Denpasar 80114 Bali, Indonesia
Phone: +62-361-227911

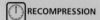 HOSPITAL

International S.O.S.
Medical Clinic & Evacuations
Jl. Bypass Ngurah Rai 505X, Kuta 80361,
Bali, Indonesia
Phone: +61-361-710505

International Tourist Medical Services
Jl. Pulau Saelus No. 2 Sesetan, Denpasar,
Bali, Indonesia
Phone: +61-361-240730

CONSERVATION SOCIETY

Bali Barat National Park in Bali is administered
by the P.H.P.A.: Cekik PHPA, Labuhan Lalang
PHPA, Jl. Suwung 40, Denpasar, Bali, Indonesia
Phone: +62-365-61060
E-mail: bali-info@promotingbali.com

DIVER'S TIP

Currents are an issue here. Look out for what
the reef fish are doing. Their body orientation
is a good indicator of the current you are
about to enter. If the fish are pointing directly
up, or directly down, think about sharing the
same piece of water very carefully!

▶ REGAL ANGELFISH

One of the many colorful fish species
found swimming the reefs of Bali.

THE DIVES

The diving industry in Bali has been established for more than twenty years, and consequently the standard of most dive operators, boats, and equipment is unmatched anywhere else in Indonesia, with the possible exception of Jakarta. However, you should be aware that there is a wide range in the standard of dive services offered on the island. Although most operations are relatively well run, there are one or two less well-funded centers. But if you choose with care and take responsibility for your own safety, you should have no problems.

Many of the dive sites are situated a long way from inhabited areas and can only be reached after a considerable drive overland or by boat. Although there is a huge variety of dives available around the island, ranging from screaming drifts over wild reefs through to sedate beach dives in sheltered inner lagoons, the best sites tend to be clustered around the northeast coast or the southeast region, including the island of Nusa Penida. Be prepared to work for your diving here—the rewards are invariably worth it!

LIBERTY WRECK

• 100 feet (30 m) • intermediate

This wreck has a fascinating history. It was torpedoed in the Lombok Strait on January 11, 1942, and her skipper nursed the stricken vessel to Tulamben Beach, where she was beached in the lee of Bali's largest mountain, the Gunung Anung volcano. In 1963 the volcano erupted, pushing the wreck back into the sea. She now lies within snorkeling distance of the beach parallel to the shore in 100 feet (30 m) of water.

Marine life absolutely swarms over the wreck, now covered in soft corals and crinoids, and great shoals of unicornfish and surgeonfish are seemingly unperturbed by the regular presence of divers. Groupers, coral trout, and regal angelfish share the superstructure, while the sand of the seafloor is home to large numbers of blue spotted stingrays. Look out for the colony of spotted garden eels on the return swim to shore.

NUSA PENIDA ISLAND

• 0 to 130 feet (0 to 40 m) • beginner to expert

Bali's finest dive site, Nusa Penida Island offers a range of diving experiences. The strong currents that wash the island are the reason for its spectacular abundance of large animals. Divers should approach the dives cautiously, mindful of their experience levels—a three-knot current over a drop-off surrounded by sharks is no fun if you are inexperienced.

Linda Pitkin

Mikayo Langhofer

At Ped a refuge from the racing currents can be found, with gently sloping reefs down to 70 feet (21 m) before shelving off more abruptly to 130 feet (40 m) and beyond. Sea snakes abound here, a fascinating encounter for any diver, and mantas may frequently be seen off the reef wall. The other great encounter is with sunfish—this distinctive, massive ocean-going fish seems to be present here in unusually large numbers.

Jurassic Point is slightly more hardcore in terms of barreling currents, but offers the opportunity to observe a range of large pelagics off its steeply stepped reef walls. Sunfish are also present at this site, sharing the waters with large groupers, sharks, mantas, and great aggregations of fantail rays.

OTHER ACTIVITIES

Although visitor numbers to Bali fell off after the terrorist bomb tragedy of 2002, tourism is slowly recovering. Kuta, on the bustling south coast, is the main center of nightlife and has some excellent surfing.

Bali, the only Hindu island in Muslim Indonesia, has a fascinating culture of dance, music, and drama, and the island offers a range of more traditional experiences. In the capital of Denpasar is the Museum of Bali, and the attractions of the artistic center of Ubud—a focal point for visitors from within Indonesia and beyond—should be investigated. Away from the well-developed tourist areas patches of rainforest still clothe the mountainous interior. The Bali Barat National Park on the western edge of Bali, covering 190,267 acres (77,000 ha), contains one of the world's most endangered bird species, the Bali starling.

☎ **TELEPHONE NUMBERS**

Recompression chamber	+62-361-227911
Hospital	+61-361-710505

🖳 **WEBSITES & E-MAIL**

Indonesian Tourist Authority	www.indonesia-tourism.com
Bali Tourism Authority	www.balitourismboard.org

▲ **COLORFUL RESIDENT**

As well as having a large number of fish species, Bali also has 75 species of prawn and lobster.

OTHER DIVE SITES

Tulamben
Amed
Gili Selang
Tepekong
Malibu
Manta Point
Menjangan Pos
Secret Bay

WAKATOBI

words by Jason Heller

THE REMOTE WAKATOBI ARCHIPELAGO IS A CORAL REEF PARADISE IN INDONESIA'S PRISTINE BANDA SEA. LUSH CORAL-COVERED WALLS OFFER DIVING AT ANY DEPTH YOU CHOOSE FROM SHALLOW REEF TOPS TO BLACK CORAL DEPTHS. MACRO LIFE IS THRIVING ON THESE REEFS. YOUR BIGGEST ISSUE IN WAKATOBI IS WHICH LENS TO PUT ON YOUR CAMERA.

Jason Heller

VISIBILITY
50 to 160 feet (15 to 50 m)

MUST SEES
Village Tour
Resort Grounds
Extended Stay in Bali

DOWNSIDE
Not much to do other than diving, but that's not much of a downside!

GETTING THERE
Many airlines offer international flights to Bali.

* Singapore Airlines
* Cathay Pacific
* Continental Airlines
* Malaysian Airlines
* Japan Airlines
* China Airlines
* EVA Air
* Thai Airways

You will need to stay overnight in Bali. The resort will fly you in for the last leg of the trip via private air charter from Bali to Wakatobi's private air strip.

VISA
Most visitors can obtain a 30-day "visa upon arrival" into Indonesia, but check with the Indonesian Consolate to ensure that your passport qualifies.

MONEY
USD ($), Euros, Indonesian Rupiah

WATER TEMPERATURE

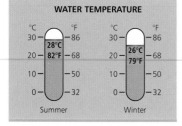

	Summer		Winter
°C	°F	°C	°F
30 — 28°C 82°F	— 86 — 68	30 — 26°C 79°F	— 86 — 68
20 —		20 —	
10 —	— 50	10 —	— 50
0 —	— 32	0 —	— 32

Diving in Wakatobi is offered via resort or live-aboard. Wakatobi Resort acquired the Pelagian Dive Yacht in 2005 and this move expanded the diving opportunities throughout this remote archipelago. However, it is the house reef at the resort that just may be the shining star.

GEOGRAPHY

Wakatobi lies smack in the middle of the "coral triangle," the most bio-diverse marine region in the world, and sits just south of the Wallace line. The archipelago receives less rain than the surrounding area, which creates a rather arid landscape, but limits runoff and siltation on the reefs.

The resort is named as an acronym from the first two letters of the main islands in the chain, namely Wangi Wangi, Kaledupa, Tomia and Binongko. The resort is actually located on Onemobaa Island, and the private resort airstrip is located on neighboring Tomia.

The Pelagian cruises throughout the archipelago north of Wakatobi where the resort's day boats could never reach including Wangi Wangi, Hoga, Kaledupa and Buton.

MARINE LIFE

Key features of the region are extremely healthy coral, and abundant and diverse macro life. This is not a big animal destination and while there is little fishing

Roma•

Table Coral City
Waitii Ridge•

TOMIA

• Blade

Magnifica   Tanjung Patok
Cornucopia•   • ✈
         Turkey Beach• ● Wakatobi Island Resort
                        •Zoo

Sawa

•Teluk Maya

Lintea Selatan

Kaledupa Reef

0 ___ 2 km
0 ___ 2mi

45

pressure, large schools of fish are sparse. However, while the critters that make up Wakatobi's usual subjects may be rare in other parts of the region, they can be found in relative abundance here.

In an effort to establish one of the healthiest marine parks in the region, Wakatobi Resort has been working with local villages to establish environmentally and culturally sound conservation programs. This has resulted in a large protected area created through the Wakatobi Collaborative Reef Conservation Program, which is now one of the world's largest privately funded marine protected areas. Consequently there is very little fishing pressure or pollution, and some of the healthiest coral reefs you will find anywhere.

The currents are manageable and range from gentle to wild, which help to feed the reef ecosystem. Hard and soft corals, sea fans, tunicates, sponges, sea whips, and crinoids all thrive in these fruitful currents.

THE DIVES
THE HOUSE REEF

• 0 to 130 feet (0 to 40 m) • intermediate

Appropriately dubbed one of the best house reefs in the world, the Wakatobi House Reef is indeed a special place to dive. It is normally unusual to find guests skipping out on boat dives so that they can dive a house reef all day long, but that is often the case here.

The reef consists of a colorful wall with a shallow drop-off that can begin in water less than 2 m (7 feet) deep during low tide and as deep as 4 m (13 feet) during high tide. In the short distance between the drop-off and the resort lies a vast ecosystem of turtle grass and isolated coral heads, a rich environment for odd and beautiful creatures such as frogfish, stonefish, blue ring octopus, moray eels, blue spotted stingrays, ghost pipefish, jawfish, shrimp and goby pairs. It also provides a safe haven for a wide variety of juvenile reef fish.

The bright blue mantles of juvenile giant clams seem to be wedged between some of the coral formations and rocks, most likely due to the shallow reef top and strong sunlight in this habitat. Beyond the reef top, you will cruise over the edge of the drop-off, where a sheer wall face is covered with hard and soft corals, sea fans, sponges, tunicates and overhangs that have become a favorite resting place for large resident turtles.

The other residents on the reef include a sizeable school of jacks that can be regularly found in front of the jetty bar at the end of the pier, which protrudes from the island to the edge of the drop-off.

◄◄ **LIONFISH**

A lionfish lies in wait atop a beautiful mound of potato coral on Roma, a wide sea mount to the west of the resort, washed with fairly strong currents throughout most of the day.

DIVE CENTERS

Wakatobi Dive Resort & Pelagian Yacht
Kuta Poleng Blok D-1
Jln Setiabudi—Simpang Siur
Kuta—Bali
80361 Indonesia
Phone: +62-361-759669
Web: www.wakatobi.com
E-mail: office@wakatobi.com

DIVING ORGANIZATIONS

The Wakatobi resort is affiliated with both PADI and TDI.

RECOMPRESSION

Closest recompression chambers are on Bali.

HOSPITAL

Emergency first aid can be administered by resort staff, and there is a basic hospital on the island neighboring Wakatobi (sufficiently equipped for most general treatments).

CONSERVATION SOCIETY

The Nature Conservancy:
Web: www.nature.org
E-mail: indonesia@tnc.org

▶ **PLEASE TAKE MY PICTURE**

Encounters with intelligent cuttlefish can last for 30 minutes or more. They are certainly not shy as long as you are respectful. It is common to find mating cuttlefish on the reefs. Some will even pose for pictures.

▶▶ **WHAT A STAR**

A blue star finds a home where the edge of the wall meets the reef top—a very special place where light dances over the sea grass and corals below.

At night, while enjoying a drink at the jetty bar after your house reef night dive (equally as rewarding as the daytime experience), you can hear the jacks hunting and splashing.

The current on the house reef can range from mild to fairly wild, and there is always a small taxi boat available to drop divers off up-current so that you can drift right back to the resort for a quick surface interval before a repeat performance. This is definitely a reef that you can dive all day long. By varying your depth and drop-off points, each dive becomes unique.

ONEMOBAA CAVERN

- **10 to 130 feet (3 to 40 m) • beginner**

An extension of the house reef, this cavern is more of an extremely large overhang carpeted with colorful soft corals, sponges and sea fans. Within the healthy corals lives a vibrant macro world, ranging from multiple species of pygmy seahorses to frogfish, commensal shrimps, nudibranchs and many others. In recent years, in an effort to conserve the health of the reef, the dive staff have asked divers to refrain from diving under the overhang in order to prevent exhaust bubbles from damaging the delicate corals.

Onemobaa Cavern is usually a scheduled boat dive (Tanjung Patok) during each diving itinerary, but can also be dived as part of a house reef dive when there is a mild current present. The taxi boats can drop you off in front of the cavern, and the current can assist in drifting you back to the resort. If you don't make it all the way back – no problem: just surface and signal for a taxi boat to pick you up.

TURKEY BEACH

- **10 to 80 feet (3 to 25 m) • beginner**

Technically this site is around the corner from the house reef, but it is inaccessible from shore due to an ever-present current, therefore Turkey Beach is scheduled only as a boat dive. The dive site gets its name from a story about how one of the owner's relatives remarked on the resident reef turkeys. Of course, she meant to say turtles, and from then on the reef had acquired its name.

Large resident turtles are indeed a prominent

Jason Heller

feature of this site. It is not uncommon to see up to five or more on one dive. The shallow sloping wall at Turkey Beach is fed by a current that seems to be nonstop, making for a fun drift dive. There are a couple of large canyons in the reef that offer refuge from the current, where often you can find small schools of batfish or snapper. Otherwise, the current feeds the abundant soft corals and sponges. A seemingly endless number of crinoids are perched on top of the sponges and sea fans, reaching out into the current for sustenance.

When the current is manageable, you can move in close to the reef to find pygmy seahorses sitting on sea fans, soft coral crabs, shrimps of every variety, the tiniest colorful nudibranchs and flatworms and other invertebrates. Apparently the recently discovered Pygmy Pipe Horse has been seen fairly consistently on Turkey Beach, otherwise this species has only been sighted in Lembeh.

BLADE

- **13 to 100 feet (4 to 30 m) • intermediate**

This is probably the unique dive site of the area, and also the furthest site accessed by the resort's day boats. Blade is a series of small sea mounts in clear, open water that apparently resemble the blade of a serrated knife, hence its name. Diving from the top of one sea mount to another is an amazing experience: less so when there is a current as it rather denies you the opportunity to "take it all in." At times, though the experience can be quite overwhelming.

Blade is about as picturesque as it gets, complete with giant sponges, sea fans and corals, and of course colorful crinoids sitting on top of everything. The red whip corals seem to be growing everywhere, and provide fantastic photo opportunities, as do the sea fans that can at times grow to upward of 6 to 10 feet (2 to 3 m) across. Only the more experienced and quicker divers will be able to visit more than the first three or four of the sea mounts on one dive as they get progressively deeper and deeper.

CORNUCOPIA AND MAGNIFICA

Some of the most lush and colorful sites are along the Sawa Reef system, which is at the edge of an immense lagoon around Sawa Island, across the channel from the resort. While there are many sites along this stretch of wall, Cornucopia and Magnifica sit on a corner that receives a particular level of current creating a jam-packed area of colorful lush soft corals, whip corals, sponges and sea fans.

On Cornucopia there is also a cleaning station for a large transient school of bumphead parrotfish. Ironically among all the large and healthy soft corals, you can also find plenty of macro critters. The dive guides have an uncanny ability to discover resident gems such as the white pygmy seahorse, a paper thin creature the size of your fingernail, which lives among one of the many, many patches of halemeda on this immense wall. Usually these critters become residents; as long as they are not bothered, they will stay in the vicinity for months. In fact, on these dives you can find three of the four pygmy seahorse species (including Denise and Bagarbunti), as well as various nudibranchs, jawfish, shrimp and goby pairs, orangutan crabs, dendronephthya crabs, xenon crabs, Zanzibar shrimp, and other magnificent feats of nature.

Sometimes the currents can be ripping on these walls, in which case you drift dive at whatever depth you are comfortable with, although it makes photography and critter spotting a little more challenging. You may appreciate the option of the large 100 cubic foot scuba tanks, which are a standard option at Wakatobi, that can maximize your "suck up the air while shooting photography in currents" possibilities.

ROMA

• **10 to 65 feet (3 to 20 m)** • **beginner (except when a strong current is present)**

This is one of the handful of non-wall dives at Wakatobi, and a true pleasure when the current isn't ripping over the site. Fortunately the tides and currents are fairly predictable so the dive guides ensure that this site is dived as much as possible during slack tide.

Essentially Roma is a large, wide pinnacle, fringed with beautiful potato coral and adorned with anemones and clownfish rising into the current. Large schools of fusiliers, anthias and snapper patrol the water column above the pinnacle, which make for a constant flittering of light on the dive site.

Banded sea snakes can be consistently found poking around the coral foraging for food. Like all the sites in Wakatobi, among the healthy coral you can discover fruitful macro life if you focus on the task.

THE ZOO

• **6 to 80 feet (2 to 25 m)** • **beginner**

Another site close by the resort, the Zoo is a patch reef just beyond Turkey Beach on the backside of the resort. Named for the plethora of critters found here, this is one of the true macro dives of Wakatobi. Residents include frogfish, ghost pipefish, mantis shrimp, leaf fish and more. One of the more unique macro critters found at the Zoo among the mushroom anemones is the mushroom pipefish, a small white creature with a triangular head, which makes it look less like a pipefish and more like a small underwater python.

The reef turns into a special place at night. At dusk the mating mandarinfish emerge from the staghorn

Jason Heller

and rubble zones. Many species of lionfish scour the reef, including the elusive twin spot lionfish. Bobtail squid and octopus seem to be found in larger numbers here than other sites, and a million glowing eyes of various shrimps and crabs peer at you from every crack and crevice in this lattice of life.

TELUK MAYA

- 20 to 80 feet (6 to 25 m) • beginner

This sloping and fringing reef sits on the north side of Lintea Island, across from the resort. A large resident school of batfish greets divers on this dive. If you observe closely you'll find a strange phenomenon among these fish: an abundance of parasitic isopods on their faces and bodies. The presence of these isopods does not seem to cause any health issues, but it is a peculiar example of an isolated infestation of a parasite among a resident school.

The batfish are often found in fairly large numbers and can present a fantastic photo opportunity. Teluk Maya has also become the home for many cuttlefish, which seem to forage, mate and lay eggs freely in the presence of divers. At the base of the fringing reef is a large sandy bottom, and home to a squadron of garden eels. You can also periodically find the odd pegasus sea moth and frogfish at this site.

WAITII RIDGE

- 20 to 100 feet (6 to 30 m) • beginner

Not far from Roma, and connected to another site with huge table corals appropriately named Table Coral City, Waitii Ridge is a long ridge along the west side of Tomia Island. As you descend from the surface, the clearly defined ridge is an impressive site, with reefs sloping down each side.

Anthias and damselfish dance in large numbers across the top of the staghorn and potato coral, keeping a keen eye on the banded sea snakes randomly foraging among them. Saron shrimp, mantis shrimp, banded pipefish, leaf fish, stonefish and other species that would be considered rare in other destinations are regularly found on this site.

▼ GARDEN OF EDEN
Prolific colors, shapes and patterns of healthy coral, sea fans and sponges are the main attraction in this reef Eden in the Banda Sea.

Jason Heller

CHEEKY BEACH, BUTON (PELAGIAN)

• 6 to 80 feet (2 to 25 m) • beginner

This is a fairly wide muck diving area inside a bay on the island of Buton, and is every bit as good as some of the top muck areas in the world, many of which are also located in Indonesia.

The site consists of a sloping mucky gravel zone where you can find seahorses, waspfish, shrimp/goby pairs, frogfish, colorful squid, magnificent urchins, zebra crabs, various moray eels, nudibranchs and other muck critters.

One of the unique and interesting features of this area is an abnormal abundance of baby porcupinefish and pipefish. There must be hundreds, if not thousands of porcupinefish hiding in every rock, log, hole in the sand, tin can, shoe and a plethora of other discarded items. Pipefish are not found in the same extraordinary numbers as the porcupinefish, but you expect to see one or two at least every few minutes, and it is not surprising to find groups of three to five foraging together.

This area still cries out for exploration, and the potential exists to discover interesting species of small and odd critters.

ASPHALT PIER, BUTON (PELAGIAN)

• 20 to 65 feet (6 to 20 m) • beginner

A wonderful muck dive on an abandoned old asphalt loading station and pier, the site consists of a shipwreck, the pier pilings and a disgustingly awesome mucky bottom.

Some of the critters you should expect to find include juvenile batfish, ornate and robust ghost pipefish, blue ribbon eels, frogfish, mantis shrimp, pipefish and nudibranchs.

At night this site offers much of the same daytime critters, in addition to octopus, squid and crustaceans of many varieties. Pipefish tend to congregate in small areas on the shipwreck, often in groups of 10 to 20. This is possibly a group mating or feeding behavior. Either way, it's a unique aggregation of a species that otherwise tends to live a more solitary or paired lifestyle.

MAGIC PIER, BUTON (PELAGIAN)

• 0 to 60 feet (0 to 20 m) • beginner

While Magic Pier is home to a diverse mix of fish and invertebrates, it is best dived at night, when you will find the large concrete blocks that make up the pier home to a variety of unique marine life. The masses of long spined urchins offer protection to small cuttlefish, shrimp, crabs and many small sole, which blend right into the sand-covered blocks.

A night dive on the pier will inevitably offer an

Jason Heller

encounter with possibly one of the largest schools of shrimpfish you will ever come across. Swimming through the dense school of vertically hovering slivers is a fairly weird, but interesting feeling as they bump into every part of your body. Sea snakes and moray eels also tend to come out at night on Magic Pier.

METROPOLIS (PELAGIAN)

• 20 to 100 feet (6 to 30 m) • intermediate

Metropolis is a unique dive site on the plateau of a sea mount in the north of the Wakatobi archipelago. The top of the plateau is covered in hard coral, including a large staghorn area.

As you descend the slope of the fairly wide sea mount, you will discover a rich coral environment fed by unpredictable currents that feed sizeable coral, sponge and sea fan growth. Large schools of barracuda are usually present above the dive site.

The currents here can be strong, but it is the reason for the coral growth. Be careful not to spend too much time at depth.

OTHER ACTIVITIES

Let's be clear, diving is the main activity in Wakatobi. The pristine beaches lend themselves to sunbathing and you can take a sea kayak out for a spin around the reef top. But generally there is not much to do other than dive, eat and sleep.

However, that's all you will want to do in this slice of diving paradise. The resort itself is beautiful, the food is good and plentiful and there is a small spa facility. On the last day of each itinerary at Wakatobi, you have the option to go on a village tour, where you can observe some of the local culture and see how the local villagers live.

◄ WHAT'S IN A NAME?
Turkey Beach consistently offers encounters with large green and hawksbill turtles, often with large remoras hanging on for the ride.

WEBSITES & E-MAIL
Wakatobi Dive Resort & Pelagian Yacht
Web: www.wakatobi.com
E-mail: office@wakatobi.com

The Nature Conservancy
Web: www.nature.org
E-mail: indonesia@tnc.org

NINGALOO
REEF

WESTERN AUSTRALIA

 VISIBILITY
90 to 140 feet (27 to 43 m) Oct–May
60 to 100 feet (18 to 30 m) May–Oct

 MUST SEES
Whale sharks
Point Murat Navy Pier

 DOWNSIDE
Remote

 GETTING THERE
Approximately 30 international airlines fly to Perth, the gateway to Western Australia. A two-and-a-half hour flight north takes you to Learmouth airport, and you can catch a bus to Exmouth.

 VISA
E.U. and U.S. citizens require a valid passport and a visa or Electronic Travel Authority (E.T.A.) to enter Australia. The latter are very simple to acquire, cost Aus.$20, and allow you to stay for three months. Go to www.eta.immi.gov.au for more information.

 MONEY
Currency is the Australian dollar, and is readily available at A.T.M.s throughout the country. Operators and hotels of any size accept all major credit cards.

WATER TEMPERATURE

°C	°F		°C	°F
30 —	— 86		30 —	— 86
20 — **30°C** **86°F**	— 68		20 — **24°C** **75°F**	— 68
10 —	— 50		10 —	— 50
0 —	— 32		0 —	— 32
Summer			Winter	

▶ **WHALE SHARK**
Ningaloo is the most well-established dive location on Earth for those wishing to encounter whale sharks.

FROM APRIL TO JULY EVERY YEAR DIVERS FLOCK TO REMOTE NINGALOO REEF IN WESTERN AUSTRALIA FOR THE CHANCE OF SEEING WHALE SHARKS, BUT THESE WATERS AND REEFS ARE SPECTACULAR IN THEIR OWN RIGHT, REASON ENOUGH TO COME HERE AT ANY TIME OF YEAR.

Dan Burton

The wonderfully scenic stretch of coastline where Ningaloo Reef is located forms part of the Coral Coast of Western Australia, the strip of shoreline extending from the Northwest Cape all the way to the Tropic of Capricorn. It is gloriously undeveloped—undoubtedly one of its great attractions. However, over the past few years a bustling diving community has grown up in the town of Exmouth, centered around the spectacular reefs of Ningaloo Reef and, in particular, the reliable presence of whale sharks. There has been a significant tourist presence here ever since word about the sensational whale shark diving got out in 1993. Each year from April through to July the population of Exmouth swells as divers from all over the world make the pilgrimage to swim with these magnificent animals.

GEOGRAPHY

Ningaloo Reef is a fringing reef that extends for 174 miles (280 km) midway up the Western Australia coastline approximately 745 miles (1,200 km) north of Perth. It is one of the only large reef systems on Earth that runs consistently close to a continental landmass, a ribbon of coral extending from within 328 feet (100 m) to 4 miles (7 km) offshore. A National Park was declared at Ningaloo Reef in 1987, covering an area of 1,544 sq miles (4,000 sq km).

MARINE LIFE

This is a hugely diverse stretch of coastline, mainly due to the merging of warm temperate, subtropical, and tropical ecosystems. Exact estimates of species numbers at any site are always sketchy, but experts believe that Ningaloo Reef has approximately 500 fish species, 200 corals, and 600 mollusk species. Added to this impressive mix are 4 of the world's 7 species of marine turtles (leatherback, loggerhead, hawksbill, and green), and 14 species of whale. Of particular note are the twice-yearly migrations of humpbacks along the reef. Two species of dolphins have been recorded in these waters, and a survey carried out in 1994 counted 1,000 individual dugongs, making this one of the most significant populations on Earth. The dugongs are resident all year round, feasting on the three species of seagrass in the area.

As if this wasn't enough, there are always congregations of the great filter-feeders to be found at Ningaloo. Mantas are present all year round but are particularly prevalent from May to October. They seem to gather in very large numbers at Maud's Landing (reports of in excess of 100 mantas on a single dive!), and anecdotal evidence suggests this is a mating area.

Finally of course there are the whale sharks—the largest fish on Earth, up to 45 feet (13 m) in length, and

NINGALOO REEF
(Australia)

```
0           20 km
|———————————|
0           15 mi
```

DIVE CENTERS

EXMOUTH DIVING CENTER
2 Payne Street, Exmouth,
Western Australia 6707
Phone: +61-8-9949-1201
E-mail: whaleshark@exmouthdiving.com.au
Web: www.exmouthdiving.com.au

VILLAGE DIVE
Corner Murat Road & Truscott Crescent,
Exmouth, Western Australia 6707
Phone: +61-8-9949-1116
E-mail: villdive@bigpond.net.au
Web: www.villagedive.com.au

 DIVING ORGANIZATIONS

None, but the Australian Government's
Marine Protection Areas Section regulates all
commerical activity in the Park:
Peter Taylor – Director
Marine Protected Areas Section
Phone: +61-2-6274-1111
Web: www.environment.gov.au/coasts/mpa/

 RECOMPRESSION

Hyperbaric Medicine Unit
Fremantle Hospital, Alma Street, Fremantle,
Western Australia 6160
Phone: +61-8-9431-2233
E-mail: jeff.pinkham@health.wa.gov.au

 HOSPITAL

Exmouth District Hospital
Lyons Street, Exmouth W.A. 6707
Phone: +61-8-9949-1011

 CONSERVATION SOCIETY

There is an alliance of local businesses,
committed to preserving the wilderness values
of Ningaloo Reef and the adjacent Cape
Range. They can be contacted at:
Web: www.save-ningaloo.org

OTHER DIVE SITES

Turquoise Bay
Turtle Mound
Blizzard Ridge
Northwest Ridge
Cod Spot

▶ **HAWKSBILL TURTLE**

As well as hawksbill, Ningaloo is home to
leatherback, loggerhead, and green
turtles.

one of only three filter-feeding sharks. These huge dappled animals descend on the reef in great numbers from March through to June, and there now exists a complex industry to spot the sharks and put divers in the water for the experience of a lifetime.

THE DIVES

As all the local operators are only too anxious to tell you, there is a great deal more to Ningaloo than whale sharks. This huge reef is a mixture of spur and groove, complex canyons and gullies, bommies and mini walls. Most of the diving here takes place in 26 to 60 feet (8 to 18 m) of water, and the best time to visit the area is certainly in the summer months—November through to March—because the swells have decreased during this period and visibility is at its greatest. However, this is just the beginning of the whale shark season, so you might want to visit the region slightly later if you have these creatures in mind.

Large schools of fish are not particularly characteristic of Ningaloo, although the marine life is certainly abundant enough. On any single dive it is possible to encounter a range of shark species, rays, reef fish aplenty, and of course the really impressive large pelagic species for which the area is famed. For these,

the optimum months for sightings are broadly speaking: March to June for whale sharks; May to October for mantas; July to November for whales; November to January for nesting turtles.

POINT MURAT NAVY PIER

15 to 65 feet (5 to 20 m) • beginner

This is one of those dives the operators are on about when they say there is more to Ningaloo than big stuff! This is a truly world-class diving experience, made all the more enjoyable by the fact that it is shallow and readily accessible. (Although permission is required from the Australian Navy before diving can commence, the local operators will seek this out on behalf of their diver groups.)

Located at the entrance of Exmouth Gulf, the Point Murat Navy Pier is a large structure jutting out into the shallow water of the bay. The area is strongly affected by tides, offering two windows for diving at slack water on high and low tide. High tide is preferable as more of the pier is accessible, allowing for two short dives during this period.

The pylons and struts of the pier are home to a dazzling array of fish life and encrusting organisms. Shoals of barracuda, sweetlips, and spangled emperors

Tony White

Linda Pitkin

are ever present, with larger species such as Queensland groupers, wobbegong sharks, and estuarine cod particularly abundant as well. Divers frequently report encounters with mantas on this dive, as well as white tips, whale sharks, and even tiger sharks. Amongst the smaller but no less spectacular members of the reef community in attendance are ghost pipefish and leaf fish. The spars and struts of the pier are coated in a gloriously eclectic mix of sponges, sea squirts, barnacles, and fire coral.

WHALE SHARK DIVES

• Snorkeling • beginner

You get an idea of just how smoothly the local whale shark dive industry swings into operation when you see spotter planes taking to the skies in mid morning to hunt for cruising specimens. The pilots are in constant communication with the waiting dive vessels below, and as soon as they get the signal, the boats speed to the relevant location for the action to begin. At the right time of year sightings are guaranteed.

The operators are reasonably co-operative in their efforts to make sure that everyone will get a chance of viewing the sharks and will do their best to allow every diver at least a quick dip for a brief in-water encounter. No more than 10 snorkelers are allowed in the water with a particular shark at any one time, and there is a strict protocol in place to avoid stressing the animals. Flash photography, touching the shark, and approaching the tail are not permitted—the latter rule more for the protection of the snorkelers than the shark! If the shark is in the right mood, it may hang around for a considerable period. Invariably, under these circumstances, the snorkelers give out before the shark does.

OTHER ACTIVITIES

Exmouth is a small town with a population around 2,200, a figure that more than doubles in the busy season. There is a full range of accommodation available, as well as some pleasant restaurants. Within a few miles are beautiful beaches and deserted coastline. Cape Range National Park is located 25 miles (40 km) south from Exmouth. It boasts spectacular gorges and an array of wildlife and wildflowers in season. A number of operators run four-wheel drive tours through the park.

▲ MANTAS AT MAUD'S

Huge aggregations of mantas at Maud's Landing have added to Ningaloo's reputation.

☎ **TELEPHONE NUMBERS**

Recompression chamber	+61-8-9431-2233
Hospital	+61-8-9949-1011
Exmouth Visitor Center	+61-8-9949-1176

💻 **WEBSITES & E-MAIL**

Western Australia Tourist Commission	www.westernaustralia.net
Australian Travel Commission	www.australia.com

KANGAROO ISLAND

words by Lesley Maw

FOR A GLIMPSE OF THE BEAUTIFUL BUT ELUSIVE LEAFY SEA DRAGON YOU CAN'T BEAT AUSTRALIA'S KANGAROO ISLAND. ENDEMIC TO THE TEMPERATE, SOUTH AUSTRALIAN WATERS, THEIR ACTUAL LOCATION IS OFTEN A CLOSELY GUARDED SECRET.

 VISIBILITY
30 to 60 feet (10 to 20 m)

 MUST SEES
Leafy and weedy sea dragons
New Zealand fur seals
Australian sea lions

 DOWNSIDE
A long way from almost anywhere

GETTING THERE
International airlines fly into Adelaide (either direct or from one of the major Australian hubs). Kangaroo Island can be reached from Adelaide by either car or coach and ferry or by local flights directly from Adelaide. There is no public transportation on the island.

 VISA
All nationalities (except for New Zealand) require a tourist visa or Electronic Travel Authority (ETA) valid for 3 months to enter Australia. (See other Australian entries in book.)

$ MONEY
Australian Dollar

Lesley Maw

WATER TEMPERATURE

°C	°F		°C	°F
30	86		30	86
20	68		20	68
21°C 70°F				
10	50		10	50
			12°C 54°F	
0	32		0	32
Summer			Winter	

Pissy Boy Bay •
•Western River Cove
Portland Maru •
• Snug Rock
Castle Rock
•Kingscote

KANGAROO ISLAND

K angaroo Island is one of earth's last unspoiled refuges, with its pure white sandy beaches, rugged inlets and secret coves. The rich diversity of flora and fauna includes colonies of fairy penguins, Australian pelicans and the endangered Australian sea lions, as well as platypus, echidnas and the island's own endemic kangaroo. Beneath the waves there is some of the best temperate water diving in Australia.

GEOGRAPHY

Seven times the size of Singapore and Australia's third largest island, Kangaroo Island lies 68 miles (110 km) southwest of Adelaide at the entrance to the Gulf St. Vincent. It was named by British explorer Matthew Flinders in 1802.

The island is 95 miles (155 km) long from east to west and about 35 miles (55 km) wide north to south. It is a mix of bush, farmland, beaches and rugged coastline with cliffs rising to over 820 feet (250 m). There are five main wilderness protected areas on the island and four marine protected areas (MPAs). The island also has its own Volunteer Marine Rescue (VMR).

MARINE LIFE

The temperate waters of Kangaroo Island are home to both the leafy sea dragon and the more common weedy sea dragon. Worried about their rapidly decreasing numbers, in 1991 the Department of Fisheries in Western Australia declared the leafy sea dragon a totally protected species. Divers come here primarily to see these fascinating creatures.

Both animals are part of the seahorse family with leaflike appendages on their heads and bodies. These provide excellent camouflage when the animal is located in its habitat of seaweed, sea grass and rocky reefs. "Leafies" can grow to about 12 inches (30 cm) while the "weedies" can grow up to 18 inches (46 cm). Playful New Zealand fur seals and the endangered Australian sea lion are also a common sight around the island.

Over 270 known species of fish can be found here, the majority of which are endemic to southern Australian waters, and it is one of the most prolific areas for soft corals, sponges and gorgonian fans in temperate zones.

Other marine life often found here include eagle rays, stingrays and over 60 types of nudibranch. The blue groupers in the area can reach up to 3 feet (1 metre) long and it is not uncommon, while diving, to be inspected by a passing pod of a dozen or so bottlenose dolphins.

During the winter months the migration route of the southern right whale takes them past Kangaroo Island.

THE DIVES

Diving is by boat and usually on the more sheltered north coast of the island. The coastline offers numerous rocky bays and inlets. Apart from a few wrecks, the underwater scenery is a mixture of white sand, the most widespread marine habitat in the world, giving way to sea grass beds, rocky reefs and walls, and kelp, all providing a perfect habitat for the rich and diverse marine life.

Being in the southern hemisphere, the Australian summer between November and April are the best months for diving.

47

◀◀ **NEW ZEALAND FUR SEAL**
These delightful creatures race around playfully while they inspect divers with a curiosity that is totally endearing.

► **WEEDY SEA DRAGON**
The male weedy sea dragon carries the eggs of his offspring on the underside of his tail.

PISSY BOY BAY

• 16 to 62 feet (5 to 19 m) • beginner

Located to the west of Western River Cove, Pissy Boy Bay lies beneath 500-foot (150 m) cliffs. It is named in typical direct Australian style after a natural vent in the rocks which, during heavy swells, sprays water out with great force.

Three different dive sites make up Pissy Boy Bay: the Amphitheatre, the Cut and the Arch, which are all situated within 550 yards (500 m) of each other in a protected area. The excellent visibility ranges from 50 to 80 feet (15 to 25 m).

The Amphitheatre drops through a gully to 56 feet (17 m) opening out in a white, circular sandy bottom. The walls are smothered with many nudibranchs and, if you look very closely, you can also see tiny black-knee sea spiders on the numerous sponges dotted over the surrounding structures. Large stingrays rest on the sandy bottom. The Amphitheatre leads to flat seabed covered in sargassum weed, which houses masses of tiny shrimps, the favorite food of both the leafy and weedy sea dragons. Look carefully and you will find one or both of these incredible creatures. Large blue groupers and many other fish can also be found here.

The Cut lies 500 feet (150 m) south of the Amphitheatre. Here, in a depth of around 30 feet (10 m), lives a small group of New Zealand fur seals always ready to frolic with the comparatively small number of divers that visit the site. You might also encounter friendly and inquisitive Australian sea lions, whose numbers are sadly in decline. The walls are covered with multicolored sponges and gorgonian fans with harlequin fish peeking out of small crevices.

The third site in this area is the Arch, named after a natural rock arch that overhangs the site. This leads to a small pool near the cliff face. Here, the resident New Zealand fur seal colony help create a truly memorable underwater experience. The diving is shallow, at about 10 to 16 feet (3 to 5 m), and the seals are often caught just hanging around on the surface in something of a comical posture with their feet in the air and their heads beneath the waves watching you with their huge eyes surrounded by long whiskers. Wait long enough and inevitably their curiosity gets the better of them. They will come and gently interact with you. It really is a very special direct yet benign encounter; something you will long remember.

PORTLAND MARU

• 50 feet (15 m) • beginner

The Japanese steamer *Portland Maru*, with a cargo of some 5,000 tons of wheat, ran aground at Cape Torrens —the highest cliffs on Kangaroo Island—during March 1935. The ship was beached approximately 550 yards (500 m) from shore; it began to sink after developing a list that had caused severe flooding. Fortunately, no lives were lost. Today, the remains of the wreck consist of little more than boilers and a number of exposed beams standing 20 feet (6 m) above the seabed in 50 feet (15 m) of water.

This wreck is very broken up so the main interest lies with the resident marine life. The good visibility here can range from 30 to 100 feet (10 to 30 m). Typical of many wreck sites, the exposed beams have become

Lesley Maw

encrusted with coral and sponges. Large schools of fish are seen all around the wreck, including red snapper and swallowtails, and it is also home to many different types of nudibranchs, crustaceans and the ubiquitous blue grouper. Blue devilfish can be seen foraging among the rubble lying on the seabed. Keep a careful eye out for the deadly blue-ringed octopus, which can also be found in this area.

Because of this site's exposed position, it can be prone to heavy swells. If you encounter these sorts of conditions be aware of the many exposed rusty objects that lie around, which can easily snag gear.

WESTERN RIVER COVE

- 30 feet (10 m) • beginner

The cove consists of a sandy bottom leading to a rocky reef with kelp and sea grass. Marine life includes stingrays, nudibranchs and starfish.

SNUG ROCK

- depth variable • intermediate to advanced

Snug Rock is a pinnacle rising out of the depths of the ocean. Depth is from the surface downward. Many colorful corals and nudibranchs adorn the walls with green grouper and blue devilfish in the nooks and crannies. Huge shoals of red snapper hang around in open water and there is a prolific selection of fish life in the area.

CASTLE ROCK

- 50 to 65 feet (15 to 20 m) • beginner

Castle Rock is a combination of sea grass, kelp and rocky walls. Marine life includes the beautiful leafy and weedy sea dragons, numerous colorful gorgonian fans, ornate cowfish, large crayfish, rays and the Australian sea lion. "Big Blue", a particularly friendly blue grouper, will often follow divers here.

The rock face contains small recesses, the walls and tops of which are covered in masses of small gorgonian fans ranging from bright yellow to deep blue in color.

Here you are most likely to encounter pods of bottlenose and common dolphins.

OTHER ACTIVITIES

If you have day or two to spare, there is cage diving with great white sharks at Dangerous Reef—run by Rodney Fox, located on the mainland at Port Lincoln.

Kangaroo Island is home to many different native animals and birds. There are many diverse attractions either rural, coastal or cultural. Over 30 percent of Kangaroo Island consists of national parks or heritage protected land. A number of good quality operators offer personalized guided 4x4 tours to see the highlights of the Island. Or rent your own 4x4 vehicle

Lesley Maw

and take a drive to Flinders Chase located at the western end of Kangaroo Island. Here you can see the amazing landscape created by the natural elements at Remarkable Rocks and see the New Zealand fur seals at Admirals Arch.

For the best of the pristine waters and pure white beaches, try Vivonne Bay, where you can catch your own dinner from the jetty. If pushed for time watch the pelican feeding at the KI Marine Centre in Kingscote, daily at 5 pm.

▲ **LEAFY SEA DRAGON**

The elusive leafy sea dragon grows leaf-like appendages that act as camouflage against predators.

☎ **TELEPHONE NUMBERS**

Recompression chamber	+61-8-8222-5116
Hospital	+61-8-8683-2288
South Australian Visitor Center	+61-13-0065-5276

💻 **WEBSITES & E-MAIL**

www.tourkangarooisland.com.au

NEPTUNES ISLANDS & DANGEROUS REEF

MADE FAMOUS BY THE DIVING MOVIE "BLUE WATER WHITE DEATH", SOUTH AUSTRALIA'S WHITE SHARK "HOT SPOTS" ARE LEGENDARY THROUGHOUT THE DIVING WORLD; HOWEVER, BY THE 1990's SHARK NUMBERS WERE TAKEN TO THE BRINK BY OVER FISHING AND PERSECUTION. SINCE THE INTRODUCTION OF TOUGH CONSERVATION MEASURES SHARK NUMBERS ARE AGAIN ON THE ASCENDANT, AND THE GREAT WHITE SHARK DIVING PHENOMENA HAS RE-EMERGED.

 VISIBILITY
80 feet (25 m) max
20 to 40 feet (6 to 12 m) on average

 MUST SEES
Great white sharks
Seal and sea lion colonies
Deep cage dives

 DOWNSIDE
Limited number of trips visiting the islands

 GETTING THERE
Many international airlines fly direct to Adelaide in South Australia. There are domestic flights from all over Australia to Port Lincoln.

 VISA
U.S. and E.U. citizens require a valid passport and a visa or Electronic Travel Authority (E.T.A.) to enter Australia. These are simple to acquire, cost Aus.$20, and allow you to stay in the country for three months. For further information go to: www.eta.immi.gov.au

$ MONEY
Currency is the Australian dollar, and cash is readily available at A.T.M.s throughout the country. Operators and hotels of any size accept all major credit cards.

WATER TEMPERATURE

	Summer		Winter	
°C	°F	°C	°F
30	86	30	86
20	68	20	68
20°C / 68°F			
10	50	16°C / 60°F	
10		10	50
0	32	0	32

▶ **MASTER PREDATOR**
The great white's massive bulk belies its graceful movement past the cage.

Contrary to what some people might believe, Dangerous Reef does not owe its name to its famous population of great white sharks, but rather to the fact that it posed a threat to ships as they approached Port Lincoln through the navigable channel at the entrance to Spencer Gulf. However, in the 1970s and 1980s its name took on a new resonance when word spread among divers that huge numbers of great whites, drawn in to feed on the large colonies of seals and sea lions, had taken up residence here.

Overfishing and persecution of the sharks subsequently took a heavy toll, and by the early 1990s the area was virtually devoid of sharks. The picture is changing again as conservation measures have brought about something of a recovery, but it is the South and North Neptunes that now see the greatest concentrations of great white sharks, with lesser—but still exciting activity—around Dangerous Reef itself.

North Shields

• Coffin Bay

SOUTH AUSTRALIA (Australia)

Boston Island

Spilsby Island

Port Lincoln ✈

Cape Donington

Dangerous Reef

0   20 km
0   14 mi

Taylor Island

Sibsey Island

Cape Wiles

Thistle Island

Liguanea Island

Cape Catastrophe

Gambier Island

• **North Neptune Island**

• **South Neptune Island**

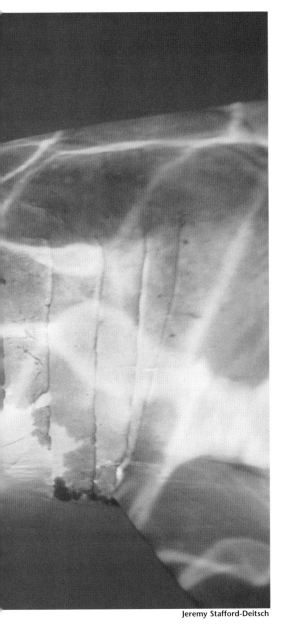

Jeremy Stafford-Deitsch

GEOGRAPHY

Dangerous Reef and the North and South Neptunes are part of a series of islands and reefs off the Eyre Peninsula coast of South Australia that serve as feeding grounds for great white sharks. Dangerous Reef lies directly east of Port Lincoln, while the North and South Neptune Islands are southwest of Thistle Island at the entrance to Spencer Gulf. Shark encounters also take place on Sibsey Island slightly to the northwest of Thistle Island and farther in to the Gulf.

MARINE LIFE

These small islands are uninhabited except for large colonies of New Zealand fur seals and Australian sea lions. There are 30 species of pinniped (a word that means "fin footed") on Earth, but these are the only two that breed in this region. Indeed, the breeding colony of Australian sea lions on Dangerous Reef is the largest in Australia, accounting for one-tenth of the species' total population of only 12,000.

It is the breeding colonies that draw the great white sharks to the Neptunes. A survey carried out in 2000 counted a total of 5,988 pups on this small island group alone, an irresistible magnet for the great whites. When the breeding season ends, numbers drop dramatically, with anything from a few dozen to a couple of hundred individuals remaining on the Dangerous Reef haulout points.

The presence of seals or sea lions in a cold-water environment does not automatically guarantee great

48

DIVER'S TIP

This delicate ecosystem should be a Marine Protected Area. If you have enjoyed your encounter with the great whites, take a moment to contact the Director of the M.P.A.S. in Australia and let your views be known.

DIVE CENTERS

FOX GREAT WHITE SHARK EXPEDITIONS
Moseley Square, Glenelg, SA 5045, Australia
Phone : +61-8-8363-1788
E-mail: expeditions@rodneyfox.com.au
Web: www.rodneyfox.com.au

DIVING ORGANIZATIONS

South Australian Diving Association
9 Sunhaven Avenue, Athelstown,
SA 5076, Australia
Phone: +61-7-3823-1444
E-mail: mgodden@ausport.gov.au
Web: www.ausport.gov.au

RECOMPRESSION

Hyperbaric Medicine Unit
Royal Adelaide Hospital
North Terrace, Adelaide, SA 5000
Phone: +61-8-8222-5116
E-mail: imirabel@mail.rah.sa.gov.au
Web: www.rah.sa.gov.au

HOSPITAL

Divers' Emergency Service
Phone: +1-800-088-200

Port Lincoln Hospital Accident and Emergency
Oxford Terrace, Port Lincoln, SA 5606
Phone: +61-8-8683-2288

CONSERVATION SOCIETY

Marine Protected Areas Section
Phone: +61-2-6274-1111
Web: www.environment.gov.au/coasts/mpa/

The Shark Trust
National Marine Aquarium, The Rope Walk,
Coxside, Plymouth, PL4 OLF, U.K.
Phone: +44-870-128-3045
Web: www.sharktrust.org

white sharks—there are huge seal colonies off Argentina, for example, with no significant shark presence. However, the undersea topography of the South Australian island group creates ideal ambush zones where deep channels running past reefs and haulout points give the sharks space to gain impetus to attack the unwary pups. Significantly, the sharks also predate on adult seals and sea lions here.

The region became a mecca for shark diving and fishing in the 1980's, when a survey noted that as many as 200 individual sharks were regularly patrolling the waters around Dangerous Reef. Although chumming for great white sharks is always an unpredictable business, dive operators were getting truly impressive results in these waters, with regular sightings of large great whites.

Subsequent events at Dangerous Reef provide a perfect example of what can happen when an apex predator is put under pressure by uncontrolled fishing and exploitation. Indeed, the history of shark diving and filming expeditions in the region bears witness to the dramatic crash in shark numbers at this time as commercial and recreational fishing gradually took their toll. By the early 1990s the waters around Dangerous Reef were almost completely devoid of great whites, a situation that became all too obvious when a well-financed filming expedition sat over one of the prime shark hotspots for three weeks, chumming continuously, and saw only three juvenile great whites, all of which moved away before being filmed.

▼ SEA LIONS

Australian sea lions need all of their intelligence and acrobatics to avoid falling prey to great whites in this region.

Legislation passed in 1998 finally gave much-needed protection to the great white sharks in these waters, and there has been a cautious recovery in their numbers since. Nevertheless, despite this official protection, 30 percent of all great whites sighted in the region still bear the evidence of injuries from commercial fishing gear, and the battle is far from won.

It is possible that Dangerous Reef is an important mating area for the great whites, as the ratio of females to males in the waters around the reef is a 6:1, a sharp contrast to the ratio of 1:20 in the nearby Neptunes. However, many of the sharks sighted at Dangerous Reef are immature and are therefore visiting it purely to feed, so this ratio actually raises rather more questions than it answers.

THE DIVES

Trips to dive the islands depart from Port Lincoln or from Adelaide, the capital of South Australia, a few miles to the south. However, dive operators tend to work Dangerous Reef and Sibsey Island less and less nowadays, and indeed both sites may well be ruled out of bounds in the near future by local legislation.

One operator has a particularly impressive record for finding sharks in these waters. Rodney Fox has had a fascination for great whites ever since he was attacked by one in 1963, and for the last 32 years he has been running diving safaris to tag individuals and record shark population numbers in the region. Out of a total of 300 trips, he saw no sharks at all on only eleven—an amazing record.

February is considered to be the best month to encounter sharks in these waters. The standard arrangement is to motor to the reef or islands in a large sailing craft, sit in place, and chum for resident sharks. It is also possible to go on organized walks amongst the seal colonies, or indeed to film them, using remote cameras, in the shallows around the island.

CAGE DIVES

- Surface • beginner
- Seabed • intermediate

The cages used on these expeditions are fairly substantial, able to hold up to four divers. While the chumming is going on, the cages can be lowered with the divers inside to observe local marine life and check for the presence of sharks in deeper water (from 40 to 80 feet/12 to 25 m). One of the advantages of the great white sites in this region as compared to South Africa is the visibility—in peak season visibility can be good enough around the Neptunes to allow for some really great photographic opportunities.

Fox Great White Shark Expeditions has perfected the use of deeper cages placed on the seabed, something

John Bantin

Jeremy Stafford-Deitsch

that is unique to its operations. Breathless divers, fresh back from the trip, describe it as the ultimate in white shark encounters. The whole cage operation is well organized, and two-way radios are used to inform any clients who are out on seal-observing excursions that the sharks have turned up—a process that can take anything from ten minutes to several days.

Most of the shark diving now takes place around the Neptunes, with consistently impressive encounters particularly in the winter months. Most trips spend about 80 percent of their time at North Neptune. But as if to show that this isn't a zoo, the great whites overturned all predictions by being present in huge numbers at Dangerous Reef during the 2002 season. The local operators are at pains to emphasize that great white sharks are nomadic creatures, a point brought home by tagging programs that show the same shark turning up at either or both of the islands, or at the reef. Indeed, one individual animal may migrate many thousands of miles in the course of its lifetime.

The recovery of this remarkable animal does seem to be ongoing in South Australia. However, something in the region of 140 are killed by accident off the coast of Australia each year, so their future can by no means be considered assured.

OTHER ACTIVITIES

Trips to see the sharks are not daily excursions in South Australia as they are at locations in South Africa. Here they are much more serious affairs, lasting up to ten days, chumming heavily and moving from island to island. For non-divers, the attractions are limited to visiting the seal and sea lion colonies, fishing, and viewing the great white sharks through remote cameras.

☎ **TELEPHONE NUMBERS**

Recompression chamber	+61-8-8222-5116
Hospital	+61-8-8683-2288
South Australian Visitor Center	+61-13-0065-5276

💻 **WEBSITES & E-MAIL**

South Australian Visitor Center	www.southaustralia.com
Australian Travel Commission	www.australia.com
Travel information	www.atn.com.au

▲ **CLOSE RANGE**
Being eyeballed at close range by a great white shark can be a disconcerting experience.

PACIFIC
OCEAN

The largest and deepest of all the oceans, the Pacific covers 33 percent of the Earth's surface and contains more than 50 percent of all the seawater on the planet. With a total surface area of 64 million sq miles (166 million sq km), it extends from the Arctic to the Antarctic and from the Americas to Asia and Australia.

Two vast circulating movements of water, known as gyres, flow around this great expanse. Moving clockwise in the northern hemisphere and counter clockwise in the southern hemisphere, they form the westward-moving North and South Equatorial Currents in the tropics. In the North Pacific the Kuroshio–North Pacific Current moves warm water up the coast of Asia and the California Current draws cold water down from the Arctic to the west coast of North America. In the South Pacific, the Humboldt (or Peru) Current moves cold water from the circumpolar Antarctic Current up the west coast of South America, and the East Australian Current carries warm water southward.

The Pacific's average depth is 2.7 miles (4.3 km); its deepest point, at 35,830 feet (10,924 m), is the Marianas Trench southwest of Guam, a massive gash in the Earth's crust that could absorb the whole of Everest and still leave the summit 1.2 miles (2 km) beneath the water's surface. This and other deep trenches mark the Pacific's "Ring of Fire", the circle of volcanic activity formed where the ocean's massive tectonic plates are sliding beneath the landmasses around its edges. Some 75 percent of the seabed, however, consists of flat and featureless abyssal plains spreading away from the line of seamounts and ridges that runs northwest to southeast down its center.

The Pacific shows the diver many different faces, but one area is irresistible—the so-called "Triangle of Diversity" lying between New Guinea, the southern tip of Sumatra, and the Philippines. These extraordinary waters contain more than 500 species of reef-building corals, compared with only 70 species in the Caribbean (hence the region's alternative name of the "Coral Triangle"), and a similar richness of fish, invertebrate, and marine life. Indonesia alone has more than 1,650 species of fish.

This amazing abundance of marine life is what makes coral reef diving in the Pacific so very exciting. But such a vast area of water has many other tremendous dive sites. Whether diving with great whites off California, snorkeling with orcas in New Zealand, or "muck" diving in search of tiny reef inhabitants off Indonesia, there is a lifetime of diving in the Pacific.

◄ FUSILIERS
The diving in the Pacific is as diverse as the marine life found there.

Linda Pitkin

CATALINA
ISLAND

 VISIBILITY
As low as 10 feet (3 m) in big swells or after storms, to 100 feet (30 m) on the outer reef.

 MUST SEE
Kelp forests

 DOWNSIDE
Cold
Rough

 GETTING THERE
Numerous international airlines flying into Los Angeles and San Diego. Both ferries and catamarans operate from this section of coastline, the latter taking about 90 minutes to make the crossing. There is a helicopter service from Los Angeles that flies to the island in 15 minutes.

 VISA
Canadians do not need a visa or passport to enter the U.S. Generally all other nationalities require a visitor's visa, though some 27 countries participate in the Visa Waiver Program. Check with a U.S. consulate or embassy.

$ MONEY
Currency is the U.S. dollar.

CATALINA ISLAND, FAMOUS FOR ITS DENSE KELP FORESTS, IS WIDELY REGARDED AS THE FINEST COLDWATER DIVE LOCATION IN THE UNITED STATES. AN OASIS OF TRANQUILITY OFF THE COAST OF CALIFORNIA, THE ISLAND'S RUGGED SCENERY ABOVE THE WATER IS REFLECTED IN THE CRAGGY REEFS BELOW.

Phillip Colla

WATER TEMPERATURE

°C	°F	°C	°F
30	86	30	86
20	68	20	68
20°C		**12°C**	
10	50	10	50
68°F		**53°F**	
0	32	0	32
Summer		Winter	

▶ **KELP DIVING**
Drifting through kelp forests is an eerie and unforgetable experience.

Catalina Island has been a popular holiday retreat for over a century and a nature reserve since 1974, but it is only in the last 30 years that divers have discovered the magic that lies beneath its dense kelp beds. Washed in the chilly current off southern California, the protected waters around the island are a mass of marine life swimming in oxygen-rich water over complex reefs and craggy drop-offs. The matchless diving experiences range from well-maintained protected shallow bays to steep cliffs that plunge beneath the waves to become precipitous drop-offs in snorting coldwater currents.

By a great stroke of good fortune Catalina Island was purchased by the Wrigley family in 1919. They took a particularly enlightened view of conservation and resisted all attempts to colonize and build on the island, ultimately setting up the Catalina Island Conservancy in 1974, which established 86 percent of the island as a nature reserve. Visitors to Catalina are encouraged to explore the natural wonders of the unspoilt interior, where buffalo (introduced from the mainland) roam.

GEOGRAPHY

Lying some 22 miles (35 km) off the coast of California and reached from the mainland ports of Long Beach or San Pedro, Catalina Island forms part of the 8-island archipelago of the Californian Channel Islands. The island itself, only 21 miles (33 km) long by 8 miles (13 km) wide, is divided in two by a narrow isthmus, with the settlement of Two Harbors on the smaller northern part, and the main town of Avalon at the southern end of the larger part of the island. There is evidence of human habitation dating as far back as 7,000 years ago. The permanent population today numbers around 3,000.

The island has a distinctly rugged appearance, with rocky hills and bushy scree slopes mixed with areas of grassy plain running down to jagged cliffs. The highest point is more than 2,000 feet (610 m) above sea level, leading the Native Americans to name the islands "The Mountains that Rise from the Sea". Such rugged topography promises great things beneath the waves, a promise that is more than fulfilled.

MARINE LIFE

The waters around Catalina Island have undoubtedly been affected by the activities of the fishing fleets that trawl this stretch of the Californian coast. In particular, the squid fishing boats seem to have swept the waters clean of this crucial link in the food chain. However, close to shore there are some wonderful areas of dense kelp and convoluted reef that have an array of sea life matching that of many a coral reef community around the world. Sheltered areas have been set up especially

CATALINA ISLAND
(California, U.S.A.)

for divers where no boat traffic is permitted, the most famous of these being the Casino Point Underwater Park.

Kelp beds are found all around the island, and some huge individuals rise more than 90 feet (27 m) from the seafloor, creating wonderfully atmospheric green forests through which a diver drifts surrounded by marine creatures that seem particularly fearless in their presence. Prime amongst these is the garishly colored garibaldi, utterly fearless and a photographer's dream against the emerald backdrop of the kelp.

Eagle rays soar through the canopy, and kelp bass share the middle reaches of the kelp beds with huge black sea bass, the latter sometimes reaching 500 lbs (186 kg) in weight. In the cracks, holes, and overhangs of the seafloor are beautiful zebra and bluebanded gobies, as well as Californian moray eels and two-spot octopuses. Californian sea lions have a number of haul-out points around the island, and blue sharks are sometimes to be seen in the deep waters off the reefs, although sightings of this beautiful animal seem, sadly, to be on the decrease.

THE DIVES

There is a complete range of dives available around the island, with massive kelp forests, rocky drop-offs, shallow, gently sloping reefs, wrecks, and sand patches. However, a constant factor is the cold! The California Current flowing southeast off the British Columbia coast towards the Baja Peninsula brings cold water to these southern shores, and even at the height of summer the water reaches a mere 20°C (68°F), dropping considerably below that in winter. A good thick wetsuit

DIVER'S TIP

Perfect your kelp swimming techniques. Locals use the "kelp crawl" when they surface away from the boat, shifting over the top of the kelp in a front crawl motion. A handy skill!

▶ **GARIBALDI FISH**

A constant feature of diving the island is the attentions of fiercely territorial garibaldi fish, which are also the official 'marinefish' of the State of California and have protected status.

 DIVE CENTERS

CATALINA SCUBA LUV
126 Catalina Avenue, P. O. Box 2009, Avalon, CA 90704, U.S.A.
Phone: +1-310-510-2350
E-mail: scubaluvcatalina@att.net
Web: www.scubaluv.biz

DBOS/CATALINA ISLAND KAYAK EXPEDITIONS
P.O. Box 386, Avalon, CA 90704, U.S.A.
Phone: +1-310-510-1226
Web: www.kayakcatalinaisland.com

 DIVING ORGANIZATIONS

U.S. Coast Guard legislates all dive vessels:
Phone: +1-800-368-5647
E-mail: uscginfoline@gcrm.com

 RECOMPRESSION

The Catalina Hyperbaric Chamber
P.O. Box 5069, 1 Big Fisherman's Cove, Two Harbors, CA 90704, U.S.A.
Phone: +1-310-510-1053
E-mail: chamber@usc.edu
Contact: Karl E. Huggins

 HOSPITAL

Avalon has a 12-bed municipal hospital with an adjoining medical clinic:
Catalina Island Medical Cente,
100 Falls Canyon Road, Avalon, CA 90704, U.S.A.
Phone: +1-310-510-0700

 CONSERVATION SOCIETY

Catalina Island Conservancy
P.O. Box 2739, Avalon, CA 90704, U.S.A.
Phone: +1-310-510-1299
Web: www.catalinaconservancy.org
There is also a dedicated diving conservation branch:
Web: www.ccd.org

OTHER DIVE SITES

Twin Rocks
Church Rock
Ragger's Point
Pedestal Rock
Kelp Point
Eagle Rock
Arrow Point
Indian Rock
Lion's Head

is essential, and at any time of year but summer a dry suit is a very good idea indeed!

The shallow water around the island is subject to strong surge, and storms in winter can reduce visibility considerably. Diving can be challenging in these conditions. Currents are also a factor, particularly on some of the island's more remote and deeper sites such as the Farnsworth Banks, and such dives are for the experienced diver only. Diving in kelp is something of an acquired skill, particularly in the surface phases of the dive, although the rewards speak for themselves.

CASINO POINT UNDERWATER PARK

• 0 to 90 feet (0 to 27 m) • beginner

This protected area, buoyed and roped off, is reserved for divers, and provides many with their first introduction to the islands. Located next to the magnificent casino building (never actually used as a casino!) just north of Avalon, the site was established as long ago as 1962, and is now beautifully set up for divers, with kit lockers at the entry point and trolleys supplied by local dive centers to ferry gear to the site.

The dive takes place in the shallow reef inside the roped-off area, sloping gently from the shoreline to about 90 feet (27 m) at the outer limit. The prevailing current running from the west sweeps over dense kelp beds and patchy rocky reefs, creating a real haven for the local marine life and presenting a microcosm of the ecosystems found all around the island. The shallow kelp beds are home to fiercely territorial garibaldi and rock wrasses, whilst the open sandy patches are ideal territory for large stingrays. An exploration of the park's smaller reefs and rocky outcrops may bring dividends in the shape of small horn sharks and numerous spiny lobsters.

A number of man-made objects are encountered during the course of the dive, including the wrecks of three small boats and a memorial plaque to Jacques Cousteau. At the eastern end of the dive you will come across the wreck of the *Sue Jac*, a 70-foot (21-m)

Phillip Colla   Phillip Colla

◄ CALIFORNIA SEA LIONS

◄ CALIFORNIA SEA LIONS
The acrobatics of sea lions have to be seen to be believed.

freighter that now lies on the rocks between 60 and 90 feet (18 and 27 m). It is a measure of just how powerful the swell is in this area that the vessel is now reduced to a random collection of crushed plates and heavily colonized metal spars.

BLUE CAVERN POINT

• **30 to 100 feet (9 to 30 m)** • **intermediate**

This popular cavern site is situated just southeast of Fisherman's Cove close to Two Harbors at the northern end of the island. The area is washed by strong currents that can generally be relied on to provide reasonable visibility. The dive itself starts at the entrance to a large cave that extends back into the island. As you descend a small wall that sinks to 100 feet (30 m) you will observe a number of smaller crags, fissures, and mini caverns along the face. The walls of the cavern are coated with sponges, hydroids, gorgonians, and cup corals. Look out for spiny lobsters and moray eels in the smaller cracks.

FARNSWORTH BANK

• **55 to 120 feet (16 to 36 m)** • **advanced**

Offering the most exciting face of the Catalina diving experience, this is a dive best undertaken in optimum conditions only by experienced divers. Located 2 miles (3.2 km) off the west coast, Farnsworth Bank is actually the top of a pinnacle that ascends from deep water and provides a guaranteed gathering point for marine life, large and small. Currents may be strong at the site, and many stories are told of divers being swept off the rock faces into blue water. The pinnacles themselves are coated with beautiful purple Californian coral, with blue sharks, bat rays, and large sea bass frequently seen in the blue water. People who have dived this site in the right conditions say there is nothing on the island to beat it.

OTHER ACTIVITIES

You cannot hire a car in Catalina, and the island can only be explored on foot along well-marked trails, by biking over mountain tracks, or taking a bus tour. There is much to see, with 15 species of plants and animals on the island found nowhere else on earth. Kayaking tours can be arranged around the wild bays and inlets of the island. Avalon is a busy vacation center and has a number of excellent restaurants, hotels, and shops. You can get around by taxi or bus, but most people travel on golf carts, bike, or walk.

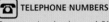

TELEPHONE NUMBERS

Recompression chamber	+1-310-510-1053
Hospital	+1-310-510-0700
U.S. Coast Guard	+1-800-368-5647
Tourism Organization	+1-310-510-1520

WEBSITES & E-MAIL

Tourist information	www.catalina.com

SEA OF CORTEZ

SEA LIONS, TURTLES, WHALES, HAMMERHEADS—YOU'LL FIND THEM ALL IN THE SEA OF CORTEZ ON MEXICO'S WEST COAST. THE SHALLOW WATERS OF THIS PROTECTED ARM OF THE PACIFIC ARE A MEETING PLACE FOR TROPICAL AND TEMPERATE MARINE LIFE, CREATING A VERITABLE FEAST FOR VISITING DIVERS.

 VISIBILITY
80 feet (25 m) plus June–Nov
30 feet (9 m) average Dec–May

 MUST SEE
California sea lion colonies

 DOWNSIDE
Thermoclines
Limited visibility in winter

 GETTING THERE
Airports at San José del Cabo and La Paz are served by a number of international airlines. Regular flights depart from Los Angeles, a journey of about 90 minutes.

VISA
Visitors require a tourist card, a single-entry document issued free of charge, and available in advance from Mexican consulates or embassies. A passport with a minimum of 6 months still to run is also required, as well as a return or onward ticket and possibly proof of sufficient funds.

 MONEY
Currency is the Mexican peso. U.S. dollars are widely accepted, particularly in resort areas. Major credit cards and traveler's checks also accepted.

WATER TEMPERATURE

°C	°F		°C	°F
30	86		30	86
20 **21°C** 68			20 **18°C** 68	
10 **69°F** 50			10 **64°F** 50	
0	32		0	32
Summer			Winter	

► **SEA LIONS**
Californian sea lions provide remarkable displays of underwater agility for watching divers.

John Bantin

SEA OF
CORTEZ
(Mexico)

Guerrero
Negro

Ciudad
Obregón

Mulege

Loreto
Isla Coronado
Isla Carmen
Los
Mochis
Loreto National Park
Isla Monserrate
Isla Catalina

Ciudad
Constitución
Isla
San José

Los Islotes
Isla Espiritu
Santo
El Baja

La Paz
Isla
Cerralvo
La Paz

0   160 km
0   100 mi

San José del Cabo
Los Cabos
Cabo San Lucas

50

John Bantin

▲ ELEPHANT SEAL

An elephant seal is a very powerful animal indeed, and this is an encounter that divers should treat with respect.

Protected on its western side by the long peninsula of Baja California and on its eastern side by the Mexican mainland, the huge, relatively shallow Sea of Cortez (also known as the Gulf of California) is noted for its exceptional wildlife and for its fine diving. Visiting divers have the opportunity to explore a variety of marine environments, ranging from reef walls to isolated pinnacles, protected bays, mangrove lagoons, and wild rocky islands. Much of this activity takes place in the company of mantas, aggregations of sharks, and passing gray whales.

GEOGRAPHY

On the southwest extremity of North America, the arid wedge of rock that is Baja California thrusts its way south, flanked by the Pacific Ocean on one side and the Sea of Cortez on the other. The whole of the mountainous peninsula lies within Mexico and is divided into two states, Baja California Norte to the north and Baja California Sur in the south. The launch point for much of the diving that takes place within the Sea of Cortez is La Paz, the state capital of Baja California Sur. The sea has some fascinating oceanographic and geological features that contribute to its diving interest, including

a number of fairly large islands, the most noteworthy of which, in diving terms, are directly off La Paz, and in Loreto National Marine Park, about 150 miles (240 km) further north up the coast. The popular holiday resort of Cabo San Lucas on the southwest tip of the peninsula also has some fine diving within a short distance of the main tourist areas.

MARINE LIFE

Tropical and temperate zones meet in the Sea of Cortez, creating a rare array of environments for marine life. Some areas within the sea have a mixture of species from both zones, and some of the smaller fish combine the body forms of temperate species with the garish coloration of their southern tropical relations. The Cortez damselfish and the rainbow wrasse both display this characteristic. The sedentary inhabitants of the reefs are also particularly striking, including several remarkable urchin species, such as the flower and slate pencil urchin.

A good idea of just how significant the Baja California is in terms of wildlife can be gleaned from the number of nature reserves, marine parks, and animal sanctuaries that dot its 2,000 miles (3,200 km) of coast-

John Bantin

► **TEMPERATE LIFE**
The marine life living in the Sea of Cortez combines the body shapes of temperate species with the coloration of their southern tropical relations.

DIVE CENTERS

UNDERWATER DIVERSIONS DE CABO
Plaza Marina Locales F5-7, Marina Blv. SN,
Cabo San Lucas, Baja California Sur,
C.P. 23410, Mexico
Phone: +52-624-143-4004
E-mail: divecabo@hotmail.com
Web: www.divecabo.com

DOLPHIN DIVE CENTER
Loreto A.P. 132, Loreto, Baja California Sur,
C.P. 23880, Mexico
Phone: +52-613-135-1914
E-mail: info@dolphindivebaja.com
Web: www.dolphindivebaja.com

DIVING ORGANIZATIONS

None. However advice on good operators is available from:
Baja California Sur Tourism Office,
K.M. 5.5, Carretera al Sur, A.P. 419,
Baja California Sur, Mexico
Phone: +52-521-124-0100
E-mail: turismo@lapaz.cromwell.com.mx

RECOMPRESSION

Local E-15, 16, 17, Plaza Las Glorias Marina,
Cabo San Lucas, Baja California Sur,
C.P. 23410, Mexico
Phone: +52-612-143-3666

Divers in the region are charged a fee of U.S.$2 per dive or U.S.$7 a day for upkeep of the chamber.

HOSPITAL

Centro Medico de Diagnóstico Integral
Ave. 5 de Mayo, entre Ramírez y Altamirano,
La Paz, Baja California Sur, C.P. 23000, Mexico
Phone: +52-612-122-3990

General Hospital
Marinos s/n Chamizal, San José del Cabo,
Baja California Sur, C.P. 23400, Mexico
Phone: +52-624-142-1510

There is also an air ambulance service:
Medcare Ambulance Services
Hidalgo y Zapata, Altos, Cabo San Lucas, Baja
California Sur, C.P. 23410, Mexico
Phone: +52-624-143-4020

CONSERVATION SOCIETY

One of the best sources for information on Mexico's National Parks is:
Mexico Affairs Office, 2455 Missouri Suite "C",
Las Cruces, NM 88001, U.S.A.
Phone: +1-505-521-2689
Web: www.nmsu.edu/~nps/

line. Among them are the Cabo Pulmo National Marine Park, which protects seven ribbon reefs, important for being the most northerly coral reefs in the Pacific Ocean, and the Underwater Wildlife Reserve at Cabo San Lucas (see below). The El Viscaino Biosphere Reserve and U.N.E.S.C.O. World Heritage Site covers an enormous area of lagoons, bays, and desert extending over 2.5 million acres (1 million ha.)

What the Sea of Cortez really has developed is a reputation for encounters with large animals. The biggest colony of Californian sea lions in Mexico is located here, and 5 of the 7 known species of turtle have been recorded around the peninsula. Large schools of scalloped hammerheads are sometimes seen off the more remote pinnacles and islands, as well as mantas and whale sharks. Finally, as many as 15 whale species are known to visit these waters, and the annual migration of gray whales, in particular, has spawned a substantial money-spinning whale-watching industry that attracts thousands of visitors to the region.

THE DIVES

The three main centers for launching dive operations in the Sea of Cortez are La Paz, Loreto, and Los Cabos in the south. The diving from La Paz and Loreto tends to concentrate on the islands just off the coast, although a substantial wreck, the 300-foot (91-m) long ferry, the *Salvatierra*, can be explored from La Paz. Los Cabos offers a year-round sea lion colony as well as a substantial seamount and a number of interesting cave and cavern formations. In addition to these traditional centers, a bustling liveaboard industry has sprung up to take divers to more remote areas, particularly the

Socorro Islands, which lie several hundred miles off the coast of Cabo San Lucas.

The diving infrastructure is particularly well organized to cater for the U.S. market. One of the advantages of diving within the Sea of Cortez is that the mountain barrier of the Baja California peninsula creates a haven from powerful Pacific swells and winds. Currents can be strong in this shallow sea, but a dive operator with good local knowledge will generally insure that these are used to the divers' benefit to provide some excellent drift dives.

LORETO NATIONAL MARINE PARK

• 30 to 130 feet (9 to 40 m) • beginner to advanced

This National Park, which is 50 miles (80 km) long and 20 miles (32 km) wide, stretches across 510,000 acres (206,397 ha), and includes areas of mountain and desert as well as sea. The diving within the park mostly takes place around five large islands, Coronado, Carmen, Danzante, Monserrate, and Catalan.

On the southeast side of Coronado Island there is a magnificent wall dive on La Lobera. After descending to nearly 100 feet (30 m), divers drift past caves and caverns on a wall festooned with sea fans and black coral trees. Morays and large groupers are normally encountered during this dive, as well as schooling tuna and bumphead parrotfish in the deeper regions. The exit point is a small sea lion colony, so you have a good chance of an encounter with these animals in the latter stages of the dive. Another fine wall dive is found at Las Tijeratas on the same island, descending to roughly 70 feet (21 m). Once again, the densely colonized walls are festooned in gorgonians, multicolored sponges, and soft corals, which are inhabited by a wide range of invertebrates. Look out for more sea lions on this dive.

Off Carmen Island a small wreck in only 35 feet (11 m) of water has become a focal point for marine life. Octopus and moray eels lurk within its darker recesses, and there are even reports that a lone whale shark frequented the wreck for quite a considerable period of time. Danzante Island, a smaller island to the south of Carmen, has a series of stepped reefs to the northeast, with canyons, gullies, and crevices lined with soft corals.

LA PAZ

• 30 to 130 feet (9 to 40 m) • beginner to advanced

The tourist infrastructure at La Paz is well-developed, and the resort offers access to some of the best diving in the Sea of Cortez. The most spectacular sites are the Pinnacles at Las Animas, and El Baja, which offers encounters with larger animals such as whale sharks, mantas, and schools of scalloped hammerheads.

One of the great diving experiences in the Sea of Cortez takes place on the small island of Los Islotes, closer to shore, where a series of rocky shelves and platforms is the site of a huge rookery of Californian sea lions. The juveniles are extremely boisterous and will hassle and harry divers throughout the dive—a tremendous experience. You can also snorkel with the sea lions.

LOS CABOS

• 30 to 130 feet (9 to 40 m) • beginner to advanced

Don't be put off by appearances—some excellent dive spots lie only a short boat-ride away from the high-rise apartments and busy sea front of this popular resort. The Underwater Wildlife Reserve at Cabo San Lucas contains the "sand falls" made famous by Jacques Cousteau, an extraodinary underwater phenomenon that has the appearance of sand tumbling like water over rock formations at the end of a large sandy plain. The Bay of San Lucas has a year-round sea lion rookery, as does Anagada Rock. Dives at Gorda Banks, 8 miles (12 km) offshore, offer classic encounters with large pelagics such as whale sharks and tuna.

OTHER ACTIVITIES

In the words of Dr. Lyall K. Watson, author of *Sea Guide To Whales of the World*, "There is probably no other body of water in the world where more species of cetacean can be seen, more often, more reliably, and more clearly than the Sea of Cortez." It would be a pity not to go on a dedicated whale-watching trip while in the area, and it's also well worth taking time off to explore the arid mountains and shores of the wildlife parks along the peninsula. For those seeking restaurants, busy beaches, and fine hotels, both La Paz and Los Cabos have plenty to offer.

☎ **TELEPHONE NUMBERS**

| Recompression chamber | +52-612-143-3666 |
| Hospital | +52-612-122-3990 |

💻 **WEBSITES & E-MAIL**

| Travel in Mexico | www.mexonline.com |
| La Paz Tourism Bureau | www.vivalapaz.com |

▼ **WHALE SHARK**
The Sea of Cortez has developed a reputation for its encounters with large animals including magnificent whale sharks.

Linda Pitkin

COCOS & MALPELO ISLANDS

DRAMATIC PINNACLES, PLUNGING WALLS, THE OPEN OCEAN, BIG ANIMALS, NOT TO SPEAK OF TIMELESS RUMORS OF BURIED TREASURE—THE ISLANDS OF COCOS AND MALPELO IN THE EASTERN PACIFIC OCEAN ARE LEGENDARY AMONG DIVERS.

 VISIBILITY
30 to 80 feet (9 to 25 m)

 MUST SEE
Scalloped hammerhead aggregations

 DOWNSIDE
Remote
Currents
Limited visibility

 GETTING THERE
Liveaboard dive vessels only. Fly to San José in Costa Rica, and for Cocos Island transfer by road to Puntarenu. For Malpelo Island fly to Golfito. Boats can be boarded from each of these ports. Exit tax U.S.$26.

 VISA
Visas are not required for 30-day stays (90-days for visitors from the U.S. and most European countries.)

 MONEY
U.S. dollars are accepted on most liveaboards, as are most major credit cards when booking.

The islands of Cocos and Malpelo are the tips of two undersea mountains, 250 miles (400 km) apart, that rise from the distant seafloor to break the surface of the eastern Pacific. The trip to the islands is long, the diving challenging, the currents severe, and visibility mediocre. Yet as soon as the diver enters the water at either place, all is forgotten in the midst of some of the most dramatic aggregations of large marine animals on Earth. As Stan Waterman, renowned underwater filmmaker and something of a diving institution, has noted, "These locations always deliver."

GEOGRAPHY

Cocos Island, the northernmost of the two, lies 300 miles (483 km) southwest of Costa Rica's Cabo Blanco.

Approximately 5 miles (8 km) long by 2 miles (3 km) wide, it is slightly the larger of the two, and ranks among the largest uninhabited islands on Earth. Cocos Island was formed 2.5 million years ago through volcanic activity. This is reflected in its precipitous cliffs and stark ridges, making up four mountain peaks, the highest of which is Cerro Yglesias at 2,080 feet (634 m). It is said that Captain Thompson, a brigand who relieved the Spanish of their wealth, hid the richest pirate treasure in the world on Cocos Island. As if this wasn't enough, another pirate named Benito Bonito is also supposed to have buried treasure here, but a total of 300 expeditions has failed to find either stash!

Some 250 miles (400 km) to the southwest of Cocos, and 300 miles (483 km) from the coast of Colombia, lies

WATER TEMPERATURE

Summer 30°C 86°F | Winter 23°C 73°F

Phillip Colla

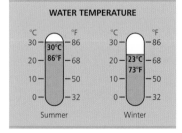
▶ **SCHOOLING MANTAS**
Aggregations of mantas, sometimes numbering as many as 10 individuals are a regular feature of both islands.

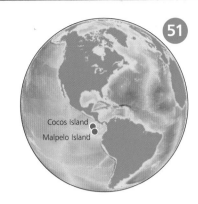

51

Cocos Island

Malpelo Island

Manuelita Island

Isla Pejora   *Chatham Bay*

Viking Rock   • **Lobster Rock**

Dirty Rock

Wafer Bay

COCOS ISLAND
(Costa Rica)

Dos migos lands   **Big Dos Amigos**

Pyramid   • **Bajo Alcyone**

o Dos migos   • **Submerged Rock**

Shark Fin Rock   **Manta Corner**

Lone Stone

The Cathedral   *Los Tres Mosqueteros*

MALPELO ISLAND
(Colombia)

The Freezer

The Fridge   • **Virginia's Altar**

Salomon Saul

La Gringa

Escuba

```
0                    3 km
0                    2 mi
```
Please note that the distance between the two island groups has been reduced and is not to scale.

The islands are 250 mi (400 km) apart.

Malpelo Island. The only visible feature of the extensive underwater Malpelo volcanic ridge, the island shares the same craggy characteristics as its remote neighbor. Although today it is only 5 sq miles (13 sq km) in area, geologists believe that Malpelo was once eight to ten times larger. It is a dramatic and forbidding sight, consisting in essence of three rugged peaks, the largest of which is El Cerro de la Mona. There are also 11 smaller rocks and islets at the north and south ends of the islands. There has been a small Colombian Navy garrison on the island since 1986.

MARINE LIFE

Both locations are very special places indeed for encounters with large pelagic animals, and possibly the two sites in the world where divers can most consistently swim with schools of scalloped hammerheads. Although the islands are justifiably famed for these features, there is much, much more going on around their rugged walls and undersea pinnacles to interest and excite the diver.

One reason for the islands' sublime marine life is their remoteness, and it is this same factor that has seen them unsullied by human colonization or the arrival of livestock or vermin. A measure of just how special these sites are is their protected status today—Cocos is a National Marine Park and was declared a World Heritage Site in 1997, whilst Malpelo was declared a Colombian Flora and Fauna Sanctuary in 1996. The latter legislation saw a protected zone put in place for 6 miles (9.5 km) around the island.

Along the dramatic walls and canyons around both islands there are aggregations of several hundred scalloped hammerheads, although in Malpelo they seem to school somewhat more shallowly than in

Cocos. White tip reef sharks, some of them extremely large, also hunt here in packs, and some divers have noted that they outnumber the hammerheads. Other shark species at both islands include aggregations of silky sharks and Galápagos sharks. In addition, Malpelo is famed for its abundance of fine spotted moray eels, so much so that it appears a veritable snake pit with some holes crammed with several animals at one time. There have even been recent reports from divers of the morays being attacked and eaten by the hammerheads—the stuff of every underwater photographer's dreams if caught on camera.

Also regular residents of the reefs around the islands are whale sharks, mantas, almaco jacks (the largest of all the jack species), and great aggregations of marbled rays. Smaller inhabitants of the reefs include the extraordinary red-lipped batfish, who look for all the world as if they have just slapped on lipstick before venturing out onto the reef. Massive schools of horse-eye jacks swirl around rocky pinnacles, and off Cocos Island sailfish are sometimes seen slashing into swirling baitballs. Indeed one of the dives here is called Baitball for this very reason.

THE DIVES

Although most of the diving at the islands is in a range between 60 and 100 feet (18 and 30 m), these sites are not for the faint hearted. Currents swirl around

---

DIVER'S TIP

Watch out for the thermoclines—you may find it advisable to dress more warmly for the dives than the surface temperature might indicate.

► **SCALLOPED HAMMERHEAD**
Great numbers of scalloped hammerheads is one of the features for which the islands are justifiably famed.

 DIVE CENTERS
UNDERSEA HUNTER
P.O. Box 025216, Dept. 314, Miami,
FL 33102-5216, U.S.A.
Phone: +1-800-203-2120
or +11-506-228-6613
E-mail: info@undersehunter.com
Web: www.undersehunter.com

 DIVING ORGANIZATIONS
The Costa Rica National Chamber of Tourism can offer advice on diving the islands:
Phone: +11-506-234-6222
E-mail: info@tourism.co.cr
Web: www.costarica.tourism.co.cr

 RECOMPRESSION
IIDEXO
Cuajinquil de La Cruz, Guanacaste, Costa Rica
Phone: +11-506-679-1053
E-mail: website@IIDEXO.com

 HOSPITAL
Hospital San José, S.A.
Sabana Oeste, Costa Rica
Phone: +11-506-2208-1000

 CONSERVATION SOCIETY
Friends of Cocos Island Foundation
276-1005, Barrio México, San José, Costa Rica
Phone: +11-506-256-7476
E-mail: info@cocosisland.org
Web: www.cocosisland.org

U.N.E.S.C.O. Office in Costa Rica
Apartado Postal 393 - 2050 San Pedro,
Montes de Oca, San José, Costa Rica
Phone: +33-1-45-68-25-72
E-mail: dl.costa-rica@unesco.org

the islands, the reefs are in the main forbidding crags and pinnacles, visibility is limited, and thermoclines are present throughout. There is a distinct lack of tropical sunshine and blue skies to illuminate the dives.

All the diving at both islands is by way of live-aboards, all of which use smaller tenders to drop divers above the key sites and recover them afterwards. Hair-raising tales record the drama of some of these dives. A common technique when diving the islands' more exposed sites is to descend rapidly to the reef wall and cram yourself into a crevice to watch the open water. One diver tells of finding just such a crevice, squeezing himself into it, and then glancing around to find it full of terrified baitfish sheltering from the predators above. Another diver relates that as he was preparing to ascend from the dive, he looked up to see several hundred large hammerheads in the swirling current above him, and realized that he would have to make his way up through them.

Recompression chambers and medical assistance are some distance away, so this location is only recommended for the more experienced diver.

MANUELITA ISLAND

• 20 to 70 feet (6 to 21 m) • intermediate

Manuelita Island off Cocos Island is most divers' introduction to diving in this location. It is a small island that has a protected coast facing shallow Chatham Bay. Batfish and morays are in residence and offer some great opportunities for macro-photography. The outer coast of the island is slightly wilder, and diving here may bring the chance of encountering hammerheads, as well as white tip reef sharks in some numbers.

BAJA ALCYONE

• 90 to 120 feet (27 to 36 m) • advanced

The most famous site in Cocos and one of the better large animal encounter dives in the world, Baja Alcyone

Phillip Colla

island where the reef walls slope gently enough to give the right conditions for dense concentrations of colonizing organisms such as sponges to develop. These attract a range of reef species including moorish idols, snappers, sea bass, and surgeonfish. This is also a good dive for sightings of Malpelo's famous fine spotted moray eels.

LA GRINGA

• 60 to 130 feet (18 to 40 m) • advanced

La Gringa is the name of a deep cave in a large rock located on the south side of Malpelo that runs from 80 to 130 feet (24 to 40 m). Residents of the cave include large scorpionfish and morays, and this dive also provides the opportunity to see hammerheads, Galápagos sharks, tuna, and eagle rays around the outer walls and nearby seamounts.

OTHER ACTIVITIES

There are limited activities for the non-diver on either islands. The terrestrial fauna is undoubtedly interesting—for example, the colony of 24,000 masked boobies on Malpelo is reportedly the second largest in the world. However, the dive safaris to Cocos and Malpelo usually last a week, and that is a long time to spend around the islands if not diving.

☎ **TELEPHONE NUMBERS**

Recompression chamber	+11-506-679-1053
Hospital	+11-506-2208-1000

🖥 **WEBSITES & E-MAIL**

Costa Rica Tourist Board	www.visitcostarica.com
Travel information	www.costaricabureau.com

OTHER DIVE SITES

Lobster Rock
Submerged Rock
Manta Corner
Lone Stone
Bajo Dos Amigos
Pyramid
Big Dos Amigos
Dirty Rock
Viking Rock
The Fridge
The Freezer
The Cathedral

▼ **WHITE TIP REEF SHARK**
Some visiting divers believe that white tip reef sharks are more numerous than hammerheads around the islands.

is a large seamount made famous by Jacques Cousteau. It takes some skill to descend through the strong currents and wedge yourself into the reef to watch the drama unfold. Scalloped hammerheads, whale sharks, white tip reef sharks, mobula rays, dolphins, tuna, and mantas are all sighted regularly on this dive.

BAITBALL

• 0 to 20 feet (0 to 6 m) • intermediate

As the name suggests, this site seems to attract regular baitballs, though they are by no means guaranteed— but spend enough time at Cocos and you may get lucky. These marine bonanzas draw in sailfish, dolphins, silky sharks, tuna, and jacks. Caution is advised when diving with a baitball, as it really is a predators' free-for-all.

VIRGINIA'S ALTAR

• 40 to 90 feet (12 to 27 m) • intermediate

On Malpelo Island, this is one of the few sites on either

John Bantin

GALÁPAGOS
ISLANDS

 VISIBILITY

Visibility ranges from 15 to 85 feet (5 to 25 m). Most of the time it is restricted to between 40 to 60 feet (12 to 18 m)

 MUST SEES

Schooling hammerheads
Iguanas
Sea lion colonies
Aggregations of rays

 DOWNSIDE

Strong currents
Rough weather
Remote

 GETTING THERE

Quito and Guayaquil both have international airports with frequent direct connections to Houston, Los Angeles, Miami and New York. However the region's main international hub is Lima, Peru, and you may find it cheaper to fly there and continue overland to Ecuador (a 24-hour bus trip). There's a U.S.$25 airport departure tax.

 VISA

Citizens of most countries can stay a maximum of 90 days in any year without needing a visa. Entry permits available on arrival at airport.

 MONEY

Currency is the U.S. dollar. Major credit cards are widely accepted in tourist areas and big hotels. Credit cards are also increasingly accepted at A.T.M.s and for cash advances at banks, though not all branches provide this service. NB: Remember your $100 parks cash payment on entering the Galápagos.

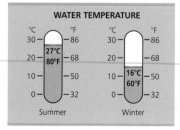

WATER TEMPERATURE

°C	°F	°C	°F
30 — 86	30 — 86
27°C / 80°F			
20 — 68	20 — 68
		16°C / 60°F	
10 — 50	10 — 50
0 — 32	0 — 32
Summer	Winter

BIG ANIMALS, WILD REEFS, AND UNIQUE SPECIES—THE GALÁPAGOS ISLANDS HAVE SOME OF THE BEST DIVING ON EARTH. IN THE LAST DECADE, THIS ECOLOGICAL JEWEL HAS BECOME A MAJOR INTERNATIONAL DIVE LOCATION AND A MUST SEE FOR THE SERIOUS ADVENTURE DIVER.

In 1535, the Spanish bishop of Panama, Fray Tomas de Berlanga, was on his way to Peru when his ship was blown off course. Arriving by chance upon a group of wild islands, beset on all sides by five mighty ocean currents and surrounded by swirling currents and pirouetting waves, he named them the *Islas Encantadas*—the "Enchanted Isles". The islands' later name of Galápagos, from an old Spanish word for saddle, comes from the shape of the shell of the islands' best-known inhabitant, the giant tortoise. It is easy to believe that the original name would have stuck if the early explorers had ventured into the enchanted world beneath the waves and observed the islands' wild reefs.

The location and environmental conditions of the Galápagos make them unique. The wildlife above the waters is well documented, with the giant tortoises in particular providing a draw for ecotourists. Visiting whalers decimated the Galápagos tortoise in the 19th century, but their numbers are slowly recovering thanks

▼ **BLACK LAVA**

The volcanic past of the Galápagos islands becomes obvious when the islands are seen from the air.

M. Espanosa

to the enlightened conservation efforts of the Ecuadorian government, to whom the islands belong.

GEOGRAPHY

The Galápagos, some 600 miles (965 km) off the coast of Ecuador, are seriously remote. The islands sprung out of the ocean 5 million years ago, and their violent volcanic birth is apparent everywhere in the twisted black lava that predominates both above and below the water's surface.

The archipelago stretches across 45,000 sq miles (116,505 sq km) of ocean. It consists of 13 main islands, and 48 smaller outcrops and islets, and has a total land area of 4,897 sq miles (12,678 sq km). The largest island is Isabela, at 1,771 sq miles (4,585 sq km).

Although the island group straddles the Equator, the climate is greatly influenced by the prevailing ocean currents. The five major currents that swirl around the islands are the cold Humboldt Current from the south, the cool Peruvian Counter Current, the Cromwell Equatorial Undercurrent, the tropical Panama Current, and the South Equatorial Current. The individual climatic conditions on a particular island are strongly influenced by its position in respect to one of these currents, or indeed the changeable paths of the currents themselves. Such vulnerability to the vagaries of ocean meant that the island group was particularly affected by the El Niño phenomenon in 1997–98.

MARINE LIFE

The British naturalist Charles Darwin, then aged 22, visited the Galápagos Islands in 1835. He stayed for only 35 days yet his visit sowed the seeds for one of the most important books in the study of natural history, *The Origin of Species*. What is perhaps less well known is that Darwin had a passion for coral and marine life, and

**GALÁPAGOS ISLANDS
(Ecuador)**

DIVE CENTERS

SCUBA IGUANA
Avenue Amazona 1004 y Wilson, Office 04,
Quito, Ecuador
Phone: +593-2-526497
E-mail: info@scubaiguana.com
Web: www.scubaiguana.com

LAMMER LAW
Trimarine Boat Co., c/o Charterport,
P.O. Box 8309, PMB 613, Cruz Bay,
VI 00831, British Virgin Islands
Phone: +1-284-494-2490
E-mail: cuanlaw@surfbvi.com
Web: www.lammerlaw.com

GALÁPAGOS SUB-AQUA
Charles Darwin Ave., Puerto Ayora,
Santa Cruz, Galápagos, Ecuador
Phone: +593-4-230-5514
Web: www.galapagos-sub-aqua.com

DIVING ORGANIZATIONS

Diving is strictly regulated by the Galápagos
National Park Authorities:
Galápagos National Park
Charles Darwin Ave., Puerto Ayora,
Santa Cruz, Galápagos, Ecuador
E-mail: info@galapagosonline.com

RECOMPRESSION

Protesub
18 de Febrero and R. Lara Street, Puerto Ayora,
Santa Cruz, Galápagos, Ecuador
Phone: +593-552-6911
E-mail: galapagos@ssnetwork.com
Website: www.sssnetwork.com

HOSPITAL

Visitors to the Galápagos Islands are advised
that acute surgical and cardiac services are not
available. Serious cases must be evacuated to
the Ecuadorian mainland.

CONSERVATION SOCIETY

Charles Darwin Research Station
Puerto Ayora, Santa Cruz, Galápagos, Ecuador
Phone: +593-52526-146/147

DIVER'S TIP

Make sure your buoyancy is in order for
the blue water dives in the channel at
Gordon Rocks and Darwin and Wolf.
These are deep waters, occasional big
currents, and there are lots of toothy
animals, so it's easy to lose concentration.

▶ WHALE SHARK

There is a genuine sense of adventure
when diving the Galápagos Islands, with
encounters with large animals such as this
whale shark always a possibility.

---

one can only speculate as to his reaction if he had been
able to explore the seas around the islands.

Although there are only 13 reef-building species of
coral in these waters, as is typical of the eastern Pacific,
there is no shortage of bustling marine life as the
pitted, scarred lava rock creates perfect hideaways for
species large and small. The huge diversity of the
islands' marine life is due partly to this characteristic of
the reefs and partly to the deep-water upwelling and
ocean currents that circulate cold water, rich in
nutrients and oxygen, through the island system. The
remoteness of the Galápagos also means that many
species are endemic (unique) to the islands.

Of the 333 species of seaweed on the islands, 35
percent are endemic. There are 24 species of sea urchin,
28 species of sea star, 600 mollusk species, and 100 different kinds of crab. Cruising above these busy reefs are
more than 300 species of fish, and feeding on them are
thousands of seals and sea lions, some 80,000 of which
are estimated to live in large colonies around the islands.

It is estimated there are 30 species of shark and 13
different species of ray. Certain sites in these waters are
famous for their giant gatherings of scalloped hammerhead sharks, as well as unusually large congregations of
mantas and eagle and cow-nosed rays. Whale species
commonly sighted here include the Brydes whale, humpbacks and sperm whales. Bottlenose and common
dolphins are also prevalent.

A famous symbol of the Galápagos are their marine
iguanas. There are in fact three different species of
iguana on the islands—one land-based, one adapted to
life in the ocean fringe, and one that is a hybrid of the
two. Diving with the iguanas is tricky, as they favor
areas of strong wave action where they use their well-
adapted claws to hook into the craters and pits in the
lava as they feed on algae. It is not difficult to approach
them on land, however, and in some places you may
find it hard to avoid them as they love to bask on the
busy jetties and in the bustling thoroughfares.

THE DIVES

One of the great draws of the Galápagos is a genuine sense of never knowing what you will encounter
on the next dive! Such is the species diversity and abundance of large animals in these waters that encounters
with turtles, groups of rays, sea lions, and sharks are
considered somewhat routine. There are, however, certain dive sites in the islands that are exceptional even by
Galápagos standards, and have gained legendary status
amongst divers and adventurers throughout the world.

Divers new to the islands should note that although
the diving is truly exceptional, the conditions can sometimes be demanding. The cold water and swirling
currents that create such an abundance of marine life

also give rise to choppy seas, racing tides, and currents that even the local guides can't accurately predict. Carefully plan each dive, and make sure that everyone is briefed on separated and lost procedures. Always dive well within your ability and experience range.

DARWIN AND WOLF

• 65 to 130 feet (20 to 40 m) • advanced

Many divers regard Darwin and Wolf—sometimes known as Wenman and Culpepper—as the two best dive sites on Earth. Located approximately 100 miles (160 km) off the northwestern tip of Isabela, the islands are the tips of two peaks arising from a volcanic ridge, the Wolf-Darwin Lineament, which extends 3,000 feet (914 m) down to the seabed. The two islands stand

▼ RICH CURRENTS
Deep-water upwelling, rich in nutrients and oxygen, attract large schools of fish.

Monty Halls

approximately 600 feet (183 m) proud of the surface, plunging off into the abyssal depths of the ridge. The upwelling of nutrient-rich, oxygenated cold water along this ridge creates an almost unparalleled abundance of big animals. At Wolf, three anchorages are possible; the pinnacle, the reef, and the south islet channel. The reef contains many warm-water varieties of fish found nowhere else in the islands and is the most consistent place to see hammerheads.

At Darwin, one site has achieved legendary status, and is truly a dive that can match anything else in the island group and, indeed, the world. Darwin's Arch is the northernmost point of the two islands. Visibility can be in the 100-foot (30-m) range, although the large swells hammering into the foot of the arch are frequently reflected in turbulent conditions beneath. The diversity of large species around this site almost defies description—large schools of hammerhead sharks, Galápagos sharks, silky sharks, manta and eagle rays, spotted morays, green and hawksbill turtles, dolphins, and sailfish. Whale sharks are particularly prevalent—throughout the whole of one season, a local operator excitedly noted, "Whale sharks were encountered up close on all but one dive at Darwin's Arch!"

This is not a dive for the inexperienced diver. The currents are powerful, the drop-offs precipitous, the swell muscular, and the large numbers of big animals somewhat daunting for the uninitiated.

GORDON ROCKS

• 30 to 130 feet (10 to 40 m)
• intermediate to advanced

This dive is readily accessible for anyone diving from the island of Santa Cruz, and is an hour's boat ride from the main port of Puerto Ayora. Gordon Rocks are actually two gigantic lumps of rock rising precipitously out of the ocean. The tide surges through the gap between the rocks, creating an influx of nutrients and oxygenated water that draws marine life large and small.

There are four classic dives around the rocks, but the best is unquestionably the one taken in the heart of the channel itself. It should be undertaken by experienced divers in the intermediate/advanced range as it involves phases of blue water diving when the action takes place away from the reef walls while hanging suspended in mid-channel.

You enter at the edge of the southeast face of the rocks in the channel and swim down toward the reef 50 to 65 feet (15 to 20 m) below. Octopus, moorish idols, harlequin wrasse, and large hawksbill turtles are present in great abundance on this well-populated reef, but it is even more thrilling to push off into the green water above the 130 feet (40 m) depths of the main channel and drift away from the reef wall.

Hanging in the water that sweeps through the channel, you have a wonderful vantage point to observe large pelagic animals as they surge between the giant rock walls below. Hammerheads are frequent here, although their numbers have diminished rapidly over the last few years in line with the catastrophic drop in their worldwide distribution. Large formations of eagle and cow-nosed rays (known locally as golden rays) may also be seen, as well as occasional visits from mantas. This is a classically unpredictable wild Galápagos dive to set the heart thumping and camera shutters clicking.

NORTH SEYMOUR ISLAND

• 30 to 100 feet (10 to 30 m) • beginner

North Seymour is a 90-minute boat ride from Puerto Ayora. Although not perhaps a classic, wild, adrenaline-surging Galápagos dive, it offers a series of encounters with big animals, some healthy reef fish populations, and some intriguing cavern formations and overhangs. It is also an opportunity for less experienced divers to enjoy the Galápagos without wrestling with currents, surge, and wild tides—although the waters can be unpredictable even here.

The reefs on the eastern edge of the island slope gently into deeper water. The area is pockmarked with caves and gullies, and is a particularly good spot to encounter sleeping white tip reef sharks, some of them of considerable size. The sharks seem used to divers, and can be approached closely if you are prepared to move slowly and patiently. On the sandy shelves below the main reef you may frequently encounter stingrays, and there is a quite beautiful colony of garden eels swaying gently in the surge. Hammerheads and Galápagos sharks are sometimes seen in mid-water.

An added bonus is the presence of a shallow channel close to the entry point that makes an excellent spot to pause between dives. On one shore is a large sea lion colony. Visibility in the shallow water and rocky seabed around the colony is consistently clear, creating an ideal snorkeling location.

ROCA REDONDA

• 55 to 100 feet (17 to 30 m) • intermediate

Roca Redonda is a large angular rock that juts from the relatively shallow seafloor about 15 miles (10 km) off the northwestern tip of the large island of Isabela. The best dives take place on the southeastern side of the rock and follow a route designed to take in the different levels of shelving rock, a remarkable warm water upwelling driven by volcanic activity beneath, and the large pelagic animal encounters that are such a strong feature of diving in the Galápagos.

Local operators like divers to enter the water on the eastern side of the rock and drift around to the south

Monty Halls

for pickup on the western edge. This dive presents a neatly spaced series of epic encounters at every depth and stage throughout, from entry to exit. During the early stages, encounters with playful sea lions on the large shelves of rocks at roughly 50 feet (15 m) are commonplace. As the diver descends, with the rock wall to the right, there is the chance of encountering stingrays on the seabed and mantas in mid water. The dive progresses towards its conclusion on the western side of the rock, where there are great opportunities to observe hammerheads in the open water toward the north of the pickup point, and a seemingly ever-present shoal of barracuda swirling above the rock wall.

OTHER ACTIVITIES

Where to begin! The wonders beneath the sea off the Galápagos certainly extend to the land. The islands are a mecca for wildlife enthusiasts, and are packed with interesting birds and animals. There are of course the giant tortoises, best seen at the Darwin Center, and the famous marine iguanas. Although the former are now extensively protected, the latter are everywhere, and are very much part of life in the Galápagos. Some of the beaches are quite beautiful, and although much of the island chain is rocky and barren, it is well worth taking a ride into the heart of the larger islands such as Isla Isabela and exploring what remains of the forest on the slopes of the highest volcano in the island chain, the 5,600 feet (1,707 m) Wolf volcano.

▲ IGUANA
There are three different species of Iguana on the Galápagos.

OTHER DIVE SITES

Academy Bay
Albany Rock
Bartolome
Champion Island
Cousin's Rock
Daphne Islet
Devil's Crown
Gardener Bay
Leon Dormido
Nameless Rock
Plaza Islands

📞 **TELEPHONE NUMBERS**

Recompression chamber	+593-552-6911
Hospital	+593-552-6103
Tourism Board	+1-863-439-2659

💻 **WEBSITES & E-MAIL**

Tourism Board

www.ecuadortouristboard.com

Charles Darwin Foundation

www.darwinfoundation.org

RANGIROA

MUCH OF FRENCH POLYNESIA REMAINS UNEXPLORED IN DIVING TERMS, BUT ONE SITE THAT HAS WON A WORLDWIDE REPUTATION FOR BIG ANIMAL ENCOUNTERS IS RANGIROA, THE SECOND LARGEST ATOLL ON EARTH, FAMOUS FOR ITS RACING CURRENTS AND DRAMATIC DRIFT DIVES.

 VISIBILITY

Spectacular on the outer reef: 100 feet (30 m) plus. Can drop to 40 feet (12 m) in the shallower regions of the channel.

 MUST SEE

Sharks in Tiputa Pass

 DOWNSIDE

Remote
Powerful drifts

 GETTING THERE

Tahiti Faaa, the international airport for French Polynesia, is served by a number of international airlines from most major hubs around the world. From Tahiti Faaa the internal airline Air Tahiti fly straight on to Rangiroa.

VISA

As a French overseas territory (T.O.M.), entry into French Polynesia is much the same as for France itself. E.U. passport holders can stay for up to three months without a visa, and most other nationalities a month.

MONEY

Currency is the C.F.P. or Pacific franc. Changing money can be expensive, so check with your host operator prior to arrival exactly how much cash will be required. Larger resorts take major credit cards.

French Polynesia is about as far from anywhere as it is possible to be—five island groups sprinkled across the vast expanse of the Pacific Ocean. It is a French overseas territory (Polynesia means "many islands"), and although its official name may not sound overly exciting, to recite the names of the individual islands—Tahiti, Bora Bora, Moorea—is to invite romantic images of the South Seas, evoking the ultimate in tropical paradises. Possibly the most famous site of all, in diving terms, is Rangiroa.

GEOGRAPHY

The islands of French Polynesia lie like strings of tiny beads amidst a serious amount of ocean. Fiji is about 1,500 miles (2,413 km) to the west, Hawaii 1,800 miles (2,896 km) to the northeast. The northernmost island group, the Marquesas, lie a few degrees south of the Equator, whilst the Australs in the south just tip over the Tropic of Capricorn. The 3 other island groups are the Tuamotu Islands running west-east across the center, the Society Islands, and the Gambier Archipelago. There are 118 recognized islands in the whole of French Polynesia, with hundreds more smaller islets, reefs, and atolls, but only 220,000 people live in this entire vast area, almost half of them in the capital of Papeete on Tahiti, the largest of the Society Islands.

Rangiroa lies at the western end of the Tuamotu group some 200 miles (320 km) northeast of Tahiti, and

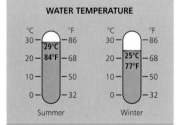

WATER TEMPERATURE

°C	°F		°C	°F
30	86		30	86
29°C			**25°C**	
20 **84°F** 68			20 **77°F** 68	
10	50		10	50
0	32		0	32
Summer			Winter	

▶ **THREAT DISPLAY**

A close pass to the diver with pectoral fins held low is a threat display. Time to move away.

John Bantin

John Bantin

◄ **BEACHES AND PALM TREES**
Rangiroa Atoll offers the quintessential Pacific Island experience.

is the second largest atoll on Earth. A 125-mile (200-km) long island chain encircles a lagoon of approximately 1,000 sq miles (2,589 sq km). Most human activity on this huge expanse of water is concentrated in the northwest between the two village settlements of Avatoru and Tiputa. Several breaks in the island chain are, of course, hugely significant in terms of the diving of the region, as the tide rushes through them twice a day.

MARINE LIFE

Although there are busy reefs along the outer walls of the lagoon and more sheltered dives on patch reefs teeming with life inside, it is the possibility of encountering big animals that draws divers to Rangiroa. The shark populations are particularly healthy. They gather in large numbers in the channel races that lead to the open ocean, classic Pacific reef species such as white tips and gray reefs sharing the water with black tip reef sharks and lemon sharks. Divers may even be lucky enough on occasion to encounter silver tip sharks, one of the shark species that demands particular respect from anyone who chooses to share its personal piece of reef. You may also meet up with hammerheads in the deeper water. The surging tides and barreling currents of these channels also attract mantas and eagle rays as well as huge schools of snappers and trevallies.

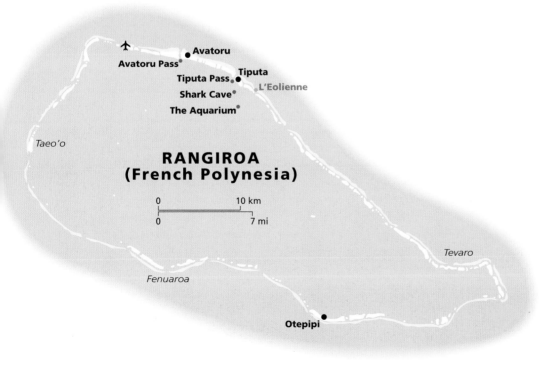

Avatoru
Avatoru Pass
Tiputa Pass
Tiputa
L'Eolienne
Shark Cave
The Aquarium

Taeo'o

RANGIROA
(French Polynesia)

0   10 km
0   7 mi

Tevaro

Fenuaroa

Otepipi

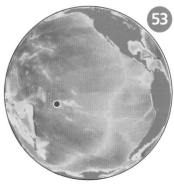

53

DIVE CENTERS

THE SIX PASSENGERS
BP 128 Avatoru, Rangiroa 98775,
French Polynesia
Phone: +689-960-269
E-mail: the6passengers@mail.pf

RAIE MANTA CLUB
P.O. Box 55 Avatoru, Rangiroa 98775,
French Polynesia
Phone: +689-96-22-53
E-mail: raiemantaclub@mail.pf

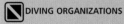 **DIVING ORGANIZATIONS**

None. Contact the Tahiti Tourism Head Office
for information on recommended operators:
Phone: +689-505-700
Web: www.tahiti-tourisme.com

 RECOMPRESSION

Centre Hospitalier Territorial
Ave Georges Clemenceau, Papeete, Tahiti
Phone: +689-466-262

 HOSPITAL

There is a large hospital in Papeete staffed by
French doctors:
Centre Hospitalier Territorial
Ave Georges Clemenceau, Papeete, Tahiti
Phone: +689-466-262

Rangiroa has a small clinic:
Centre medical d'Avatoru

CONSERVATION SOCIETY

The Polynesian Coastal Conservation Agency
has set up three protected areas in French
Polynesia. It can be contacted through the
French Government's environmental website
for the region:
Web: www.environnement.gouv.fr.

OTHER DIVE SITE

L'Eolienne

THE DIVES

Rangiroa's world-class status as a diving destination rests on the racing waters of the channels, which provide some of the most dramatic drift dives anywhere in the Pacific. Be warned, however—they do demand a certain level of experience and preparation. The standard technique here is to follow the divers' bubbles in a maneuverable small boat or deploy an S.M.B. Diver recovery is a key factor at every stage of the dive.

Much of the coral within the lagoon has undoubtedly been impacted by bleaching—according to some reports up to 50 percent of the hard coral in this region shows signs of the effects of increased water temperatures—and there is significant storm damage in the shallower sections. All the same, there are still some excellent dives to be had in the more sedate waters within the lagoon itself over patch reefs and small bommies where you come face to face with the smaller representatives of the Rangiroa fish community.

TIPUTA PASS – THE VALLEY

- **60 to 130 feet (18 to 40 m)** • **advanced**

Hang on to your hats! This is a drift dive that lives long in the memory. A fly-by through Tiputa Pass in the teeth of the incoming tide, it can only be done one way; to go with the outward tide would be far too dangerous because the broad shelf leading to the open ocean runs down to 130 feet (40 m) and beyond. The reef bordering the channel is steep-sided (hence the name of the Valley), and it is this additional feature that makes it such a great dive—the Valley gradually narrows as it approaches the inner lagoon whilst gently rising at the same time, so the dive is completed in about 60 feet (18 m) of water. This acts as a bottleneck for the incoming sea, creating a tremendous sensation of flying and swooping over the reef walls and sandy seabed—a truly hair-raising experience.

The dive can begin at Shark Cave, one of Rangiroa's iconic sites. Here, on the outer wall of the channel at about 100 feet (30 m), is an area protected from the current by a large overhang where you can sit, giving you a grandstand view of the shark and ray action in the mouth of the pass. Grays, white tips, silver tips, eagle rays, mantas, and napoleon wrasses are all seen regularly at this extraordinary site.

As soon as you move out of Shark Cave the current quickly sweeps you into the Valley itself. Hammerheads frequently lurk in the deeper recesses of the Valley, but by this stage of the dive it is probably prudent to allow yourself to be taken gradually shallower on to the narrow lip at the entrance to the lagoon. As well as the lively pelagic action, keep an eye out for the schools of blue-stripe snappers and double-saddle butterflyfish that frequent this site.

John Bantin

AVATORU PASS

- **50 to 70 feet (15 to 21 m)** • **beginner**

A scaled-down version of the Tiputa Pass, this dive offers a similar range of pelagic species, with the added bonus that manta encounters here seem to be a regular feature. Look out for large silver tip sharks; deep-bodied sharks with wide pectorals that are held in some reverence by the locals. The drift is considerably less forceful here, making this an ideal site to introduce a new diver to the joys of drift diving.

THE AQUARIUM

- **10 to 30 feet (3 to 9 m)** • **beginner**

A tremendous dive on the edge of the wash created by the incoming currents blasting through Tiputa Pass, this site is a sheltered zone that offers a haven for a wide

variety of local reef fish, but because of its proximity to the pass there is every likelihood of encountering some larger animals as well. Indeed, many a beginner diver has been surprised with his or her first sight of a passing manta, eagle ray, or shark here.

The jumbled contours of the shallow reef provide a wide range of habitats for resident fish, and the Aquarium is alive with triggerfish, surgeonfish, wrasses, and butterflyfish. This is a perfect introductory dive to Rangiroa, or alternatively a fine stand-alone dive for the enthusiastic underwater photographer.

OTHER ACTIVITIES

While on Rangiroa, the Blue Lagoon is a beautiful spot for a day-trip and some snorkeling, as is the Island of the Reefs to the east of the main atoll. Rangiroa is also famous for its production of black pearls, and it is well worth taking the time to visit a number of farms in the region.

Further afield in French Polynesia, a particularly special encounter takes place in the southern island group of the Australs. Here you can snorkel with the humpback whales that use the warm waters of the region as a nursery through the months of July to October.

☎ TELEPHONE NUMBERS

Recompression chamber	+689-466-262
Hospital	+689-466-262
Tourist Board	+689-505-700

🖥 WEBSITES & E-MAIL

| Tourist Board | www.tahiti-tourisme.com |

▲ **SILVER TIP REEF SHARK**
Silver tip reef sharks have a well-deserved reputation as a bold, curious shark.

DIVER'S TIP

Be seen on the surface! A deployable S.M,B. is a wise precaution for the more dramatic drifts.

BORA BORA

THE MOST BEAUTIFUL OF THE ISLANDS OF FRENCH POLYNESIA, BORA BORA HAS BEEN A SOURCE OF INSPIRATION FOR WRITERS AND ARTISTS ALIKE. FOR DIVERS, INSPIRATION ALSO EXISTS IN THE WARM, SHELTERED WATERS OF THE LAGOON, A MAGNET FOR MANTAS, SHARKS, AND PASSING HUMPBACK WHALES.

 VISIBILITY

Spectacular on the outer reef—100 feet (30 m) plus. Can drop in the shallower regions of the channel to 40 feet (12 m.)

 MUST SEE

Mantas

 DOWNSIDE

Remote

 GETTING THERE

Tahiti Faaa, the international airport for French Polynesia, is served by a number of international airlines from most major hubs around the world. From Tahiti Faaa the internal airline Air Tahiti flies straight on to Bora Bora.

VISA

As a French overseas territory (T.O.M.), entry into French Polynesia is much the same as for France itself. E.U. passport holders can stay for up to three months without a visa, and most other nationalities a month.

$ MONEY

Currency is the C.F.P. or Pacific franc. Changing money can be expensive, so check with your host operator prior to arrival exactly how much cash will be required. Larger resorts take major credit cards.

Bora Bora has long been regarded as among the most magical islands in the Pacific. The novelist James Michener, who served with the U.S. forces in the Pacific and wrote a story that later became the screenplay for the musical *South Pacific*, that epitome of alluring island romance, was not usually short of a dramatic phrase or two. But even he admitted defeat when it came to Bora Bora, saying only "the central lagoon is so stunning, there really are no words to describe it." One of the many websites devoted to the praises of Bora Bora encapsulates its delights in one simple line: "The most beautiful island in the world."

GEOGRAPHY

Bora Bora is one of the Society Islands belonging to the French overseas territory of French Polynesia, and lies about 170 miles (273 km) northwest of Tahiti, the site of the capital, Papeete. The main island of Bora Bora is only 6 miles (9 km) long by 4 km wide, and is almost completely encircled by a wide lagoon about three times larger than the land it surrounds. The airstrip serving Bora Bora is on the small island of Motu Mute, a 20-minute boat ride away from the main settlement of Viatape, where most of Bora Bora's 4,650 residents live. The island is dominated by the twin peaks of

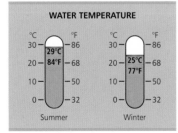

WATER TEMPERATURE			
°C	°F	°C	°F
30 —	— 86	30 —	— 86
29°C			— 68
20 — **84°F**	— 68	20 — **25°C** **77°F**	
10 —	— 50	10 —	— 50
0 —	— 32	0 —	— 32
Summer		Winter	

John Bantin

▶ **RUGGED LANDSCAPE**

Bora Bora's volcanic origins are unmistakable in the rugged contours of the main island.

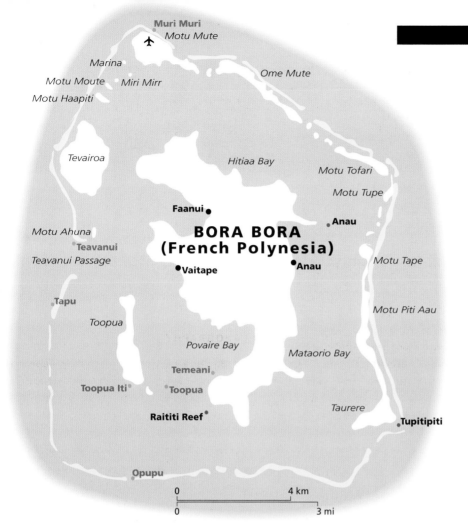

Muri Muri
Motu Mute
✈
Marina
Motu Moute   Miri Mirr
Motu Haapiti
Ome Mute

Tevairoa   Hitiaa Bay
                                              Motu Tofari
                                              Motu Tupe

Faanui •   • **Anau**

BORA BORA
Motu Ahuna   **(French Polynesia)**
    Teavanui
Teavanui Passage   Motu Tape
                    • **Vaitape**   • **Anau**

Tapu   Motu Piti Aau
    Toopua

            Povaire Bay   Mataorio Bay

        Temeani •
Toopua Iti •   • **Toopua**

Raititi Reef •   Taurere
                                        • **Tupitipiti**

Opupu

0   4 km
0   3 mi

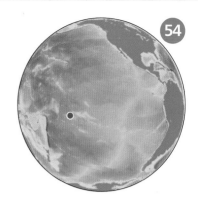

Mount Pahia and Mount Hue, while the even larger Mount Otemanu provides a stunning backdrop to the dives in the eastern sections of the lagoon. The islands are volcanic in origin, and the mountain slopes are mostly covered in dense forest.

During World War II Bora Bora served as a strategic staging post for U.S. forces fighting in the Solomons, and at one point there were 5,000 servicemen based on this tiny island. The vestiges of this period can be seen in the seven huge guns that still guard the entrances to the island, guns that were—thankfully—never fired.

MARINE LIFE

More than 500 fish species and 170 coral species have been recorded at Bora Bora, and the actual number for both is almost certainly more. But there is one particular aspect of the lagoon that sets it apart as a diving location. While sheltered, it has eddies and currents from small cuts in the reef, providing a rich source of nutrients and oxygen in this warm sea. Where there is planktonic food, the big animals assuredly follow, and Bora Bora has become well known for its manta ray population. There are also healthy populations of eagle rays, batrays, gray and spotted stingrays, some of which congregate in groups of considerable size. Local operators have been feeding the stingrays for many years, and they positively welcome the presence of divers.

There are also large populations of sharks including the ubiquitous gray reef and white tips, as well as lemons and silvertips, although not quite in the same number as at other Polynesian sites such as Rangiroa. Humpbacks are also seen in the area from August through to October.

▼ **CLARKS ANEMONEFISH**
A Clarks anemonefish stays close to the protection of its host's stinging tentacles.

John Bantin

DIVE CENTERS

TOPDIVE BORA BORA
P.O. Box 515, Vaitape, Bora Bora 98730,
French Polynesia
Phone: +689-60-50-50
Web: www.topdive.com

BORA DIVE CENTRE
B.P. 182, Bora Bora 98730, French Polynesia
Phone: +689-677-184
E-mail: boradiving@mail.pf
Web: www.topdive.com

DIVING ORGANIZATIONS

None. Contact the Tahiti Tourism Head Office
for information on recommended operators:
Phone: +689-505-700
Web: www.tahiti-tourisme.com

RECOMPRESSION

The Centre Hospitalier Territorial in Papeete,
Tahiti, has a large modern chamber:
Phone: +689-466-262

HOSPITAL

The large hospital in Papeete is staffed by
French doctors:
Centre Hospitalier Territorial
Ave Georges Clemenceau, Papeete, Tahiti
Phone: +689-466-262

Bora Bora has a small clinic:
Centre medical de Bora Bora

CONSERVATION SOCIETY

The Polynesian Coastal Conservation Agency
has set up three protected areas in French
Polynesia and can be contacted through the
French Government's environmental website
for the region:
Web: www.environnement.gouv.fr.

OTHER DIVE SITES

Muri Muri
Teavanui
Tapu
Toopua Iti
Temeani
Toopua
Opupu

THE DIVES

There is only one navigable pass leading to the open sea from the Bora Bora lagoon, but the numerous smaller cuts and the extensive reefs within the lagoon itself offer a host of diving opportunities. The great advantage of Bora Bora is that very few of the sites are extreme, which means that even the most spectacular (with the notable exception of Tupitipiti) can be dived by every level of diver from beginner to highly experienced. The lagoon to the east of the island is a shallow body of water throughout, rarely dipping below 60 feet (18 m), and yet it is the site of one of the best manta dives around the whole island.

Bora Bora has five established dive centers, while smaller operations run from several hotels. The diving industry has been set up to cater for a clientele that has the means to travel across the world to dive, and is at the top end of the market, offering very comfortable accommodation. But you should also be able to find options to suit the less well-padded wallet.

As there is no recompression chamber on the island, emergencies have to be evacuated to Papeete on Tahiti. Luckily, the medical evacuation services on Bora Bora are efficiently organized and, because of the nature of the diving, incidents are, thankfully, extremely rare.

ANAU

• 30 to 70 feet (9 to 21 m) • beginner

This channel has become the manta hotspot in Bora Bora, and is a delightfully simple dive that can be attempted by anyone who wants to swim in controlled conditions with these great rays. The best time is said to be from May to December.

The dive itself is located about a third of a mile (500 m) off Tuivahora Point on the east of the island. It begins in shallow water on the reef top and drops down the gently sloping reef to reach a large channel running north to south at the bottom, with a maximum depth of approximately 70 feet (21 m). Part of the channel is at the tail end of the influence of tidal water running through the cut in the reef to the east, and this seems to be the region favored by the mantas. Your best chance of a close encounter is to sink gently to the seabed and let the mantas swoop towards you, although they will also allow you to swim with them if you do not approach too closely. Be sure to keep your

▶ BLACK TIP REEF SHARK
A pack of black tip reef sharks hunt over one of Bora Bora's healthy hard coral reefs.

John Bantin

movements relaxed and leisurely (not easy to do when you are next to a manta!).

Look out for black tip reef sharks on this dive, as well as the fish life on what is a very busy reef due to the nutrient-rich water and tidal movements here. Angelfish, snappers, morays, and napoleon wrasses are the usual companions on this dive.

TUPITIPITI

• 30 to 130 feet (9 to 40 m) • advanced

This dive does not take place very often, requiring the happy coincidence of calm seas and limited currents at what is one of the most exposed sites in Bora Bora. Tupitipiti is at the far southeastern end of the long coral island of Motu Piti Aau, and the dive itself takes place on the southern end of the wall off Tupitipiti Point.

The reef wall is a mass of canyons, caves, gullies, overhangs, and cuts, presenting a wonderful series of habitats for the residents of the reef, both large and small. There is tremendous drama on this dive; gray and white tip reef sharks patrol the blue water, and the many nooks and crannies in the wall are occupied by marbled groupers and large morays. Eagle rays and

John Bantin

napoleon wrasses cruise overhead, and schools of trevally hunt immediately off the reef. The coral growth here is also spectacular, with soft and hard corals mixed in with multicolored sponges and delicate gorgonians.

RAITITI REEF

• 10 to 40 feet (3 to 12 m) • beginner

Used as an introductory dive, this is a very pleasant reef in the heart of the lagoon. The reef is shallow and swarms with clouds of damselfish, lone parrotfish, and small schools of snapper. Triggerfish seem to be here in some numbers, and there is also the chance of encountering eagle and stingrays. The perfect gentle introduction to Bora Bora.

OTHER ACTIVITIES

There is a road that completely circles the main island of Bora Bora, a mere 20 miles (32 km) long, which is surely one of the most beautiful seafront drives in the world. Do take the time to drive around it if you can; I promise it will be one of the more memorable drives in your diving life. Local guides will also take you to see the huge U.S. gun emplacements, with the guns still in place and gently rusting away. It is also well worth visiting the *marae*, the ceremonial centers of the Polynesians. The *marae*—open meeting places with stone platforms for worship and ritual—were destroyed by European missionaries in the 18th century, but the sites still remain and can be located quite easily by dint of a quick drive and some brisk footwork.

▲ **FISH GALORE**
Bora Bora has over 500 recorded fish species and 170 coral species living in its surrounding reefs.

DIVER'S TIP

When swimming with mantas, don't let your bubbles connect with the underside of the mantas—they don't seem to like it and will disappear. Never try to ride or touch them, and—as is the case with many large animals—they will be happier with your presence if you stay within their line of vision.

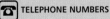 **TELEPHONE NUMBERS**

Recompression chamber	+689-466-262
Hospital	+689-466-262
Tourist Board	+689-505-700

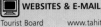 **WEBSITES & E-MAIL**

Tourist Board   www.tahiti-tourisme.com

BIKINI ATOLL

WATER TEMPERATURE

°C	°F	°C	°F
30	86	30	86
29°C		**29°C**	
20 **85°F**	68	20 **85°F**	68
10	50	10	50
0	32	0	32
Summer		Winter	

► SARATOGA

A diver swims past an open bomb-elevator on the deck of the *U.S.S. Saratoga*.

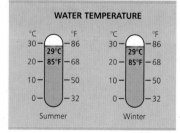

NOT ONLY DID BIKINI ATOLL GIVE ITS NAME TO A SCANT ITEM OF SWIMWEAR, THE NUCLEAR TESTS THAT TOOK PLACE THERE CREATED A WRECK SITE ON THE SEAFLOOR THAT MUST SURELY BE RECKONED AS AMONG THE MOST STAGGERING ANYWHERE ON THE PLANET.

But for the series of American nuclear weapon tests that took place in its crystal waters between 1946 and 1958, Bikini Atoll would have remained an anonymous set of tiny islands at the northern end of the Marshall Islands. In the uneasy political climate of the developing Cold War, the United States warily eyed its superpower opponent and former World War II ally, Soviet Russia. The U.S. pushed ahead vigorously with a nuclear weapons program, choosing as its testing ground two tiny clusters of coral islands in the western Pacific—Enewetak and Bikini Atolls—that had recently passed into its hands as part of the Pacific Islands Trust Territory at the end of World War II.

To test the destructive efficiency of some of the largest bombs ever detonated, the Americans assembled an enormous fleet in Bikini Atoll, consisting of 84 warships of varying styles and vintages, with the intention of sinking the lot. All were primed for war, with fuel in their tanks, aircraft in their hangers, and ammunition in the breeches of guns that would never be fired again. Among this fascinating array of fighting vessels was one of the largest aircraft carriers ever built, the *U.S.S. Saratoga*, as well as a captured German battle cruiser, the *Prinz Eugen*, and the battleship the *Nagato*, former flagship of the Japanese fleet. Alongside these great vessels were submarines, and a World War I Dreadnought. The atoll's 167 inhabitants were forced to leave the islands. Told they would be allowed to go back to their homes once the tests were over, the majority still wait to return to this day.

The first two bombs tested, Able and Baker, were impressive enough. The first detonation was about the same magnitude as the atomic bomb dropped over the Japanese city of Nagasaki in 1945, and created a 65-foot (20-m) high wave that sunk the vessels within a short distance of the central blast. The second bomb was much larger still, and sent millions of tons of water skywards, sinking the majority of the attendant fleet.

On March 1, 1954, the United States set off the largest device yet tested, a hydrogen bomb with a yield equivalent to 15 million tonnes of T.N.T.. The detonation vaporized three islands, blew a hole 250 feet (76 m) deep and 650 feet (198 m) wide in the atoll, and produced a contamination cloud that spread for many hundreds of miles.

Bikini Atoll has now been declared safe for visitors, although unacceptable amounts of cesium remaining in the soil mean that all foodstuffs have to be imported. The legacy of the tests are the wrecks that scatter the seabed, a potent symbol of the power of the bombs and the wanton destruction of a Pacific paradise that had ironically been completely untouched by war up until this time.

GEOGRAPHY

The Marshall Islands are located in the central western Pacific. Independent since 1986, they consist of a small group of 33 islands with a land area of only 70 sq miles (180 sq km) scattered over 750,000 sq miles (1,900,000 sq km) of ocean. The capital is Majuro, which also acts as a gateway for visitors. Bikini Atoll is at the northwestern end of the archipelago. It is a large atoll that is almost a self-contained sea, although there are a number of channels leading to the open ocean.

MARINE LIFE

The atoll's combination of intricate reef systems along the walls and large bommies that almost break the surface within the lagoon itself harbor the tremendous diversity of marine life associated with this part of the world—some 2,000 species of fish and 500 species of coral. But it is the breaks in the ring of islands that have found a place in diving lore—these tidal channels attract large numbers of cruising sharks, though these have recently been affected by long-line fishing. It is also quite possible to spot marlins and sailfins here.

THE DIVES

The dives here are deep—right on the limits of recreational diving, at an average of 160 to 180 feet

Bukor Island
Oddik Island
Lomlik Island
Aom-en Island

Nam Island

Bokobyaadaa Island
Bravo Crater

Bikini Island

U.S.S. Apogon
U.S.S. Arkansas
H.I.J.M.S. Nagato
U.S.S. Saratoga U.S.S. Carlisle
U.S.S. Pilotfish U.S.S. Gilliam
U.S.S. Anderson U.S.S. Lamson
H.I.J.M.S. Sakawa

Eomlan Island

BIKINI ATOLL
(Marshall Islands)

Rojkora Island

Bokororyuru Island
Shark Passage
Bokaetokutoku Island (Bird Island)

Bokaetokutoku Passage

Eneu Island

Jelete Island
Lukoj Island
Rukoji Passage

Aerkojlal Island

Eneu Channel

Lete Island

Enemaan Island
Jabej Island
Edboot Island
Aerkoj Island

DIVER'S TIP

Take a computer that can cope with a complex decompression plan, including changing mixes in water. It is no use hanging in water on an air computer while using a nitrox mix for accelerated decompression and counting down the minutes as your buddies soak up the sun on the boat!

John Bantin

John Bantin

 DIVE CENTERS

Bikini Atoll Divers, a part of the Bikini Atoll Local Government Council, owns and operates the dive program on Bikini Atoll:

BIKINI ATOLL DIVERS
C/o Kili/Bikini/Ejit, Local Government Council,
P.O. Box 1096, Majuro, Marshall Islands
MH 96960
Phone: +692-625-3177
For Customer Service:
E-mail: saratoga@ntamar.net
For technical dive info/Operations Manager:
E-mail: bikini@ntamar.net
Web: www.bikiniatoll.com

 DIVING ORGANIZATIONS

Marshall Islands Visitors Authority
P.O. Box 5, Majuro, Marshall Islands
MH96960
Phone: +692-625-6482
E-mail: tourism@ntamar.com
Web: www.visitmarshallislands.com

 RECOMPRESSION

There is no recompression chamber on Bikini. The nearest chamber is at Kwajalein. This is a U.S. Armed Forces facility, so use is not guaranteed. Contact them at:
Kwajalein Hospital, Ocean Road,
P.O. Box 1607, Kwajalein Atoll, Marshall Is
Phone: +805-355-2019

 HOSPITAL

Majuro Hospital
P.O. Box 16, Majuro, Marshall Islands
Phone: +692-625-3355

Each outer island community has a health assistant connected by marine high-frequency radio to the main center in Majuro.

 CONSERVATION SOCIETY

There are currently no protected areas in the Marshall Islands.

I.A.E.A.'s (International Atomic Energy Agency) Bikini Advisory Group has conducted studies on radiation on Bikini Atoll. Reports can be ordered from
E-mail: sales.publications@iaea.org

OTHER DIVE SITES

U.S.S. Apogon
U.S.S. Arkansas
U.S.S. Carlisle
U.S.S. Pilotfish
U.S.S. Gilliam
U.S.S. Anderson
U.S.S. Lamson
H.I.J.M.S. Sakawa

(50 to 55 m). The checkout dive is at 110 feet (33 m), and the remainder of the dives demand the use of some fairly advanced, albeit well-established, deep-water techniques such as decompression trapezes, nitrox mixes supplied by hookah on stops, and deep-water graded ascents with numerous stops. Although this can be daunting, the operators on Bikini are highly experienced in such techniques, and if a diver is prepared to absorb new methods and not be put off by racking up decompression times, the lack of currents and ready access to shot lines make this diving both enjoyable and educational. The local government council that operates the dive program on Bikini insists that all visiting divers have a medical evaluation by their own doctor prior to arrival, and that they read the radiological status report on the atoll, copies of which are supplied.

U.S.S. SARATOGA

• **110 to 180 feet (33 to 55 m) plus • intermediate**

The best wreck dive in Bikini, if not the world. The *U.S.S. Saratoga*, only the third aircraft carrier ever built, has a flight deck length of 888 feet (271 m), longer than the *Titanic*! She displaced a massive 33,000 tonnes, and everything about her is so big it almost defies description. The Japanese claimed to have sunk her seven times, and she enjoyed a distinguished career in the Pacific before suffering her incongruous end at Bikini.

Saratoga sits bolt upright in 190 feet (58 m) of water. It is quite impossible to explore her in a single visit and she should be dived several times to do her justice. Her bridge lies a mere 40 feet (12 m) below the surface, but all of the classic dives lie on the flight deck or within the eight decks that extend below—these

spaces, however, are largely unexplored due to depth restrictions and the vessel's deterioration over time.

The wreck is buoyed at three points—bow, stern, and bridge—and is used by the operators as a checkout dive. This is probably the most dramatic checkout dive on Earth, as the flight deck at 110 feet (33 m) appears below you, stretching into the distance. The bridge, still containing a battery of instruments, consoles, and voice tubes, can be visited on this dive. Dropping onto the flight deck, it is a long swim to the port side, passing the colossal forward elevator en route. At the edge of the flight deck are 22-mm Oerlikon antiaircraft guns and an abandoned forklift truck.

The hanger on the *Saratoga* is also a tremendous dive, in which you swim past rows of 500-lb (225-kg) bombs before arriving at the remains of four aircraft—three Helldiver single engine bombers and an Avenger. The bow also merits a separate dive. To hover slightly off the bow and look down at the sharp prow disappearing for 100 feet (30 m) into the gloom beneath is reminder of just how large this vessel really is.

H.I.J.M.S. NAGATO

• **160 feet (50 m) plus • advanced**

The *Nagato*, the first warship to be armed with 16-inch (405-mm) guns, was probably the fastest battleship in the world when she was launched in 1920. At 708 feet (216 m) in length and weighing 38,500 tonnes, here is another ship that almost defies description. She is a truly historic vessel, having acted as the flagship for the Japanese attack on Pearl Harbor in December 1941, as well as taking part in the official surrender of Japan in Tokyo Bay in 1945.

The *Nagato* flipped over on sinking and settled belly up in 170 feet (52 m) of water, a feature that is characteristic of many large battleship wrecks around the world. Despite this, her immense superstructure held her off the seabed, and it is possible to inspect her gun turrets quite easily.

From the shot line the best dive is to drop down onto the battleship's starboard side (the diver's port side, as the ship is upside down) and follow the line of the deck. This leads directly to the massive forward gun turrets. The gun barrels alone are 60 feet (18 m) long, and have a circumference of 5 feet (1.5 m) at the base. Enjoy the spectacle—this is the only place in the world where it is possible to dive on 16-inch (405-mm) guns. On returning, it is possible to explore a section of the bridge that has fallen beside the wreck.

A further dive to explore the stern of the *Nagato* is well worth the effort. You will be able view the propellers, each a total of 20 feet (6 m) across consisting of four massive blades, still perfectly visible as the ship is in an inverted position.

OTHER ACTIVITIES

It is the diving that draws visitors to Bikini Atoll, although you can explore some of the military bunkers on the islands if that appeals to you. One activity not to be missed is the shark diving, a recent development in the atoll, and yet such a success that it is almost eclipsing the attractions of the wrecks. The long line fishing fleets, which have plundered shark populations in other areas, tend to avoid Bikini, and as a result it has some of the healthiest shark populations on Earth.

TELEPHONE NUMBERS

Recompression chamber	+805-355-2019
Hospital	+692-625-3355
Tourism Organization	+692-625-6482

WEBSITES & E-MAIL

Tourism Organization

www.visitmarshallislands.com

▼ APOGON

A binocular gun-sight, with rubber eyecaps still in place, on the deck of the submarine *U.S.S. Apogon*.

John Bantin

CHUUK LAGOON

VISIBILITY

Ranges from 40 to 100 ft (12 to 30 m) depending on local conditions. Visibility can be affected by summer rains

MUST SEES

Coral on *Shinkoku Maru*
Fujikawa Maru

DOWNSIDE

Remote
Expensive

GETTING THERE

By air via Hawaii or Guam to Weno. A departure tax of U.S.$15 per person is payable before leaving.

VISA

Each island airport has its own customs and immigration officers. If you plan on visiting several islands on one trip, you will be passing through customs and immigration lines at each stop and filling out the usual paperwork. As a rule you will need a valid passport with at least 120 days left in it. You may also need to show proof of onward passage. Visitors will be issued an entry permit for an additional period not to exceed 60 days.

MONEY

Currency is U.S. dollar. Most operators take all major credit cards.

WATER TEMPERATURE

°C		°F		°C		°F
30		86		30		86
20	29°C 84°F	68		20	29°C 84°F	68
10		50		10		50
0		32		0		32
	Summer				Winter	

BENEATH THE WATERS OF CHUUK LAGOON LIE THE REMAINS OF A JAPANESE FLEET DESTROYED BY U.S. PLANES IN WORLD WAR II. DIVING HERE IS AN UNFORGETTABLE EXPERIENCE, WITH EACH WRECK A TIME CAPSULE WITH ITS OWN STORY.

Chuuk Lagoon is ringed by 140 miles (225 km) of outer reef. In early 1944, the Japanese were using this circular natural harbor as a supply base for their fleet. On February 17 and 18, at the start of Operation Hailstone, some 450 U.S. aircraft swept in to attack it from 9 aircraft carriers positioned below the horizon. During the ensuing battle for Chuuk (then known as Truk) at least 60 Japanese vessels, some 220,000 tonnes of crucial shipping, were sunk. The remnants of this fleet still lie on the seabed.

GEOGRAPHY

Chuuk lies within the Caroline Islands about 617 miles (993 km) southeast of Guam and is one of four states that make up the Federated States of Micronesia. It consists of 15 inner islands and numerous outer islands and atolls. Although it covers a total area of 822

▼ SILENT TANK
One of the three *Ha Go* tanks sits silently on the deck of the *San Francisco Maru* wreck. The wreck also has a cargo of lorries, shells, and a steamroller.

Kevin Davidson

sq miles (2,104 sq km), its land area is a mere 77 sq miles (199 sq km). Weno is the commercial center and capital. Five deepwater channels between the outer islands allow the passage of large vessels. The lagoon, 40 miles (65 km) across, is one of the largest in the world.

Chuuk was once an ancient volcano. The inner islands are the remnants of its cone. Over geological time the weight of the coral forming on the shallow outer edges of the volcano forced it beneath the waves. The coral continued to grow as the volcano sank, and an atoll—a circle of coral islands—developed above the volcano's sunken coastline. The waters within the atoll are shallower than the surrounding ocean, with a maximum depth of 280 feet (85 m).

MARINE LIFE

The sunken vessels provide Chuuk Lagoon with some of the finest coral reefs in Micronesia. The shallow wrecks in particular are the foundation for some tremendous coral formations, both hard and soft, as well as clouds of associated fish species.

THE DIVES

The ferocious bombardments from February to April 1944 rendered 400 Japanese aircraft inoperable, and sank at least 60 ships, large and small. Thirty-eight of these wrecks have been charted, although—to deter treasure hunters and souvenir collectors—not many are buoyed. They are mostly tenders, cargo vessels, tankers, and submarine support vessels, but a submarine and a destroyer have also been found.

Much of the diving in Chuuk Lagoon is deep. While visibility is almost invariably good and there are few currents, only divers with appropriate qualifications should attempt the deeper dives, and all must be accompanied by an experienced guide. Good buoyancy control is a key skill here—the interiors of the wrecks are very silted, and a single clumsy sweep of a fin can ruin a dive for everyone else in the group.

You may choose to dive from one of the shore dive centers, but they offer limited numbers of dives. Several liveaboards operate in the lagoon. They sit at key points in the lagoon within easy reach of a large number of the best wrecks, and most will only move two or three times in a single week's diving. Nearby wrecks are accessed by tenders, making it possible to dive up to five times a day.

THE FUJIKAWA MARU

- 20 to 120 feet (6 to 36 m)
- beginner to intermediate depending on depth

This dive really has it all. The wreck, a 437-foot (133-m) long armed cargo vessel, lies upright on the seabed with her bow facing east by southeast. It slopes gently toward deeper water, with the encrusted bow gun at 40 feet (12 m) and the stern gun at 60 feet (18 m). The relatively shallow superstructure is cloaked with tremendous soft and hard coral growth, while the wreck itself, and the water column above it, are dense with jack, Spanish mackerel, and juvenile barracuda. Much of the best photography on the wreck is of the tiny occupants of the soft corals, sea fans, and sea anemones that cover the bow. Particularly notable are the purple anemone shrimps, and the profusion of nudibranchs and pink anemone fish.

An enduring image of Chuuk Lagoon is of the broken and twisted fuselages of Zero fighters that lie within the large hold of the *Fujikawa Maru*. Penetrating this hold presents no serious problems as well-lit over-hangs provide clear views of large exit points through-out. Most dives begin by exploring this area, then drift over the superstructure. Passing alongside the wheel-house you can enter the hold behind the bridge and sink toward the impact hole created by the torpedo that sank the ship. The spectacular bow is an awesome sight when standing on the seabed looking up the port anchor chain, but do not overlook the stern—there are extensive safe passages through well-lit spars and passageways, most of which offer a clear path to the surface if required. Crisscrossing your path are beautiful sea fans and whip corals; this is a fine site for atmos-pheric natural light wide-angle photography. The officers' tiled bathroom aft of the wheelhouse is a real highlight toward the end of the dive. It is shallow enough to allow easy access and leisurely exploration.

Map

CHUUK (TRUK) ISLANDS (Micronesia)

Pis
Larnoil
North Passage
Tonclik
Tora
Tora Island Passage
Holap
Falalu
Falas
Oite
Northeast Is
Yawata
Quoi
Northeast Passage
Katsuragisan Maru
Ealo
Fealealloj Passage
WENO
Moen
Fumitzuki
Shinkoku Maru
Shinkoku Maru
Nippo Maru
Pata
Udot
Eot
Param
I-169
Dublon
San Francisco Maru
Piaanu Passage
Polle
Hanakawa Maru
Fala-Beguets
Betty Bomber
Fefan
Fujikawa Maru
Torres
Tol
Tarik
Taiho Maru
Uman
Rio de Janeiro Maru
Pisar
Bernard Is
Uliperu
Tsis
Amagisan Maru
Salat
Ollan
Pones
Fanan
South Passage
Otta Passage
Otta
Uijee
Udidan
Mesegon
Givry
Royalist Lagoon
Eauvergne South

0 — 15 km
0 — 10 mi

56

DIVER'S TIP

You will need the widest of wide-angle lenses to do justice to this vast collection of wrecks. However many photographic treats lie hidden among the coral growth on the decks and superstructures. Don't forget your macro lens and, even if you are a non-photographer, take some time to peer at some of the busiest coral communities in Micronesia.

DIVE CENTERS

S.S. THORFINN
Seaward Holidays Micronesia Inc., P.O. Box
1086, Weno, Chuuk State, F.M. 96942
Phone: +691-330-3040
E-mail: Seaward@mail.fm
Web: www.thorfinn.net

AGGRESSOR FLEET
P.O. Box 1470, Morgan City, LA 70381, U.S.A.
Phone: +1-800-348-2628
E-mail: info@aggressor.com
Web: www.aggressor.com

BLUE LAGOON DIVE SHOP
P.O. Box 429, Truk Moen, E.C.I., FM 96942
Phone: +691-330-2796
E-mail: bluelagoon@truk-lagoon-dive.com
Web: www.truk-lagoon-dive.com

 DIVING ORGANIZATIONS

None. Contact Chuuk Visitors Bureau for
information on operators:
Phone: +691-330-4133

 RECOMPRESSION

There is a hyperbaric chamber run by
volunteers in Neaou village, Weno. This
chamber may or may not be available.
A further chamber is available in Guam at the
U.S. Naval Hospital:
Phone: +1-671-344-9340

 HOSPITAL

Chuuk State Hospital
Chuuk, F.M. 96942
Phone: +691-330-2210

 CONSERVATION SOCIETY

The Chuuk State Government take a very dim
view indeed of anything being removed from
the wrecks. Equipment confiscation is the least
a diver can expect. Contact Chuuk Marine
Resources for information on marine
conservation:
Phone: +691-330-2660

THE SHINKOKU MARU

- **70 to 130 feet (20 to 40 m)**
- **beginner to intermediate**

This 541-foot (165-m) vessel sits upright with her prop at 138 feet (42 m) and her bow rising to 39 feet (12 m). A fleet oiler, the *Shinkoku Maru* had an interesting history. One of the few vessels in the lagoon actually constructed in Japan, she was at the vanguard of the fleet that launched the assault on Pearl Harbor in December, 1941, and was anchored in Chuuk Lagoon awaiting repairs to an earlier torpedo strike when Operation Hailstone struck. She was quickly sunk.

The coral growth on this wreck is notable, particularly on the bow section all the way back to the bridge. Some of the soft corals here are breathtaking, and are mixed in with multicolored sponges, anemones hydroids, and hard coral species. Beautiful black crinoids wave in the current, set on a backdrop of red sea fans. Groupers, anemone fish, and small morays jostle for position in this kaleidoscopic coral garden, enlivened by brightly colored nudibranchs and shrimp.

Among the treats on this dive is a swim through the wheelhouse where the telegraph is still intact. A further exploration of the bridge section reveals a sick bay with an operating table in place. The interior can be safely penetrated in the company of a local guide, and provides interesting glimpses of the crews' quarters and the engine room. There is a large hole towards the stern in the port side, its entrance clouded by shoals of glass-fish and various juvenile species. The rudder and screws are also still intact, lying at 125 feet (38 m).

The abundance of colorful growth on the *Shinkoku Maru* makes this the most outstanding night dive in Chuuk Lagoon, to the extent that tales are told of one visiting diver who had a powerful religious conversion during the course of just such a dive!

BETTY BOMBER

- **50 feet (15 m)** • **beginner**

This is an excellent shallower dive towards the end of the day. The Betty bomber is a twin-engined Mitsubishi G4M3 attack bomber ("Betty" was the nickname given these aircraft by the Allies). It sits upright in 49 feet (15 m) of water, only just short of the former airstrip on Etten Island.

This large aircraft has a 72-foot (22-m) fuselage and a 88-foot (27-m) wingspan. Both engines have fallen off, and are lying close together within 330 feet (100 m) of the main fuselage—relatively intact, although the cockpit has been twisted off. This allows easy access into its extremely clean interior. It is an eerie sensation to drift through the inside of the aircraft illuminated only by the ghostly green light from the oval hatches on the side of the fuselage. The radio is still in place in the main body of the fuselage. Interesting coral and sea fan formations hang beneath the large wings, and scattered in the sand around the bomber are a machine gun and various bits of debris.

▼ **SOFT CORAL SHRIMP**
As well as the wrecks Chuuk Lagoon offers great opportunity to see and photograph many of the reefs smaller residents including purple anemone shrimps.

Kevin Davidson

THE SAN FRANCISCO MARU

• 130 to 240 feet (40 to 73 m) • advanced

The so-called "Million Dollar Wreck", the *San Francisco Maru* was a big freighter, 426 feet (130 m) long. Her 4,000 horsepower engines gave her a cruising speed of 14 knots. It needed six 500 lb (227 kg) bombs to sink her, and she was completely ablaze as she went down. The "million dollar" tag stems from the sheer volume of cargo she was carrying, including three tanks, lorries, a steamroller, shells, depth charges, torpedoes, and mines. The latter are still occasionally plundered by local fishermen for the explosives they contain.

This is the most exciting deep dive in Chuuk. The bridge is at 130 feet (40 m), the deck at 165 feet (50 m), and the seabed a maximum of 240 feet (73 m) at the stern. Even the deck and bridge are exceptionally deep dives on scuba, and some parts of the wreck are beyond the limits of recreational diving. Appropriate training, equipment, experience, and suitable conditions are crucial when diving the *San Francisco Maru*.

Perhaps the best-known feature of this wreck are the three Type 95 Ha Go tanks on the deck forward of the bridge. These are light tanks, designed to take a three-man crew (although this is difficult to believe given the size of the tanks themselves). To trim the ship, there would have been two heavy vehicles on each side, and indeed a glance over the port rail shows a steamroller lying on the seabed. Moving forward, to Hold Number Two, the diver can see several vehicles including tankers and a staff car, as well as a large collection of tableware. Hold Number One, further toward the bow, is full almost to the brim with hemispherical beach mines. These Model 96 mines each weigh 106.5 lbs (47.9 kg), with an explosive charge of 46 lbs (20.8 kg), and any gaps in the neat rows of the mines can be explained by theft by local dynamite fishermen. There is a bow gun in immaculate condition on the foredeck.

Immediately aft of the bridge there is considerable bomb damage. Toward the stern, Hold Number Four contains the remains of four lorries, and a considerable quantity of ammunition, mostly 3- and 4-inch (7- and 10-cm) shells. Hold Number Five contains many torpedoes in various states of storage and disrepair.

OTHER ACTIVITIES

On Weno, Chuuk's main island, visitors can experience a taste of island life by visiting the local stores jammed with everything from kerosene stoves to ladies' wear and handicraft. For an outstanding view of Weno and the lagoon, climb into the old light house built during the Japanese occupation and visit the Blue Lagoon Resort for a stroll in the coconut palm groves with splendid views across the water to Dublon Island, formerly the Japanese Military Headquarters.

Dan Burton

TELEPHONE NUMBERS

Recompression chamber	+1-671-344-9340
Hospital	+691-330-2210
Chuuk Visitors Bureau	+691-330-4133
F.S.M. Visitors Board	+691-320-5133

WEBSITES & E-MAIL

South Pacific Organization	www.southpacific.org
F.S.M. Visitors Board	www.visit-micronesia.fm
Bob Hampton's Ghost Fleet	bobhampton@kwajonline.com

▲ CORAL GROWTH

All the wrecks around Chuuk are now covered by a profusion of coral growth making the diving even more spectacular.

YAP
ISLAND

VISIBILITY
150 feet (46 m) on reefs & walls
30 feet to 100 feet (9 to 30 m) in the channels

✓ MUST SEES
Manta rays
Yap Caverns

✗ DOWNSIDE
Remote
Expensive

✈ GETTING THERE
The main gateways into the Federated States of Micronesia are Honolulu, Manila, and Guam. There are also twice-weekly flights from Taipei. A Circle Micronesia air pass will let you hop around the islands. Yap has no departure tax.

👤 VISA
Not required for tourist visits of up to 30 days. Your 30 days start afresh each time you move to a different island group. U.S. citizens can extend their permit for up to a year.

$ MONEY
U.S. dollars are the official currency. U.S. dollar traveler's checks are accepted at most large hotels, restaurants, and shops. Credit cards are gaining in use.

YOU CAN BE SURE OF A WARM WELCOME IN THESE IDYLLIC ISLANDS, WHERE THERE IS SPECTACULAR DIVING AMONG EXCEPTIONAL HARD CORALS. BUT ASK ANY DIVER WHY THEY MAKE THE LONG PILGRIMAGE TO YAP, AND THERE IS LIKELY TO BE ONLY ONE ANSWER—MANTA RAYS. YAP IS MANTA RAY HEAVEN.

Dan Burton

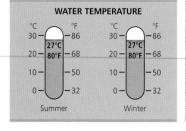

WATER TEMPERATURE

°C	°F	°C	°F
30 —	— 86	30 —	— 86
20 — 27°C 80°F	— 68	20 — 27°C 80°F	— 68
10 —	— 50	10 —	— 50
0 —	— 32	0 —	— 32
Summer		Winter	

To see a giant manta materialize out of the gloom and hover a few feet above you is one of the great experiences of world diving. These huge fish can grow to as much as 27 feet (8 m) across and weigh a ton and a half. But manta rays are not the only reason for visiting Yap. It is a truly magical place, apparently unspoiled by the modern world, and is one of the last places in Micronesia to preserve its distinctive culture largely unchanged.

GEOGRAPHY

Yap is the most westerly of the four states that make up the Federated States of Micronesia. It consists of 4 large islands, 7 small islands, and 134 atolls spread over 600 sq miles (1,553 sq km) of ocean, with a total land area of 46 sq miles (119 sq km). The Yap Trench, a deep ocean trench, lies some 17 miles (27 km) away. The

▼ MANTA HEAVEN

The mantas of Yap, some of which have a wing span of over 20 feet (6 m), have ensured its fame as a top diving destination.

state capital, Colonia, is on the main island of Yap, and is the closest these idyllic islands get to the modern world. In the small villages of the scattered islands the men still fish the reefs in the traditional way from large single outrigger canoes, women weave mats of pandanus leaves, and both men and women wear the traditional island garb of loin cloths and grass skirts.

MARINE LIFE

In addition to its world-famous manta rays, Yap has hard coral reefs of exceptionally high quality. In part, this is due to the presence of the Yap Trench, which protects the islands from violent swings in water temperature. Thus its reefs have escaped the worst effects of the El Niño climate event that has proved so catastrophic for other tropical reefs in Micronesia. A recent typhoon, however, has had a major impact on the reef.

Another factor is the traditional custom of allocating particular reefs to certain villages or families so that the marine life of the reefs is sustainably exploited. Because

> **DIVER'S TIP**
>
> The tide really snorts through the manta channels, so be prepared. Descend quickly and hug the bottom. It's a good idea to take a separate line to attach to the shot line to avoid being battered by other divers when recompressing.

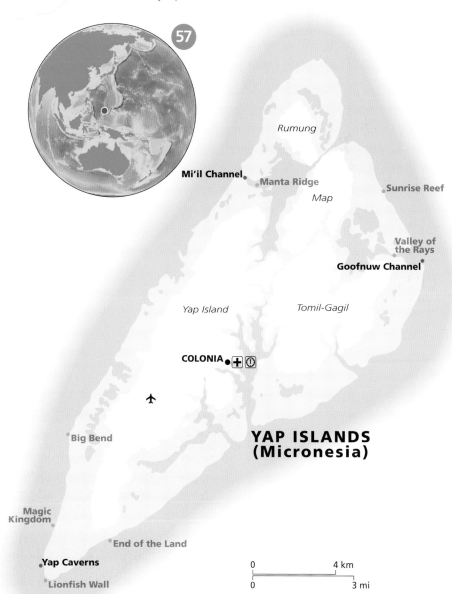

57

Rumung

Mi'il Channel

Manta Ridge

Map

Sunrise Reef

Valley of the Rays

Goofnuw Channel

Yap Island

Tomil-Gagil

COLONIA

Big Bend

YAP ISLANDS (Micronesia)

Magic Kingdom

End of the Land

Yap Caverns

Lionfish Wall

| 0 | | 4 km |
| 0 | | 3 mi |

Dan Burton

► **MACRO SHRIMP**
The macro life of Yap's healthy hard coral reefs is a worthy distraction from the mantas.

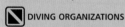

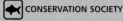
of these powerful local traditions, human impact on the reefs has remained minimal. Some 80 percent of the reefs around Yap remain undived, and hopefully they will stay this way for a very long time.

A very healthy population of reef sharks patrol the reefs and drop-offs of Yap for prey, and you are likely to observe white tips and grays on virtually every dive on the fringing reef. Yap also has a noteworthy array of tropical fish species, and the numbers of mandarin fish it boasts are unmatched anywhere else in the islands of Micronesia. Cruising the blue water above the reefs are schools of bigeye jack, blackfin, and barracuda, as well as two species of sea turtle.

For the macrophotographer, Yap's coral reefs have a wide range of nudibranch species, as well as numerous rare small fish species such as the fire goby, leaffish, ghost pipefish, longnose filefish, sea horses, shrimpfish, and dragon wrasses.

THE DIVES

Diving in Yap divides very neatly between the gently sloping reefs on the east of the island and the more severe drop-offs to the west. There are numerous individual dives within both of these areas. Cutting through the island is Mi'il Channel, and to the east is Goofnuw Channel. Both attract manta rays, drawn in by the racing tide and the presence of several cleaning stations within each channel.

MI'IL CHANNEL

• 25 to 70 feet (8 to 21 m) • beginner

Cutting into the northwestern coast of the island, Mi'il Channel experiences a strong tidal race and has a very large population of mantas. Some operators guarantee the sight of a manta on every dive, and it is not uncommon to see up to ten of these magnificent animals on a single dive. To observe the mantas, you drop down the walls of the channel, frequently in the teeth of some strong currents, and make your way to the lee of one of several cleaning stations. There you will be rewarded with the sight, unparalleled in diving, of a manta stopping inches overhead for a thorough grooming by several cleaner wrasses.

GOOFNUW CHANNEL

• 25 to 70 feet (8 to 21 m) • beginner

Slightly wider and more exposed than Mi'il Channel, Goofnuw Channel experiences the same racing tides that draw the manta in. The routine for a manta sighting is the same. You make your way down to the seafloor, frequently battling against a racing tide, to wait at one of several cleaning stations. It is worth noting that visibility in both channels can be severely restricted by the movement of the currents and tides.

YAP CAVERNS

• 10 to 60 feet (3 to 18 m) • beginner

This is a spectacular dive for those who have had enough of manta sightings. Located on the southern tip of the island, this dive offers a series of spectacular swims through caverns that honeycomb the reef from the surface down to a depth of 60 feet (18 m). Visibility is often very good at this site, offering a chance to view the patrolling white tip and gray reef sharks in the blue water beyond the reef wall. Lionfish are plentiful, and schools of tuna and amberjacks have been sighted around the entrance to the caverns.

OTHER ACTIVITIES

An island of rolling green hills, Yap has a fascinating past and is famous for its ancient stone remains—especially the large stone disks that are a form of money that is still in use today, and are well worth going to see.

Yap is one of the few places where Micronesian culture has survived the passage of time. Dance forms an important part of Yap cultural life. It is the way that the islanders pass on their legends and history, and men and women learn to dance from an early age.

The islanders are warm and welcoming, and are usually happy to talk to visitors. Most hotels lay on formal tours to outlying villages, but it is often just as satisfying to explore on your own—seek advice on where to go though, as some villages are more accepting of visitors than others. When exploring the villages, take a leaf with you as this is the universal sign in Yap that you are a visitor with no ill intentions.

☎ **TELEPHONE NUMBERS**

Recompression chamber	+691-350-2115
Hospital	+691-350-2115

🖥 **WEBSITES & E-MAIL**

Yap Visitors Bureau	www.visityap.com
Micronesia Visitors Center	www.visit-fsm.org

OTHER DIVE SITES

Manta Ridge
Sunrise Reef
Valley of the Rays
Big Bend
Magic Kingdom
End of the Land
Lionfish Wall

▼ **BARRACUDA**
Large schools of barracuda can be seen cruising the clear blue water above the reefs of Yap.

Monty Halls

THE PALAU ARCHIPELAGO

THE BEAUTIFUL ARCHIPELAGO OF PALAU HAS EVERYTHING THE ADVENTUROUS DIVER COULD WISH FOR—WRECKS, DRIFT DIVES, BLUE HOLES, AND VAST CAVERNS. THE ONLY DOWNSIDE TO THIS PACIFIC PARADISE IS ITS REMOTENESS, BUT ONCE THERE YOU WON'T WANT TO LEAVE.

 VISIBILITY

150 ft (46 m) June–July (flood tide)

60 ft (18 m) Jan–Feb (ebbing tide)

 MUST SEES

Blue Corner

Ngmelis Wall

Blue Holes

Jellyfish Lake

Numerous wrecks

 DOWNSIDE

Remote

Expensive

Strong currents on some dives

 GETTING THERE

Flights to Guam from the U.S., Japan, and certain other countries connect with regular flights to Koror, Palau's capital. Most good dive operators within the islands have their own pick-up and drop-off service at Koror.

 VISA

Visas are not required. Non-U.S. citizens must have a valid passport. Visitors' permits for those planning to stay more than 30 days must be obtained from the Chief of Immigration for a fee of U.S.$100.

$ MONEY

Currency of choice for the visitor is the U.S. dollar.

The diving in Palau is truly amazing: spectacular drop-offs policed by vast schools of predators, swirling cylinders of barracuda and jacks, and big pelagic species. The famed Blue Corner may just be one of the finest single dives anywhere on Earth.

GEOGRAPHY

The Palau archipelago is made up of 307 islands, the tops of a mountain chain thrust up from the ocean bed when the Pacific and Philippine plates of the Earth's crust collided some 35 million years ago. The significance of this from a diver's point of view is that the islands consist of a mixture of volcanic rock and porous limestone, creating exactly the right foundation for extensive coral reefs and tunneling cave systems leading to cathedral-like caverns.

Palau (formerly Belau) lies at the western end of the Caroline Island chain of Micronesia. The economy of this tiny state, which became fully independent of the United States in 1994, is heavily reliant on diving

WATER TEMPERATURE

	Summer		Winter
°C	°F	°C	°F
30	86	30	86
28°C			
20 — 82°F	68	20 — 24°C 75°F	68
10	50	10	50
0	32	0	32

▶ **MANY SPOTTED SWEETLIPS**

Although most divers come to Palau for the larger residents of the reef, the smaller animals found in and around the reefs should not be overlooked.

Kevin Davidson

Kevin Davidson

▲ PALAU

With over 300 islands, the Palau archipelago has many isolated islands to visit—all with stunning scenery and clear blue water.

Map labels:

Ngeruangel
Blue Hole
Kayangel Atoll
Kayangel Islands
Kayangel Passage
Kossol Passage
Kossol Reef
Coromoran Reef
East Entrance
Ngamegi Passage
Konrei
Aiwokako Passage
Ngardmau
West Passage
Babelthuap
Melekiok
PALAU
Mukeru
KOROR
Garusuun
Pincher's Lagoon
Chandelier Cave
Sias Tunnel
Malakal
Aulong
Rock Islands
Iro Maru
Shark City
Bichu Maru
Urukthapel
Orukuizu
Jellyfish Lake
Eil Malk
Blue Corner
Blue Holes
Ngemelis Islands
New Drop
Ngmelis Wall
Big Drop Off
Ngercheu (Carp Island)
Ngedebus Wall
Omok
Ngardolok
Peleliu
Peleliu Wall
Saipan
Angaur

0   15 km
0   10 mi

tourism, particularly from the affluent end of the international market. The government, dive operators, and fishermen cooperate together, through a raft of local initiatives and the careful policing of the heavily dived reefs and wrecks, to conserve the unique quality of Palau's underwater environment, thereby insuring that it remains a mecca for divers. The population of the islands is a mere 17,000, administered from the capital city of Koror on the island of Arakabesan.

MARINE LIFE

Some of the richest coral reefs on the planet cover the protected gullies and walls of rock that surround the islands of Palau, although the El Niño event did have an undoubted impact on much of the hard coral on the shallower reefs. There are approximately 700 species of coral, and 1,500 resident species of fish, while 50 species of bird fly overhead. This ecological richness is sustained by a mixture of ancient tradition and modern legislation. The Palauan menfolk take great pride in their fishing skills, enforcing ancient taboos called *bul* designed to maintain fish populations and preserve

breeding grounds. Government regulations ensure that designated reserves and parks are patrolled by the Koror State Rangers, a body set up specifically to guard the fragile ecosystems of the land and the sea.

THE DIVES

One of the attractions of Palau is the range of dives available just a short boat-ride away from the main dive centers. Wrecks such as the *Bichu Maru* and the *Iro* are well preserved monuments to the battles of World War II, and crumpled aircraft fuselages litter the seabed. You can enjoy fabulous wall-diving along the edge of the

58

DIVE CENTERS

SAM'S DIVE TOURS
P.O. Box 7076, Koror, Palau 96940
Phone: +680-488-1062
E-mail: info@samstours.com
Web: www.samstours.com

NECO MARINE
P.O. Box 129, Koror, Palau 96940
Phone: +680-488-1755
E-mail: info@necomarine.com
Web: www.necomarine.com

PELELIU DIVERS
P.O. Box 8071, Koror, Palau 96940
Phone: +680-345-1058
E-mail: pdivers@palaunet.com
Web: www32.ocn.ne.jp/~palau/pd02_e.htm

 DIVING ORGANIZATIONS

Koror State Rangers
Phone: +680-488-2150

 RECOMPRESSION

Belau National Hospital, Koror, Palau
Phone: +680-488-1755

 HOSPITAL

Belau National Hospital, Koror, Palau
Phone: +680-488-1411

 CONSERVATION SOCIETY

Palau Conservation Society
P.O. Box 1811, Koror, Palau 96940
Phone: +680-488-3993
E-mail: pcs@palaunet.com
Web: www.palau-pcs.org

island plateaus as they plunge into the ocean depths, the best sites being Blue Corner, the Ngmelis Wall, and the Big Drop-Off. Most are drift dives, but less experienced divers can safely explore sheltered atolls such as Pincher's Lagoon and Kayangel Atoll.

Caves and caverns riddle the islands, including stunning stalactite formations in Chandelier Cave, Sias Tunnel, and the gigantic cathedral-like cavern at Blue Holes. Palau also guarantees big animal encounters at most dive sites. True shark junkies should not miss Blue Corner, one of the best places to observe life at the top of the food chain, from stalking sharks to manta ray fly-bys.

BLUE CORNER

• **30 to 60 feet (10 to 20 m)** • **advanced**

Blue Corner offers true world-class diving. The scope of marine life is of a consistently high quality and includes rich coral reefs and guaranteed encounters with big pelagic animals. Blue Corner, situated on the edge of a shallow plateau to the southwest of Ngerukewid (Seventy Islands) is washed by powerful currents that create an incredible foodweb. This is an advanced dive. Divers have to hook themselves onto the reef—using patches of dead coral and small reef hooks—to observe the gray and white tip reef sharks hovering in the crystal-clear water at the edge of the drop-off. Visibility on this dive can be up to 150 feet (45 m), although it has been as low as 60 feet (18 m). Along with sharks, there are king mackerel, giant and bluefin trevallies,

and dogtooth tuna. Back from the edge of the plateau, the reef is policed by large napoleon wrasses, lionfish, spotted eagle rays, and the ubiquitous clownfish, as well as many other well-known species.

The end of this dive is a decompression stop that involves stepping off into the blue water beyond the continental shelf and drifting surrounded by schools of blackfin barracuda and various pelagic species.

NGMELIS WALL

• **10 to 100 feet (3 to 30 m)** • **beginner to expert**

Another dive that has a near mythical reputation with divers throughout the world, Ngmelis Wall is a wall dive that will appeal to raw amateurs and experienced pros alike. Options on this dive are limitless—you can choose a long shallow drift through the dense coral gardens close to the surface or a bounce dive among the patrolling predators at depth. Every depth along the wall offers a myriad of activity, with charismatic larger species drifting in the blue water alongside the reefs.

In the shallow sections of the wall, large napoleon wrasses can be seen hugging the reef, while in mid water the stealthy silhouettes of white tip reef sharks accompany virtually every dive. Deeper still, divers at dawn or dusk have the opportunity to observe the non-stop action of big bluefin trevallies hunting along the wall and the dogfights with scattering shoals of bait fish in the middle distance. Behind the divers, the gullies and caves of the wall are occupied by a resident population of moray eels.

Dan Burton

WRECK OF THE BICHU MARU

• 30 to 130 feet (10 to 40 m) • intermediate

Wrecks litter the seabed around the Palau Islands, a legacy of the ferocious fighting that took place in the region between U.S. and Japanese forces during World War II. One of the finest is the *Bichu Maru*, a 360-feet (110-m) long army cargo ship that is lying on its port side in 131 feet (40 m) of water. The wreck is largely intact, with the starboard rail amidships about 33 feet (10 m) from the surface.

Although the ship sustained damage when sunk by American bombers on March 30, 1944, she nonetheless retains most of her superstructure and hull. Her holds are empty, which allows divers to penetrate deeply into the wreck all the way through to the engine room to observe a matrix of valves and pipes.

In the galley just aft of the engine room, stoves, kettles, and rice pans are still lying around, and as you exit the galley to return to the exterior of the wreck, it is worth giving the silt below the wreck a brief search for pieces of unbroken china that were lost from the galley during the sinking.

Swirling over the superstructure of the wreck are juvenile harlequin sweetlips, along with six-banded anglefish and eight-banded butterflyfish. Some beautiful sea whips are growing from the starboard anchor, which is still in its stowed position. On the deck itself the stunning nudibranch, *Glossodoris egretta*, is particularly abundant.

CHANDELIER CAVE

• 0 to 60 feet (0 to 18 m) • intermediate

This exquisite dive gives even divers of intermediate standard the opportunity to explore the interior of a cave system. The cave is entered via a hole that is found only a few feet beneath the water surface in Malakal Harbor. After passing through the hole, the system immediately opens into a series of caves that extend for hundreds of feet into the island. Four large air pockets (or sumps as they are known in the trade) provide cavernous spaces for the diver to surface, and the natural light levels keep claustrophobia to a minimum.

Throughout the caves are beautiful stalactites that contribute to the overall impact of this unique, safe diving experience for those not used to diving cave systems. On exiting the cave, divers can see mandarin fish, crocodile fish, cuttlefish, and gobies in the sheltered waters of the lagoon.

JELLYFISH LAKE

• Snorkeling • all levels

The geology of Palau, with its tunneling systems of caves into porous rock, lends itself to the formation of marine lakes. Jellyfish Lake is one of 70 such systems

Kevin Davidson

dotted around the archipelago. Although several of these lakes support populations of jellyfish, Jellyfish Lake is the only one that can be visited by the public.

One of the most photographed dives on Palau, Jellyfish Lake is a quirky dive that has become a real "must see" for the experience of being immersed within a great mass of jellyfish (happily with no stinging cells.) The lake is also home to populations of cardinal fish, mangrove gobies, small bait fish, crabs, mussels, and sponges. In short, it offers something completely different for the visiting diver who is replete with coral reefs and bustling drop-offs.

BLUE HOLES

• 100 feet (30 m) • intermediate

Another stunning dive, combining a spectacular cavern system with safe access to the surface at all times, the Blue Holes are a worthy addition to the world-class attractions of Blue Corner. Located slightly to the north of the main point of Blue Corner are several large holes in the flat surface of the reef. In placid conditions, divers can enter these holes directly. On rougher days the Blue Holes can be accessed by a large entrance halfway down the reef wall.

The diver descends a large tube decorated with hydroids and emerges into a great open space that appears to be supported by four massive pillars of light streaming in from the entrances above. The holes are relatively devoid of marine life, save for the frequent presence of Randall's fairy basslet and the lyre-tail wrasse, but this is a never to be forgotten dive as you

◄ **CHANDELIER CAVE**
Situated in Malakal Harbor, Chandelier Cave is a thrilling dive, especially for those who haven't experienced a cave dive before.

◄◄ **JELLYFISH LAKE**
One of 70 marine lakes around Palau, Jellyfish Lake is a truly unique dive. As well as masses of jellyfish, the lake is also home to cardinal fish and mangrove gobies.

► SNORKELING

Palau's many islands are surrounded by calm shallows that are ideal for snorkeling.

Kevin Davidson

float through the cavern with the light dappling the jumbled rocks of the floor beneath. Access to the surface is always available through the large skylights in the cavern roof, and on completion of the dive, it is easy to drift through one of the holes and, keeping the reef wall on the left, move toward Blue Corner.

GERMAN CHANNEL

• **30 to 80 feet (10 to 25 m)** • **intermediate**

A monument to human engineering and persistence, German Channel is a large man-made cut through to the outer reef. The sea is funneled through this cut, creating nutrient-rich waters and sweeping currents that attract the big filter feeders and their attendant entourage of cleaners and parasites.

German Channel can only be dived on an incoming or slack tide. Dives tend to focus on the cleaning stations that dot the channel, although divers may initially drift over white sand and sparse reefs where the occasional stingray or sleeping white tip reef shark may be encountered. On coming across a cleaning station, it is worth spending some time waiting for a manta to turn up, as there are resident populations in the region of the channel throughout the year. In the shallower fringes at the edge of the channel, generally investigated toward the end of the dive, you may meet with leopard sharks sleeping in protected gullies. There is also the possibility of an encounter with the occasional turtle feeding on the channel wall.

JAKE SEAPLANE

• 50 feet (15 m) • novice

Sitting upright on the bottom, this largely intact aircraft wreck is located about 0.6 miles (1 km) north of Meyens Island. This dive offers particularly good opportunities for wide-angle photography as the main fuselage is still intact, the engine cowling and propeller leans drunkenly into the seabed, and the tail section lies close by. The fuselage is encrusted in hydroids and corals, while the tail section is carpeted in sponges. There are virtually no currents in this area, and the 37-foot (11-m) long wreck is therefore suitable for novices and makes an ideal second dive.

ZERO FIGHTER

• 10 feet (3 m) • snorkel

Another iconic image of Palau among the international diving fraternity is this Japanese light fighter aircraft lying in shallow water. The canopy and cockpit instruments are missing, as is the left wing. The propeller curves out of the cowling half-buried in coarse coral sand, and at low tide the tip stands proud of the water.

This is a poignant reminder of the conflict that raged through Palau during World War II. It is a good opportunity for a snorkel and to take some interesting wide-angle photos, as you make your way back to Malakal Harbor at the end of a day's diving.

TEMPLE OF DOOM

• 130 feet (40 m) • expert

Beneath Blue Corner, at the very back of the Blue Holes, is the entrance to the Temple of Doom. This is a vast cavern, stretching back more than 328 feet (100 m) into the reef. Whereas other cave dives within the archipelago lend themselves (uniquely) to amateur exploration, the Temple of Doom (as its name suggests) is unequivocally a dive for the qualified and experienced diver, for once you are through the small entrance, there is no direct access to the surface. Be warned—at least three divers, in recent years, have lost their lives as a result of becoming disorientated in the cave.

On entering the cavern, divers should follow the line laid by local dive operators along the left-hand wall of the cavern. The silt of the cave floor is extremely fine, demanding excellent buoyancy control to avoid stirring up a dense cloud and reducing visibility. The complete skeletons of three turtles are present in the cavern, the first of which lies partially buried 60 feet (18 m) from the entrance. Drifting over the top of these jumbled bones, divers should follow the line back to the rear of the cave where, on top of a silt ledge, a magnificent complete turtle skeleton is visible. Should time permit, divers can take a turn around the gigantic stalactite at the rear of the cavern before returning to the entrance and the safety of the main reef.

OTHER ACTIVITIES

Although diving is its main tourist attraction, Palau also offers visitors world-class game fishing, kayaking, and the chance to explore World War II memorabilia on islands such as Peleliu (also famous for its bat-filled caves). Sailing tours of the islands range from single-day trips through to longer excursions of up to a week. These can generally be arranged through your dive operator.

Palauans are extremely friendly people. Most speak English, although some of the older generation still speak Japanese, a legacy of the period from 1914 until 1944 when the islands were under Japanese mandate. In 1947 they become part of the U.S. Trust Territory of the Pacific Islands. Palauans today are eager to retain their rich local traditions while adapting themselves to the needs of the global tourist market.

▼ **ZERO FIGHTER**

Situated in the shallow waters below Malakal Harbor this wrecked Japanese fighter plane is a reminder of the conflict that took place in the region during World War II.

☎ TELEPHONE NUMBERS

Recompression chamber	+680-488-1755
Hospital	+680-488-1411
Palau Visitors Authority	+680-488-2793
Office of Environment	+680-488-6950

🖥 WEBSITES & E-MAIL

Palau Visitors' Authority	www.visit-palau.com
	pva@visit-palau.com
Palau National Information	www.palaunet.com
Palau International Coral Reef Center	www.picrc.org

Kevin Davidson

TUBBATAHA
REEFS

 VISIBILITY
Up to 130 feet (40 m)

 MUST SEE
Jessie Beazley Reef

 DOWNSIDE
Remote
Strong currents
Limited window of opportunity to visit

 GETTING THERE
Most tourists fly into Manila. You can either take a liveaboard directly from here, or make the 70-minute flight to Puerto Princessa in Palawan, where it is a 12-hour boat ride to the islands. Trips to Tubbattaha are all by liveaboard and and you should plan them a minimum of 6 weeks ahead of departure to ensure a successful booking.

 VISA
For most foreign visitors, visas are not needed for stays of less than 21 days. Three-month visas can be obtained in advance and cost around U.S.$35.

 MONEY
Currency is the Philippines peso; U.S. dollars are also widely accepted. A.T.M.s are found in most larger towns, and leading credit cards are accepted by established tourist facilities.

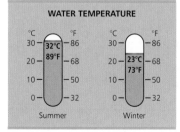

WATER TEMPERATURE

°C	°F	°C	°F
30 — 32°C — 86		30 — — 86	
20 — 89°F — 68		20 — 23°C — 68	
10 — — 50		10 — 73°F — 50	
0 — — 32		0 — — 32	
Summer		Winter	

▶ **SOFT CORAL**
Multi-colored soft corals and tube sponges enjoy the strong currents and nutrient-rich upwelling of a typical Tubbataha Reef wall.

THE NEAREST INHABITED ISLANDS ARE 80 MILES (128 KM) AWAY—THIS IS A SERIOUSLY REMOTE DIVE! BUT IT IS WORTH EVERY MILE OF THE JOURNEY FOR THE WONDERFUL ARRAY OF LIFE ON THESE EXQUISITE REEFS AT THE HEART OF THE PACIFIC OCEAN'S "TRIANGLE OF DIVERSITY".

John Bantin

At the center of the deep Sulu Sea, off the southwest Philippines, sits a small collection of reefs and atolls called Tubbataha Reefs. This is a classic tropical dive site, with steep walls swept by strong currents and busy reef tops leading to shallow lagoons. The tiny set of sandbars, reefs, and islets sits at the heart of the famed "Triangle of Diversity", and plays host to scores of hundreds of reef species as well as larger visitors from the open ocean.

Tubbataha Reefs are many miles from civilization and accessible for only a brief period every year. The very epitome of isolation, they have been spared the ravages of the singularly destructive fishing methods employed elsewhere in the Philippines, although there is evidence of reef destruction even here.

GEOGRAPHY

The Sulu Sea is a deep basin covering an area of 100,386 sq miles (260,000 sq km), with a deepest point of 18,308 feet (5,580 m). Tubbataha Reefs lie at the center of the sea, 113 miles (181 km) southeast of Puerto Princessa, the capital city of the large island of Palawan in the west of the Philippines archipelago. The reefs and islets of Tubbataha are part of the Cagayan Ridge, which runs from San Miguel Island in the southwest to Sultana Shoal in the northeast.

The reefs themselves, both classic atoll-style lagoons surrounded by emergent sandbars and islands, may be divided into two different groups. To the southwest is South Atoll, a small triangular-shaped atoll approximately 1.5 miles (2 km) across, with a prominent black rock to the north and a solar-powered lighthouse to the south. To the east of the lighthouse, stark and skeletal above the reef, are the remains of the wreck of the *Delsan*, an old merchant vessel slowly rusting in the spray and salt. Separated by a 4-mile (6-km) channel from its smaller neighbor is North Atoll. This larger atoll is approximately 3 miles (5 km) wide, and has a small sandbar to the northeast called Bird Islet, an important roosting and breeding area for seabirds.

The islands are uninhabited for most of the year, although small groups of fishermen move in from elsewhere in the Philippines during peak fishing periods. There is also a small ranger station at Tubbataha, set up through the fees paid by visiting divers.

MARINE LIFE

The area around Palawan contains 40 percent of the Philippines' 13,127 sq miles (34,000 sq km) of coral reef. The reefs of the Philippines are some of the most damaged on Earth due to the destructive methods used by local fishermen. Although blast fishing has had its impact on Tubbataha Reefs, damage is confined to the reef tops and even this is receding as a result of the hard

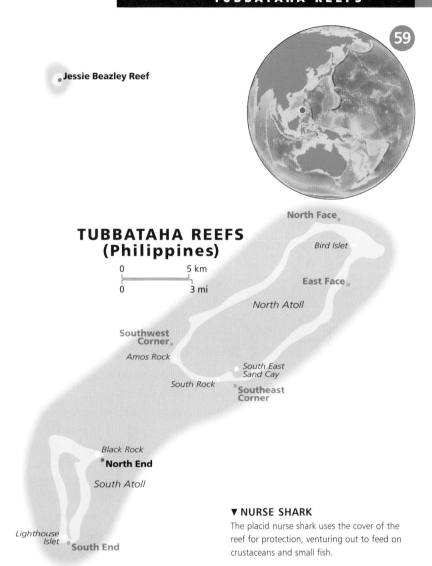

59

Jessie Beazley Reef

TUBBATAHA REEFS
(Philippines)

0   5 km

0   3 mi

North Face

Bird Islet

East Face

North Atoll

Southwest Corner

Amos Rock

South East Sand Cay

South Rock

Southeast Corner

Black Rock
North End

South Atoll

Lighthouse Islet

South End

▼ NURSE SHARK
The placid nurse shark uses the cover of the reef for protection, venturing out to feed on crustaceans and small fish.

John Bantin

► **ZEBRA CRABS**

With 396 recorded species of coral, and 415 fish species, Tubbataha Reefs marine diversity is astounding.

Tony White

 DIVE CENTERS

REEF & RAINFOREST DIVE AND
ADVENTURE TRAVEL

400 Harbor Drive Suite D, Sausalito,
CA 94965, U.S.A.

Phone: +1-415-289-1760

E-mail: info@reefrainforest.com

Web: www.reefrainforest.com

DIVE BUDDIES DIVE CENTER

G/F Robelle Mansion Bldg., 877 J.P. Rizal St.,
1200 Makati City, Philippines

Phone: +63-2-899-7388

E-mail: center@divephil.com

Web: www.divephil.com

 DIVING ORGANIZATIONS

The diving activities around the reefs are monitored by the Tubbataha Project of the W.W.F. See below for contact details.

 RECOMPRESSION

Armed Forces of the Philippines (A.F.P.)
Medical Center

V. Luna Road, Quezon City, Philippines

Phone: +63-2-920-7183

Contact: Jojo R. Bernardo, M.D.

✚ **HOSPITAL**

Palawan Adventist Hospital

P.O. Box 94, San Pedro,

5300 Puerto Princessa City, Philippines

Phone: +63-48-433-2244

 CONSERVATION SOCIETY

Tubbataha Project

W.W.F.-Philippines, 57 Kalayaan Ave.,
LBI Building, 1101 Diliman,
Quezon City, Philippines

Phone:+63-48-434-4156 (Puerto Princessa)

E-mail: mariveld@mozcom.com

U.N.E.S.C.O. provide information on the reef system (a World Heritage Site) at:

Web: www.unesco.org

OTHER DIVE SITES

North Face

East Face

Southwest Corner

Southeast Corner

South End

---

work of the resident rangers and the conservancy boats that patrol the waters frequently.

The unique nature of these reefs is acknowledged in the fact that they were established in Philippine law as a Marine Reserve in 1988. Perhaps even more significantly, the reefs were recognized by U.N.E.S.C.O. as a World Heritage Site in 1993, one of only three in the Philippines. Both anecdotal and scientific evidence suggests that since the inception of the system of zoned protection areas throughout the 82,037 acres (33,200 ha) of the reserve, there has been a notable recovery in the marine life of the reefs, which now appears to be in excellent condition. In 2000 a total of P1.6 million (U.S.$28,445) was collected from visiting divers, helping to fund the conservation effort.

A survey carried out in 2001 recorded 396 species of coral and 415 fish species (although the latter is almost certainly an underestimate.) There are also 6 species of marine mammals, while two species of turtle are known to nest on the islands. Add to this the 7 species of marine plants and 71 of algae that have been recorded here, and the 23 species of seabirds that hunt in the shallows and roost on the sandbars and islands, and you begin to form an idea of the marvelous diversity of these reefs.

The reefs themselves have two very different characters, with smaller animals and juvenile species concentrated on the shallow reef tops, and big pelagics cruising off reef walls crowded with coral fish species. The reef walls themselves are a mass of sponges, soft and hard corals, gorgonians, and hydroids. Caves in the drop-offs shelter sleeping nurse and white tip reef sharks, while close into the walls angelfish, butterfly fish and moorish idols vie and jostle for position. These are hectic, crowded, healthy reef systems, and divers will find the full gamut of animals, big and small, present at most of the dive sites.

THE DIVES

All diving at Tubbataha Reefs is from liveaboards, and there is a relatively narrow window of opportunity to visit the islands because of their considerable distance from viable ports in the Philippines. Most operators visit the islands from Manila, Puerto Princessa, or Cebu City, and make the trip with any reliable consistency only from March through to June.

In broad terms, the shallow reef tops are good snorkeling areas with some shallow dives, but the real action is on the drop-offs and walls around the islands. One of the better-known dives—Jessie Beazley Reef—is actually 14 miles (22 km) north west of the island group, a considerable distance.

The precipitous drop-offs around Tubbataha Reefs are swept by strong currents and play host to magnificent animals in crystal visibility. This is a potent combination in safety terms, and it is easy to lose a sense of depth and time. It is a long haul back to the nearest chamber, so caution should be the order of the day.

NORTH END

• 50 to 120 feet (15 to 36 m) • intermediate

There is a white sandy slope at the start of this dive that leads down to some large coral heads at 50 feet (15 m.) Amongst the gullies and sandy run-offs there are guitar sharks and blue spotted lagoon rays, and it is occasionally possible to see young mantas in this region. Look in the smaller holes for redtooth triggerfish.

The wall itself is truly spectacular, with numerous

grooves, small caverns, and overhangs. Look out for huge numbers of sabre squirrelfish, black and white snappers, and spotted squirrelfish nestling beneath coral outcrops. The wall itself is a mass of sponges and gorgonians with black coral also present. Up close look out for some exquisite hawkfish. Out in mid water there is every chance of seeing some huge mantas, tuna, trevallies, napoleon wrasses, and sharks.

JESSIE BEAZLEY REEF

• **30 to 130 feet (9 to 40 m) • advanced**

Essentially a massive pillar of coral that rises from deep water to just below the surface, the top of this reef is a small green patch below the water's surface. It is not a large reef and can be circumnavigated in its shallower sections in a single dive. However, it is in the reef's precipitous deeper walls and dark overhangs that the action really happens.

The walls are a colorful mass of sponges, sea whips, soft and hard corals, and gorgonians. Royal, emperor,

and yellowmask angelfish swarm over the reef, dotted among multicolored schools of dusky and racoon butterflyfish. Large groupers drift and hide in the many small caverns in the reef, while off the walls schools of jack and barracuda seem ever present. Eagle and manta rays add to the mix.

OTHER ACTIVITIES

This is very much a site for divers. Unless you happen to be an avid bird watcher, it is probably best to remain on the main island of Palawan!

☎ **TELEPHONE NUMBERS**

Recompression chamber	+63-2-920-7183
Hospital	+63-48-433-2558

🖥 **WEBSITES & E-MAIL**

Philippines Government	www.tourism.gov.ph
Philippine Tourist Authority	www.philtourism.com
Palawan Visitors Authority	www.palawan.com

▼ **FEATHERSTARS**

Multi-colored featherstars secrete a mucus slime that traps planktonic organisms carried on the currents.

John Bantin

LAYANG LAYANG

words by JP Trenque

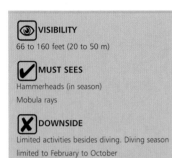

VISIBILITY
66 to 160 feet (20 to 50 m)

MUST SEES
Hammerheads (in season)
Mobula rays

DOWNSIDE
Limited activities besides diving. Diving season limited to February to October

GETTING THERE
Three flights a week from Kota Kinabalu (Terminal 2) to Layang Layang. There is a 25kg (55-pound) luggage allowance on the flight from KK to Layang-Layang but storage can be arranged on the mainland for non-essential baggage items.

Daily flights to Kota Kinabalu with Air Asia, Malaysia Airlines and Royal Brunei.

VISA
None required

MONEY
Malaysian Ringgit
Payments by credit card are accepted.

RISING FROM THE ABYSS IN AN AREA WHERE THE DEPTH AVERAGES 6,500 FEET (2,000 M), LAYANG LAYANG IS A HAVEN FOR PELAGICS AND FOR DIVERS KEEN TO ENJOY CLOSE ENCOUNTERS WITH THE SCALLOPED HAMMERHEAD SHARKS KNOWN TO FREQUENT THE ATOLL BETWEEN APRIL AND JUNE.

JP Trenque

WATER TEMPERATURE

°C	°F	°C	°F
30 — — 86		30 — — 86	
20 — **30°C** — 68		20 — **25°C** — 68	
10 — **86°F** — 50		10 — **77°F** — 50	
0 — — 32		0 — — 32	
Summer		Winter	

▶ **CLOSE ENCOUNTERS**
A diver enjoys a close encounter with one of the numerous hammerhead nudibranchs.

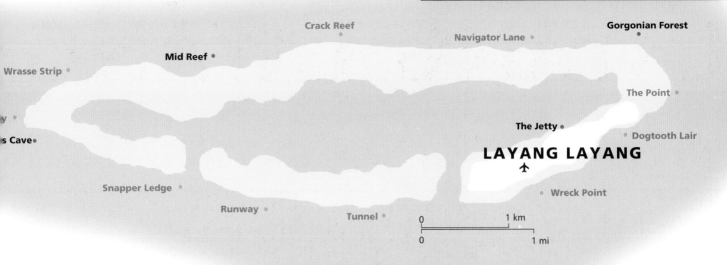

Crack Reef
Navigator Lane
Gorgonian Forest
Mid Reef
Wrasse Strip
The Point
The Jetty
Dogtooth Lair
LAYANG LAYANG
s Cave
Snapper Ledge
Wreck Point
Runway
Tunnel

| 0 | | 1 km |
| 0 | | 1 mi |

N ot many people know about this Malaysian resort. A tiny speck of land off Borneo, it is often overshadowed by the more popular Sipadan, famous for its turtles and action-packed dives in the middle of schooling barracuda and jacks.

The Layang Layang experience starts at Kota Kinabalu airport, where a special flight is chartered several times a week. After a quick weight check where passengers step on the scale with their hand luggage, you board the aging, windowless twin-prop Russian aircraft through the tailgate while your 25 kg (55-pounds) of allowable luggage is secured in nets behind the seats.

GEOGRAPHY

Situated off Malaysian Borneo, nearly 200 miles (320 km) northwest of Sabah's capital known affectionately as KK, the island is part of a 5-square-mile (13 sq km) atoll made up of 13 coral reefs in an area called the Spratly Islands. The Spratly archipelago's ownership is disputed by several nations including China, Taiwan, Vietnam and the Philippines, which have all shown an interest in the rich oil reserves discovered in the late 1960s. Brunei has also established an exclusive fishing zone in the south. Swallow Reef—the international name for Layang Layang—has allowed Malaysia to stake its claim on a small section of the Spratlys.

The Layang Layang Island Resort was built on an island that was practically manmade by the Malaysian government when it connected two isolated reefs. It shares the highly strategic piece of land with a Malaysian navy base (built in 1983) that is sensibly offlimits to the tourists (despite the absence of a fence).

Being close to the equator, the region enjoys year-round warm temperatures, with a rainy season around Christmas. Layang Layang Island Resort is closed during the monsoon season between November and January.

MARINE LIFE

Many divers travel to Layang Layang to swim with the scalloped hammerhead sharks that hang around the atoll predominantly between April and June. While one would be rather unlucky not to come across at least one shark during a weekly stay during that period, it would be a mistake to choose the destination solely for the purpose as there is so much more to see.

There are schools of mobula rays, often described as a miniature version of manta rays, and sizeable healthy barrel sponges and corals smothering the rock and teeming with life in an explosion of colors. Resting on

60

▼ **PRETTY BOY**
As they rest on top of coral heads, ringeye hawkfish are a photographer's dream model.

JP Trenque

JP Trenque

▲ BEWARE OF THE LION

Elegant lionfish are very succesful predators as they slowly patrol the reef.

DIVE CENTERS

Layang Layang Dive Center is the only operator on the island.

DIVING ORGANIZATIONS

PPADI, NAUI

RECOMPRESSION

Labuan Pejabat Selam
Markas Wilayah
Laut Dua, 87007
Labuan
Phone: +60-87-412-122

HOSPITAL

Queen Elizabeth Hospital
Karung Berkunci No 2029
88586 Kota Kinabalu
Sabah
Phone: +60-88-517-555

top of coral heads and moving very little, inquisitive ringeye hawkfish are a photographer's dream model.

Other sedentary critters such as pygmy seahorses are masters of disguise and prove to be a lot more difficult to spot, let alone photograph, as they blend with their fan coral host. Nudibranch aficionados are rewarded by an abundance of hammerhead nudibranchs.

Predators such as lionfish are present in significant numbers and territorial triggerfish are often seen ambushing divers who inadvertently venture too close to their nests.

Less visited, the lagoon area close to the dive center's jetty is also rich in critter life and is well worth a few shore dives. Care must be taken, however, not to disturb the fine sand or the visibility will quickly be impaired. To maximize chances of spotting small animals it is well worth going with a dive guide whose trained eye will save a lot of critter-hunting time.

THE DIVES

Three daily boat dives are arranged in boatloads of about 10 to 12 guests. The sites are organized by the staff so that each group can have the reef to itself. To prevent overcrowding at the dive center, briefing session and boat departure times are staggered.

Although Layang Layang is great for wall dives and pelagic sightings, currents can occasionally be strong

and some of the sites should be considered as advanced. To make the most of their stay, beginner divers would be wise to gain experience on drift dives and practice their buoyancy skills.

A dozen dive sites are located outside the lagoon where the visibility is often excellent. They are usually reached after a 5 to 10 minute boat ride and the farthest ones take about 15 minutes to reach. The water ranges from 26 to 30°C (79 to 86°F), but with a thermocline on some sites that can reduce the temperature by some 20 percent. In addition to the boat dives and while not considered a dive site per se, the jetty next to the dive center is a magnet for critter life often favored by underwater photographers.

GORGONIAN FOREST

• 130 feet (40 m) • advanced

An ideal morning dive for experienced divers, Gorgonian Forest offers the chance of hammerhead shark encounters in season. It is best to start the dive swimming away from the reef and drift gently with the current for a few minutes as barracuda and tuna often patrol in the blue. It is easy to get disoriented as the reef fades away in the distance and care must be taken not to drop too deep.

Heading back toward the reef, it's easy to understand why this site was given its name, as the wall is covered in sea fans displaying their warm colors from a depth of about 50 to 130+ feet (15 to 40+ m). Reef life is abundant among the soft corals with sweetlips, groupers and myriad colorful fishes darting among the giant barrel sponges.

SHARK'S CAVE 1

• 100 feet (30 m) • intermediate

One of the furthest sites, Shark's Cave is reached after a 15-minute boat journey across the lagoon. More an overhang than an actual cave, this site is a good place to find resting leopard sharks, whitetip reef sharks or rays lying on the sand at about 100 feet (30 m). Although they are easily spooked, it is possible to get relatively close to them by moving very slowly.

Further up near the ceiling, various species of smaller fish can often be seen schooling. On the sheer wall outside the cave, the soft corals are worth a close inspection, with gorgonian fans and black coral often hiding interesting marine creatures such as lionfish. The dive finishes on a shallow plateau covered in hard corals.

MID REEF

• 130 feet (40 m) • advanced

Mid Reef is not as well known as other sites around the lagoon. Many dives in Layang Layang start with a quick exploration in the blue away from the wall, and this one is no exception as schooling devil rays can often be encountered at any depth.

Back on the reef, the staghorn corals offer shelter to a variety of colorful fish, the most popular of which is possibly the ringeye hawkfish with its characteristic horseshoe mark behind the eye. Several varieties of clownfish, including the bridled anemonefish, are also found there, hiding in their host anemone.

THE JETTY

• 16 feet (5 m) • beginner

Accessible by walking down the steps at the dive center, the sandy area around the jetty is a prolific site for macro photographers who could easily spend a couple of hours in depths of no more than 10 to 16 feet (3 to 5 m). Although the visibility is somewhat reduced owing to the fine sand particles in suspension, it is possible to spend a great deal of time here watching silversides, conchs, clams, upside-down jellyfish and a whole array of strange-looking critters as they go about their daily routine.

Aside from the jetty, a few rocks and manmade objects litter the seabed and provide a habitat for various species of gobies. Small patches of sea grass may also hide camouflaged animals.

OTHER ACTIVITIES

There is little to do at the resort besides scubadiving, chilling out by the pool or watching the colony of seabirds that have taken residence on a rock at the end of the runway. Back on the mainland though, northeast Borneo has a lot to offer, such as treks up Mount Kinabalu or rain forest walks around KK. Venturing further, the town of Sandakan is only a short flight away where the Sepilok Orang-utan Sanctuary is worth spending half a day. Wildlife amateurs will also enjoy boat trips up the Kinabatangan River to see proboscis monkeys, famous for their long noses, or visit the Gomantong Caves where edible bird nests are harvested.

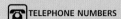

TELEPHONE NUMBERS

Recompression chamber	+60-87-412-122
Hospital	+60-88-517-555

▼ **SCHOOL'S OUT**
Schools of pelagic and reef fish can be seen on most sites.

SIPADAN
ISLAND

FIRST MADE FAMOUS BY JACQUES COUSTEAU, TINY SIPADAN ISLAND HAS BECOME A LEGEND IN THE WORLD OF DIVING. CHIEF DRAWS ARE THE BARRELING SHOALS OF BARRACUDA AND HUGE NUMBERS OF TURTLES THAT SWARM AROUND THIS BEACON OF LIFE ARISING FROM THE DEPTHS OF THE CELEBES SEA.

 VISIBILITY
60 to 130 feet (18 to 40 m) plus

 MUST SEES
Green turtles
Barracuda and jack shoals

 DOWNSIDE
Remote
Nothing for non-divers

 GETTING THERE
International flights to Kuala Lumpur and Kota Kinabalu, overnight and then fly to Tawau. Two-hour bus ride to Sêmporna, then an hour's ferry-ride to Sipadan.

 VISA
U.S., Commonwealth, and most European citizens do not need visas for visits of less than 3 months. Visitors are usually issued an extendable 30 or 60-day visa on arrival.

 MONEY
Currency is the ringgit. U.S. dollars are accepted everywhere.

It is fair to say that Jacques Cousteau knew a good dive site when he found one. After anchoring his research ship *Calypso* off Sipadan and exploring the waters around the island, the great man was moved to remark "I have seen other places like Sipadan…45 years ago. Now again we have found an untouched piece of art." Unfortunately, so too have many thousands of divers, and more than 20 years later Sipadan is feeling the impact of relentless diver traffic.

The upside is that the presence of so many divers has brought an end to dynamite-fishing and gill netting around the reefs. However, the unavoidable downside is broken coral and harassed marine life.

The Malaysian government now sets limits on diver numbers, and several of the more reputable operators have made commendable efforts to put in place a code of practice that it is hoped will reap rewards. This has also lead to a number of operators closing down.

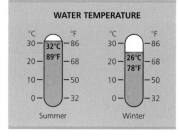
WATER TEMPERATURE

	Summer		Winter	
°C		°F	°C	°F
30		86	30	86
	32°C / 89°F		26°C / 78°F	
20		68	20	68
10		50	10	50
0		32	0	32

Jane Morgan

▶ **TURTLE HEAVEN**
Sipadan's healthy turtle populations ensure encounters on virtually every dive.

Monty Halls

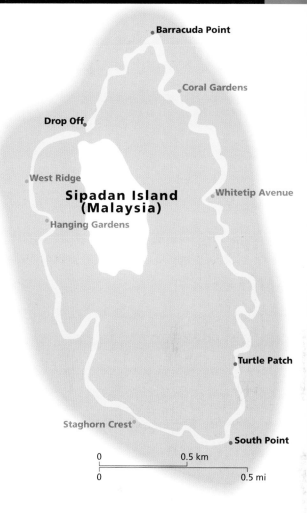

Barracuda Point

Coral Gardens

Drop Off

West Ridge

**Sipadan Island
(Malaysia)**

Whitetip Avenue

Hanging Gardens

Turtle Patch

Staghorn Crest

South Point

0   0.5 km

0   0.5 mi

▲ BARRACUDA

Barracuda Point plays host to large schools of barracuda.

GEOGRAPHY

Sipadan is a tiny 34-acre (14-ha) island some 22 miles (35 km) off the coast of Sabah, Malaysia, in the northeast corner of Borneo. The island sits on top of a lozenge-shaped reef in the Celebes Sea, a massive basin that plunges to depths of more than 4 miles (6 km) at its deepest point. Sipadan is Malaysia's only oceanic island, arising from the abyssal depths 7 miles (11 km) south of the continental shelf, and is the top of an ancient volcano.

The shallow reef surrounding the island is not large, covering approximately six times the area of the island itself. At one point to the north of the island, the wall of the reef actually touches the shoreline, so the diver can step off the land, walk several steps, and swim into water more than 2,000 feet (610 m) deep.

MARINE LIFE

More than 3,000 separate fish and coral species have been recorded on the reefs of Sipadan, making it one of the most diverse marine ecosystems on Earth. But Sipadan is particularly well known for green turtles,

and surely has some claim to be the turtle capital of the diving world. All year round the waters around the island witness nearly every stage in the life cycle of these animals, with baby turtles swimming furiously for the open ocean and adults coming on shore to create the next generation. It is forbidden to walk on the beaches at night during this period when the hatchlings are making their perilous journeys down to the surf line and the tracks of nesting turtles criss-cross the white sand in the morning light. Such huge populations of hatchling turtles support a network of predators, with large numbers of white tip reef sharks zooming in to enjoy the feeding bonanza. Hawksbill turtles are also found around the island.

Among Sipadan's enduring features are two massive shoals of fish—one of barracuda and one of jack—that appear to be always present somewhere around the reef. Indeed, the first of these has given its name to one of the best-known dives in Sipadan, Barracuda Point, although the shoal is frequently on the move and may or may not be present at the point itself. Mantas, eagle rays, reef sharks, leopard sharks, and hammerheads are also in attendance.

To concentrate only on such larger attractions is to ignore the exceptional life on the reefs themselves.

61

▶ **BIGEYE TREVALLY**

Huge shoals of trevally are a constant feature around Sipadan.

 DIVE CENTERS

BORNEO DIVERS & SEA SPORTS

(K.L.) Sdn. Bhd. (Co. No. 309257-H), 115M
Jalan SS21/37, Damansara Utama, 47400,
Petaling Jaya, Malaysia
Phone: +60-88-222226
E-mail: informationl@borneodivers.info
Web: www.borneodiverskl.com

 DIVING ORGANIZATIONS

There is a Sipadan Resort Operators Consortium which can be contacted through Borneo Divers. See above.

 RECOMPRESSION

The nearest major hyperbaric center is at:
Republic of Singapore Navy
AFPN 6060, 36 Admiralty Rd. W,
Singapore 759960, Singapore
Can be contacted through Borneo Divers. See above.

There is also a chamber on the island itself.
Contact Borneo Divers for more details:
Phone: +60-377-273-066

 HOSPITAL

Queen Elizabeth Hospital, Beg Berkunci 2026
Kota Kinabalu, 88586 Malaysia
Phone: +60-88-517555

CONSERVATION SOCIETY

The island is covered by government legislation and is a marine reserve. The authority for these reserves is:

Department of Wildlife and National Parks
Peninsular Malaysia
Km. 10, Jln. Cheras, 56100, Kuala Lumpur,
Malaysia
Phone: +60-390-752-872
Web: www.wildlife.gov.my

OTHER DIVE SITES

Coral Gardens
Whitetip Avenue
Staghorn Crest
Hanging Gardens
West Ridge

Linda Pitkin

There are delicate leaf fish, gorgonian fans, huge barrel sponges, and several exquisite nudibranch species.

THE DIVES

No dive on Sipadan is more than a 10-minute boat-ride away, and this is one of the joys of the island. But this concentration of dive sites comes with a down-side—there are many stories of turtles suffering injury from speeding boats and of coral being damaged by clumsy divers. Examples of this are most obviously found on the reef shelf, some areas of which come close to resembling the dynamited reefs found farther north. Although the local operators insist that this damage is the result of severe weather, there appears to be some evidence that the steady flow of heavy diver traffic over this area is having severe impact on the reef and its inhabitants.

The island enjoys a reputation for having access to some easy diving with limited currents, although there are certainly brisk currents and upwellings off the walls. Suffice it to say that the diving off Sipadan is the last word in convenient sites, offering short boat rides to precipitous walls, or shore dives over shallow reefs leading to steep drop-offs.

The present quota of divers is 14 per operator, and there are moves afoot to limit diver numbers further. However, these regulations do not take into account operators working from adjacent islands, and numbers are difficult to monitor anyway. Diver pressure remains intense off Sipadan.

SOUTH POINT

• **70 feet (21 m)** • **intermediate**

South Point is one site in Sipadan where the current really does flow, being the sloping shoulders of the reef shelf leading to a precipitous drop-off. The notable feature of this reef shelf is the perpetual lurking presence above it of two massive shoals of barracuda and jack. The shelf varies between 15 and 70 feet (5 and 21 m) in depth, although the deeper reef terraces, and of course the drop-off itself, take the diver deeper still. The current is fairly unpredictable here, splitting and flowing in different directions on different days.

There are overwhelming sights to be seen in the blue of the open ocean next to the reef wall where mantas regularly cruise and green and hawksbill turtles rise slowly from the deep toward the island. But do not forget to make time to observe the smaller members of the reef community tucked away in the jumbled coral, sponges, and gorgonians. Look out for some of the 9 species of clownfish that live around Sipadan, as well as scorpionfish, leaf fish, and octopuses on the shoulder of the reef itself.

BARRACUDA POINT

• **50 to 130 feet (15 to 40 m)** • **intermediate**

The other dive on Sipadan that is a must see, it owes its name to the massive school of chevron barracuda that seems to be a permanent feature of this site. Sadly, the steady stream of divers is having a deleterious effect judging from the amount of broken coral apparent on the reef shelf, but nonetheless Barracuda Point remains a classic dive.

The dive is located on the northern edge of the island next to Borneo Divers' base. After descending the wall at this point, the diver moves onto a gentler slope at about 50 feet (15 m), the location of the only eel garden in the whole of Sipadan. Look out for large crocodile fish here, as well as leaf fish and nudibranchs. Currents can be significant on this dive, and may be strong enough to carry divers off the reef, so careful pre-planning and briefing is required.

Deeper still, in the region of 110 to 130 feet (34 to 40 m), it is sometimes possible to encounter huge schools of big eye trevally and barracuda. Gray and white tip reef sharks are a permanent feature of this site, as well as some hefty groupers and, of course, green turtles at the right time of year.

Several other dives in Sipadan have achieved similar cult status to these two, including Turtle Patch and Drop Off. Each of them offers divers the classic Sipadan experience—big walls, big animals, and busy reefs.

OTHER ACTIVITIES

Sipadan is unequivocally a divers' haven, although there are some watersports facilities available for non-divers. Both the nearby islands of Mabul and Kapalai are worth a visit on a degassing day, but really any diver in Sipadan wants to optimize his or her dive time! The Mabul Island resort offers a range of alternative activities including fishing and organized beach activities.

Sipadan suffered bad publicity after the kidnapping of 21 tourists and staff members from the island made international headlines in April 2000. Since then, the Malaysian authorities have placed an almost permanent military presence on Sipadan. Divers who have visited the island since the incident report that the security is excellent and they have felt perfectly safe, so there seems to be no reason to be deterred.

☎ **TELEPHONE NUMBERS**

Recompression chamber	+60-377-273-066
Hospital	+60-88-218-166

🖥 **WEBSITES & E-MAIL**

Tourism Malaysia	www.tourism.gov.my
Sabah Tourism	www.sabahtourism.com

▼ **CLOWNFISH**
In addition to larger pelagic attractions Sipadan's reefs have much to offer by the way of colorful marine life.

Mikayo Langhofer

EASTERN FIELDS & KIMBE BAY

ONE OF THE LAST TRULY WILD DIVING DESTINATIONS LEFT TO EXPLORE, PAPUA NEW GUINEA OFFERS SOMETHING UNIQUE ON EVERY VISIT—STEEP WALLS, WRECKS, LAGOONS, BIG ANIMALS—AND ALL IN A VAST EXPANSE OF THE MOST SPECIES-RICH SEAS ON THE PLANET.

 VISIBILITY

From 50 feet (15 m) in Milne Bay to 165 feet (50 m) in Eastern Fields

 MUST SEES

Diverse reefs

Smaller rare fish species

☒ DOWNSIDE

Remote

Limited tourist infrastructure

Expensive

✈ GETTING THERE

Visitors fly into Port Moresby, the largest international gateway, from Australia. There are also connections with Singapore, Manila, (Philippines), and other Pacific countries. A new international airport has opened at Alotau (Milne Bay Province). The departure tax is about U.S.$7. Air Niugini, the national airline, operates a number of domestic flights—the easiest way to get around the islands given the limited infrastructure.

 VISA

Although you can obtain a visa on arrival for a maximum stay of 60 days in any 12 months, it is wisest to obtain one in advance. Overstaying the period of the visa leads to steep fines on departure.

$ MONEY

Currency is the kina. Most traveler's checks will be accepted.

Papua New Guinea (usually referred to as P.N.G.) was the last great diving frontier to open up to the outside world. Even today, visits to these islands have a pioneering feel to them, with wild reefs set against a backdrop of uninhabited shorelines where precipitous mountains cloaked in rainforest plunge into the sea. There are opportunities here to encounter species that are genuinely new to science or exquisitely rare. Much of the beauty of diving in Papua New Guinea is provided by the tiny creatures of the reefs. This has given rise to the practice of "muck" diving—the investigation of relatively featureless sites made fascinating by the abundance of smaller inhabitants. The islands and their dive sites, especially Eastern Fields and Kimbe Bay, have something special for every diver. Many of those who visit P.N.G. rate it as the greatest diving experience of their lives.

▼ WAITING IN AMBUSH

This small grouper lies in ambush within a reef crevice, watchful for passing baitfish.

Dan Burton

WATER TEMPERATURE

°C	°F		°C	°F
30 —	— 86		30 —	— 86
20 —	— 68		20 —	— 68
29°C			**24°C**	
84°F			**75°F**	
10 —	— 50		10 —	— 50
0 —	— 32		0 —	— 32
Summer			Winter	

Karkar Island

Madang

Long Island

Umboi

Lama Shoal

Kimbe Bay

Rabaul

New Britain

Lae

PAPUA NEW GUINEA

Kiriwina Island

Goodenough Island

D'Entrecasteaux Islands

Fergusson Island

PORT MORESBY

Tufi

Observation Point

Normanby Island

Eastern Fields

Alotau

Banana Bommie

Milne Bay

0   120 km

0   80 mi

GEOGRAPHY

The main territory of Papua New Guinea occupies the eastern half of the island of New Guinea, and lies immediately off the northeastern tip of Australia. Port Moresby , the capital, is a mere 130 miles (209 km) from the Australian mainland. P.N.G. also has more than 600 islands spread over 289,275 sq miles (748,933 sq km) of ocean. Eastern Fields are reefs in the Gulf of Papua southwest of Port Moresby, and Kimbe Bay is a large inlet on the north coast of New Britain in the Bismarck Archipelago.

More than 70 percent of P.N.G.'s land area is still covered in rainforest, including the highest peak of Mount Wilhelm at 14,970 feet (4,563 m). Some 75 percent of the population of just over 5 million are subsistence farmers. The majority live in the remote Central Highlands and are divided into 1,000 tribes speaking 700 languages. This really is an ancient land where true exploration is still possible both above and below the sea.

MARINE LIFE

Papua New Guinea lies within what biologists term the "Triangle of Diversity" or the "Coral Triangle", an area of the Pacific Ocean widely regarded as having the greatest diversity of coral and fish species on Earth. Kimbe Bay alone is home to at least 860 species of reef fish and 360 species of coral. As there are more than 15,444 sq miles (40,000 sq km) of coral reefs along P.N.G.'s coastline, much of this array of life remains unexplored, one of the great attractions of diving in this remote region.

To study the extraordinary range of life inhabiting the reefs, seagrass beds, and mudflats of P.N.G.'s coastline, divers there developed "muck diving", a diving technique that involves exploring the silty or sandy bottom beneath an anchored liveaboard boat. Among the small, well-camouflaged inhabitants revealed by "muck diving" are leaf fish, some remarkable examples of colorful scorpionfish, mantis shrimps, beautiful mandarin fish, and several species of sea horse and pipefish. A startling demonstration of the richness of P.N.G.'s reefs was the discovery (albeit in deeper water) of a new species of sea horse—the pygmy sea horse—as recently as 1997. Reaching a maximum size of only 0.8 inch (2 cm), this tiny animal disguises itself in the gorgonian which is its home. It was found through the persistent efforts of two researchers, Kim and Alan Payard.

Papua New Guinea is also famous for its larger residents, including some stunning gatherings of scalloped hammerheads and the altogether more menacing silver tip sharks. Whale sharks and mantas are also frequently sighted at certain sites, as well as a number of species of dolphins and whales.

▲ B17 BOMBER

Papua New Guinea has some tremendous World War II wrecks to explore.

OTHER DIVE SITES

Banana Bommie
Lama Shoal

62

DIVE CENTERS

MADANG RESORT HOTEL & NIUGINI DIVING
ADVENTURES
P.O. Box 707, Madang, Papua New Guinea
Phone: +675-854-1300
E-mail: melanesian@mtspng.com
Web: www.meltours.com

M.V. GOLDEN DAWN
P.O. Box 1335, Port Moresby, N.C.D.,
Papua New Guinea
Phone: +675-325-6500
E-mail: enquiry@mvgoldendawn.com
Web: www.mvgoldendawn.com

WALINDI PLANTATION RESORT
& M.V. FEBRINA
P.O. Box 4, Kimbe, W.N.B.P.,
Papua New Guinea
Phone: +675-983-5441
E-mail: info@walindi.com
Email: info@febrina.com
Web: www.walindi.com
Web: www.febrina.com

DIVING ORGANIZATIONS

Papua New Guinea Divers' Association
P.O. Box 1646, Port Moresby, N.C.D. 121,
Papua New Guinea
Phone: +675-320-0211
E-mail: info@pngdive.com
Web: www.pngdive.com

RECOMPRESSION

Melanesian Hyperbaric Services
Jackson's Airport, Port Moresby,
Papua New Guinea
Phone: +675-693-0305
E-mail: peter@walindi.com

HOSPITAL

Port Moresby General Hospital
Taurama Road, Boroko, Port Moresby,
Papua New Guinea
Phone: +675-324-8200
Papua New Guinea

Alotau Hospital
Alotau, Milne Bay, Papua New Guinea
Phone: +675-641-1200
E-mail: alotaugh@daltron.com.pg

CONSERVATION SOCIETY

The Nature Conservancy runs a number of
projects in Papua New Guinea:
The Nature Conservancy
4245 North Fairfax Drive, Suite 100,
Arlington, VA 22203-1606, U.S.A.
Phone: +1-703-841-5300
E-mail: comment@tnc.org
Web: nature.org/contactus/

▶ **MANTA RAY**
Papua New Guinea's reputation for
regular encounters with large ocean going
species is well deserved.

THE DIVES

Diving in Papua New Guinea. is notable for the range of dives on offer, with steep walls, shallow lagoons, busy channels, and some tremendous World War II wrecks. It also remains relatively remote, so the sites tend to be quiet, although the diving infrastructure has become well established over the last 20 years.

Eastern Fields has the best wild diving in the region. It takes place on pristine reefs, where divers are almost virtually guaranteed encounters with some impressive pelagic species. Kimbe Bay has sheltered lagoons that create areas rich in juvenile fish species and delicate coral formations. The best W.W. II wrecks in P.N.G. are found at Rabaul on the northeast end of New Britain; they have survived the huge volcanic eruptions that rocked the area and destroyed the town in September 1994.

One of the great attractions for divers in P.N.G. is the proximity of deep water to shore, some of the best sites for this being along the northern coast and areas around Milne Bay on New Guinea. Day trips can be organized from Port Moresby to many of the dive sites on the southern coast, and a well-established diving infrastructure exists at Milne Bay, on the island's extreme southeast tip. However, if you want to explore the islands fully, you should investigate options with liveaboards—although they are more expensive, they are the only way of accessing some of P.N.G.'s truly unexplored remote areas.

EASTERN FIELDS

· 60 to 130 feet (18 to 40 m) · advanced

One site that can only be accessed on liveaboards is Eastern Fields, located approximately 120 miles (193 km) southwest of Port Moresby, which possesses some of the most unspoiled reefs on Papua New Guinea's south coast. The diver who makes the long trip to these remote reefs won't regret it—they really are worth the trip!

Eastern Fields is a classic submerged atoll that covers an area of about 60 sq miles (155 sq km) and rises from deep clear water. Currents can be strong here, bringing water rich in nutrients but demanding good buoyancy skills from divers as the racing water

Kevin Davidson

Linda Pitkin

can be rather unforgiving. This is particularly true of the channels and cuts in the atoll ring, which are the site of some of the best dives.

Although a number of individual sites within Eastern Fields have achieved cult status, in broad terms the atoll offers divers guaranteed encounters with a number of shark species—including wobbegongs and hammerheads—as well as opportunities to explore craggy reef walls split by overhangs, channels, gulleys, and swimthroughs. Off the reef wall are huge schools of jacks and barracuda, together with some large groupers and napoleon wrasses. The reefs themselves are a bewildering combination of huge barrel sponges, sea whips, gorgonians, and brightly colored crinoids.

KIMBE BAY

• 10 to 130 feet (3 to 40 m) • beginner to advanced

A huge sheltered bay offering the full gamut of diving experiences. There are nearly 200 recognized dive sites in the bay, providing a range of dives from gentle drifts to epic pelagic encounters with resident dolphin and shark populations. Most diving is done at the western end of the bay where, unusually for Papua New Guinea, there is some distinctly luxurious land-based accommodation available.

MILNE BAY

• 20 to 130 feet (6 to 40 m) • beginner to advanced

Another area offering an excellent array of options for the diver all the way from racing drifts over shallow reefs to steep drop-offs patrolled by hammerheads through to one of the most active manta cleaning stations in the Pacific. Observation Point offers some great opportunities for classic muck diving, whereas Veale Reef has splendid steep walls coated in large hard coral formations and patrolled by tuna, eagle rays, and sharks. There are also some great World War II wrecks to explore in Tufi, including two torpedo boats and a B17 bomber.

OTHER ACTIVITIES

Port Moresby is not recommended as a casual tourist venue. Social problems and unrest have led to a culture of violence and crime in many areas of the city, and it is best avoided completely. Some other urban centers in the Highlands are also reported to be somewhat risky for the traveler. Nonetheless there are some wonderful parks close to Port Moresby including the Varirata National Park, and if the traveler is prepared to rough it off the beaten track, the Central Highlands and the outlying islands are truly fascinating. The species diversity of the reefs is reflected on land, and a number of trekking and cruising operations exist to take visitors around the islands.

☎ TELEPHONE NUMBERS

| Recompression chamber | +675-693-0305 |
| Hospital | +675-324-8200 |

🖥 WEBSITES & E-MAIL

| Travel information | www.diversionoz.com |
| Papua New Guinea Tourism | www.pngbd.com |

▲ BIG-EYED TREVALLY

Huge schools of big-eyed trevally, jack, and barracuda patrol between the reef walls and the open ocean.

GIZO & UEPI ISLANDS

THE SOLOMONS ARE NOTED FOR THEIR HUGE ARRAY OF WORLD WAR II WRECKS BUT THE ISLANDS' BUSTLING REEFS ALSO OFFER DIVES OF OUTSTANDING QUALITY, AND THEY ARE FAST BECOMING ONE OF THE ESSENTIAL DESTINATIONS FOR THE MODERN ADVENTURE DIVER.

 VISIBILITY

Can be affected by run-off from the land, particularly in areas where logging occurs. Offshore 130 feet (40 m.)

 MUST SEES

Tao Maru
Big pelagics

 DOWNSIDE

Remote
Limited tourist infrastructure

 GETTING THERE

The small number of international flights connecting directly to the Solomons is part of its charm for the adventurous diver. The international airport, Henderson, is 7 miles (11 km) east of the capital, Honiara, on Guadacanal. It is tiny, but is due to be upgraded. Regular flights depart from Brisbane, Australia (three flights a week) and a small number of South Pacific Islands. There is a U.S.$8.50 airport tax payable on arrival.

 VISAS

Visitors planning to stay less than 3 months don't require entry visas.

 MONEY

Currency is the Solomon Islands dollar. Branches of the main bank (N.B.S.I.) are available at fifty locations around the islands. Traveler's checks and credit cards accepted in towns and by most of the larger operators.

WATER TEMPERATURE

°C	°F		°C	°F
30	86		30	86
28°C				
20 **82°F**	68		20 **23°C**	68
			73°F	
10	50		10	50
0	32		0	32
Summer			Winter	

▶ **WAR WRECK**
The Solomons saw some of the most ferocious fighting in the whole Pacific region during World War II.

Still being developed as a holiday destination, the Solomons are the new frontier of Pacific diving. Starting south of Bougainville Island in the Papua New Guinea archipelago, the chain of rugged islands runs south and east into the Pacific for more than 900 miles (1,450 km.) The history books record that some truly ferocious fighting took place here between Japanese and American troops in 1942–43, resulting in the islands' liberation from Japanese rule. The legacy of the war are the wrecks that dot the sea-bed and reefs of the Solomons in such numbers that one area off Guadacanal is known as Iron Bottom Sound. However, visiting divers today are discovering that the island reefs have just as much to offer as the wrecks.

GEOGRAPHY

The Solomons consist of 6 large islands (Choiseul, New Georgia, Santa Isabel, Guadacanal, Malaita, and Makira) arranged in a double chain. They are volcanic islands, ruggedly mountainous and cloaked in rain-forest. In addition, there are 992 smaller islands, atolls, and reefs. The islands cover a total land area of 18,750 sq miles (48,544 sq km) and are spread over a massive 800,000 sq miles (2,071,200 sq km) of ocean.

This vast area is inhabited by around 509,000 people, mostly subsistence farmers and fishers. Most people live on the large islands of the chain, together with the Shortland Islands in the north. The islanders are predominantly Melanesian in origin, but living in

John Bantin

SOLOMON ISLANDS

0   90 km

0   100 mi

▼ SCORPIONFISH

The scorpionfish has venomous spines in its dorsal fin which can cause intense pain.

Colin Bateman

scattered, isolated communities divided from each other by craggy mountains and wide seas, they have developed a rich cultural diversity, creating a glorious pot pourri of island traditions. More than 100 languages are spoken in the Solomons, with pidgin being the main language of communication.

The dive sites are concentrated in three main areas: off Guadacanal, the largest island in the group; in Morovo Lagoon at the south end of New Georgia, including the tiny island of Uepi; and in the small island group of Gizo, northwest of New Georgia.

MARINE LIFE

The Solomon Islands lie on the eastern edge of the the area of the Pacific known to biologists as the "Triangle of Diversity", as is reflected in its extremely species-rich coral reefs. In the more remote diving sites there is some excellent big pelagic action, with areas such as Gizo playing host to big aggregations of barracuda, an array of shark species including seasonal gatherings of hammerheads, mantas, eagle rays, and even the occasional passing orca.

The Solomon Islanders consume more fish per capita than any other race on Earth. For centuries they have sustainably fished the reefs and lagoons, but now commercial interests are moving in. Tuna fishing is becoming one of the major exports of the Solomons, bringing a significant threat to marine life in many areas.

On the islands themselves, logging is also taking place on an industrial scale, and the run-off of effluent and silt from the large-scale clearance of mountain slopes is beginning to cloud the reefs, particularly in the once pristine Marovo Lagoon.

Tony White

► MANDARIN FISH

The tiny mandarin fish is one of the many residents of the reefs around the Solomons.

DIVE CENTERS
BILIKIKI CRUISES
P.O. Box 656 , Iroquois Falls, Ontario,
POK 1GO, Canada
Phone: +1-705-363-2049
E-mail: bilikiki@bilikik.com
Web: www.bilikiki.com

TROPICAL PARADISE PTY LTD
P.O. Box 149, Mt. Eliza, VIC 3930, Australia
Phone: +61-3-9787-7904
E-mail: info@uepi.com
Web: www.uepi.com

DIVERSION DIVE TRAVEL
P. O. Box 191, Redlynch (Cairns),
QLD 4870, Australia
Phone: +61-7-4039-0200
E-mail: info@DiversionOz.com
Web: www.diversionoz.com

DIVING ORGANIZATIONS
None, although the South Pacific Tourism Organization may be able to provide information on appropriate operators:
South Pacific Tourism Organization,
P.O. Box 13119, Suva, Fiji Islands
Phone: +679-330-4177
Web: www.spto.org

RECOMPRESSION
Melanesian Hyperbaric Services
P. O. Box 111, Jacksons Airport, Port Moresby,
Papua New Guinea
Phone: +675-693-0305
E-mail: peter@walindi.com

HOSPITAL
There is a large hospital in Honiara, and the advice on their website is to contact them should you wish to find out about clinics further afield within the Solomons.

National Referral Hospital
P.O. Box 349
Honiara, Guadalcanal,
Solomon Islands
Phone: +677-2-3600
E-mail: nrh@solomon.com.sb
Web: www.hermannoberli.ch/general_e.htm

CONSERVATION SOCIETY
The World Wildlife Fund Pacific run a series of programs on the Solomons, including terrestrial and marine conservation projects. Their website is at: www.wwfpacific.org.fj/where_we_work/solomons

THE DIVES

Dive operators are centered on the three main diving areas of Guadalcanal, Gizo, and Marovo Lagoon, and there are also a number of liveaboards that cruise to the more remote parts of the archipelago. Local knowledge is a key factor of diving in the Solomons, as the coastline and reefs are very extensive, and the classic sites well spread throughout the archipelago. Significantly, 88 percent of all land and marine resources are owned by local families or clans, a measure of the extent to which the traditional way of life still predominates among the islanders.

There are some severe issues of local politics surrounding the diving off Guadalcanal, and diving activities are periodically suspended as negotiations grind on. Although the area around Guadacanal can be regarded as a mere point of departure to the outer islands or boarding point for liveaboards, there are some dives of genuine quality here. This includes some shallow World War II wrecks easily accessible from shore, and some deeper wrecks penetrable only with technical diving equipment.

Marovo Lagoon and Gizo are less well developed, and are all the more exciting for it. They provide a mix of drop-offs and wrecks, as well as some thumping big pelagic activity.

GIZO

• 20 to 130 feet (6 to 40 m) • beginner to advanced

Gizo is the center of a collection of atolls, reefs, and tiny islands offering an array of diving experiences. Of the numerous wreck sites to be found in the area, perhaps the most famous is the *Tao Maru*, one of the best-preserved wrecks in the Solomons. This 6,700 tonne Japanese merchant vessel lies on her starboard side at depths ranging from 25 to 130 feet (8 to 40 m), and contains an eclectic mix of cargo and personal possessions, from saki bottles to tanks. She is in good condition, and guided penetrations allow a thrilling exploration of a vessel frozen in time.

Gizo is also famed as the spot where future U.S. President John F. Kennedy had his torpedo boat rammed by a Japanese destroyer, resulting in a desperate swim to safety on a small island. This island was, by a happy coincidence, at the head of a magnificent wall, now named the Kennedy Wall. Large shoals of jacks and barracuda patrol the wall as well as reef sharks and the occasional visiting manta.

If the visiting diver is after diversity of fish species combined with big pelagics, a visit to Grand Central Station is a must. Two currents meet at this point, and the drift dive here reveals a cornucopia of groupers, eagle rays, napoleon wrasses, sharks, and mantas moving over some of the busiest reefs in the entire Solomons archipelago.

UEPI ISLAND

• 20 to 130 feet (6 to 40 m) • beginner to advanced

Marovo Lagoon to the south of New Georgia is officially recognized by the World Wildlife Fund as the longest island-protected lagoon on Earth. Uepi Island is located at its southern edge. This is a seriously remote location, 6 miles (10 km) from the nearest village and 100 miles (160 km) from the nearest large settlement. The island itself is on a raised coral reef, and has its own mini ecosystem. It offers a tremendous range of diving experiences from the moment the diver enters the water at the resort edge. Venture farther afield into the Chaparoana channel that divides Uepi from nearby islands, and you'll find some tremendous pelagic action.

Notable dives include the Elbow, a vertical wall dropping into a 1,970-foot (600-m) trench. This wall, pitted and cratered with caves, caverns, channels, and overhangs, is festooned with sponges and fans, among which you may be lucky enough to find the occasional resting turtle. Off the wall are tuna, barracuda, eagle rays, and king trevallies.

OTHER ACTIVITIES

The Solomons are a true wilderness, and for the intrepid trekker there are riches indeed in the wilder areas of rainforest. For the bird lover, of the 163 species of land birds that breed in Solomon Islands, 44 are found nowhere else in the world. Such diversity has led to the creation of a small eco-tourist industry offering hiking, caving, climbing, canoeing, and cycling tours. For a real slice of island culture, take time out to explore the traditional village lodges around Marovo Lagoon.

☎ TELEPHONE NUMBERS

Recompression chamber	+675-693-0305
Hospital	+677-2-3600

🖥 WEBSITES & E-MAIL

Travel information	www.solomonislands.cc

OTHER DIVE SITES

Cave of the Custom Shark
Rainbow Passage
Passage Rocks
I-23
Bonegi

▼ DOUGLAS DAUNTLESS
One of the many World War II wrecks, many of which are still reasonably intact and give a haunting reminder of the conflict.

John Bantin

S.S. PRESIDENT
COOLIDGE

THE LARGEST ACCESSIBLE SHIPWRECK IN RECREATIONAL DIVING, *S.S. PRESIDENT COOLIDGE* SAW SERVICE AS A LUXURY CRUISER BEFORE BEING REQUISITIONED AS A TROOP CARRIER IN WORLD WAR II. SHE LIES OFF THE NORTHERN COAST OF VANUATU, AND GUARDS A LADY IN HER HEART.

 VISIBILITY

50 to 165 feet (15 to 50 m)

Cyclone Season: Nov - Apr

Wet Season: Feb - Apr

 MUST SEE

S.S. *President Coolidge*

 DOWNSIDE

Remote

Limited tourist infrastructure

 GETTING THERE

There is an international airport at Bauerfield, 10 minutes north of Port Vila. Aircalin and Air Vanuatu are the only international airline providing direct services to Vanuatu. Air Pacific, Qantas, and Solomon Airlines have code-sharing arrangements with Air Vanuatu. Departure tax is around U.S.$20.

 VISA

U.S. and E.U. citizens, those of the Commonwealth, Fiji, Japan, Norway, the Philippines, South Korea, South Africa, and Switzerland do not require visas for stays of up to 30 days.

 MONEY

Currency is the vatu (VT). Most establishments in Vila and Luganville can handle traveler's checks in major currencies, but hotels elsewhere may only accept Australian or U.S. dollars. It's wise to take 500 and 1000 VT notes as well as VT coins for smaller purchases. Major credit cards are accepted in most major stores.

WATER TEMPERATURE

°C	°F	°C	°F
30 —	— 86	30 —	— 86
28°C			
20 — **82°F**	— 68	20 — **24°C**	— 68
		75°F	
10 —	— 50	10 —	— 50
0 —	— 32	0 —	— 32
Summer		Winter	

Launched in 1930, *S.S. President Coolidge* is a monument to the golden era of sea travel, a time when white-coated stewards padded across pile carpets to bring drinks to elegant socialites lounging in mahogany smoking rooms, and passengers sunned themselves on the artificial sand beach of one of its two saltwater swimming pools. Some 654 feet (199 m) long, she displaced 21,936 tonnes, and would carry 988 passengers at 21 knots on the Sunshine Route from San Francisco to Honolulu, Yokohama, Shanghai, and Hong Kong. But even the *S.S. President Coolidge,* luxurious though she was, could not escape the consequences of war. In 1941 she was requisitioned by the U.S. Government for service as a troop carrier.

On October 26, 1942, *President Coolidge* was steaming through the channel to the south of Espiritu Santo on her way to the Solomon Islands. Packed into her elegant saloons and lounges were 4,800 soldiers of the 43rd Infantry Division and the 172nd Combat Team to reinforce the troops fighting in Guadalcanal. She was also carrying crucial medical supplies, including 519 lbs (235 kg) of quinine—the entire reserve supply for the American forces in the South Pacific. Her captain had not been informed that the U.S. marines had laid mines in the channel, and at 9:45 a.m. she struck two in quick succession. This great ship took a mere 90 minutes to sink. Due to the quick thinking of her captain, who drove her hard into shore, only two lives were lost, and now she lies on her port side with her bow at 70 feet (21 m) and her stern at 240 feet (73 m).

GEOGRAPHY

Espiritu Santo is the northernmost island of the state of Vanuatu, formerly the New Hebrides. The wreck of the *S.S. President Coolidge* is located only a few miles from Luganville, the second largest town in Vanuatu. She lies within 300 feet (90 m) of the shore.

Dan Burton

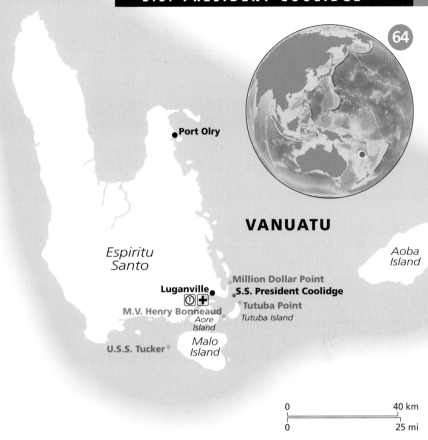
MARINE LIFE

The *President Coolidge* is not a highspot for marine life, as it is relatively free of coral growth and the large fish species normally associated with wrecks. However, there are numerous large lionfish around the wreck, and a night dive among the flashlight fish that inhabit the main holds should not be missed. But the best marine life of this wreck is on the decompression platforms created by the local dive operators. Here, over the years, small coral gardens have grown up that are alive with clown fish and anemones. Watch out for mantis shrimps in the sandy slopes leading to the platforms. Amongst the larger residents is the famous grouper Boris, a thumping 440 lb (200 kg) animal who is extremely familiar to divers. You may also be lucky enough to spot a dugong passing through.

THE DIVES

The *Coolidge* can be dived by boat, but as the ship was beached in the moments following the attack and only slipped off the foreshore in the final moments of her sinking, she is readily accessible from the shore. The local dive operators have laid a neat selection of lines to guide divers to the wreck and have also created clear decompression platforms of flattened sand on the fringing reef that line the shore. These platforms have stage cylinders in place, and are fitted with bars to secure the overly buoyant diver.

The dive protocol is well defined for the *Coolidge*, with local operators insisting on limited bottom time on all dives, and clearly staged decompression stops. This is because the ship's aft section lies in deep water, extending down to 196 feet (60 m). Although the local conditions are benign, it is essential that anyone diving the *Coolidge* at depth is experienced and holds appropriate qualifications for deep diving.

Many of the classic dives on this vessel—for example, the Lady, the Swimming Pool, and the Engine Room—are at considerable depth and involve full penetration of the wreck, which the dive operators encourage. Make sure that you follow normal precautionary routines at all times. There are considerable risks to some of the dives, and divers should not attempt them without an experienced local guide. Beware—it is very easy to lose track of time and depth when exploring this massive wreck.

◄ THE LADY

This statue, called "The Lady", sits at the end of the First Class Dining-room.

DIVER'S TIP

Keep a close eye on decompression times as they can swiftly rack up on these dives. The *Coolidge* is deceptive, and it is very easy to go deeper than planned and end up embarrassed at the decompression stop!

DIVE CENTERS

ALLAN POWER DIVE TOURS
S-8285, Box 233, Espiritu Santo, Vanuatu
Phone: +678-36-822
Web: www.allan-power-santo.com

BOKISSA ISLAND RESORT
Bokissa Island, Espiritu Santo, Vanuatu
Phone: +678-36-913
Web: www.bokissa.vu

PRO DIVE ESPIRITU SANTO
Aore Resort, Espiritu Santo, Vanuatu
Phone: +61-2-811-61100
E-mail: travel@prodive.com.au
Web: www.prodive.com.au

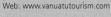
DIVING ORGANIZATIONS

None, but Vanuatu Tour Operators Association
may provide some useful information. They
have a set of rules by which local operators
must abide. Find them at:
Web: www.vanuatutourism.com

RECOMPRESSION

Luganville Hospital
Luganville, Espiritu Santo, Vanuatu
Phone: +678-25566

HOSPITAL

Luganville Hospital
Luganville, Espiritu Santo, Vanuatu
Phone: +678 -36-216

Vila Central Hospital,
Port Vila, Vanuatu
Phone: +678-22-100

Medical facilities are limited. The nearest
reliable medical facilities are in Australia or
New Zealand. Medical conditions resulting
from diving accidents may require evacuation
to Australia or New Zealand.

CONSERVATION SOCIETY

No dedicated marine organization in Vanuatu.
The Vatthe Conservation Area is the first
national forest park in Vanuatu. It protects
11,045 acres (4,470 ha) of rich and diverse
forests on the north coast of Espiritu Santo.
Information can be found at:
Web: www.unescap.org

▶ **SHIPS ANCHOR**

S.S. President Coolidge lies on her port
side with her bow section at a depth of
70 feet (21 m). The area around the bow
is littered with debris, including one of the
ships anchors.

THE PROMENADE DECK

• 80 to 105 feet (25 to 30 m) • intermediate

The local guides often use this dive as an introduction to the *Coolidge*, as it offers a dive along one of the most picturesque areas of the wreck, littered with interesting artefacts. It has clear access to the surface at all times, and is therefore suitable for intermediates.

The upper Promenade Deck—originally reserved for First Class Passengers only—was later lined with bunks when the ship was converted to a troop carrier. On the order to abandon ship, the soldiers quartered on the Promenade Deck were told to discard their helmets and rifles to avoid the risk of injury to those below them if they dropped them as they slid down the evacuation nets. These weapons and other personal effects lie where they were discarded. Other examples of the detritus of war—bayonets, respirators, a pistol, plates, cups, and phials of medicine—are scattered about this deck, and most dive operators can show you where to look for them. Meanwhile, the backdrop of the deck sweeps away behind you like a grand avenue lined with pillars of light arcing in from the windows in the superstructure above.

At the end of the deck, at 105 feet (30 m), you turn for home. Look for the lines of toilets glimpsed through the superstructure as you go. Moving up over the hull you can return via the discarded shark cage resting on the hull. Large coral trout may occasionally be seen hunting in this area. From here you simply follow the hull to the bow, and return up the slope to the decompression platform.

THE LADY

• 125 feet (38 m) • intermediate

The wreck's most famous passenger lies at the end of the First Class Dining-room, gazing down on divers who come to pay their respects. Known simply as "the Lady," this statue of an Elizabethan woman standing in front of a unicorn was discovered by *Coolidge* diving legend Allan Powers in 1981. The significance of the statue is not really known, but may have something to do with the fact that the *Coolidge* was built and launched in Virginia, the state named by explorer Sir Walter Raleigh for the virgin Queen Elizabeth of England. Unicorns are visible only to virgins, so it is remarkable that most divers who visit the wreck see the whole statue!

The Lady used to look down from the mantelpiece of the First Class Smoking-room, a dive of considerable depth. Allan Powers moved her to her present location, at a depth of 120 feet (35 m), after she was damaged in an earthquake several years ago.

Divers enter the hold in front of the bridge and move directly below the bridge along the deck toward the dining-room. This is a room of considerable size, and of course is tipped up on its side, so moving along it is akin to journeying along a very high corridor. After a distance of about 195 feet (60 m), the Lady looms up out of the gloom like a ghost.

Many divers act in a peculiar way when they see the Lady for the first time—indeed, a tradition has grown up of planting a kiss on her cheek before leaving. However, this should not be encouraged as the repeated contact is probably detrimental to the statue's preservation. Tales abound of furious exchanges between photographers bustling for position in front of the Lady, and patience and good buoyancy control are the two qualities required from the groups of divers who dance in attendance before her.

THE SWIMMING POOL

• 180 feet (55 m) • advanced

This is the First Class pool—the Second Class pool was removed to allow access to the aft hold when the ship was adapted for wartime service. It is actually a very simple dive, but the depth calls for a certain level of experience and qualification. The best way to conduct the dive is to begin with a long surface swim to the buoy tied just aft of the second funnel. From here you can drop straight onto the end of the Promenade Deck, requiring only a short swim at depth to the pool.

As you drop down to the pool, the top end is at 160 feet (50 m). The far end is below you, at 180 feet (55 m). The pool is in excellent condition, with the mosaic tiling still clearly visible. Both ladders are in place, and it even still has water in it!

As you return from the pool allow yourself a leisurely swim along the length of the *Coolidge*. Should decompression times and air supply permit, don't forget to pop in to see the barber's chair in the beauty salon, and of course take in the Promenade Deck in the final stages of the dive leading to the bridge.

THE ENGINE ROOM

• 150 feet (45 m) • advanced

This dive has claimed the lives of two divers, and should be taken seriously. A knowledgeable guide is essential. From the bow drop down diagonally toward the starboard side, where there is a large hole cut by salvagers in 1976. Passing through this hole, you then travel down the face of a giant condenser. Some 20 feet (6 m) further down is a small hatch giving access to the control room itself, a confined space containing numerous dials and telegraphs. It is tempting to linger here to take photographs, but it is wise not to stay too long as the decompression time quickly mounts up, and you still have a swim of some 130 feet (40 m) to exit the hull through the aft funnel shaft, at a depth of 150 feet (45 m). Then you still have the final swim back along the

▲ GHOSTLY LIGHT
A table lamp still stands in the remains of a stately lounge.

length of the hull to the decompression stop. On exiting the engine room, therefore, you must still have ample air supply to allow for the 20 to 25 minutes of stops you will inevitably require.

DOCTOR'S OFFICE

• 150 feet (45 m) • advanced

This is another dive that involves a deep penetration, and requires meticulous planning and briefing.

On this dive you enter the wreck through "Euart's Door" on C Deck, so named after an army officer who died on board rescuing his men. Then you follow a passage through the dining-room and upwards to

reach the doctor's office itself. The room is in total darkness, but a flashlight reveals many artefacts of interest, including ampoules of white powder, as well as a telephone. You exit by the same route, allowing yourself time for an easy swim back along the hull to the bow and the decompression stop.

FLASHLIGHT FISH DIVE

• 115 feet (35 m) • intermediate

This is a wonderful night dive, and a surreal experience for those not familiar with flashlight fish. The diving group enters the main hold at dusk, making sure that enough light is present to follow the guide without the

Dan Burton

warm crystal-clear water of brilliant blue. Only an hour and a quarter from Luganville, it is an ideal location for swimming and snorkeling and is widely regarded as one of the finest beaches in the South Pacific.

The Vatthe National Park contains 82 percent of Vanuatu's native land and freshwater species. Whilst visiting Santo Espiritu, it is well worth taking time off to climb the 1,473-feet (449-m) high Mount Wimbo or, if you are feeling particularly adventurous, make a journey to admire the famous bungee vine-jumpers of Pentecoste Island, about 60 miles (96 km) away to the southeast.

☎ TELEPHONE NUMBERS

Recompression chamber	+678-25566
Hospital	+678-36-216
Vanuatu Tourism (Europe)	+33-04-90-72-23-40

🖥 WEBSITES & E-MAIL

Vanuatu Government	www.vanuatugovernment.gov.vu
Vanuatu Tourism	www.vanuatutourism.com

OTHER DIVE SITES

U.S.S. Tucker
M.V. Henry Bonneaud
Tutuba Point
Million Dollar Point

▼ FIRST CLASS RESIDENT

A hawkfish takes refuge within a porthole on the *Coolidge*.

use of torches. The reason for this becomes apparent as soon as the divers enter the really dark spaces in the large hold and are surrounded by great shoals of flashlight fish, a species that has a light-emitting organ below each eye, creating a strobe effect in the black water of the hold. This amazing dive is a must for anyone visiting the *Coolidge*.

OTHER ACTIVITIES

There is much to take in on the island of Espiritu Santo, which is wonderfully wild and has a vibrant local culture. Local attractions include Champagne Beach, a sweeping crescent of purest powdery white sand with

Monty Halls

FIJI
ARCHIPELAGO

VOLCANIC PEAKS CLOAKED IN RAINFOREST LOOM ABOVE THE REAL HIDDEN TREASURES OF THIS SCATTERED TROPICAL ISLAND PARADISE—THE CRYSTAL LAGOONS AND BUSY CORAL REEFS THAT MAKE UP ONE OF THE MOST DIVERSE MARINE ENVIRONMENTS ON EARTH.

 VISIBILITY

Visibility is greatest during Fiji's winter months, June to October. Clarity soars to well over 100 feet (30 m) around most islands. In the summer, plankton blooms can reduce visibility to 60 feet (18 m) on occasion.

 MUST SEES

The White Wall
Aqua Trek 3D

 DOWNSIDE

Some sites only accessible by liveaboard

 GETTING THERE

Fiji is one of the main hubs of the South Pacific, well served by international airlines from countries around the Pacific Rim. Many people come on a round-the-world ticket or as a stopover between Australia or New Zealand and North America. Most travelers arrive and depart from Nadi International Airport on Viti Levu. There is a U.S.$9.50 departure tax. Internal travel around Fiji is easy, both by plane (expensive), ferry, or charter boat.

 VISA

Four-week visas issued automatically on arrival to visitors from the U.S., Canada, most Commonwealth countries, South and Central America, Western Europe, Israel, and Japan.

 MONEY

Currency is the Fiji dollar. Traveler's checks and major credit cards are accepted just about everywhere. U.S. and Australian dollars are also accepted.

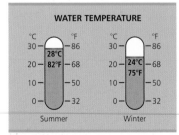

WATER TEMPERATURE

°C	°F		°C	°F
30	86		30	86
28°C				
20 **82°F**	68		20 **24°C**	68
			75°F	
10	50		10	50
0	32		0	32
Summer			Winter	

▶ **CORALS GALORE**
Soft and hard corals create rich multi-colored reefs throughout Fiji.

Kevin Davidson

Cikobia

Qele Levu

Nukubasaga

Labasa

Vanua Levu

Rainbow Reef

Savusavu

Somosomo Strait

Matagi Island

Mariah's Cove

The White Wall

The Purple Wall

Taveuni

Naitaba

Malima

Vanua Balavu

Yasawa

Yasawa Islands

Nacula

Bligh Water

Vatu-i-Ra Channel

Koro

Makogai

Wakaya Channel

Yacata

Kanacea

Munia

Vatu Vara

Mago

Yaqeta

Naviti

Waya

Tavua

E6

Lomaiviti Group

Tuvuca

KORO SEA

Cicia

Mamanucas Islands

Lautoka

Supermarket

"W"

Nadi

Viti Levu

Batiki

Nigali Passage

Nairai

Gau

FIJI

Nayau

Lau Group

Lakeba

SUVA

Beqa

Navua

Lagoon

Aqua-Trek 3D

Caesar's Rocks

Frigate Passage

Beqa

Vatulele

Oneata

0   50 km

0   40 mi

Moala

Komo

Moce

Vuaqava

Namuka-i-Lau

Kadavu

Ono

Naingora Pass

Totoya

Kabara

Galoa

Aquarium I & 2

Matuku

Fulaga

Ogea Levu

Ogea Driki

For divers, Fiji offers experiences that are truly out of the ordinary. Only 12 percent of its coral-fringed islands are inhabited, and it still has places that can be described as genuine tropical wildernesses, both above and below the waves. Away from major population centers, many of Fiji's reef systems have not been over-exploited, over-fished, or damaged.

GEOGRAPHY

A chain of more than 800 islands strung out in the the South Pacific approximately 1,700 miles (2,735 km) northeast of Australia, Fiji has a total land area of 7,000 sq miles (18,130 sq km) amidst 80,000 sq miles (208,000 sq km) of ocean. The population of 840,000 is made up of Pacific islanders and Indians descended from sugar plantation workers brought here in colonial times. More than 75 percent of people live on the largest island, Viti Levu (with its capital at Suva), the rest on Vanua Levu, Taveuni, and Kadavu.

The islanders traditionally live in villages along the coast and their culture has grown up in harmony with the sea. Fiji's traditional land tenure system rigorously protects tribal land and waters from misuse, ensuring that areas reserved for fishing are preserved.

The islands are mostly shallow atolls with large platforms and lagoons leading to deep channels such the Somosomo Strait. This is a heady mix for the diver, creating a wide variety of marine habitats.

MARINE LIFE

Many of the Fijian islands are cloaked in lush natural vegetation, while the surrounding waters have extensive and diverse coral reefs, mangroves, and seagrass beds. Reefs have been sustainably harvested here for millennia using wisdom passed down through local knowledge and custom. They are also a crucial asset to

▼ CLOWNFISH

A clownfish balances on top of its host, protected from the stinging cells by its unique protective slime.

Colin Bateman

DIVE CENTERS

AQUA TREK TAVEUNI
P.O. Box 1, Waiyevo, Taveuni, Fiji
Phone: +679-345-0324
E-mail: bega@aquatrek.com
Web: www.aquatrek.com

DIVE KADAVU
P.O. Box 8, Vunisea, Kadavu, Fiji
Phone: +679-368-3502
E-mail: admin@divekadavu.com
Web: www.divekadavu.com

SUBSURFACE FIJI
P.O. Box 3002, Nadi, Fiji .
Phone: +679-666-738
E-mail: info@subsurfacefiji.com
Web: www.fijidiving.com

AGGRESSOR (FIJI) LTD
P.O. Box 3174, Lami, Suva, Fiji
Phone: +679-361-382
E-mail: aggressorfiji@is.com.fj

DIVING ORGANIZATIONS

There is a Fiji Diving Operators Association, which requires members to adhere to certain safety standards. They can be contacted through:
Subsurface Fiji
P.O. Box 3002, Nadi, Fiji
Phone: +1-985-385-2628
E-mail: info@subsurfacefiji.com
Web: www.fijidiving.com

RECOMPRESSION

Suva Private Hospital
120 Amy Street, Suva, Viti Levu, Fiji
Phone: +679-330-3404

HOSPITAL

Healthcare facilities in Fiji are barely adequate for routine medical problems. Doctors and hospitals often expect immediate cash payment for health services.

Lautoka Hospital
Lautoka, Viti Levu, Fiji
Phone: +679-660-399

The Colonial War Memorial Hospital
Suva, Viti Levu, Fiji
Phone: +679-313-444

CONSERVATION SOCIETY

British-based conservation group Coral Cay Conservation have projects running in the Mamanucas Their website also offers some excellent general information on conservation problems in Fiji:
Coral Cay Conservation
The Tower, 13th Floor, 125 High Street, London SW19 2JG, United Kingdom
Web: www.coralcay.org
E-mail: info@coralcay.org
Phone: +44-7620-1411

Fiji's tourism—the country's main generator of foreign exchange.

Fed by the rich nutrients streaming up from the Tonga Trench to the southeast, and—on the large islands at least—influenced by several rivers, the reef ecosystem of the Fiji Islands is noted for its complex nature. The total of 6,000 sq miles (15,534 sq km) of reef is home to 398 coral species, whilst 9 separate species of mangrove grow along the island shores. Soft coral is spectacularly abundant; indeed, the islands are famed as one of the soft coral hot spots of the world.

There are 1,200 recorded fish species in Fiji, with more than 35 species of angelfish and butterflyfish alone. Some 12 species of whale and dolphin have been recorded in Fijian waters, using the deep channels and warm waters around the islands as part of their migration routes. Five of the 7 species of turtle found on Earth are seen off Fiji—namely, the green, hawksbill, leatherback, olive ridley, and loggerhead turtles.

THE DIVES

All major types of coral reefs are present in Fiji, including barrier reefs and fringing reefs. This gives the visiting diver a wide variety of options, with the marine life over the reefs holding a wealth of smaller attractions for the macro-photographer, while the healthy population of large pelagics offers plenty for the thrill-seeker.

Pelagics are particularly abundant in the tidal races through the gaps and channels around atolls, although these dives are recommended only for the more experienced diver. Another benefit of these areas of strong currents is the abundance of soft coral growth, something for which Fiji is justifiably famed. Other areas such as Beqa's Lagoon offer more sheltered dives, although at the cost of possibly finding less abundant coral. This area also offers some great drift dives between the outlying islands.

There is a genuine air of exploration on some of the more remote sites in Fiji. With many thousands of miles of reef to explore and hundreds of tiny islands as yet undived, there is a lifetime's diving here.

The diving industry in Fiji is well developed, and has been catering for the demanding American and Japanese markets for many years. Equipment is therefore likely to be of a high standard, and the boats well maintained and fitted out with appropriate communications and safety equipment.

BEQA LAGOON

• **20 to 120 feet (6 to 37 m)** • **beginner to advanced**

The rim of an ancient volcano, Beqa is a chain of islets surrounding a lagoon, a massive 17 miles (27 km) across. Nutrient-rich water rushes daily through breaks

in the walls of this underwater mountain, supporting the rich diversity of soft and hard corals that are found here, along with large purple, tan, and green sea fans. Altogether, the lagoon contains more than 100 breathtaking coral, wall, and cave dive sites, and its profusion of marine life includes sharks, turtles, lionfish, and blue ribbon eels.

Among the sites particularly worthy of note in Beqa Lagoon are Aqua-Trek 3D, Caesar's Rocks, and Frigate Passage. Each of them offers a completely different

experience, and they represent a cross-section of Fijian diving's many faces.

Lying off the village of Wainiyabia, Aqua-Trek 3D is a shark encounter that has to rank among the best in the world. There are 7 separate species of shark that frequent this site, including bull, gray reef, nurse, silver tip, lemon, black tip, and white tip reef sharks! Shark feeding does take place at this site—a sensitive issue for many divers, but nonetheless something that occurs at a number of top dive locations around the world. The

area of this dive is a Marine Park and, added to the obvious thrills of the shark encounters, there are some beautiful smaller reefs nearby.

Caesar's Rocks are a series of coral pinnacles rising almost to the surface. Well-protected from currents and tidal surges, this is a wonderful site for the more inexperienced diver. Attractions include some tremendously complex coral structures, huge numbers of anemones and clownfish in the shallow tops of the pinnacles, and a tunnel through one of the pinnacles

▲ AQUA-TREK 3D

Grey reef sharks are just one of the seven shark species commonly encountered at the Aqua-Trek 3D dive site.

Colin Bateman

▲ **SEA TURTLE**
A turtle hugs the reef to avoid predators in mid-water.

OTHER DIVE SITES

Matagi Island

Wakaya Channel

at a depth of 50 feet (15 m). Visibility can be rather limited at this site depending on the prevailing weather conditions.

At the southwest corner of Beqa Lagoon is Frigate Passage. This is a classic drift dive through a large channel guarded by two big coral bommies at the entrance, which make for a fascinating beginning to the dive. Riddled with overhangs, caves, and holes, yet washed by powerful tides, the bommies are home to a whole range of the smaller inhabitants of the reef. Look out for big pelagics during this dive, with mantas and eagle rays drifting through the channel and white tips sleeping on the sand below with stingrays half buried in the sand alongside.

SOMOSOMO STRAIT

• **30 to 130 feet (9 to 40 m)** • **beginner to advanced**

This is the location of Fiji's most famous dive of all—the White Wall—and is a large channel running between Vanua Levu to the north and Taveuni to the southeast. The famous Rainbow Reef is 20 miles (32 km) of exquisite soft and hard corals that cuts into the channel, creating powerful currents and a steady flow of nutrient-rich water over its kaleidoscopic walls and

canyons. The reef itself is subdivided into smaller sites beloved of local operators and visiting divers alike.

The Purple Wall is a dive located between Taveuni and Qamea, with a colorful reef wall beginning at 30 feet (9 m) and ending at 80 feet (24 m) where it turns into a more gradual slope. The drift takes place in a current running at 1-3 knots, and provides divers with a whistlestop tour over the bustling small drop-off, resplendent with masses of soft corals, crinoids, gorgonians, and sea whips.

Mariah's Cove is a ridge extending from the point of a peninsula off the north of the island of Qamea. The wall itself begins at 30 feet (9 m), and is a riot of soft corals down to 80 feet (24 m.)

The famous White Wall begins at around 75 feet (23 m) and is generally approached by drifting up from the channel. The reefs on either side, creating some very powerful currents at this site, prevent the diver from approaching the wall of the channel. As you punch your way out of the channel through a narrow passageway at 80 feet (24 m), the splendor of the wall is revealed, completely festooned with beautiful white soft corals. The drift continues along this wall, and as the face drops away to more than 200 feet (60 m) below the

diver, it is covered in soft corals as far as the eye can see. The strength of the currents in this region, together with the depth of the walls, render this dive one for the advanced diver.

NAINGORA PASS

• 20 to 130 feet (6 to 40 m) • intermediate

Naingora Pass is located at the northeast corner of the southern island of Kadavu, and begins in only 10 feet (3 m) of water, gradually sloping down to 200 feet (60 m) plus. The current here is not particularly excessive, and this is an ideal drift dive along reefs coated with soft corals and gorgonians.

This is big pelagic country, with large Maori wrasses, barracuda, and jacks ever present. Look out for mantas, and most thrilling of all, the occasional sighting of large tiger sharks. In the Astrolobe Reef to the north are two large blue holes, known as Aquarium 1 and Aquarium 2. Both are 180 feet (55 m) across and 130 feet (40 m) deep, and as they are surrounded by very shallow water it is only possible to access them at high tide.

This northern section of the reef offers what many regard as the best diving in Fiji. The area around the island of Gau and Namena is renowned for crystal visibility, big animals, and busy reefs. It is mostly only accessible by liveaboards, and offers a glimpse of truly wild Fijian diving with drifts along precipitous walls and narrow channels swept by powerful currents. Nigali Passage off Gau is a tremendously exciting drift dive, with current speeds of up to 4 knots amongst schools of mantas, hammerheads, and jacks. Reach the narrow constriction at the end of this drift before moving into wider calmer areas, passing over a huge area of stony corals called the Cabbage Patch, before slowing down to watch a conveyor belt of Fiji's more spectacular marine residents sweep past.

MAMANUCAS ISLANDS/YASAWA CHAIN

• 20 to 130 feet (6 to 40 m)
• beginner to advanced

The soft corals for which Fiji is renowned are not much in evidence here. However the Mamanucas Islands and the Yasawa Chain to the north are sites of consistent large pelagic activity, with schooling hammerhead, numerous turtles, and dolphin in considerable numbers.

Dive sites of note include the Supermarket, a shallow reef lying off Mana Island guaranteeing large schools of barracuda as well as white tip and bronze whaler sharks. The 9-mile (14-km) Malolo Barrier Reef has a number of tremendous sites, including the famous "W", a double reef point jutting out into deep water. Off this wall are likely sightings of mantas, whale sharks, and dolphins. The E6 site is the top of a massive seamount or pinnacle rising from 3,000 feet (915 m) all the way to

the surface. The top of the mount is pockmarked with small caverns and caves, the most famous of which is the Cathedral. Look out for barracuda, eagle rays, mantas, and hammerheads swimming in the blue water off the walls.

OTHER ACTIVITIES

Fiji is well set up for tourists and divers, and there are facilities everywhere offering equipment for hire and day tours. All manner of interesting cultural and adventurous activities are available. The natural wonders of the reefs are reflected in the species diversity on land. Island fauna includes endemic bats, 20 reptile species, and 100 varieties of birds. Undisturbed islands provide nesting sites for seabirds including great crested terns, lesser frigates, and Gould's petrels. One-third of Fiji's 3,000-odd plant species are endemic, and for centuries Fijians have used plants for hundreds of purposes, ranging from dyes and medicines to clothes and building materials. For the surfing fanatic there is some good surf off the Mamanucas, with several resorts dedicated entirely to the big waves.

TELEPHONE NUMBERS
Recompression chamber +679-330-3404
Hospital +679-660-399

WEBSITES & E-MAIL
Fiji Visitors Bureau www.bulafiji.com
Fiji Government Online www.fiji.gov.fj
Fiji Dive Operators www.fijidive.com

DIVER'S TIP

Not exactly diving related, but do try kava (also known as yaqona)! This traditional local brew made of chewed or pounded roots is frequently drunk with great ceremony and is always a novel experience. Perhaps best left for a non-diving day!

▼ **RED SEA HORSE**
As well as the bigger species of marine life Fiji also offers a multitude of smaller reef inhabitants.

Kevin Davidson

GREAT BARRIER
REEF

THE GREAT BARRIER REEF OFF THE QUEENSLAND COAST OF NORTHEASTERN AUSTRALIA IS A DIVER'S PARADISE, NOT LEAST FOR THE STAGGERING RICHNESS OF ITS MARINE LIFE. OVER 30 PERCENT OF THE REEF ENJOYS A HIGHLY PROTECTED STATUS, MAKING IT THE LARGEST MARINE PARK ON EARTH.

The dimensions of the Great Barrier Reef are so great that no one is certain just how large it really is. All the figures for the reef are impressive: it is approximately 1,400 miles (2,253 km) long, is made up of more than 2,000 individual reefs, covers more than 134,633 sq miles (343,700 sq km), and is visible from outer space. It is constructed of hundreds of species of coral and contains more than a thousand species of fish.

GEOGRAPHY

 The Great Barrier Reef begins off the coast of Papua New Guinea and ends at Lady Elliot Island, 248 miles (400 km) north of Brisbane, Queensland's capital city. Its 2,000 individual reefs are in turn divided into smaller strips and patches of coral. Particularly notable are the famous "Ribbon Reefs" to be found north of Cairns in the central section of the main reef. In addition, there are 71 islands sprinkled along its length.

 VISIBILITY
50 to 100 ft (15 to 30 m)

 MUST SEES
Hard coral formations
Large approachable animals

 DOWNSIDE
Strong currents at some sites
Crowded dive sites

GETTING THERE
Around 30 international airlines fly to Australia. Cairns is the gateway to the Great Barrier Reef, and has a large international airport. Domestic flights are relatively cheap, and can be taken to Port Douglas or Townsville for access to the northern sections of the reef.

 VISA
All nationalities except New Zealanders require a tourist visa or Electronic Travel Authority (E.T.A.), valid for 3 months, to enter Australia. These cost Aus.$20 (U.S.$11.)

 MONEY
Currency is the Australian dollar. Cash is readily available at A.T.M.s throughout the country. Operators and hotels of any size accept all major credit cards and traveler's checks.

WATER TEMPERATURE
Summer: 27°C / 80°F
Winter: 24°C / 75°F

Monty Halls

▶ **HUMPHEAD WRASSE**
This large humphead wrasse typifies the impressive fish to be found on the outer edges of the Great Barrier Reef.

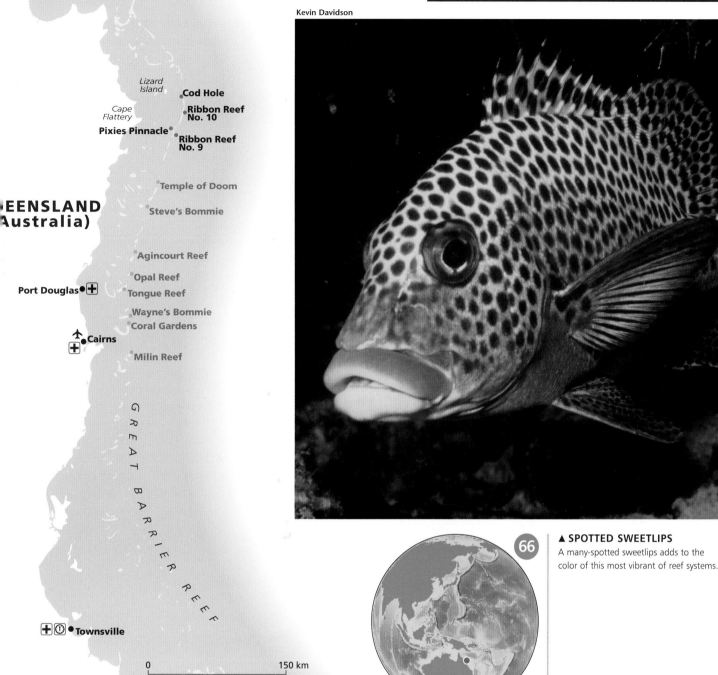

Kevin Davidson

Lizard
Island
•Cod Hole
Cape
Flattery •Ribbon Reef
No. 10
Pixies Pinnacle•
•Ribbon Reef
No. 9

Temple of Doom

EENSLAND
Australia) Steve's Bommie

Agincourt Reef
Opal Reef
Port Douglas•⊞ Tongue Reef
Wayne's Bommie
Coral Gardens
✈
⊞⊞•**Cairns**
Milin Reef

G
R
E
A
T

B
A
R
R
I
E
R

R
E
E
F

⊞◫•**Townsville**

0 ———————————— 150 km
0 ———————————— 100 mi

66

▲ SPOTTED SWEETLIPS
A many-spotted sweetlips adds to the
color of this most vibrant of reef systems.

The Great Barrier Reef divides into two broad habitats. The first is the Great Shallow. This inshore section of the reef averages 45 to 90 feet (14 to 27 m) in depth and is never more than 200 miles (322 km) wide, creating a complex matrix of shallow reefs. In many parts of the Great Shallow the large tidal range of the inshore waters rushes through these reefs at speeds of up to 8 knots. The second habitat begins as the reef reaches the deeper water of the oceanic shelf, where it becomes characterized by large bommies and plunging drop-offs. This is the wilder side of the Great Barrier Reef, where ocean meets coral to create upwellings and turbulent water that draw in large oceanic predators.

The wall and drift dives of the outer reef are full of stupendous drama.

The Great Barrier Reef was established as a Marine Park in 1975 and as a World Heritage Site in 1981. There is a now a zoning system in place that ensures that certain areas (known as General Use and "B" Zone regions) are open to all types of use. This allows both recreational and commercial fishing, as well as diving and other water sports, and covers 71 percent of the total area of the reef. The highest classification of protection is a Preservation Zone. In order for the reef to be allowed to develop entirely naturally, there is strictly no entry to this zone for anyone except

► HARD CORALS

Convoluted gardens of hard coral create a maze of reefs throughout the inner Great Barrier Reef.

 DIVE CENTERS

CAIRNS DIVE CENTER

121 Abbott St., Cairns, QLD 4870, Australia

Phone: +61-7-4051-0294

E-mail: info@cairnsdive.com.au

Web: www.cairnsdive.com.au

MIKE BALL DIVE EXPEDITIONS

143 Lake Street, Cairns, QLD 4870, Australia

Phone: +61-7-4053-0509

E-mail: mbde@mikeball.com

Web: www.mikeball.com

GINGARA ECOTOURS

P.O. Box 997, Townsville, QLD 4810, Australia

Phone: +61-7-4771-6187

 DIVING ORGANIZATIONS

The Queensland Government produces guidelines for the recreational diving industry accessible on their website at:

Web: www.whs.qld.gov.au

 RECOMPRESSION

Townsville General Hospital

Eyre Street, Townsville, QLD 4810, Australia

Phone: +61-7-4796-2080

The Wesley Center for Hyperbaric Medicine, Suite 53, Sandford Jackson Building, Wesley Hospital, Auchenflower, Brisbane, QLD 4066, Australia

Phone: +61-7-3371-6033

 HOSPITAL

Cairns Base Hospital

The Esplanade, Cairns, QLD 4870, Australia

Phone: +61-7-4050-6333

Fax: +61-7-4031-1628

Ingham Hospital

McIlwraith Street, Ingham, QLD 4850, Australia

Phone: +61-7-4776-2000

Fax: +61-7-4776-3624

The Mossman Hospital

Hospital Street, Mossman, QLD 4873, Australia

Phone: +61-7-4098-2444

For information on health facilities in specific areas go to:

Web: www.health.qld.gov.au

 CONSERVATION SOCIETY

Great Barrier Reef Marine Park Authority

P.O. Box 1379, Townsville, QLD 4810, Australia

Phone: +61-7-4750-0700

Fax: +61-7-4772-6093

E-mail: info@reefHQ.org.au

Web: www.gbrmpa.gov.au

researchers with permits to conduct very limited scientific studies. These areas are vital as they will make it more likely that the reef will continue to prosper and develop as a complete system.

MARINE LIFE

The marine life of the Great Barrier Reef, even in areas heavily impacted by tourism, is breathtaking. Although not at the absolute peak of diversity in terms of species numbers (for higher numbers of fish and coral species you need to travel further north to the Pacific reefs), it is still one of the richest marine habitats on Earth. The reef itself is made up of an estimated 400 species of coral, through and over which swim 1,500 fish species, and within which lurk 4,000 species of mollusk. Cruising throughout its length are 23 species of marine mammal, while 53 species of bird swoop over its waters and dive-bomb the surface in search of food. Of particular interest to the diver are the hard corals, the foundation of the reef itself, which are truly staggering

John Bantin   Kevin Davidson

in their range and size. At almost any point on the reef it is possible to swim through a labyrinth of coral alley-ways, surrounded by gloriously convoluted structures that give shelter to a multitude of rainbow-colored inhabitants.

One of the advantages of visiting the heavily dived areas of the reef is the relaxed attitude of the larger residents to the presence of divers. This allows you to observe these animals much more closely than is possible on the reef's wilder stretches. The latter, of course, have their own unique attractions, not the least of which is the possibility of encountering great oceanic predators. Divers here also have the opportunity to explore healthy reefs away from the hustle and bustle of the mass diving fraternity.

THE DIVES

Much like the reef itself, the diving on the Great Barrier Reef can be divided into two distinct types. There are the numerous large-scale operations, many of them

▲ ANTHIAS

Anthias and other multi-colored fish live in and around the hard coral reefs of the Great Barrier Reef.

Monty Halls

operating out of Cairns, that place hundreds of divers every day in the waters of the stretch of reef between Port Douglas and Cairns. The reefs in this region have naturally begun to degrade under this sustained impact. However, there is still some fine diving to be had in this zone for those who know where to look for it.

The shallow reefs of this region are easily accessed, and there is excellent visibility. All this makes it an ideal location to introduce beginners to the sport of diving. On the downside, there can be considerable tidal range in this part of the reef, and therefore strong currents. The sheer numbers of divers also mean that you are rarely able to dive here alone, which unfortunately detracts from the pleasure of the dives, particularly for more experienced divers.

Liveaboards can be chartered from this stretch of coast to explore the more remote areas of the Great Barrier Reef. These can be three-day excursions to visit classic sites such as the wreck of the *Yongala*, or still longer forays into the Coral Sea. In addition, several island resorts along the reef—notably Heron and Lizard Island—cater for residential diving. These resorts have gained a reputation with the diving community for allowing particularly easy access to the wonders of the Great Barrier Reef, as they are invariably situated in the heart of the reef itself.

BACK DOOR TO RIBBON REEF NO. 10

• 30 to 100 feet (9 to 30 m) • **advanced**

Ribbon Reef No. 10 has been identified as a bio-physically special and unique site by the Great Barrier Reef Marine Park Authority, and as such could well have a heavily protected status in the near future. It lies northeast of Cape Flattery, near Lizard Island, and is the location of world-renowned dives such as Cod Hole and, at the junction of Ribbon Reef No. 10 and No. 9, the famous Pixies Pinnacle.

The Back Door dive takes place on the seaward side of the ribbon reef, and involves a dramatic drift along the face of the reef. This site is not normally visited by dive operators, and so you have the chance to dive here in freedom without the hassle of the crowds drawn to the more popular sites.

Here on the seaward side of the reef the corals are particularly magnificent, with some spectacular table corals. In attendance are all the large charismatic animals associated with the Great Barrier Reef—if you are lucky, you may encounter schools of large bump-head parrotfish, giant potato cod, and Queensland groupers, as well as white tip reef sharks.

The strong tidal currents that wash over this section of reef are responsible for drawing in this profusion of life, and divers are well advised to take appropriate drift-diving measures when conducting this dive. It is no fun to be swept seaward, all the while waving at a disappearing boat!

COD HOLE

• 65 feet (20 m) • **beginner**

Located 118 miles (190 km) north of Port Douglas, Cod Hole is a 12-hour boat trip to a site famed throughout the world for its resident population of massive potato cod. An alternative and much closer launch point to reach the hole is Lizard Island, which also offers the opportunity to dive other similarly remote sections in this relatively wild zone of the Great Barrier Reef.

The large potato cod for whom the site is named were first discovered by the famous Australian under-water filmmakers Ron and Valerie Taylor and have been hand-fed by dive operators for the past 20 years. There has been a growing tendency for divers also to feed the fish with all manner of inappropriate foodstuffs. While the opportunity to come close to these impressive animals—some individuals weigh more than 300 lbs (136 kg)—is tremendous, there is concern that their health may be declining as a result of the poor diet they receive and the constant attention and handling by divers. General opinion now is that the hand-feeding of the cod is unnatural and intrusive but is so well established that the behavior of the fish has been

> ### DIVER'S TIP
>
> Always take a number of diver location devices when diving anywhere on the Great Barrier Reef. The presence of large numbers of divers, combined with strong currents, can endanger even the best-planned dive, and a whistle, flag, or large S.M.B. could be a life saver.

◄ **SWIRLING SCHOOLS**
Even when juveniles, barracuda form impressive schools for protection from predators hunting the shallow reef tops.

▼ **POTATO COD**
The large potato cod frequenting Cod Hole have had their behavior radically altered due to being hand-fed for many years.

John Bantin

Dan Burton

▲ BUMPHEAD PARROTFISH

Schools of bumphead parrotfish can be seen cruising the waters around the Great Barrier Reef.

OTHER DIVE SITES

Temple of Doom

Steve's Bommie

Agincourt Reef

Opal Reef

Tongue Reef

Wayne's Bommie

Coral Gardens

Milin Reef

permanently altered by it. Rather than ban the feeding altogether, it is proposed that only approved dive operators should be allowed to do so in order to minimize the amount of handling the animals are subjected to and to ensure that they receive a more suitable diet. Divers often forget, moreover, that the cod are large predators—a fact readily acknowledged by the more prudent divemasters who wear a large chainmail glove to protect themselves while feeding the fish.

A number of large maori wrasse (so called because of the elaborate swirling pattern markings on their heads) are likely to be in attendance in the hole. Although the coral cover in this part of the reef is of only an average standard, it is still possible to see giant clams, pyramid butterflyfish, trigger fish, large moray eels, white tip reef sharks, camouflage cod, coral trout, and trevallies. It is well worth taking the opportunity to explore the area around the feeding site, far from the madding crowd, and to enjoy the spectacle of marine life on the fringes of the main dive area.

PIXIES PINNACLE

• **0 to 100 feet (0 to 30 m)** • **intermediate**

Located at the northwest corner of a small plug reef between Ribbon Reefs Nos. 9 and 10, this site has a justified reputation for offering a mixture of all the best elements of the inshore Great Barrier Reef.

Pixies Pinnacle is a vertical pillar of coral that rises from 100 feet (30 m) to within a few feet of the surface. This tower of coral measures only 50 feet (15 m) across, and is a beacon for surrounding marine life. A popular site, it shows signs of the heavy traffic of divers upon its kaleidoscopic faces. However, it is positioned within a large channel that offers nutrient-rich currents, and as such has remained in reasonable condition.

This is a tremendous dive for viewing the different types of activity to be found at different levels of the reef, and is an added attraction for the more experienced diver when visiting the more "touristy" Cod Hole nearby. Beautiful black corals adorn the lower faces of the pinnacle, as well as the normal range of hard and soft corals higher up the precipitous walls. Mixed in among these are gorgonians, brightly colored sponges, and exquisite hydroids. Under the many overhangs of the pinnacle lurk lionfish, emerging at night to hunt the shimmering schools of fry and silversides around the reef walls. Numerous stonefish peer out from heavily camouflaged positions, while trevallies, barracuda, sharks, batfish, and large groupers cruise around the pinnacle.

OTHER ACTIVITIES

The more heavily dived areas of the Great Barrier Reef are well set up to support the tourist trade. The centers of Cairns, Townsville, and Port Douglas all have different characters, and yet share the vibrant personalities associated with towns born to serve tourists.

Cairns, the jumping-off spot for the Great Barrier Reef, is a youth-oriented, tropical city with plenty of hotels and restaurants. Cairns' "beach" is a mud flat dotted with roseate spoonbills and other tropical birds, and you can visit the reptile farm to see saltwater crocodiles eating chickens, or take the Kuranda Railway for a look at a magnificent waterfall. Townsville has a more outback feel to it, with a number of backpackers' bars and hostels an indication of its more itinerant atmosphere. Magnetic Island just off the coast contains a large National Park, and there is also Reef H.Q., a beautifully set-up aquarium and education center. The Billabong Wildlife Sanctuary offers the chance to interact with animals in rainforest, wetlands, and eucalyptus forest. Port Douglas has the Habitat Wildlife Sanctuary, with a similar arrangement, plus the added attraction of a large grassland area.

All along the Queensland Coast are thriving adventure sports such as skydiving and rafting. There is also some excellent fishing on designated areas of the reef.

TELEPHONE NUMBERS

Recompression chamber	+61-7-4796-2080
Hospital	+61-7-4796-2080
Marine Park Authority	+61-7-4750-0700

WEBSITES & E-MAIL

| The Australian Travel Commission | www.australia.com |
| Barrier Reef | www.barrierreefaustralia.com |

▼ **COLORFUL RESIDENT**
Though the Great Barrier Reef does not have the diversity of dive locations further north, an estimated 1,500 different fish species are found swimming in its waters.

Kevin Davidson

CORAL SEA

IT WAS NOT UNTIL 1972 THAT THE MORE ADVENTUROUS LIVEABOARD DIVE BOATS BEGAN TO VENTURE OUT INTO THE OCEAN BEYOND THE GREAT BARRIER REEF TO EXPLORE THE REEFS OF THE CORAL SEA. HERE THEY DISCOVERED SOME OF THE FINEST ADVENTURE DIVE SITES ON THE PLANET.

👁 **VISIBILITY**
130 feet (40 m) plus

✔ **MUST SEES**
Guaranteed pelagics
Huge walls
Crystal visibility

✖ **DOWNSIDE**
Strong currents
Remote

✈ **GETTING THERE**
About 30 international airlines fly to Australia. Cairns is the gateway to the Great Barrier Reef, and has a large international airport. Domestic flights are relatively cheap and can be taken to Port Douglas or Townsville for easier access to the northern sections of the reef.

VISA
U.S. and E.U. citizens require a valid passport and a visa or Electronic Travel Authority (E.T.A.) to enter Australia. These are simple to acquire, cost Aus.$20, and allow you to stay in the country for three months. For further information go to:
Web: www.eta.immi.gov.au

$ **MONEY**
Currency is the Australian dollar, and cash is readily available at A.T.M.s throughout the country. Operators and hotels of any size accept all major credit cards.

The Coral Sea reefs are a series of mountain-tops that rise precipitously from the ocean bed more than half a mile (1 km) below. The reefs are oases of life in the surrounding deep water, creating huge walls and rich upwellings that support extraordinary coral communities and attendant predators. Divers who endure the lengthy (and frequently rough) sea crossing to reach them will find exceptional diving among incredibly dramatic reefs dominated by gigantic sponges and large coral formations. They will enjoy some of the most impressive encounters with pelagic creatures to be found in the world of diving. All this takes place in crystal-clear water that many a dumb-struck diver has described as the best visibility they have ever encountered. Dive boats moor alongside atolls and reefs that are surrounded on all sides by an unbroken blue horizon and the deep blue Pacific sky above. All in all, one of the great experiences in Australian diving.

GEOGRAPHY

Some 100 miles (160 km) off the Queensland coast east of Townsville is Flinders Reef, a popular dive site that lies at the southwestern edge of the Coral Sea reef

▼ STEEP WALLS
Healthy reef tops plunging over steep walls are a characteristic of many Coral Sea dives.

John Bantin

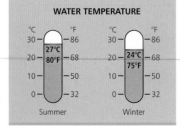

WATER TEMPERATURE

	Summer		Winter	
°C	°F		°C	°F
30	86		30	86
20	**27°C 80°F**	68	20	**24°C 75°F** 68
10	50		10	50
0	32		0	32

Bougainville
Reef

C O R A L
S E A

✈ ●Port Douglas

✈ ●Cairns

Holmes
Reefs

Diane Bank

Golden Wall

QUEENSLAND
(Australia)

Flora Reef

Willis
Group

Herald
Cays

**Watanabe
Bommie**

°Herald Cays

Magdelaine
Cays

Flinders
Reefs

Cod Wall

G
R
E
A
T

B
A
R
R
I
E
R

R
E
E
F

Diamond
Islets

Malay Reef

Abingdon
Reef

Tregrosse
Reefs

Lihou Reefs

●Townsville

| 0 | | 150 km |
| 0 | | 100 mi |

system—a glorious collection of walls, reefs, and atolls covering over 38,000 sq miles (100,000 square km). Close to Flinders are North and South Boomerang Reefs. North Boomerang is particulaly popular with visiting divers. The more intrepid diver should visit the outer reefs—such as Lihou, Diamond, and Marion—as well as Willis Islet and Holmes Reef farther north. All these sites have their own characteristics, and yet present a consistently high standard of diving for those with the budget and time to make the journey beyond Australia's main Barrier Reef.

MARINE LIFE

The marine life and coral formations of the Coral Sea are similar to those of the Great Barrier Reef, but it is the size of the reef animals to be met here that consistently impresses visiting divers. An individual gorgonian sea fan at Flinders Reef measures 16 feet (5 m) across, probably the largest known specimen in the world. Huge sponges cling to steep walls covered in sea whips and plentiful hard and soft corals. Particularly exciting for the diver is the presence of many large pelagic species from the open ocean around the Coral Sea reefs, which cruise the walls and reefs to prey on the inhabitants. Tales abound of encounters with huge sharks, including tigers and hammerheads, and the ubiquitous gray reef and white tip sharks. Huge schools of jacks and blackfin barracuda patrol specific sections of reef wall and can be revisited dive after dive. Sites such as Flinders Reef have vast fields of garden eels, and Marion Reef is famous throughout the diving world for its population of sea snakes.

THE DIVES

Some sections of the Coral Sea reef system are more than 180 miles (300 km) away from mainland Australia, so they can only be explored on liveaboards. Vessels visiting the Coral Sea reefs operate out of the three principal Queensland diving centers of Cairns, Port Douglas, and Townsville. A trip to the outer reefs, allowing time to explore them in any detail, will take 10 days. The crossing can be rough, particularly during the best diving periods from May to January.

DIVER'S TIP

Making yourself seen on the surface here is important. Take a flag or a large S.M.B. on every dive.

Monty Halls

DIVE CENTERS

DIVE DIRECTORY
P.O. Box 5264, Cairns, QLD 4870,
Australia
Phone: +61-7-4046-7304
E-mail: info@divedirectory.com.au
Web: www.dive-australia.com

MIKE BALL DIVE EXPEDITIONS
143 Lake Street, Cairns, QLD 4870, Australia
Phone: + 61-7-4053-0509
E-mail: mbde@mikeball.com
Web: www.mikeball.com

GINGARA ECO TOURS
P.O. Box 997, Townsville,
QLD 4810, Australia
Phone: +61-7-4771-6187

DIVING ORGANIZATIONS

The Queensland Government produces
guidelines for the recreational diving industry
that can be accessed on their website at:
Web: www.whs.qld.gov.au

RECOMPRESSION

Townsville General Hospital
Eyre Street, Townsville, QLD 4810, Australia
Phone: +61-7-4781-9211
Contact: Dr. D. Griffiths

HOSPITAL

The Wesley Park Haven Private Hospital
9-13 Bayswater Road, Hyde Park,
QLD 4810, Australia
Phone: +61-7-4722-8822

Townsville General Hospital
Eyre Street, Townsville, QLD 4810, Australia
Phone: +61-7-4796-2080

**CONSERVATION SOCIETY**

Great Barrier Reef Marine Park Authority,
P.O. Box 1379, Townsville,
QLD 4810, Australia
Phone: +61-7-4750-0700
Fax: +61-7-4772-6093
E-mail: info@reefHQ.org.au
Web: www.gbrmpa.gov.au

OTHER DIVE SITES

Golden Wall
Herald Cays

▶ CORAL FORMATIONS

The Coral Sea has similar coral formations
to the Great Barrier Reef but they can be
far more impressive.

Choice of liveaboard operator is important. Many of these reefs are remote and not well established as dive sites, and experience and local knowledge are vital. There are a number of stories of divers being taken out to these reefs, only to find themselves diving on flat sand and featureless sites. Having endured the crossing, it would be a great pity not to visit the dozen or so Coral Sea "classics".

The enduring feature of the Coral Sea for most divers is the massive walls cruised by impressive pelagics. Many of the sites are drift dives, and the operators who visit this area are well versed in this form of diving. The strong currents and upwellings that create such species-rich reefs also create a number of hazards for the diver, and should be treated with respect. It's a long swim to the next island!

COD WALL

• **30 to 130 feet (10 to 40 m) • advanced**

This is one of the real classics of the Coral Sea. As it is located just south of Flinders Reef it is also a popular site. This does not mean that hundreds of divers a day visit the reef—this is the Coral Sea after all—but simply that it is one of the few places where there is a high chance of encountering other boats.

Cod Wall is essentially a very large drop-off between North and South Boomerang Reefs, descending to 1,312 feet (400 m) on the south side. The wall itself is cut by a series of deep grooves. The diver drops off the shallow lip of the wall, which rises to within 25 feet (7 m) of the surface. A substantial ledge running along the length of the main wall at just above the 130-feet (40-m) mark serves as a good maximum depth guide. The visibility of this site is mind-blowing, often more than 150 feet (45 m.) This allows ample opportunity to view the large tuna and several shark species that cruise in the blue water beyond the wall. The wall and shelf are covered by huge sea fans and beautiful red sea whips. As you ascend the wall towards the end of the dive, also make time to observe the large schools of blackfin barracuda that hover motionless in the current just off the wall. You should also observe a large cave at about 50 feet (15 m) on the bommie side that is festooned with soft corals.

It is worth noting that the currents in this region can be very strong, and the diver should be prepared for a powerful drift throughout this dive.

WATANABE BOMMIE

• **30 to 100 feet (10 to 30 m) • intermediate**

This is a huge coral bommie extending to within 30 feet (10 m) of the surface. The bommie is located on the western edge of Flinders Reef and is covered in schooling fish. There is a large cavern at 100 feet (30 m),

Kevin Davidson

which is a good target for this dive as to reach it the diver has to pass through the dense shoals of large barracuda, tuna, and jacks that swirl in the shallower regions of the reef staying tight to the bommie. The cavern itself has rich colonies of gorgonians and sea whips clinging to stark overhangs, and beautiful smaller reef inhabitants cluster around the entrance. As on all dives in this region, look out for the larger animals cruising in the blue water around the bommie.

OTHER ACTIVITIES

As this is strict liveaboard territory, the attractions aside from the diving are somewhat limited! Those interested in activities other than diving are better served staying within the Barrier Reef, so that they can enjoy the numerous land-based activities of the Queensland Coast.

☎ **TELEPHONE NUMBERS**

Recompression chamber	+61-7-4796-2080
Hospital	+61-7-4796-2080
Marine Park Authority	+61-7-4750-0700

💻 **WEBSITES & E-MAIL**

The Australian Travel Commission	www.australia.com
Barrier Reef Australia	www.barrierreefaustralia.com

▲ **COLORFUL FISH**
Although it is the large pelagic species that draw divers to the Coral Sea, the smaller residents of the reef have a fascination of their own.

YONGALA

 VISIBILITY
Average visibility: 40 feet (12 m)

 MUST SEE
Sea snakes

 DOWNSIDE
Rough sea conditions

GETTING THERE
Around 30 international airlines fly to Australia. Cairns is the gateway to Great Barrier Reef, and has a large international airport. Many flights are heavily booked, so make plans well in advance. Departure tax on international flights is U.S.$19. This tax is usually included with the price of your airline ticket. Domestic flights are relatively cheap, and can be taken to Port Douglas or Townsville for access to the northern sections of the reef.

VISA
All nationalities except New Zealanders require a tourist visa or Electronic Travel Authority (E.T.A.), valid for 3 months, to enter Australia. These cost Aus.$20 (U.S.$11); standard visas cost U.S.$35. Longer-term visas can be applied for before leaving.

$ MONEY
Currency is the Australian dollar, and cash is readily available at A.T.M.s throughout the country. Operators and hotels of any size accept all major credit cards and traveler's checks.

THE WRECK OF THE YONGALA IS A BIOLOGICAL WONDER, AN OASIS OF LIFE IN THE SURROUNDING DESERT OF THE SANDFLATS OF THE QUEENSLAND SEABED. HERE YOU CAN OBSERVE GRAZING HERBIVORES ROAMING THE ENCRUSTED HULL AND DOG-FIGHTING PREDATORS WHEELING OVERHEAD—TRULY ONE OF THE WORLD'S GREAT WILDLIFE DIVES.

No one knows precisely what happened on board the S.S. *Yongala* in the early hours of March 24, 1911, but whatever it was caused her to go down with all hands inshore of the Great Barrier Reef. One of the smartest vessels working the Queensland Coast at that time, she was only on her 99th voyage, and had made this particular passage from Melbourne to Cairns many times before. It is possible that the cargo in her holds shifted as she battled her way through a fierce cyclone, or she was simply battered into submission by the gigantic waves in this notoriously rough area of inshore water. The *Yongala* had missed warnings of the cyclone, as she carried no telegraph equipment, an omission that cost the lives of all 121 of her passengers and crew.

▼ DEEP CORAL
The hard and soft coral growth on the *Yongala* completely covers the superstructure.

WATER TEMPERATURE

°C	°F	°C	°F
30 —	— 86	30 —	— 86
	27°C		24°C
20 —	80°F — 68	20 —	— 68
			75°F
10 —	— 50	10 —	— 50
0 —	— 32	0 —	— 32
Summer		Winter	

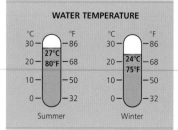

John Bantin

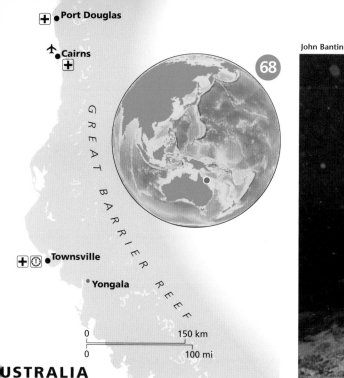

Port Douglas

Cairns

68

G R E A T   B A R R I E R   R E E F

Townsville

Yongala

| 0 | 150 km |
| 0 | 100 mi |

John Bantin

USTRALIA

The *Yongala* lay undiscovered for many years. In 1947 an Australian minesweeper clearly identified an object on the seabed as a wreck, but it was a further 11 years before it was definitively proved to be that of the *Yongala* after two salvage divers identified the name on the port side (she is lying on her starboard side.) The *Yongala* had lain untouched on the seabed for 41 years, time enough for a reef to develop. Since her discovery she has become a popular site with recreational divers, but despite this attention, she remains one of the finest wildlife wrecks on Earth. In 1981 she was given official protection under the Historic Shipwrecks Act.

GEOGRAPHY

The *Yongala* lies inside the Great Barrier Reef approximately 55 miles (90 km) southeast of Townsville, and a mere 6 miles (10 km) off the coast directly opposite Cape Bowling Green. Her uppermost rail is 40 feet (12 m) below the surface and her starboard side is on the seabed at 92 feet (28 m.) She is still facing in her original northerly direction of travel.

MARINE LIFE

Corals, with all their attendant species, large and small, have colonized the wreck of the *Yongala* in glorious profusion—indeed, many divers have compared the site to several miles of coral reef compressed into the 360-feet (109-m) length of the ship's hull, so vibrant is it with life. Hard corals grow abundantly along the wreck's entire length, mixed in with brightly colored soft corals and beautiful sea fans. Sponges and encrusting organisms cover the few exposed areas of the hull itself. Through this spectacular coral system move clouds of juvenile fish, fed on in turn by the top predators of the reef's food chain—jewfish, groupers, morays, and trevallies. Within the holds and recesses of the hull lurk sea snakes and octopuses, whilst in the blue water fringing the wreck you may be lucky enough to sight bull and tiger sharks as well as the occasional cruising loggerhead turtle.

THE DIVES

The *Yongala*'s wooden superstructure disappeared long ago, leaving only the steel hull and stark framework of struts and metal spars. As the wreck is a protected historic site, divers are strictly forbidden from penetrating the interior. Don't be tempted, however enticing the overhangs and doorways—one overzealous diver was recently fined Aus.$1500 for doing so. In any case, the wonders of the *Yongala* do not lie inside the wreck; they coat the exterior in great masses of corals and encrusting organisms on the hull, in the open water, and on the seabed around the wreck.

For the sake of simplicity, two separate dives are described, although it is possible to explore the whole ship's length in a single dive.

▲ OLIVE SEA SNAKE

An olive sea snake moves along broken coral on the seabed next to the *Yongala*.

Dan Burton

► QUEENSLAND GROUPER
An underwater cameraman encounters a Queensland grouper close to the bow of the *Yongala*.

 DIVE CENTERS

GINGARA ECO TOURS
P.O. Box 997, Townsville,
QLD 4810, Australia
Phone: +61-7-4771-6187

PRO DIVE PTY LTD
34/330 Wattle St., Ultimo,
NSW 2007, Australia
Phone: +61-2-8116-1100
E-mail: Travel@prodive.com.au
Web: www.prodive.com.au

DIVING ORGANIZATIONS
The Queensland Government produces guidelines for the recreational diving industry that can be accessed on their website at:
Web: www.whs.qld.gov.au

RECOMPRESSION
Townsville General Hospital
Eyre Street, Townsville,
QLD 4810, Australia
Phone: +61-7-4796-2080

HOSPITAL
The Wesley Park Haven Private Hospital
9-13 Bayswater Road, Hyde Park,
QLD 4810, Australia
Phone: +61-7-4796-2080

Townsville General Hospital
Eyre Street, Townsville,
QLD 4810, Australia
Phone: +61-7-4796-2080

CONSERVATION SOCIETY
Great Barrier Reef Marine Park Authority
P.O. Box 1379, Townsville,
QLD 4810, Australia
Phone: +61-7-4750-0700
Fax: +61-7-4772-6093
E-mail: info@reefHQ.org.au
Web: www.gbrmpa.gov.au

THE BOW

• 40 to 65 feet (12 to 20 m) • beginner

This dive takes you down the shot line on the wreck. As the shape of the bow swiftly emerges from the seabed, pause at the base of the line to glance along the side of the hull where hunting trevallies prowl above the encrusting coral and sponges, ambushing anything unwise enough to venture from the safety of the reef.

Dropping beneath the gloom of the hull, you are guaranteed an eyeball to eyeball encounter with at least one giant Queensland grouper. Look down toward the white sand beneath the bow where you will see bull rays and guitar sharks on the seabed. In the blue water around the entire wreck there is the distinct possibility of observing bull and tiger sharks—indeed some operators advise divers not to swim away from the wreck for this very reason.

As you move along the superstructure of the wreck, you are rewarded with an awe-inspiring display of reef life. Beautiful hard and soft corals abound, sea fans wave in the current, and moving in and out of them are a host of multicolored crustaceans and mollusks. Best of all is the sight of large coral trout ambushing prey from their lairs beneath the hard corals that coat the davits and spars emerging from the hull.

Moving back up the hull, you return to the shot line along the port side. During this phase of the dive you find yourself in the midst of the killing grounds above the protection of the reef—a boiling mass of furious predatory activity. It is also an ideal opportunity to peer into the blue water above the wreck seeking larger predators and passing pelagics.

THE MAIN HULL

• 40 to 100 feet (12 to 30 m) • intermediate

This dive takes in the entire wreck, and allows you to form an overall impression of the intense aggregation of life that has colonized the *Yongala*. Starting at the shot line on the bow, you drop immediately to the seabed at 100 feet (30 m) on the superstructure side of the wreck. Initially you travel along the starboard rail, gradually rising up the wreck all the way to the stern, encountering rays, guitar and angel sharks as you go. Do not forget to take a good look up into the mass of life that inhabits the coral growth on the top of the wreck superstructure.

Peer into—but do not enter—the hold, where you will see millions of juvenile cardinal fish. Groupers, lionfish, trevallies, and jewfish compete for the small pilchards and glassfish swarming around encrusted spars. Particularly exciting is the presence inside and around the wreck of several rare animals that divers do not generally encounter. Especially famous are the large numbers of olive sea snakes. Anyone who dives the *Yongala* for more than a couple of days is almost certainly guaranteed a hair-raising encounter with at least one of these creatures.

For a breathtaking experience, make your return to the shot line by swimming along the port side of the hull—a 360-feet (109-m) journey that offers you an exciting passage through large predators. You will find yourself in the midst of hunting trevallies and jewfish who appear completely undisturbed by the presence of divers. They race along the side of the hull, twisting inches away from your mask as they hurtle into silver shoals of baitfish.

OTHER ACTIVITIES

The *Yongala* is accessed from Townsville, a town with an outback feel to it, containing a greater than average number of backpackers' bars and hostels. For a more general view of Queensland's wildlife during time away from diving, visit Magnetic Island just off the coast, which contains a large National Park. There is also Reef H.Q., a beautifully set up aquarium and education center. The Billabong Wildlife Sanctuary offers the chance to interact with animals in rainforest, wetlands, and eucalyptus forest. The Habitat Wildlife Sanctuary at Port Douglas is set up on a similar basis, with the added attraction of a large grassland area.

☎ TELEPHONE NUMBERS

Recompression chamber   +61-7-4796-2080
Hospital   +61-7-4796-2080
Marine Park Authority   +61-7-4750-0800

🖥 WEBSITES & E-MAIL

Travel Commission   www.australia.com
Info site   www.barrierreefaustralia.com

▼ BULL RAY
Large bull rays are frequently seen cruising the seabed or lying under the sandy surface.

Dan Burton

RAINBOW
WARRIOR

words by Jane Burnett

BLOWN UP BY THE FRENCH SECRET SERVICE IN AUCKLAND HARBOUR IN 1986, THE PRIDE OF GREENPEACE NOW MAKES A FASCINATING, IF POIGNANT, DIVE.

VISIBILITY

Variable depending on weather conditions

DOWNSIDE

Cold water

Remote

Occasional poor visibility

GETTING THERE

To the north of tourist hotspot, the Bay of Islands, Matauri Bay can be reached by driving north from Auckland on State Highway 1 to Pakaraka, then taking the scenic route (highway 10) towards Whangaroa. About two-thirds of the way along this road, turn right for Matauri Bay.

VISA

A valid passport is all that is necessary for citizens of most countries.

$ MONEY

Currency is the N.Z. dollar. You'll have no trouble with major traveler's checks and credit cards.

I n July 1986, the Greenpeace flagship *Rainbow Warrior* was campaigning in the South Pacific against French Government nuclear testing in Moruroa atoll, French Polynesia. On a brief stopover in Auckland Harbour on July 10, two mines were detonated, sinking the ship and killing the Greenpeace photographer, Fernando Pereira. The event shocked the world. Eventually, responsibility was traced to the French Secret Service.

Two years later the *Rainbow Warrior* was refloated, towed north of the Bay of Islands and sunk once more to become an artificial reef. It was felt to be a suitable end for a vessel that had campaigned so effectively on environmental issues.

GEOGRAPHY

The *Rainbow Warrior's* final resting place is in the Cavalli Islands just off Matauri Bay. New Zealand's most northern region, Northland, stretches from Auckland to the tip of North Island, Cape Reinga. Matauri Bay is about two-thirds of the way up on the east.

The Pacific coast's volcanic past has created a rocky, uneven shoreline with numerous bays, headlands and islands. The gentler Tasman Sea side has fabulous beaches including the incorrectly named Ninety Mile Beach—it's actually a mere 55 miles (88 km)!

MARINE LIFE

After 20 years, the *Rainbow Warrior* is well on its way to becoming one with its environment. The wreck is completely encrusted with luxuriant marine growth. Most dominant are the jewel anemones. In every color imaginable, they have colonized almost every square inch of the ship. The hull, a patchwork of vibrant color as the polyps reproduce themselves across its surface, provides an ideal position for the filter-feeders to take advantage of the currents swirling around the wreck.

Fish life is abundant on the wreck, on the surrounding reef and in the water column. One of North Island's most plentiful residents is the two-spot demoiselle. Bright blue with, unsurprisingly, two white spots on its back, the demoiselle seems to turn up everywhere. Over the summer breeding season the female lays her eggs and then departs without so much as an adieu, abandoning the male who is left guarding

Jane Burnett

WATER TEMPERATURE

°C	°F	°C	°F
30	86	30	86
20	68	20	68
22°C			
10 72°F	50	10 14°C	50
		57°F	
0	32	0	32
Summer		Winter	

69

• Rainbow Warrior

0   200 km

0   200 mi

• Auckland

NEW ZEALAND
North Island

▼ **PARENTAL DUTY**

A two-spot demoiselle guards its eggs on the deck of the *Rainbow Warrior*.

DIVE CENTERS

None, but First Light Travel and Global Dive can arrange individualized itineraries that include the *Rainbow Warrior*.
www.firstlighttravel.com/dive.html
www.globaldive.net

▶▶ NEW LIFE IS VERDANT

Anemones festoon the wreck and make it a colorful dive.

▼ GHOSTS OF THE PAST

Diving a wreck that has such a tragic and well-known history can be an eerie experience.

Jane Burnett

the eggs until they hatch. The soon-to-be fathers can get quite agitated if they feel you are a threat to their precious offspring.

Red pigfish and leatherjackets are both common fish on the wreck. The pigfish are especially keen to introduce themselves to divers and will come in close to admire themselves in your camera lens as you take their picture.

If you decide to do a nonwreck dive in the area, you will find the surrounding reefs very pleasant if not exactly stunning. New Zealand kelp is a gorgeous golden-green, and there's a lot of it here, providing a rich backdrop for some of the local characters. This is the domain of Sandager's wrasse, a large, territorial fish that hunts in packs across the reefs of northern New Zealand. Brilliantly colored and unmistakable, the male Sandager starts life as a female, only changing gender when a vacancy arises. When the incumbent male dies, the most dominant female transforms to takes his place as leader of the harem.

As you fin across the reef, enjoying the "silent world," you may be startled by a sudden loud, repetitive noise. You could be forgiven for thinking you were listening to parrotfish feeding as the sound is not too dissimilar, but there are no parrotfish in New Zealand. The culprit is the red moki, a big bruiser of a fish, a real "fish with attitude." With their distinctive reddish brown vertical stripes and huge fleshy lips, they move slowly across the reef. The sound is their lips hitting rock surfaces as they attempt to dislodge food. One of the reef's great characters, they are reputed to live for up to 60 years. This longevity, together with their friendliness, has led to overfishing in the past. Many now consider it bad form to spearfish them, as they are so easy to catch.

You may also glimpse a stingray in the kelp, which will add a frisson of excitement to your dive.

OTHER ACTIVITIES

Don't miss the Greenpeace memorial. The ship's propeller provides a striking monument to its untimely and cruel loss and to Fernando Pereira who so tragically died in the incident. The nearby signpost points to all the places involved—Auckland, Moruroa Atoll, Paris and the current site of the *Rainbow Warrior*. A quick hike up the hill as the sun rises will bring home just what an idyllic spot has been chosen as the *Warrior's* last resting place.

DIVING PERHAPS THE WORLD'S MOST CONTROVERSIAL WRECK

Most divers visiting New Zealand make straight for the world famous Poor Knights Islands (see page 336). They are closer to Auckland and offer a range of organized dive operations. However, diving the *Rainbow Warrior* will make an interesting and poignant side trip. Bear in mind that there is no dive center on site so you will have to organize the diving in advance (see box to the left).

As wreck dives go, the *Warrior* does not rate high in the excitement stakes. It's a small ship and you can take in all there is to see in one dive. It sits proudly on the seabed at 90 feet (27 m) with its deck at about 50 feet (15 m) and is still fairly intact, although signs of deterioration are becoming more noticeable. Covered with the growth of 20 years, the *Warrior* makes an absorbing dive, particularly for those who remember it from her heyday and the shock felt around the world at its demise. As mentioned earlier, the propeller, has been removed and is the basis of the memorial overlooking the bay.

Originally a fishery research trawler (the *"Sir William Hardy"* built in 1955), the *Rainbow Warrior* was bought by Greenpeace in 1978. After a coat of paint and with the dove of peace displayed on its bow, she set off on her first mission to save the whales. Later its campaigning widened to include leading protests against nuclear testing by the French, whose intelligence operatives (the DGSE) sank the ship with explosives.

You dive the *Rainbow Warrior* for what it represents, for its fascinating life story and adventurous achievements, not for what it is now.

POOR KNIGHTS
ISLANDS

KILLER WHALES, MAKO SHARKS, AND STINGRAYS CAN ALL BE SEEN IN THE COLD WATERS THAT SWIRL AROUND THE POOR KNIGHTS, A GROUP OF ISLANDS, SACRED TO THE MAORI PEOPLE OF NEW ZEALAND, THAT OFFERS SOME OF THE BEST TEMPERATE-ZONE DIVING IN THE SOUTHERN HEMISPHERE.

 VISIBILITY

90 to 150 feet (27 to 46 m) Jan–May

10 to 100 feet (3 to 30 m) May–Dec

 MUST SEES

Southern Arch

Rikoriko Cave

Tie Dye Arch

Stingray gatherings

Dense invertebrate life

 DOWNSIDE

Cold water

Remote

Occasional poor visibility

 GETTING THERE

By international flight to Auckland, then on to Whangarei. The Poor Knights Islands can be reached from Tutukaka Harbor, 18 miles (30 km) from Whangarei. A number of charter boats operate from Tutukaka. Departure tax on international flights is N.Z.$25.

 VISA

A valid passport is all that is necessary for citizens of most countries.

 MONEY

Currency is the N.Z. dollar. You'll have no trouble with major traveler's checks and credit cards.

The Poor Knights lie 14 miles (22 km) off the northeast coast of New Zealand's North Island amidst cold, nutrient-rich water that are a beacon for marine life—the rocky margins of the islands contain the greatest diversity of fish and invertebrate species in New Zealand. The islands themselves, separated from the mainland more than two million years ago, are densely forested and are home to rare species of wildlife.

In the past the islands had a bloody history, but following a terrible massacre in 1820 the local Maori tribe declared them *tapu* (sacred). In 1977 their unique ecosystems were granted the highest form of protection under New Zealand law and since that date the only people to set foot on the Poor Knights have been conservationists, scientists, and Maori leaders—and even these visits take place very occasionally.

▼ SHARKS FIN CAVE

The caves, caverns, tunnels, and arches within the Poor Knights create an underwater labyrinth.

Monty Halls

	WATER TEMPERATURE		
°C	°F	°C	°F
30	86	30	86
20 **24°C 75°F**	68	20	68
10	50	10 **15°C 59°F**	50
0	32	0	32
Summer		Winter	

Ngaroimata Bay

Northern Arch

Barren Arch

Cleanerfish Bay

Cave Bay
Middle Arch — Tawhiti Rahi — Dark Forest
Bernie's Cave — Island

POOR KNIGHTS ISLANDS (New Zealand)

Air Bubble Cave
Rocklilly Inlet

Landing Bay Pinnacle

Maomao Arch

Motu Kapiti Island

Deep Forest

Sand Garden
Nursery Cove

Bennett's Bommie

El Torito Cave

Fred's Pinnacle

Rikoriko Cave
Aorangi Island
Foam Bay

The Chimney
Runaway Bay

The Tunnel
South — Aorangaia Island
Harbour — Shaft Cave
Jan's Tunnel — Blue Maomao Arch

Archway Island
Southern Arch

0 ———————— 3 km
0 ———————— 2 mi
Please note that the distance between the
main island group and The Pinnacles has
been reduced and is not to scale.

The Pinnacles
Tie Dye Arch

GEOGRAPHY

The Poor Knights rise some 295 feet (90 m) from the seabed. They are made up of two main islands and ten smaller islets, the remnants of a long extinct volcano. The two largest islands, Tawhiti Rahi and Aorangi, have a total land area between them of only 494 acres (200 ha). The violent volcanic upheavals of the distant geological past are obviously reflected in the dramatic convoluted reefs and walls beneath the water that surrounds the islands, making them so attractive to both fish and visiting divers.

MARINE LIFE

What strikes anyone diving the Poor Knights is the sheer numbers of fish that swarm in, over, and around this twisted and contorted collection of arches, gullies, and overhangs. Incredibly dense aggregations of certain

Glenn Edney

70

▲ POOR KNIGHTS ISLANDS
The volcanic origins of the Poor Knights Islands are apparent both above and below the water's surface.

resident species may be found beneath arches and within caves. Marine biologists estimate that the Poor Knights shelter some 120 species of resident fish, more than anywhere else in New Zealand.

This abundance of year-round residents attracts periodic visits from numerous predators, including killer whales and mako sharks. In recent years, a population of bronze whaler sharks has taken up residence at the Poor Knights—an indication that the islands' bustling ecosystem is in good health, able to accommodate the permanent presence of apex predators in its foodweb. But the outstanding event at the Poor Knights is the seasonal gatherings of mating congregations of stingrays under Southern Arch. Sometimes hundreds of animals will be stacked up from seabed to surface.

THE DIVES

Most of the dives take place either under arches or within small caverns, or along beautifully colonized walls. There are certain areas where relatively shallow patches of sand and kelp exist, and at the right time of year these are the perfect places to find numbers of stingrays. Most operators run out of Tutukaka. The 14-mile (22-km) journey in powerful dive boats takes about

DIVER'S TIP

Landing on any of the islands, stacks, or rocks of the Poor Knights Islands, including the Sugarloaf and High Peaks (Pinnacles) to the south, is prohibited without a permit from the Department of Conservation. Boats must not be tied to any part of the shoreline.

Glenn Edney

▶ SHORT-TAILED STINGRAY

Although present in small numbers throughout the year, the aggregations of short-tailed stingrays from December to March have made the Poor Knights particularly renowned.

DIVE CENTERS

DIVE TUTUKAKA

Poor Knights Dive Centre
Marina Road, Tutukaka, RD3, Whangarei, New Zealand
New Zealand toll free: +0-800-288-882
Phone: +64-9-434-3867
E-mail: info@diving.co.nz
Web: www.diving.co.nz

OCEAN BLUE ADVENTURES

Tutukaka, Whangarei, New Zealand
Phone: +64-274-880-459
E-mail: info@oceanblue.co.nz
Web: www.oceanblue.co.nz

DIVING ORGANIZATIONS

The New Zealand Underwater Council
1/40 Mt. Eden Road, Auckland, New Zealand
Phone: +64-9-623-3252
Web: www.nzunderwater.org.nz

RECOMPRESSION

Slark Hyperbaric Unit
Te Taua Moana O Aotearoa,
Navy Hospital, 91 Calliope Road,
Devonport, H.M.N.Z.S. Naval Base,
Private Bag 32901, Auckland, New Zealand
Phone: +64-9-445-5920

HOSPITAL

Whangarei Area Hospital
Northland Health Limited, Hospital Road,
Whangarei, New Zealand
Phone: +64-9-430-4100

Bay of Islands Hospital
Maunu Road, Kawakawa, New Zealand
Phone: +64-9-404-0280

CONSERVATION SOCIETY

Department of Conservation,
59 Boulcott Street, P.O. Box 10420,
Wellington, New Zealand
Phone: +64-4-472-5821
Web: www.doc.govt.nz

90 minutes. The diving infrastructure here is truly top-class. One operator in particular (Dive Tutukaka) runs one of the slickest dive operations a diver is likely to encounter anywhere in the world.

The water can be nippy, especially in the winter, and on the exposed seaward side of the islands (particularly when diving the wreck of the Tui) it can get fairly rough. One of the great advantages of the rugged topography of the islands is the fact that even in fairly unpleasant weather, there is always a sheltered spot to be found somewhere.

TIE DYE ARCH

• **15 to 50 feet (5 to 15 m)** • **beginner**

Situated to the south of Aorangi Island, Tie Dye Arch is a typical Poor Knights' dive—a large arch busy with fish swimming in all directions over rockfaces and densely colonized boulders and reefs. You enter the arch and swim along a shallow wall until the seabed drops away and the walls on either side of the channel draw closer together to form a natural tunnel. This is inhabited by large schools of demoiselles and blue maomao, as well as sandager's wrasse, ubiquitous residents of the Poor

Knights. Study the faces of the rock walls carefully—there is every chance you will spot large scorpionfish and moray eels, five species of which are to be found at the Poor Knights. At the right time of the year, you may also encounter long- and short-tailed stingrays in the arch.

SOUTHERN ARCH

- 15 to 70 feet (5 to 20 m) • intermediate

In the summer months, this dive is one of the best in New Zealand. Indeed, when huge mating congregations of short-tailed stingrays are present in the arch, it rates as one of the finest large animal encounters in the world. Each animal has a wingspan of up to 6 feet (2 m) and the groups of rays may stretch from seabed to surface—an awesome sight. (You also get congregations of stingrays in the Northern Arch, not described here.)

Whether or not the rays are present, Southern Arch is still a fine dive. You begin by moving along a large wall towards the arch that plunges to a considerable depth. Colonies of sponges, bryozoans, and cnidarians festoon these walls so thickly that there are very few places where bare rock can be sighted. Swimming off the rockface are the usual wrasse and demoiselles, and in mid water you may spot hunting shoals of trevallies pursuing swarms of mysid shrimp that congregate here.

Just before the arch there is a cave in the rockface. Use caution when entering this cave as, once inside it, there is no clear passage to the surface. Nevertheless, it is a spectacular system, opening out into a large cavern that is dimly lit from light filtering through the entrance, so it is well worth exploring.

On leaving the cave, you encounter the arch itself a few yards further along the wall. The entire area under the arch is lit by an eerie light filtering down from the surface. Here you will meet of shoals of blue and pink maomao and some extremely large scorpion fish. Stingrays are frequently encountered on the seabed at the entrance to the arch, and inspection of the arch walls and scattered boulders on the seabed will reveal the presence of many moray eels.

BLUE MAOMAO ARCH

- 15 to 60 feet (5 to 18 m) • beginner

As its name suggests, the distinguishing feature of this dive is the permanent population of blue maomao you meet up with on the left-hand wall as soon as you enter the arch. The shoal numbers several thousand individuals, each one approximately 12 inches (30 cm) long. The shoal has become quite accustomed to being disturbed and will part to accommodate divers as they swim through the tunnel created by the arch. As the huge shoal of beautifully colored fish swarms around a diver or group of divers, there are opportunities for really spectacular photographs, lit by the green glow of the light filtering through the far end of the tunnel.

RIKORIKO CAVE

- 30 feet (10 m) • beginner

Rikoriko is a Maori word meaning "cave of dancing light and echoes." Formed from a gigantic lava bubble, this is one of the largest sea caves on Earth, and is a sphere 250 feet (76 m) in diameter. Only half of the cave is filled with water, but this still allows room for a large dive boat to enter.

This fascinating dive can be undertaken by relative novices. Most of the dive takes place at the rear of the cave in the darkness of the far wall. The marine life here is generally less abundant than in the rest of the Poor Knights, but there are species not seen anywhere else in the archipelago. These include some deep-water invertebrates normally found at depths of 300 ft (90 m), as well as gigantic salps. No dive at Rikoriko is complete without testing the echoes of the cave after exiting the water—the booming lingering sound leaves you in no doubt as to how the cave got its name.

OTHER ATTRACTIONS

This is a stunning area of New Zealand coastline, with miles of deserted beaches and picturesque coves and bays. There is an excellent restaurant in Tutukaka called Schnappa Rock, which is an absolute must. About an hours drive down the coast is the market town of Whangarei, providing banks, internet services, and all the other requirements of the modern traveler. To the north of Tutukaka are some splendid surfing beaches.

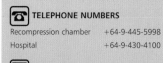

TELEPHONE NUMBERS

Recompression chamber	+64-9-445-5998
Hospital	+64-9-430-4100

WEBSITES & E-MAIL

Tourism Organization	www.purenz.com
Dive site	www.divenewzealand.com

OTHER DIVE SITES

Barren Arch
Dark Forest
Air Bubble Cave
Maomao Arch
Deep Forest
Bennett's Bommie
Fred's Pinnacle
The Tunnel
Shaft Cave
Jan's Tunnel
The Chimney
El Torito Cave
Nursery Cove
Sand Garden
Landing Bay Pinnacle
Bernie's Cave
Middle Arch
Northern Arch

▼ **YELLOW MORAY**
A yellow moray peers out from a crevice colonized by ascidians.

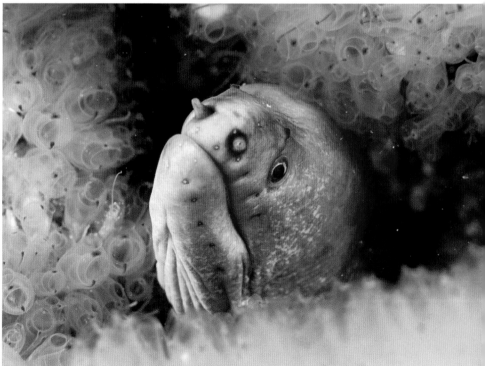

Glenn Edney

THE LERMONTOV

THIS MIGHTY RUSSIAN CRUISE LINER MET HER END IN MYSTERIOUS CIRCUM-STANCES OFF THE NORTHERN TIP OF NEW ZEALAND'S SOUTH ISLAND. THE SUBJECT OF MYTH AND RUMOR, HER SECRETS SANK WITH HER, LEAVING ONLY A REMARK-ABLE DIVING EXPERIENCE IN THE COLD WATERS OF MARLBOROUGH SOUNDS.

 VISIBILITY

Varies from 10 to 100 feet (3 to 30 m) depending on swell and tidal currents. Sites close to run-offs can have very low visibility after heavy rains.

✔ **MUST SEES**

Mikhail Lermontov
Killer Whales

✗ **DOWNSIDE**

Cold
Limited visibility
Hazardous wreck

✈ **GETTING THERE**

Auckland is the major exit/entry point for international flights to New Zealand, but you can also fly to Wellington or Christchurch and Queenstown. Departure tax on international flights is N.Z.$25. It is possible to take a ferry to Picton from Wellington, or alternatively fly to Nelson Airport on South Island from Auckland, Wellington, and Christchurch. Both Nelson and Picton are within striking distance of Marlborough Sounds.

🛂 **VISA**

Only a valid passport is necessary for citizens of most countries.

$ **MONEY**

Currency is the N.Z. dollar. You'll have no trouble with major traveler's checks and credit cards. Banks will give cash advances on Visa and MasterCard, but for American Express card transactions you must go to an American Express office.

WATER TEMPERATURE

°C	°F	°C	°F
30 – 86		30 – 86	
20 – 68		20 – 68	
22°C **71°F**			
10 – 50		10 – **14°C** **57°F** – 50	
0 – 32		0 – 32	
Summer		Winter	

The *Mikhail Lermontov*, launched in 1973, was the pride of the Soviet Union's passenger fleet—a massive vessel at 578 feet (176 m) long, she had a gross tonnage of just over 20,000 tonnes. On her maiden voyage she became the first Russian liner to enter New York Harbor for 25 years, and she continued visiting New York until the Soviet invasion of Afghanistan in 1980 soured U.S.-Soviet relations. She was refitted in the mid-1980s at a cost of $15 million, and switched to cruising in southern waters. She carried 550 passengers, their experience enhanced by the presence of 330 crew catering to their every whim. The great ship had a pool, a cinema, five bars, shops, a library, and a ballroom where shows were staged every night.

In February 1986, the *Mikhail Lermontov* left Sydney, Australia, on a two-week cruise to New Zealand with virtually a full complement of passengers and crew on board. On February 16, she was cruising in the spectacular waters of Marlborough Sounds on a clear calm day. The skipper handed the vessel over to local harbor pilot Don Jamieson, a man with 20 years' experience of guiding vessels through the Sounds. Jamieson steamed the liner between the Cape Jackson headland and the light on Walker Rock a mere 164 feet (50 m) away, a suicidally narrow gap for such a large vessel. The *Mikhail Lermontov* was making a speed of 15 knots when she inevitably struck the rocks and sustained a mortal blow on her port side. She limped into the bay at Port Gore listing heavily. The captain did not send out any mayday signal, and it took a flotilla of boats mobilized by watching locals to ensure that all the passengers and crew reached safety, although one crew member was lost in the initial impact with the reef. The ship drifted onto a sandbank, but was lifted off into deeper water by the rising tide, and sank.

Don Jamieson refused to speak publicly about the disaster, and later surrendered his pilot licence. The cause of this extraordinary sinking will remain a tantalizing mystery because the subsequent formal inquiry by the Ministry of Transport was conducted behind closed doors. Not surprisingly, all kinds of theories proliferate.

Some people have cited K.G.B. plots, claiming that the Russians needed a sunken navigation marker for their submarines, whilst others hint at inebriation and deceit—all very intriguing. The site today retains a very compelling air of mystery, and is one of New Zealand's premier big wreck dives.

Dan Burton

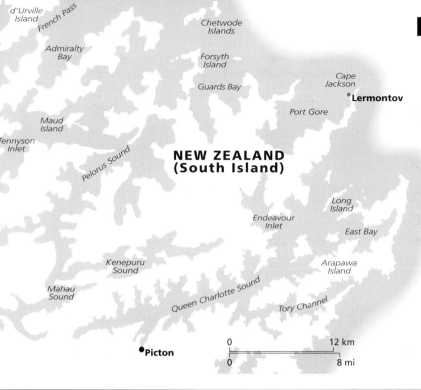

d'Urville
Island
French Pass

Admiralty
Bay

Chetwode
Islands

Forsyth
Island

Guards Bay

Cape
Jackson
Lermontov

Maud
Island

Port Gore

Tennyson
Inlet

Pelorus Sound

NEW ZEALAND
(South Island)

Long
Island

Endeavour
Inlet

East Bay

Kenepuru
Sound

Arapawa
Island

Mahau
Sound

Queen Charlotte Sound

Tory Channel

Picton

0   12 km
0   8 mi

▼ **LIMITED VISIBILITY**
Though the visibility might not be the greatest, however, the planking on the deck is clearly visible when diving the *Lermontov*.

► **SCORPIONFISH**

Large scorpionfish lurk in ambush on the wreck of the *Lermontov*.

Glenn Edney

GEOGRAPHY

Port Gore is located on the northeastern tip of South Island on the other side of Cook Strait from Wellington. The bay where the wreck lies is enclosed within a great amphitheater of green hills that plunge toward the water. The scenery is tremendously dramatic, with the odd house here and there clinging to the hillside at the end of a sinuous ribbon of road.

MARINE LIFE

The wreck itself is not too overgrown, and is mainly covered in a fine layer of algae and filamentous weed. Hidden among this are some tremendously large scorpionfish, worthy of note for both the experienced underwater photographer and the ham-fisted diver. There are also some large conger, as well as ling and hundreds of blue cod. Look out for octopuses in the numerous dark mini caves and caverns created by the wreck's superstructure and decaying decking.

Killer whales are occasionally seen in the bay of Port Gore, and seem relatively at ease with the presence of boats. Actually entering the water with the killer whales is a question of personal choice; the limited visibility of the area can make it somewhat daunting, although the rewards are obvious. However, the whales often seem to move away as soon as snorkelers enter the water, so

it may in fact be more fulfilling to stay on the boat and observe them from close range on the surface. This can be a tremendous experience set against the stunning backdrop of the hills surrounding Port Gore.

THE DIVES

The depth, low water temperature, and limited visibility, combined with the scale and deterioration of the wreck, make this a potentially hazardous dive. Four divers have lost their lives in the labyrinth of passageways and pitch-black cavernous open spaces of the *Lermontov*, and penetrations of this wreck should be taken very seriously. The interior of the wreck is deteriorating fast, and is heavily silted—a distinctly unforgiving environment for the foolhardy. A knowledgeable guide is an absolute must for any intended deep penetrations, as well as the prerequisite level of experience and appropriate equipment.

The wreck lies on her starboard side on a gentle 10 degree slope in 120 feet (37 m) of water, with the port bridge wing a mere 40 feet (12 m) below the surface. Visibility varies around the wreck from a maximum of 50 feet (15 m) to a minimum of virtually nil, and seems to be strongly affected by run-off from the surrounding hills after rainfall. The last 30 feet (10 m) of the shot is a massive chain, and is secured to the upper promenade deck at about 50 feet (15 m) depth. Many divers compare diving the *Lermontov* to the wrecks of Scapa Flow—a massive structure to explore in sometimes limited visibility, cold water, and considerable depth. The comparison is a good one, and the rewards of taking on such challenging sites are similar.

The dives listed here are simple explorations of the outside of the *Lermontov*. More complex penetrations are omitted as they have to be briefed in considerable detail. One penetration particularly favored by local divers is the ballroom.

THE BOW AND BRIDGE

• 80 feet (25 m) • intermediate

This is almost as simple as a dive on this wreck gets, and allows the diver to experience the scale of the vessel as well as glimpse the remarkable state of preservation of some of the open spaces.

From the shot line drop slightly down the top of the superstructure to outside the promenade deck. Turning right, fin past the empty lifeboat davits until the bridge wing emerges from the gloom. There is an open hatch on the side of the bridge allowing a very clear view into the bridge itself illuminated by the front windows, several of which have been put-through to allow divers access. Whether entering through one of these windows or the open door on the wing, you will find it something of a tight squeeze. Once in the bridge take some time to find the ship's con, still marvelously well preserved, as well as the instrument banks of the bridge itself. Take care not to stir up silt when exploring this area. Exit the bridge and continue forward to the bow using a large cable running from the wing to navigate— it's a considerable distance so watch your air for the return journey. Worthy of note is the decking on the bow, still well preserved, and of course the great sweep of the bow itself.

THE SWIMMING POOL AND STERN

• 80 feet (25 m) • intermediate

On reaching the base of the shot line move left following the outside of the promenade deck. At the end of the promenade deck move over and down the superstructure of the large clear upper deck (look out for a substantial cargo net as a location marker), and from there continue toward the stern and the glass-covered swimming pool. From the pool ascend slightly and explore the glass panels of the stern promenade area, following it left to the outside of the stern before moving back up and over the hull to return toward the shot line.

OTHER ACTIVITIES

It is well worth making the three-hour drive from the ferry port of Picton to French Pass just for the sake of scenery alone, which is reminiscent of the lochs and hills of the Scottish Highlands. However, French Pass is a narrow passage that has one of the strongest tidal races on the planet, so it should not be missed for this reason. Slack tide lasts a mere 12 minutes, and it is truly a great experience to swing and corkscrew through whirlpools and eddies in a local boat as the tide rushes beneath you. Killer whales are also sighted in this region fairly frequently.

TELEPHONE NUMBERS

Recompression chamber	+64-9-445-8454
Hospital	+64-3-548-3455
Ministry of Tourism	+64-4-917-5400

WEBSITES & E-MAIL

Ministry of Tourism	www.tourisminfo.govt.nz
Diving in New Zealand	www.divenewzealand.com
New Zealand Tourist Board	www.purenz.com
Local travel site	www.destinationmarlborough.com

▼ **DRAMATIC SCENERY**
The scenery on the way to French Pass is as dramatic as the diving when you get there.

Dan Burton

Wakatobi

imagine the most amazing resort you will visit. Ever.

DECOMPRESSION SICKNESS & SAFE DIVING

Go beyond the physical limits of your body's capacity to absorb nitrogen by staying too deep for too long, ascend too quickly, or dive again too soon after a short surface interval, and you will very likely fall a victim to Decompression Sickness (D.C.S.), or the "bends"—a physical constraint that limits divers today just as it did Jacques Cousteau when he first used scuba to explore the ocean in 1943. However, the modern diver has the luxury of an array of systems to ensure that D.C.S. remains a remote risk. Detailed dive tables developed during years of research, combined with computers that monitor the diver's exposure to nitrogen absorption, have brought about a marked decrease in very serious D.C.S. incidents.

Yet incidents still occur. Diver error, equipment malfunction, or lack of appropriate training are often the obvious cause, but some divers appear to suffer from the random onset of D.C.S. symptoms although they have stuck assiduously to the rules. Naturally, they are left bewildered and upset, but almost invariably, when such cases are investigated, contributory factors emerge. Obesity, age, water temperature, an intense repetitive dive program, repeated ascents, the presence of an old injury, dehydration, or fatigue may all contribute to a so-called "unearned" D.C.S. incident.

Recent research indicates that a direct ascent to the first decompression stop, often at 30 or 20 feet (9 or 6 m), may cause micro bubbles to merge into larger bubbles in the blood, leading to the emergence of D.C.S. symptoms over time. Many operators who have dived the deeper sites around the world for decades have adopted the following simple measures to counter D.C.S. These measures are standard at deep sites such as Chuuk Lagoon, for example, where they have led to a considerable decrease in number of Decompression Sickness incidents.

• Divers should be rested, prepared, and briefed for the dive ahead.

• Divers should be well hydrated before and after the dive (certain operators insist that water or juice is drunk on completion of the dive.)

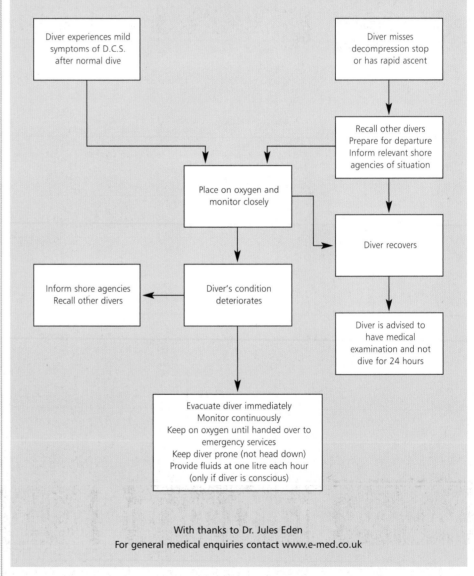

D.C.S. INCIDENT DIAGRAM

This guide tells you what simple actions to take in a suspected D.C.S. incident. Symptoms can appear minutes after a diver surfaces, and in about 80 percent of cases do so within 8 hours. Frequently, the first indications are tingling in the extremities. Subsequent pain, which ranges from mild to severe, is usually limited to the joints, but can be felt anywhere. Severe itching (pruritis), skin rashes, and skin mottling (cutis marmorata) are other possible symptoms.

Diver experiences mild symptoms of D.C.S. after normal dive

Diver misses decompression stop or has rapid ascent

Recall other divers
Prepare for departure
Inform relevant shore agencies of situation

Place on oxygen and monitor closely

Diver recovers

Inform shore agencies
Recall other divers

Diver's condition deteriorates

Diver is advised to have medical examination and not dive for 24 hours

Evacuate diver immediately
Monitor continuously
Keep on oxygen until handed over to emergency services
Keep diver prone (not head down)
Provide fluids at one litre each hour (only if diver is conscious)

With thanks to Dr. Jules Eden
For general medical enquiries contact www.e-med.co.uk

• Graded ascents should take place from deep dives; for example, decompression stops of two to three minutes at 60 and 40 feet (18 and 12 m) before the stops at 30 and 20 feet (9 or 6 m.)

• Decompression trapezes/lines should be a standard measure on any deeper dive. Some dive operators suspend a cylinder containing a nitrox mix (i.e. an increase in the amount of oxygen in the gas mix) at the shallower stops to help the decompressing diver get rid of excess nitrogen more rapidly.

• Ascent rates are extremely slow.

DIVE ORGANIZATIONS

		ADDRESS	PHONE	WEBSITE
DIVE FEDERATIONS & SOCIETIES				
Confederation Mondiale des Activites Subaquatiques	C.M.A.S.	World Underwater Federation, Viale Tiziano 74, 00196, Rome, Italy	+39-636-858-480	www.cmas2000.org
The Underwater Society of America	U.S.O.A.	53C Appian Way, South San Francisco, CA, 94080, U.S.A.	+1-650-583-8492	www.underwater-society.org
DIVER TRAINING				
American Nitrox Diving International	A.N.D.I.	74 Woodcleft Avenue, Freeport, NY, 11520-3342, U.S.A.	+1-516-546-3342	www.andihq.com
International Association of Nitrox & Technical Divers	I.A.N.T.D.	9628 NE 2nd Avenue, Suite D, Miami Shores, FL, 33138-2767, U.S.A.	+1-305-751-4873	www.iantd.com
National Assoc. for Cave Diving	N.A.C.D.	P.O. Box 14492, Gainesville, FL, 32604, U.S.A.	+1-888-565-6223	www.safecavediving.com
National Assoc. of Underwater Instructors	N.A.U.I.	P.O. Box 89789, Tampa, FL, 33689-0413, U.S.A.	+1-800-553-6284	www.nauiww.org
Professional Assoc. of Diving Instructors – Americas	P.A.D.I.	30151 Tomas Street, Rancho Santa Margarita, CA, 92688-2125, U.S.A.	+1-949-858-7234	www.padi.com
Professional Diving Instructors Corporation	P.D.I.C.	P.O. Box 3633, Scranton, PA, 18505, U.S.A.	+1-570-342-1480	www.pdic-intl.com
Scuba Diving International	S.D.I.	18 Elm Street, Topsham, MN, 04086, U.S.A.	+1-888-778-9073	www.tdisdi.com
Scuba Schools International	S.S.I.	2619 Canton Court, Fort Collins, CO, 80525-4498, U.S.A.	+1-970-482-0883	www.ssiusa.com
Y.M.C.A. Scuba	Y.M.C.A.	Y.M.C.A. of U.S.A. Scuba, 101 N. Wacker Drive, Chicago, IL, 60606, U.S.A.	+1-800-872-9622	www.ymcascuba.org
Diver Certification Board of Canada	D.C.B.C.	Suite 503, 5121 Sackville Street, Halifax, Nova Scotia, B3J 1K1, Canada	+1-902-465-3483	www.divercertification.com
Professional Assoc. of Diving Instructors – Canada	P.A.D.I.	107, 680 Broadway Street, Port Coquitlam, BC, V3C 2M8, Canada	+1-604-552-5969	www.padi.com
Professional Assoc. of Diving Instructors – International	P.A.D.I.	Unit 7 St Philips Central Albert Road, St Philips, Bristol, BS2 0PD, U.K.	+44-117-300-7234	www.padi.com
Sub-Aqua Association	S.A.A.	Space Solutions Business Centre,Sefton Lane, Maghull, Liverpool, L31 8BX, U.K.	+44-151-287-1001	www.saa.org.uk
The British Sub-Aqua Club	B.S.A.C.	Telford's Quay, South Pier Road, Ellesmere Port, Cheshire CH65 4FL, U.K.	+44-151-350-6200	www.bsac.com
The Scottish Sub-Aqua Club	S.S.A.C.	The Cockburn Centre, 40 Bogmoor Place, Glasgow, G51 4TQ, Scotland, U.K.	+44-141-425-1021	www.scotsac.com
Irish Underwater Council (Comhairle fo Thuinn)	C.F.T.	78a Patrick Street, Dun Laoghaire, Co. Dublin, Ireland	+353-1-284-4601	www.scubaireland.com
Professional Assoc. of Diving Instructors – Europe	P.A.D.I.	Oberwilerstrasse 3, CH-8442, Hettlingen, Switzerland	+41-523-041-414	www.padi.com
Verband Internationaler Tauchschulen	V.I.T.	VIT, Klaus Klink, Raunheimer Str. 44, D-55246, Mainz-Kostheim, Germany	+49-613-426-0489	www.vit-2000.de
Professional Assoc. of Diving Instructors – Norway	P.A.D.I.	PADI Nordic AS Oslo, Hyggenveien, 35, Royken, Norway	+47-31-292-750	www.padi.com
Professional Assoc. of Diving Instructors – Sweden	P.A.D.I.	Guilbergs Strandgarta 36E, 411-04 Gothenburg, Sweden	+46-31-808-840	www.padi.com
Professional Assoc. of Diving Instructors – Asia Pacific	P.A.D.I.	3/4 Skyline Place, French's Forest, New South Wales, Sydney 2086, Australia	+61-294-512-300	www.padi.com
Professional Assoc. of Diving Instructors – Japan	P.A.D.I.	1-20-1 Ebisu-Minami Shibuya-ku, Tokyo 150, Japan	+81-357-211-731	www.padi.com
DIVING WITH DISABILITIES				
Handicap Scuba Association International	H.S.A.	1104 El Prado, San Clemente, CA, 92672-4637, U.S.A.	+1-949-498-4540	www.hsascuba.com
Scuba Trust		13 Lade Fort Crescent, Lydd-On-Sea, Kent, TN29 9YG, U.K.	+44-798-502-5385	www.scubatrust.org.uk
International Association for Handicapped Divers	I.A.H.D.	Hazelaarlaan 47, 1775 EE Middenmeer, Netherlands	+31-227-503-631	www.iahd.org
MEDICAL				
e-Med		Hospital St John, 60 Grove End Road, St John's Wood, London NW8 9NH, U.K.	+44-207-806-4028	www.e-med.co.uk
U.K. Sport Diving Medical Committee	U.K.S.D.M.C.	Merryweathers, 34 Blackacre Road, Theydon Bois, Essex, CM16 7LU, U.K.	Not disclosed	www.uksdmc.co.uk
DIVER SAFETY				
American Academy of Underwater Sciences	A.A.U.S.	430 Nathant Road, Nathant, MA, 01908, U.S.A.	+1-781-581-7370	www.aaus.org
Dive Rescue International		201 North Link Lane, Fort Collins, CO, 80524-2712, U.S.A.	+1-970-482-0887	www.diverescueintl.com
Divers' Alert Network	D.A.N.	The Peter B. Bennett Center, 6 West Colony Place, Durham, NC 27705, U.S.A.	+1-919-684-2948	www.diversalertnetwork.org
International Association of Dive Rescue Specialists	I.A.D.R.S.	201 North Link Lane, Fort Collins, CO, 80524, U.S.A.	+1-970-482-1562	www.iadrs.org
Health & Safety Executive	H.S.E.	Caerphilly Business Park, Caerphilly, CF83 3GG, Wales, U.K.	+44-870-154-5500	www.hse.gov.uk
Cave Divers Association of Australia	C.D.A.A.	P.O. Box 290, North Adelaide, SA 5006, Australia	+61-408-374-112	www.cavedivers.com.au
Divers' Alert Network – S.E. Asia Pacific	D.A.N.	P.O. Box 384, Asburton, Victoria 3163, Australia	+61-82-129-242	www.danseap.com.au
CONSERVATION				
Conservation, Education, Diving, Archaeology & Museums	C.E.D.A.M.	One Fox Road, Croton-on-Hudson, NY, 10520, U.S.A.	+1-914-271-5365	www.cedam.org
Cousteau Society		710 Settlers' Landing Road, Hampton, VA, 23669, U.S.A.	+1-757-722-9300	www.cousteau.org
Marine Conservation Biology Institute	M.C.B.I.	15805 NE 47th Court, Redmond, WA, 98052, U.S.A.	+1-425-883-8914	www.mcbi.org
National Marine Sanctuaries		1305 East West Highway, Silver Spring, MD, 20910, U.S.A.	+1-301-713-3125	www.sanctuaries.noaa.gov
National Oceanic & Atmospheric Administration	N.O.A.A.	14th Street, NW, Room 6217, Washington DC, 20230, U.S.A.	+1-202-482-6090	www.noaa.org
Ocean Futures Society		325 Chapala Street, Santa Barbara, CA, 93101, U.S.A.	+1-805-899-8899	www.oceanfutures.org
Oceanic Research Group	O.R.G.	59 Old Andover Road, North Reading, MA, 01864, U.S.A.	+1-978-664-9091	www.oceanicresearch.org
Pacific Whale Foundation		300 Maalaea Road, Suite 211, Wailuku, HI, 96793, U.S.A.	+1-808-249-8811	www.pacificwhale.org
Reef Environment Education Foundation	R.E.E.F.	P.O. Box 246, Key Largo, FL, 33037, U.S.A.	+1-305-852-0030	www.reef.org
Reef Guardian International		2829 Bird Avenue, Suite 5, P.M.B. 162 Miami, FL, 33133, U.S.A.	+1-305-358-4600	www.reefguardian.org
The Coral Reef Alliance	CORAL	417 Montgomery Street, Suite 205, San Francisco, CA, 94104, U.S.A.	+1-415-834-0900	www.coralreefalliance.org
The Nature Conservancy		4245 North Fairfax Drive, Suite 100, Arlington, VA, 22203-1606, U.S.A.	+1-703-841-5300	www.nature.org
The Ocean Conservancy		1725 DeSales Street, NW, Suite 600, Washington DC, 20036, U.S.A.	+1-202-429-5609	www.oceanconservancy.org
Marine Conservation Society	M.C.S.	3 Wolf Business Park, Alton Road, Ross-on-Wye, Herefordshire, HR9 5NB, U.K.	+44-198-956-6017	www.mcsuk.org
The Historical Diving Society	H.D.S.	29 Pringle Croft, Woodend, Chorley, Lancashire, PR6 7UL, U.K.	+44-173-724-9961	www.thehds.com
The Shark Trust		National Maritime Aquarium, Plymouth, Devon, PL4 0LF, U.K.	+44-870-128-3045	www.sharktrust.org
White Shark Trust		P.O. Box 1258, Strand Street 6, Gansbaai 7220, Western Cape, South Africa	+27-283-840-331	www.whitesharktrust.org

worldwide diving holidays to suit all levels

more destinations
more flight options
more flexibility

learn to dive
land based extensions
liveaboards
photography trips with Tony White
special offers & late deals

sea of cortez . galapagos . caribbean . mediterranean . red sea
east & south africa . indian ocean . east asia . micronesia . pacific

email: us@divetours.co.uk

www.divetours.co.uk

+44 (0) 1244 401177

ATOL: T7057

GLOSSARY

Abyssal
Ocean features occurring at great depth, usually at more than 10,000 feet (3,000 m).

Atoll
A ring-shaped coral reef enclosing a lagoon that has grown up on top of a sunken volcano.

Baitball
Defensive formation assumed by small fish when under attack from predators.

Barotrauma
Pressure-related injury when diving at depth or decompressing.

Barrier reef
A coral reef that forms parallel to the shore but is separated from it by a wide strip of water.

Bends
See Decompression sickness

Biogeographic region
Term used by biologists for a geographical region and its distinct distribution of plants and animals.

Bleaching
Whitening of coral due to the expulsion of zooxanthellae, microscopic plants living within the coral polyps, thought to be caused by increased temperatures or stress.

Blue water
Any expanse of water where the diver cannot see the seabed.

Bommie
Isolated coral formation, generally fairly large.

Bounce dive
A single dive, normally to depth with very limited bottom time.

Build-up dive
Preparation dive in advance of more serious diving.

Cay or caye
Coral island, generally a term used in the Caribbean.

Check-out dive
Dive run by operator or center to check the proficiency of the diver.

Chum
Mix of fish, oil and offal used as bait to attract sharks to a dive boat.

Chumsicle
Large frozen block of chum that dissolves slowly in order that sharks will remain in the area to feed.

Cleaning station
Area of a coral reef that has a resident population of cleaner wrasses, small fish that feed by removing parasites from the skin of larger fish that gather there to be cleaned. The arrangement benefits both partners, and the cleaner wrasses even enter the mouth and gills of their "clients."

Coral reef
An underwater rocky formation made up of the chalky skeletons of hard corals.

Decompression
The gradual reduction of air pressure on a diver who has been diving at depth.

Decompression sickness (D.C.S.)
Onset of symptoms caused by the formation of nitrogen bubbles in the tissues resulting from too rapid decompression; also known as the bends. Symptoms include joint pain, numbness, nausea, and paralysis. Also known as decompression illness (D.C.I.).

Decompression stop
Planned stop on a diver's ascent toward the surface to allow nitrogen to leave the bloodstream by natural means.

Decompression trapeze
Structure suspended beneath the dive boat to allow divers to rest at specific depths when decompressing.

Divemaster
Dive supervisor and guide on dive boats or shore dives.

Drift dive
The use of currents to cover large areas in a single dive.

Drop-off
A precipitous wall of reef leading to deep water.

Ecosystem
A biological community of interacting plants and animals and their environment, including physical conditions of heat, light, etc.

El Niño
An irregular warm surface current that flows in the equatorial Pacific toward the South American coast, and suppresses the upwelling of cold, nutrient-rich water; its name, Spanish for "the (Christ) child", refers to the fact that the current commonly occurs around Christmas. It is part of a wider weather pattern which is called the El Niño–Southern Oscillation that in some years affects climate and water temperature as far away as the United States, Australia, Southeast Asia, India and East Africa.

Food chain and food web
The predatory relationship between animals in a particular ecosystem. In a marine food chain, microscopic plants (phytoplankton) are eaten by primary consumers—krill and other tiny animals—which in turn are eaten by secondary consumers, meat-eaters such as jellyfish, anchovy, and herring. They make food for larger fish, up to apex predators such as tuna, sharks and dolphins. The food web is the interconnections between food chains.

Fringing reef
A reef growing in shallow water parallel to a shore and closer in than a barrier reef.

Global Positioning System (G.P.S)
A system that uses a series of geostationary satellites to plot precise locations on the Earth's surface.

Hard coral
Coral species that have a rigid exoskeleton (external covering) of limestone. Coral polyps live in colonies, and new polyps grow on the skeletons of dead ones to create hard, rocklike coral formations that develop into coral reefs and atolls.

Hookah gear
An airline for divers to hook up to that runs from a compressor on a dive boat to a regulator below the surface.

House reef
A reef directly in front of a dive operator's facility.

Lagoon
The enclosed water, generally shallow, of a coral atoll or barrier reef.

Liveaboard
A vessel specifically geared for diving that provides accommodation for overnight trips.

Mangroves
Salt-tolerant trees and shrubs with interlacing aerial roots that form dense thickets along the shores of shallows and mudflats in tropical and semitropical regions.

Muck dive
Diving an otherwise unpromising dive site to observe, and usually to photograph, small fish and animals.

Nitrogen narcosis
Feeling of intoxication experienced by divers at depth, caused by excess nitrogen dissolving in the blood while breathing air at high pressure.

Nitrox
Artificial mix of nitrogen and oxygen that decreases the risk of narcosis and decompression sickness.

Non-decompression dive
A dive that does not require a decompression stop to release accumulated nitrogen.

Overhang
Any reef, wreck, or rock formation that creates an overhanging wall.

Patch reef
An isolated reef surrounded by featureless seabed.

Pelagic
Any animal that lives in the upper layers of the open ocean.

Penetration diving
Entering a wreck or a cave system beyond the reach of natural light or where no exit point is visible.

Plankton
Plants or animals that float in the sea and lack the means to drive themselves actively through the water.

Reef balling
The dropping of artificial spheres to provide a substrate for reef formation.

Ripping tide
A tide running very fast, generally through a narrow opening in the reef.

Runoff
Fresh water draining from the land into the sea via streams and rivers. It often contains high amounts of nitrates and other pollutants, and may be harmful to nearby reefs.

Sea grass
Green, photosynthesizing plants with roots, stems and leaves (unlike seaweed) that grow in large beds in shallow water, sheltering juvenile animals.

Sea mount
An underwater mountain that rises 3,300 feet (1,000 m) or more above the ocean floor.

Shot line
Line from the surface to the seafloor or wreck that divers use for descents and ascents.

Slack water dive
A dive that takes place between tides when the water is still.

Soft coral
Corals that lack a bony exoskeleton or hard covering.

Spur and groove reef
Zig-zagging reefs of alternating outcrops and cuts.

Surface Marker Buoy (S.M.B.)
A marker on the surface to indicate the position of divers beneath.

Swell
Wave formations that provide a slow, regular movement of water.

Technical diver
Diver trained in the used of mixed gas systems and techniques.

Thermocline
A layer in the water column in which the temperature drops abruptly.

Triangle of Diversity
Area in the Pacific Ocean that has greatest diversity of marine species in the world.

Upwelling
Water rising from depth to the surface, generally cold and rich in oxygen and nutrients.

Wallace Line
An imaginary line drawn through Indonesia that separates the Australasian and Asian biogeographical regions.

Water column
The column of water between the surface and the seabed.

PICTURE CREDITS

ALL PHOTOGRAPHY IN THIS BOOK HAS BEEN REPRODUCED BY KIND PERMISSION OF THE FOLLOWING PHOTOGRAPHERS:

JOHN BANTIN
Web: www.johnbantin.co.uk

TONY BASKEYFIELD
E-mail: tony@plustwodesign.com

COLIN BATEMAN

PAUL BIGGIN
E-mail: paulbiggin@googlemail.com

VICKI BILLINGS
E-mail: vbillings@btinternet.com

CAIO BORGHOFF
Web: www.caioborghoff.fot.br

ANDY BOTHA
Web: www.aqua-africa.com

JANE BURNETT
E-mail: janeburnett@btinternet.com

DAN BURTON
Web: danburton.deeperblue.net

PHILLIP COLLA
Web: www.oceanlight.com

CROATIA DIVERS
Web: www.croatiadivers.com

KEVIN DAVIDSON
Web: www.underwatercolours.com

GLENN EDNEY
Web: www.diving.co.nz/gallery/

CHARLES ERB
Web: www.undersea-images.com

MARK EVANS
E-mail: mark.evans@archant.co.uk

MONTY HALLS
Web: www.fullcircleexpeditions.com

JASON HELLER
Web: www.divephotoguide.com

ANTHONY HOLLEY
Web: www.holleyuwphoto.com

IMAGES DOMINICA
Web: www.imagesdominica.com

ARTHUR KINGDON
E-mail: akingdon48@aol.com

TOBIAS KLOSE
Web: www.dive.is

MIKAYO LANGHOFER
Web: www.mikayo.com

LESLEY MAW
E-mail: lesleymaw@hotmail.couk

GILLIAN MCDONALD
E-mail: divegem@yahoo.com

JANE MORGAN
Web: www.morganreefphotography.com

ALEXANDER MUSTARD
Web: www.amustard.com

NATURALIGHT PRODUCTIONS LIMITED
Web: www.naturalightproductions.com

MALCOLM NOBBS
Web: www.malcolmnobbs.com

GAVIN PARSONS
E-mail: photo@gavinparsons.co.uk
Web: www.gavinparsons.co.uk

LINDA PITKIN
Web: www.lindapitkin.net

SEAPICS.COM
E-mail: info@seapics.com
Web: www.seapics.com

JEREMY STAFFORD-DEITSCH

DAVID & TRACEY STEPHENS
Web: www.underwater-photography.co.uk

JP TRENQUE
Web: www.jptrenque.com

TONY WHITE
Web: www.seaofdreams.co.uk